RECONSTRUCTIONS
of
CANADIAN IDENTITY

RECONSTRUCTIONS
of
CANADIAN IDENTITY
Towards Diversity and Inclusion

Edited by

VANDER TAVARES AND MARIA JOÃO MACIEL JORGE

UNIVERSITY OF MANITOBA PRESS

Reconstructions of Canadian Identity: Towards Diversity and Inclusion
© The Authors 2024

28   27   26   25   24   1   2   3   4   5

University of Manitoba Press
Winnipeg, Manitoba, Canada
Treaty 1 Territory
uofmpress.ca

Cataloguing data available from Library and Archives Canada
ISBN 978-1-77284-069-8 (PAPER)
ISBN 978-1-77284-070-4 (PDF)
ISBN 978-1-77284-071-1 (EPUB)
ISBN 978-1-77284-072-8 (BOUND)

Cover art by Andrew Ostrovsky, Shutterstock image 1778950316.
Cover design by Kirk Warren
Interior design by Karen Armstrong

Printed in Canada

This book has been published with the help of a grant from the
Federation for the Humanities and Social Sciences, through the Awards
to Scholarly Publications Program, using funds provided by the
Social Sciences and Humanities Research Council of Canada.

The University of Manitoba Press acknowledges the financial support for
its publication program provided by the Government of Canada through
the Canada Book Fund, the Canada Council for the Arts, the Manitoba
Department of Sport, Culture, and Heritage, the Manitoba Arts Council,
and the Manitoba Book Publishing Tax Credit.

Funded by the Government of Canada | Canada

CONTENTS

RECONSTRUCTIONS
of
CANADIAN IDENTITY

INTRODUCTION

Rethinking National Identity in Multicultural Canada

VANDER TAVARES AND MARIA JOÃO MACIEL JORGE

The impetus for this volume emerged in a Zoom conversation between us, the editors, in the summer of 2021. Two years prior we had been involved in a collaborative writing project that focused on establishing cultural links to the Portuguese-speaking community in Toronto for undergraduate students through experiential education initiatives embedded in lusophone-related language and literature courses at York University (Dodman et al., 2022). This project cultivated important reflections and reinforced existing concerns between and within us with respect to the positions, images, and contributions of othered communities in the Canadian context—in this case, the "lusophone" community, a term employed to refer to Portugal along with countries and territories that have been forced, through colonization, to adopt and develop various forms of the Portuguese language and culture.

We had been particularly concerned about the peripheralization of Portuguese-speaking groups in Canada. Such a complex process has materialized through different mechanisms, including stereotyping, discrimination, and erasure of the contributions made by this group to Canadian society. For instance, the role played by early Portuguese immigrant women in Canadian society and its economy has always been neglected since generally it has consisted of "unskilled," low-wage jobs in the cleaning industry (Giles, 2016). Lusophone Canadians continue to face issues of legitimacy and "space" within the social and cultural milieux of Canada, as this volume will also demonstrate.

Our own lived experiences have also been affected by cultural stereotypes and the acute awareness of a multiculturalism in which our association with Portuguese-speaking immigrant groups encircled and isolated us as a distinct "community" apart from others. Our experiences of Canadian multiculturalism resulted in the simplistic notion that other "communities" also existed. Yet there was no intercommunity integration. These and other issues ultimately pointed us to the prevailing view and discourse of (one) "Canadian identity" that sustains patterns of otherness for those labelled "ethnic Canadians" of a non-Anglo or francophone background, whose Canadianness must be *marked*, most often as a hyphenated identity through which it is made partial, classified, and secondary.

Our Zoom conversation, inspired by the ramifications of our collaborative writing project into 2021, led us to problematize Canadian identity from a perspective of diversity and inclusion. However, such an issue is not new. Yet we wanted to approach it from a different angle. First, many existing volume-length works have addressed such questions within a single "discipline" or domain of study (e.g., Conrick et al., 2017) or around the experiences of one particular group (e.g., Barber & Watson, 2015). Our intention has been to produce a volume that spans different domains—or what we call here a multidisciplinary perspective. Second, we were interested in learning more about the multifaceted ways in which other(ed) groups experience Canadian identity so as to foster a more intimate dialogue among these groups through scholarship.

But we were equally interested in how such experiences, of both challenge and success, could contribute to re-envisioning the construct of Canadian identity. Thus, we wanted this contribution to be different both in its scope and in its conceptualization of inclusivity. On the one hand, our goal was to include a wider diversity of experiences and voices, some completely unrecognized and/or absent from official discourses and/or previous research. On the other hand, we envisioned this volume as a catalyst for change by informing conversations and future research regarding diversity, inclusion, decolonization, reconciliation, and belonging in relation to being Canadian. These goals became even more timely for us in light of the events that we discuss in the next section. Indeed, what makes this volume unique are its contributions by and about Canadians who have remained unheard despite multicultural discourses on Canada.

In this introduction, we seek to contextualize further the need for this volume. In the following section, we discuss global trends and national events that have intensified the urgency to not only include "others" in conversations about Canadian identity but also to rethink who leads the conversation. We point to some of the ways in which multicultural policies clash with the lived experiences of othered Canadians and in particular how Canadian identity has been exclusive by replicating structures of dominance and erasure. We provide a brief overview of persisting colonial and historical barriers and emerging issues that serve to inform the value of this volume and the wide-ranging interdisciplinary research being conducted by the authors included in it. We conclude the introduction by presenting the organ-ization of the volume.

Context: Why Now?

The year 2021 marked fifty years since Canada's official declaration and implementation of bilingual and multicultural policies for Canadian society. According to a report titled *Canadian Multiculturalism: An Inclusive Citizenship* by the Government of Canada (2012, para. 1), "Canada was the first country in the world to adopt multiculturalism as an official policy." The move signified recognition of "the value and dig-nity of all Canadian citizens regardless of their racial or ethnic origins, their language, or their religious affiliation" (para. 1). The government report also states that the implementation of such policies confirmed the Aboriginal and treaty rights of Indigenous peoples and the use of English and French in the country. The fact that fifty years have passed since the implementation of such policies affords us an important op-portunity to revisit the social, cultural, and political developments since then and to continue to problematize the notion of multiculturalism in Canada. We should ask ourselves how far have we come, who has benefited, and what is the work ahead.

The report proposes key aspects of being Canadian in relation to multiculturalism that are worth critically reflecting on. For instance, the report states that "through multiculturalism, Canada recognizes the potential of all Canadians, encouraging them *to integrate* into their society" (Government of Canada, 2012, para. 4; emphasis added). The idea of Canadian society as a space already defined socio-culturally stands out to us with respect to its potential to include existing (and future) cultural contributions that have remained excluded. In a similar vein, the report also proposes that multiculturalism "ensures that all citizens can keep their identities, can take pride in their ancestry and have a sense of belonging" (para. 2). However, as the contributions in this volume demonstrate, not all identities and ancestries are seen and treated equally in a hierarchical space that has privileged anglophone and francophone identities.

The year 2021 also brought to light the tragic discovery of unmarked graves located at former Indian residential school sites, first in Kamloops and not long after on Penelakut Island, British Columbia. The Canadian Multiculturalism Act came at a time when residential schools were still operated across Canada (1870s to 1990s) (Miller, 2012). The conflict between diversity and inclusion within Canadian identity becomes even more evident in that many Indigenous children came to "lose their language, culture, and in many cases, their lives" (Norris, 2021, pp. 1–2) through forced conversion and assimilation because they were "Indian." A statement by Penelakut Chief Joan Brown outlined that more than 160 undocumented and unmarked graves were found in 2021 (CBC News, 2021), in addition to other discoveries. The National Centre for Truth and Reconciliation estimates that the overall number of missing, and undocumented deaths of, Indigenous children at residential schools in Canada is about 4,100, but likely the number is much higher. Privileged anglophone and francophone identities have been prioritized at the cost of Indigenous identities, which have been erased through historical genocide.

This volume also emerges against the backdrop of the past decade, in which a rise in neo-nationalist attitudes has put into question the often celebratory discourse that through multiculturalism all identities are valued. From the withdrawal of the United Kingdom from the European Union to the election of Jair Bolsonaro in Brazil and the presidency of Donald Trump, among other key global events, we have witnessed various attempts to restore Old World notions of cultural, ethnic, and linguistic singularity within multicultural spaces. Despite the recent change in the political leadership in the United States, the aforementioned issues have not been resolved. Considering that the discovery of unmarked graves in Canada has only further exposed deep-seated racism and discrimination, the growing attacks on and constant aggressions against all ethnic and racial identities must not be ignored or dismissed.

Canada has not been immune to such turmoil. Both scholarship and the media reveal the rise in neo-nationalist attitudes manifested in marginalizing discourses and politics that aim to preserve and protect "real" Canadians from the influence and presence of the other (Raney, 2009). More recently, CBC's investigative journalism series *The Fifth Estate* (CBC News, 2022) has exposed the nation's homegrown White supremacy groups and their rise in popularity (Shephard et al., 2021). A singular, White, and Eurocentric identity is particularly conflicting and threatening in a country that has officially celebrated multiculturalism for fifty years now and has committed to increasing the number of new permanent residents to 431,645 in 2022, 447,055 in 2023, and 451,000 in 2024 (Government of Canada, 2022). Will they be welcomed?

It is impossible not to see these new target numbers in light of the popularity of far-right ideologies, such as the People's Party of Canada (PPC) and its vision for the country. One PPC proposition targets the number of newcomers to Canada by capping it at 150,000, but more alarmingly, another seeks to implement in-person interviews with each potential immigrant so that immigration officials can determine whether the values and ideals of the newcomer align with Canada's "societal norms" (Shivji, 2019). Based upon a speech given by Maxime Bernier, "immigrants whose responses or background checks demonstrate that they do not share mainstream Canadian values will be rejected" (Shivji, 2019, para. 9). In the following section, we contextualize what the "mainstream" can refer to within multiple disciplines.

From a Point of Departure in Literature and Language to Multidisciplinarity

Considering Canada's apparent commitment to cultural and linguistic diversity, the need to (re)define Canadian identity might seem to be unnecessary or contradictory. MacGregor (2008) proposed that the central feature of being Canadian is its very undefined identity. Indeed, this stance has been problematized by other scholars, such as Mayer (2014, p. 148), who argued that "Canada is almost too diverse and multifaceted to talk about a singular Canadian identity, since both identity markers, that is, 'Canadian' and 'identity,' are multiple, plural, and elusive." However, in attempts to recognize multiculturalism from a strictly bilingual and bicultural approach (Haque, 2012), research, policy, and national discourse point to a dominant Anglo-Saxon construction of

Canadian identity that both subtly and saliently sustains patterns of othering, exclusion, marginalization, and ghettoization (Beavon et al., 2005).

As we have discussed, neo-nationalist cultural attitudes that support a narrowly exclusionary construction of Canadian identity have been on the rise. Research conducted outside Quebec has found that being born in Canada, living most of one's life in Canada, having Canadian citizenship, and being a Christian are considered "very important" to "being Canadian" (Raney, 2009, p. 14). These notions are extremely problematic given their blatant exclusion of Indigenous peoples and considering that in Canada's large urban centres residents of transnational backgrounds generally account for 50 percent of the population, not taking into account those of refugee status who, from such a nationalist perspective, are delegitimized from having a Canadian identity because they do not hold Canadian citizenship or conform to the dominant linguistic, ethnic, cultural, and religious composition tied to the Canadian identity. In Toronto in 2016, for instance, 51.2 percent of the population was born outside Canada (City of Toronto, 2017). In our view, despite the commitment to multiculturalism, such socio-demographic trends have only further demarcated the boundaries between "Canadians" and "ethnic" or othered Canadians. As Raney (2009, p. 21) said,

> although Canada has always been an ethnically diverse country (including its First Nations and francophone populations), the rate of ethnic diversification over the past few decades has increased, which may explain why some members of the racial majority are seeking to define their national identity along racial lines to help clarify who belongs (and who does not). While recent data have been made available that show how some members of minority racial groups express lower levels of Canadian identity (Reitz and Banerjee 2007), less attention has been paid to how members of the majority racial group define their national identities as a possible reaction to perceived threats to the national group.

Old World ideologies continue to advance racial, ethnic, and linguistic forms of discrimination that directly subvert multiculturalism and, by nature, the possibility of an inclusive, multicultural Canadian identity. Through a range of socio-cultural media, such as literature, sports, journalism, and popular culture, such ideologies have maintained a fixed and static construction of Canadian identity across time and space (Downey, 2018; Sumara et al., 2001). Additionally, the nation's colonial past and the systematic exclusion of Canada's Indigenous population point to a present in which British and French traditions continue to be not only preserved but also favoured. These trends have prevented expansions of the dominant construction of Canadian identity by offering immigrant, non-anglophone, and non-francophone Canadians a marginal space, one of often "hyphenated" or "hybrid" identities that face issues of legitimacy and recognition. These partial identities allude to the imagined Canadian state as multicultural or culturally diverse; however, the lived experiences of plurality illustrate how Canadian identity remains hierarchically exclusive on the basis of race, sex, gender, language, ethnicity, religion, nationality, and class.

This marginality is pervasive in the nation's cultural expressions and productions. In the Canadian literary landscape, writers of backgrounds other than French or English find themselves occupying a marginal third space. This space is one of exclusion from mainstream literature since the traditional labels of ethnic, immigrant, or multicultural literature hold negative connotations. As Hutcheon (1990, p. 2) points out, the term "ethnic" is not applied to the two dominant cultures—French and English—despite growing recognition of their settler positionality in Canada: "The fact that the word is not used points to a hierarchy of social and cultural privilege." Earlier associations of the term with pagans and heathens or, more recently, foreigners signal that "the word 'ethnic' always has to do with the social positioning of the 'other'... and is thus never free of relations of power and value" (p. 2).

English, particularly outside Quebec, remains socially and culturally privileged, a fact evident from the dominance of English publications and translations. Conversely, only 2 to 3 percent of works written in other languages are translated into English. However, Canadian writers of a "hybrid" identity, who write in English but deviate from an Anglo-Saxon ethic and aesthetic by often writing against the sameness established by literary elites and their imagined literary audiences, also presumed to be Anglo-Saxon, must navigate issues of legitimacy within the Anglo-Saxon monoculture (Marques, 2016). From this third place, ethnic, immigrant, Indigenous, or multicultural writers have destabilized and continue to destabilize notions that define Canadian identity in and through literature. In so doing, these authors set forth critical discussions regarding identity labels of exclusion while claiming their places at the centre rather than the margin.

In second language education, issues of representation also persist. In teaching materials, the imaginary, monolingual, native speaker of "standard" English is constructed as the ideal speaker whom English as a Second Language (ESL) teachers and learners are expected to resemble rather than a plurilingual speaker with knowledge and experience of and within more than one language and culture. So-called standard English is presumably neutral. However, in Canada, it reflects the language of White Canadians since racialized and accented forms are met with suspicion and discrimination (Creese, 2010; Fadden & LaFrance, 2010). Moreover, teaching materials in second language education tend only superficially to expose learners to Indigenous and multicultural representations of Canadian culture. Readings that reflect diverse cultural representations are often positioned as supplementary material.

Although our problematization departs from our research and teaching disciplines, it has always been clear to us that such issues of marginalization and exclusion are not unique to literature or language education. As the responses to our "call for chapters" quickly contextualized, these issues exist across a range of disciplines, some of which are reflected in this volume: sociology, anthropology, geography, business, Indigenous studies, ethnic and cultural studies, religious studies, and gender studies, among others. We have organized this volume into seven thematic sections, which we describe below. Based upon the themes included in the volume, we envision that it will be of great interest to educators, researchers, graduate students, and policy makers in Canada and internationally.

Multidisciplinary Contributions and Volume Design

The seven sections of our volume address its intention to present critical and interdisciplinary theoretical, conceptual, and empirical reconstructions of "Canadian identity." The contributions not only challenge the dominant construction of Canadian identity but also, individually and collectively, move traditionally othered identities to the forefront. The seven parts are "Multiculturalism from Historical and Indigenous Perspectives" (Part 1), "Redefining Identities in Educational Contexts" (Part 2), "Beyond Marked Identities in Literature" (Part 3), "Elevating

Transcultural Identities in National Spaces" (Part 4), "Belonging in Foreign Spaces" (Part 5), "Rethinking 'Canadian Identity' from Socio-Cultural Perspectives of Inclusion" (Part 6), and "Gendered, Racialized, and Transnational Identities Reconstructing 'Canadian Identity'" (Part 7).

In the opening chapter in Part 1, "Fifty Years of Multiculturalism: A Riddle, a Mystery, an Enigma," Augie Fleras sets the tone by offering a critical assessment of fifty years of Canadian multiculturalism. As the title of the chapter indicates, the official policy and its practice are riddled with complexities and ambiguities that expose not its proclaimed success but a problematic lack of progressive values and meaningful transformation. It is time, as Fleras suggests, and inspired by Winston Churchill's oft-quoted assessment of pre–Second World War Russia as "a riddle wrapped in a mystery inside an enigma," to frame official multiculturalism along similar lines—as a riddle, a mystery, and an enigma—that can provide a new interpretive lens to an exhausted topic. Or, to rephrase this epigram in a framework for analysis, what is meant by multiculturalism as governance (riddle), is it working and how (mystery), and has it made any appreciable difference (enigma)? In the second chapter, Jennifer Adese argues that multiculturalism was never intended for Indigenous people and points to its origin in the Royal Commission on Bilingualism and Biculturalism. Adese considers the exclusion of Indigenous peoples from the commission's terms of reference, how Indigenous peoples insisted on participating in some way, and how the commissioners attempted to reconcile their mission with the fact of Indigenous presence. In "Toward an Emotional Geography of Language for Rethinking Canadian Identity in a Transnational World," Anwar Ahmed considers the connection between home language and ethnocultural identity in the contemporary transnational world and Canadian society, where identities and language practices are becoming increasingly fluid. Ahmed approaches the intersection of Canadian identity and home-/heritage-language maintenance of allophones through the conceptual lens of emotional geography. Ahmed proposes that policies and pedagogies should be informed by the affective dimensions of language and identity, especially in the case of intergenerational challenges to home-language maintenance for allophones in Canada.

Part 2 includes three chapters and focuses on redefining dominant constructions of Canadian identity in educational settings. In

"Canadian Identity from a Multicultural Perspective: Foregrounding Immigrant and Indigenous Voices in an ESL Course," Vander Tavares examines Canadian identity from a multicultural perspective in the context of an ESL course taught to international and transnational students at York University. Tavares exposes and problematizes the archetype of the ideal speaker of English and the dominant construction of Canadian identity. Through a multiculturally oriented curriculum in second language education, such dominant constructions of Canadian identity are challenged by integrating immigrant and Indigenous Canadian voices into the curriculum. Similarly, Jacqueline Ng's chapter, "Reconstruction of Canadian Identity in Second Language Education: Creating an Inclusive Classroom for English Language Learners," builds upon linguistic and cultural diversity as a path to disrupting the construction of a one-dimensional Canadian identity. Ng discusses how English language learners (ELL) critically reflect on and negotiate their hyphenated, diasporic identities based upon their experiences of transnationalism in Canada and how plurilingual ELL educators can create an inclusive, equitable classroom through a transformative pedagogy that enhances learning and reaffirms the multicultural identities of students. The last chapter in this section is by Judith Patouma. In "Les enjeux du plurilinguisme en milieu scolaire francophone minoritaire: Inclusion et construction identitaire polymorphe," Patouma focuses on recent research on plurilingualism, pluriculturalism, and new classroom pedagogies to explore issues of inclusion and identity faced by teachers and learners in francophone minoritized communities. Patouma considers how the school, despite being a microsystem in which national and international cultures are in contact and influence the identities of the actors involved, is affected by a prevailing "Canadian" culture.

Part 3 is attentive to issues of identity within literary representations. In "The Case for Literary Extroversion and Human Consciousness Expansion in Canadian Literature: Writing, Identity, and Belonging beyond the Anglo-Saxon Ethic and Aesthetic," Irene Marques argues for the advancement of plural identities toward the forging of a more transcultural society in Canada, one that, by reflecting a multitude of ethics and aesthetics, will pave the way for an expanded collective human consciousness. Marques draws from linguistic and literary diversity as well as her own experiences as a bilingual writer to confront the predominant Anglo-Saxon literary paradigm in Canada so that our multicultural theoretical proclamations become a practice that validates plural identities and literary voices. In "Confronting Exclusion in English Canadian Literature: Portuguese Canadian Hybrid and Hyphenated Voices and Identities," Maria João Maciel Jorge examines the role and the positionality of Portuguese Canadian writers within English Canadian literature. Dodman and colleagues (2022) consider that mainstream Canadian literature, originally driven by British tradition, perceived market tastes, and imagined audiences, perpetuates a colonial and divisive attitude vis-à-vis Canada's obvious cultural diversity and official commitment to multiculturalism. Maciel Jorge discusses the works of two bilingual Portuguese Canadian writers who, by promoting transnational, hybrid, and hyphenated identities as models for inclusion and belonging, contribute to destabilizing persistent nationalistic attitudes in one of the world's most diverse nations, both imagined and real.

In Part 4, contributors examine the positionings of the "transnational" within the "national." Shamette Hepburn leads this section with "A Transcultural Reconstruction of Identity and Inclusion: The Cambodian Canadian Experience." Hepburn explores the multilayered process of identity formation and expression of Cambodian Canadians (see also Wong, 2023). Hepburn's research findings shed light on this community's lived experiences as well as the facets of their transcultural identity that help to displace the apparent monocultural fixity of Canadian identity. From another perspective, Chapter 9 approaches diversity within Canadian identity from intersecting identity positions. In Chapter 10, "The Conundrum of Reconstructing Canada's Identity without Reconciliation," Catherine Longboat, Snežana Obradović-Ratković, Esther Wainaina, and Reshma Rose Tom reflect on their individual and collective experiences of identity and belonging through the Two-Row Wampum Belt story. The authors identify issues in the domains of language, education, and identity, and they reinforce that addressing the complexities of settler relationships with original peoples is a necessary path to building an inclusive Canadian identity. In this section's closing chapter, Veronica Escobar Olivo dives into the experiences of Central Americans growing up in Toronto. Escobar Olivo employs narrative inquiry to understand the experiences of twenty first-and-a-half-generation and second-generation Central Americans who grew up in Toronto. Escobar Olivo documents the tensions and conflicts that these Canadians encountered in developing a sense of identity since they could neither relate directly to their parents' experiences nor feel accepted as fully Canadian. Experiences characterized by discrimination led to a sense of unbelonging and exclusion as Canadians of Central American backgrounds.

The chapters in Part 5 consider the relationship between space and identity through the lens of belonging. Anuppiriya Sriskandarajah opens this section with "Reimagin(in)g Neighbourhood and Belonging: Youth Citizenship in Practice." Sriskandarajah examines how space plays an important role in intergenerational expressions of ethnic identities, participation, belonging, and exclusion in neighbourhoods of Toronto. Drawing from Lefebvre's "right to the city," Sriskandarajah utilizes a photovoice project to analyze how neighbourhood space informs young Canadians' sense of belonging and citizenship. In "Suppression for the Sake of Survival: Multisectoral Rural Voices on Belonging and Anti-Racism," Michelle Lam tackles the experiences of newcomers in a small prairie city. As Lam explains, and contrary to proclaimed pathways for inclusion and belonging, the lived experiences of newcomers in rural contexts are far from ideal and filled with hurtful "choices" that suppress their sense of identity. Lam presents the results of a community-based, collaborative research project that involved an interdisciplinary examination of what belonging and anti-racism might look like in rural Canada. She proposes a collaborative reconstruction of identity that validates plural identities in the hope for a more equitable future. In "Diversifying Unity and Unifying Diversity: Christian Hospitality in Multicultural Presbyterian Churches in Toronto," Lisa Davidson presents the results of ethnographic fieldwork that considers the narratives and experiences of racialized churchgoers and their negotiation of belonging, hospitality, and integration into Canadian social life vis-à-vis a Christian worldview. Uneven, fraught experiences and racialized Christian identity are aspects of concern that challenge Protestant churches to engage with Canadian multicultural sociopolitics through a framework of Christian hospitality in promoting belonging for racialized Christians. Norman Ravvin's chapter discusses "Yiddish in Canada: A Study of the Rise and Fall of a Unique Form of Cultural and Linguistic Diversity." Ravvin explores the shifts in Yiddish brought about by immigration patterns and associated global and local dynamics. In Canada, the Old World ideology associated with Yiddish asserted a global multicultural worldview that, in the decades following the Second World War, were overwhelmed by Canadian assimilationist trends. This chapter focuses on both parts of this narrative.

Part 6 deals with matters of racial exclusion and cultural discrimination. Joseph Mensah's chapter, "'But Some Are More Equal than Others': On Black Canadians' Sense of Belonging and Truncated Citizenship," with reference to Orwell's *Animal Farm*, examines Black disillusionment regarding Canadian citizenship as evident from the experiences of racism in many spheres of Canadian life, notwithstanding the professed egalitarianism of Canadian citizenship. Mensah demonstrates that Black Canadian identity is often stereotyped as the dialectical opposite of White Canadian identity. He contextualizes how Blacks bear much of the brunt of racism in Canada by discussing exclusionary and discriminatory practices in areas such as the labour market, education, law enforcement, housing, and most recently the COVID-19 pandemic. In "Canadian Multiculturalism in the Neo-Liberal Era: Discourses of Race, Asianness, and Assimilation in *Maclean's* 'Too Asian?'" Elena Chou explores racist representations of Asian and Asian Canadian students in the publication of *Maclean's* now infamous article originally entitled "Too Asian? Some Frosh Don't Want to Study at an Asian University," published in November 2010 and revisited in 2020. Chou examines not only the effects of neo-liberalism on the logics and processes of assimilation for racialized bodies in Canada but also how race and practices of racialization continue to trouble commonly held ideas and national myths about inclusion/exclusion, assimilation, multiculturalism, and national identity in the Canadian context. In "Intercultural Mediation: A Necessity for Identity Reconstruction Observed in Contemporary Quebec," Marie-Laure Dioh and Julie Bérubé speak to the barriers faced by immigrants, including current debates related to Bill 21: An Act Respecting the Laicity of the State and, previously, to the bill on the Quebec Charter of Values, rekindling conflicts and social fractures between the host society and immigrants. Dioh and Bérubé propose intercultural mediation as a solution to a divided identity.

The seventh and final part includes two contributions. In "Self-Employment among Immigrant and Migrant Women and Reconstruction of Canadian Identity from Intersecting Marginal Positions," Sepideh Borzoo and Pallavi Banerjee illustrate how professional and migration trajectories intersect with race, class, and gender within the process of developing Canadian identities among immigrant and refugee women. By focusing on the "ethnic" cosmetic industry, Borzoo and Banerjee highlight how immigrant business-women reconstruct their identities at the margins of the dominant Canadian identity, which also manifests itself in colonial standards of beauty. The volume concludes with "Migration and the Paradox of Canadian Bilingualism: The Experience of Sub-Saharan African Francophone Immigrants in the Minoritized Francophone Community of the GTA," by Gertrude Mianda. In this chapter, Mianda reveals how French-speaking immigrants from Africa rarely benefit from the symbolic capital of speaking French and are victimized by triple marginalization because of living in minoritized francophone communities, their race, and their French-language accents, acquired through colonial processes. Bilingualism, in this case, as promoted by multiculturalism, denies them access to Canadian identity.

By providing diverse contributions from a wide range of disciplines, this volume links Canadian identity to the latest conversations on multiculturalism in Canada. All chapters problematize the notion of Canadian identity by exposing divisive and exclusionary practices that reveal the challenges faced by Canadians of various ethnoracial groups, many of them under-represented in scholarship. Simultaneously, the chapters also propose possibilities for ways forward by the very Canadians who have traditionally remained unheard. In other words, the insights that this volume offers further expose the need to revisit multiculturalism from the viewpoint of systemic marginalization experienced by racially and ethnically diverse Canadians. We hope that this volume will stimulate an even greater discussion and analysis to foster inclusion, reconciliation, and belonging within and beyond academia.

References

Barber, M., & Watson, M. (2015). *Invisible immigrants: The English in Canada since 1945.* University of Manitoba Press.

Beavon, D. J., Voyageur, C. J., & Newhouse, D. (Eds.). (2005). *Hidden in plain sight: Contributions of Aboriginal peoples to Canadian identity and culture* (Vol. 1). University of Toronto Press.

CBC News. (2021, 12 July). B.C. First Nation says more than 160 unmarked graves found. *CBC News.* https://www.cbc.ca/news/canada/british-columbia/penela-kut-kuper-residential-school-1.6100201

CBC News. (2022, 22 February). The convoy and the questions: How a protest paralyzed a capital [video]. *CBC News.* https://www.cbc.ca/news/canada/convoy-and-questions-fifth-estate-1.6360859

City of Toronto. (2017). *2016 Census: Housing, immigration and ethnocultural diversity, Aboriginal peoples.* Toronto. https://www.toronto.ca/wp-content/uploads/2017/12/9282-2016-Census-Backgrounder-Immigration-Ethnicity-Housing-Aboriginal.docx

Conrick, M., Eagles, M., Koustas, J., & Chasaide, C. N. (Eds.). (2017). *Landscapes and landmarks of Canada: Real, imagined, (re)viewed.* Wilfrid Laurier University Press.

Creese, G. (2010). Erasing English language competency: African migrants in Vancouver, Canada. *Journal of International Migration and Integration, 11*(3), 295–313.

Dodman, M. J., Cardoso, I., & Tavares, V. (2022). Communicating and understanding *the other* through experiential education: Portuguese language and culture in Toronto. In F. Carra-Salsberg, M. Figueredo, & M. Jeon (Eds.), *Curriculum design and praxis in language teaching: A globally informed approach* (pp. 131–143). University of Toronto Press.

Downey, A. (2018). *The creator's game: Lacrosse, identity, and Indigenous nationhood.* UBC Press.

Fadden, L., & LaFrance, J. (2010). Advancing Aboriginal English. *Canadian Journal of Native Education, 32,* 143–155.

Giles, W. (2016). *Portuguese women in Toronto.* University of Toronto Press.

Government of Canada. (2012). *Canadian multiculturalism: An inclusive citizenship.* Government of Canada. https://web.archive.org/web/20140312210113/http://www.cic.gc.ca/english/multiculturalism/citizenship.asp

Government of Canada. (2022). *Notice—Supplementary information for the 2022–2024 Immigration Levels Plan.* Government of Canada. https://www.canada.ca/en/immigration-refugees-citizenship/news/notices/supplementary-immigration-levels-2022-2024.html

Haque, E. (2012). *Multiculturalism within a bilingual framework: Language, race, and belonging in Canada.* University of Toronto Press.

Hutcheon, L. (1990). Introduction. In L. Hutcheon & M. Richmond (Eds.), *Other solitudes: Canadian multicultural fictions* (pp. 1–16). Oxford University Press.

MacGregor, R. (2008). *Canadians: A portrait of a country and its people.* Penguin Canada.

Marques, I. (2016). Notes on the incestuous and monocultural nexus of the literati. *Maple Tree Literary Supplement, 21.* https://www.mtls.ca/issue21/irene-marques

Mayer, E. P. (2014). The significance of the United States and the Canada-US border for Canadian national identity construction. *Placing America: American Culture and Its Spaces, 3*, 145–157.

Miller, J. R. (2012, 10 October). Residential schools in Canada. In *The Canadian encyclopedia*. https://www.thecanadianencyclopedia.ca/en/article/residential-schools

Norris, T. (2021). Editorial: Memorialization, decolonization, and schools: Memorializing forced forgetting. *Brock Education Journal, 31*(1), 1–6.

Raney, T. (2009). As Canadian as possible . . . under what circumstances? Public opinion on national identity in Canada outside Quebec. *Journal of Canadian Studies, 43*(3), 5–29.

Shephard, M., Mak, A., & Kaschor, K. (2021, 10 November). White not hate. *CBC News*. https://newsinteractives.cbc.ca/longform/undercover-investigation-patrick-mathews/

Shivji, S. (2019, 24 July). Maxime Bernier says his party would cap immigration levels at 150K. *CBC News*. https://www.cbc.ca/news/politics/maxime-bernier-immigration-speech-mississauga-1.5224114

Sumara, D., Davis, B., & Laidlaw, L. (2001). Canadian identity and curriculum theory: An ecological, postmodern perspective. *Canadian Journal of Education, 26*(2), 144–163.

Wong, A. (2023). *Laughing back at empire: The grassroots activism of The Asianadian magazine, 1978–1985*. University of Manitoba Press.

PART 1

MULTICULTURALISM FROM HISTORICAL
and
INDIGENOUS PERSPECTIVES

Chapters in this section engage with issues of Canadian identity at a broader scale that includes national discourses, policies, and politics. In doing so, these chapters set the tone for the overall thematic thread of this volume by addressing systemic issues that consider, on the one hand, the multiple and often contradictory assumptions of Canadian multicultural inclusion through language policies and, on the other, the absence of Indigenous sovereignty and knowledge from colonial discourses of Canada's "two founding nations." In fact, the official policy of multiculturalism can be understood as a product of internal pressures from a range of ethnic groups of predominantly European backgrounds, which led to valuing "racial" and "cultural" diversity. Meanwhile, Canada's Indigenous peoples were subjected to policies aimed at assimilation and erasure, thereby suppressing the already-existing cultural diversity.

Equally relevant to the discussions in this section is the contradiction of multiculturalism within a bilingual, bicultural framework. As they stand, official bilingual policies not only marginalize other languages but also discourage heritage language maintenance and, by extension, an inclusive multiculturalism. Minoritized linguistic identity is always weakened by power relations in which Canada's imposed settler identities—French and English—are perceived to be best suited for social integration and financial success. In sum, the chapters in this section reveal and dismantle myths of inclusivity and multicultural well-being, a necessary critical step from which fresh insights can rise to rebuild the foundations for meaningful transformation.

In Chapter 1, Augie Fleras offers a historical overview of fifty years of official multicultural policy and demonstrates that little has changed to make Canada more inclusive. The path forward must include new assessments and perhaps even the consideration that the twentieth-century policy no longer applies in twenty-first-century realities. In Chapter 2, Jennifer Adese considers Indigenous perspectives despite their absence in official documents and consultations, in particular in the Bilingualism and Biculturalism Commission. A reckoning that accounts for the systemic violence committed against Indigenous peoples is necessary to draw them into the multicultural mosaic independent of political discourse and settler governance. In Chapter 3, Anwar Ahmed tackles the matter of language policy in determining the need to move away from bilingualism in a multilingual society to truly represent Canada's diversity. Ahmed focuses on language and emotion as an important element of identity construction and maintenance through the conceptual framework of emotional geography and offers insights into how language pedagogy can best value all languages beyond the bilingual limitations of French and English.

1

Fifty Years of Multiculturalism:
A Riddle, a Mystery, an Enigma

AUGIE FLERAS

Introduction: A Mixed Milestone

Much of value can be invoked in defence of Canada's official multiculturalism. A commitment to multiculturalism as a model of diversity
governance has presided over a remaking of Canada's national identity
along more inclusive lines (Ruble, 2018). From an openly White society and racialized regime, Canada has evolved into a cosmopolitan
domain increasingly attuned to the principles of diversity, inclusion,
and equality regardless of (or, perhaps, precisely because of) people's
race, ethnicity, or nationality. The impact of an official multiculturalism
reflects its importance in rethinking the very idea of what it means to be
Canadian in addition to reshaping how public institutions are responding to calls for diversifying rules and modifying practices. Reference to
it as a brand that "works" is justified on grounds that Canada is one of
the world's few jurisdictions to openly and unequivocally endorse an
official multiculturalism (Marche, 2016, 2018). Many Canadians tend
to concur with this observation. They believe that, in advancing a multicultural template for living together differently without drifting apart,
multiculturalism represents Canada's foremost contribution to global
peace (Adams & Neuman, 2018). Canadians are not the only ones who
lavish praise on multiculturalism (Dervin, 2017; Heath, 2014). The
popularity and success of official multiculturalism are globally admired

and widely acclaimed as a uniquely progressive model that advances the multicultural streams of social equality and cultural respect without losing sight of the national picture (Fleras, 2019).

Central to any assessment of an official multiculturalism is its durability as a mainstay of Canada's governance agenda. A Canada that recently commemorated fifty years of official multiculturalism puts the onus on deconstructing the worth of this milestone by reassessing its contribution—or lack thereof—as a political project (Adams, 2021; Cardozo, 2021; Paikin, 2021). However much it is valued or supported, an official multiculturalism also embeds a set of uncertainties and contradictions that amplifies its ambiguous status as a "solution" in search of a "problem." Yes, there is much to like about an official multiculturalism in presiding over a multicultural makeover of Canada that some anoint as revolutionary (Cowen, 1999; Sandercock, 2003). Yet it is dismaying to see how little has changed in advancing a more inclusive Canada. Multicultural success stories are offset by program failures; its popularity masks deep pockets of indifference or hostility; its impact is not nearly as pervasive or progressive as widely believed. Canadian attachment to multiculturalism continues to be conditional, comes with strings attached, and conceals substantial levels of resentment or indifference. Even the notion that multiculturalism "works" raises questions of "how," "why," and "for whom"? Paradoxes persist as well. Despite Canada's much-ballyhooed dislike of an American melting pot as a metaphor of governance, Canadians generally prefer an assimilationist model of multiculturalism (Research Co., 2019) in which newcomers blend ("melt") into Canada as the price of admission and success. No wonder critics pounce on an official multiculturalism as a kind of "assimilation in slow motion" (Forrest et al., 2006, p. 441) that masks an "assimilation by stealth" (Hansen, 2014).

The ambiguities, messiness, and ironies that inform fifty years of Canada's official multiculturalism offer the possibility of a discursive reassessment. The interplay of mixed messages and unresolved tensions exerts pressure for a new explanatory framework if only to make sense of things not normally seen or routinely voiced. Instead of approaching multiculturalism in the language of "is" or "ought" or "success," perhaps now is the time to rethink this Canada-building project along lines that embody its puzzling and paradoxical dimensions as both progressive and transformative yet also contested and controlling (see Barrett, 2015).

In casting about for a turn of phrase that captures the gist of multi-culturalism's complexities and contradictions without falling into the trap of carping negativity or treacly platitudes, what comes to mind is Winston Churchill's oft-quoted assessment of pre–Second World War Russia as "a riddle wrapped in a mystery inside an enigma." Framing an official multiculturalism along similar lines—as a riddle, a mystery, and an enigma—offers a new interpretative lens that yields fresh insights into calling out difficult issues that need to be problematized. Attention is drawn to how promises that once justified multiculturalism can prove to be increasingly irrelevant because of changing circumstances, including the term itself, which tends to mislead rather than enlighten.

Concepts and assumptions that informed multiculturalism—from ethnicity to integration to citizenship—are now dismissed as simplistic and naive and contrary to the goal of good governance in a profoundly more complex world (Kymlicka, 2015; Triandafyllidou, 2017). Multicultural myths and misconceptions are exposed as well as a precondition for unmasking the inconvenient truths that hide behind polite fictions (see Dhamoon, 2021). Finally, reference to its future viability also taps into a riddle-mystery-enigma nexus (Fleras, 2019, 2021b). Multiculturalism might have been of service in moving the national needle toward greater inclusiveness. But there is no assurance that it will continue to work without a major reset in light of the risks in coaxing new meanings into a dated governance concept already fraught with ambiguity and freighted with paradoxes. In short, the deeper that we delve into the murky depths of Canada's official multiculturalism, the greater the urgency to look at it through a prism that exposes its mixed and messy status. Or, to put this epigram into an analytical framework for discussion and debate, what does Canadian multiculturalism mean (riddle), is it working (mystery), and does it matter (enigma) (Fleras, 2020)?

Multiculturalism as Riddle: What Does It *Really* Mean?

Fifty years of official (also federal or Anglo) multiculturalism have made it abundantly clear: An official multiculturalism as a minority governance and diversity management turns on a riddle. All analyses of, debates on, and assessments of multiculturalism flow from how it is framed and defined. But multiculturalism has proven to be impossible to define to everyone's satisfaction primarily because the concept is so opaque and malleable that a mix of meanings fall under its eponymous label (Paquet, 2008). Multiple references roughly linked to each other and to a general source tend to congeal around a multicultural axis so that the same term connotes vastly different realities and fundamentally diverse programs. Frames of reference range from the formal (policies and programs) to the vernacular (everyday realities), from cultural maintenance to social justice, from group-specific minority rights to the individualistic ethos of liberal universalism, from conservative and consensus-oriented approaches to a more critically informed agenda. Assessments of multiculturalism as governance must contend with a spectrum of contradictory discourses (Fleras, 2021b). Multiculturalism can be framed simultaneously as (a) progressive, regressive, or hege-monic; (b) as conservative, liberal, or plural; or (c) as revolutionary, reactionary, or moderate. It can be criticized as too conservative or too radical; as fostering too much unity or not enough diversity; as too powerful or not powerful enough; as too outward looking or too inward looking; as too focused on preserving ethnocultural tradition or too preoccupied with the Canadianization of newcomers. It has been taken to task for taking differences too seriously or not seriously enough—either as a grave danger that lurks behind a smokescreen of reassuring bromides ("a wolf in sheep's clothing") or as a national sym-bol full of sound and fury yet signifying little of substance ("a sheep in wolf's clothing"). Compounding the conceptual disarray is an awareness that Canadian multiculturalism may be wilfully misrepresented—such as opposing multiculturalism to integration (Ambrosch, 2019) while ignoring how diverse multiculturalisms define it differently (Modood, 2014)—particularly by those intent on erecting a multicultural straw figure for the fun of toppling it.

Intense scrutiny often yields more confusion than clarity. In much the same way as a snowflake melts when examined more closely, the veneer of an official multiculturalism crumbles under sustained obser-vation, especially if interpreted too literally or too loosely. References to multiculturalism exemplify a kind of *double talk* (saying one thing while meaning another); an *irony* (what appears on the surface differs from what is actually the case); a *misnomer* (misnamed as an inaccur-acy that can easily mislead if interpreted at face value); a *red herring* (a distraction intended to deceive or disorient); a *double bind* (a damned-if-you-do, damned-if-you-don't dilemma because, no matter what it does, it invariably invites criticism from all sides [Nagle, 2008]); a *hypocrisy* (the appearance of virtue that conceals nefarious motives); an *oxymoron* (a figure of speech that combines contradictory concepts—for example, "plural monoculturalism" [Sen, 2006]); a *paradox* (advancing the seemingly counterintuitive notion that promoting ethnicity will bolster national unity); and a *contradiction* (the improbability of distinct cultures occupying the same shared space without coming to blows [Salzman, 2018]). Surprisingly, perhaps, though Canada might be the world's quintessential multicultural society because of its rootedness in the 1971 policy statement, constitutional protection under the 1982 Charter of Rights and Freedoms, and the 1988 Multiculturalism Act, no government has opted to formally define multiculturalism (Thurairajah, 2017). Any reference to an official multiculturalism subsequently reflects a largely unplanned and ad hoc trajectory bereft of conceptual clarity or prone to theoretical imprecision (Wood & Gilbert, 2005)—a situation that, paradoxically, might work to Canada's advantage (Kymlicka, 2015). Evidence suggests increased support if multiculturalism is construed in general terms rather than pinned down on specifics. In that the devil is indeed in the details, as goes the saying, there is a payoff in concealing the fine print, thus allowing people to read into multiculturalism whatever they want to project (Paquet, 2008).

An official multiculturalism that encapsulates multiple meanings across competing domains and around clashing interests renders it a riddle. Compounding the idea of multiculturalism as a riddle is an inclination to say one thing but mean another, with the intention of dodging any fixed position. Multiculturalism represents one of those curious turns of phrase that rarely means what it says or says what it really means ("polysemous"), with the result that it can mean everything ("a floating signifier") yet nothing ("an empty signifier") (de B'béri & Mansouri, 2014) or whatever the context requires (a "sliding signifier") (Giddens, 2006; Hall, 2017). Misconceptions abound because the term itself remains a misnomer. Canada's multiculturalism is not about making Canada more multicultural and diverse, as implied by the term "multi" + "cultures." Rather, it is inclined toward making Canada more inclusive through minority accommodation and migrant integration that ensure full and equal participation, accelerated access to citizenship, and enhanced sense of identity and belonging to Canada. For example, changes to the Royal Canadian Mounted Police uniform that permitted the Sikh turban alongside the Mountie Stetson did not necessarily render the national police more multicultural (if more inclusive). Or consider how Canada's multicultural model eschews the promotion of differences, instead preferring a *depoliticizing* of diversity by channelling it into harmless outlets to abort the possibility of messy ethnic entanglements. Nor is it about promoting ethnicity per se; to the contrary, the idea is to capitalize on the ethnodiversity of people as a stepping stone for facilitating their integration into Canada on terms that work for them. And, though multiculturalism seemingly targets migrants and minorities, it is also aimed at modifying mainstream mindsets and institutional structures to ensure that they play their parts in moving over and making inclusionary space.

In saying one thing but doing something else, Canada's multiculturalism is "riddled" with inconsistencies and contradictions. An official multiculturalism can come under fire for promoting too much diversity to the detriment of societal unity and national identity. But it is also criticized for promoting too much unity by not taking differences into account when necessary in levelling an uneven playing field. This disconnect between opposing demands exposes the *hypocrisies* (pretending to be something that they are not) that inform an official multiculturalism. In the final analysis, what a multiculturalism says that it will do or what the public thinks that it should be doing rarely aligns with what it can realistically accomplish. The rationale behind Canada's official multiculturalism as a state project of social engineering (see Scott, 1998) eschews the idea of celebrating many ("multi") cultures, promoting minority groups per se, or encouraging the creation of ethnic communities. More accurately, the logic of an official multiculturalism embraces a commitment to the principles of redistribution over recognition, disadvantage over diversity, equality over ethnicity, integration over division, commonalities over differences, and social justice over cultural expression (Fries & Gingrich, 2009; Kymlicka, 2012). Multiculturalism in the Canadian context transforms narratives of cultural pluralism into discourses of social justice by promoting the principles of inclusion, social equality, and anti-racism, *in the process aiming to create a Canada more inclusive of migrants and minorities rather than more multiculturally diverse.* In doing one thing yet taking refuge in another, in part to deceive or confuse audiences, multiculturalism embodies a classic example of *double talk*. Canada might be at the forefront in expounding the virtues of a multicultural society, yet, paradoxically, it also epitomizes one of the world's most comprehensive integration regimes (Rao, 2007; Smith, 2018).

Multiculturalism as Mystery: Is It Working?

References to multiculturalism as mystery tiptoe around a corpus of questions that eludes simple responses. Is an official multiculturalism working? Who says so? On what grounds can such an assessment be made (i.e., how do we find out)? For whose benefit? How does it work? Is it possible to operationalize the concept of "it works" for the purposes of measurement? If yes, then can multiculturalism be disaggregated from other relevant factors associated with its success? Does it work in facilitating the settlement and integration of newcomers to Canada? Or does it work primarily to distract from a racialized-in-Whiteness status quo, with its prevailing distribution of power and privilege? Why does an official multiculturalism seemingly work in Canada but rarely elsewhere? Will it continue to work in the future? That answers are difficult to articulate to everyone's satisfaction compounds the mystery of Canadian multiculturalism.

For some, reference to "it works" points to the popularity of and support for multiculturalism. A commitment to multiculturalism endorses the idea of a post-racist Canada that repels the primacy of a White supremacy complex, rejects racism and discrimination, dismisses race as a determinant of life chances, and endorses the principle of inclusion. For others, multiculturalism "works" in Canada, albeit rarely elsewhere, because it represents a low-risk option for accommodating minorities and integrating migrants who have arrived through documented channels, possess liberal values, and are job ready for the modern labour market (Kymlicka, 2012). For still others, multiculturalism "works" in Canada to the extent that, as a polite fiction, it conceals yet perpetuates unmulticultural realities that conveniently sanitize the historical violence of a settler/monocultural regime. For others yet, multiculturalism "works" because it keeps Canada afloat by depoliticizing the potency of diversity to fragment or foment. To complicate matters further, minority perceptions of what "works" differ from those of the mainstream. For example, new Canadians might perceive multiculturalism as a platform for maintaining multiple identities that allow them to engage with homeland politics. Yet this aspiration can be dismissed as un-Canadian by those who insist that newcomers discard their pasts as the price of admission into Canada (Thurairajah, 2017).

The best spin? Multiculturalism "works" because it has contributed to a multiculturalizing of Canada along diverse, equitable, and inclusive lines (Jedwab, 2021). From a transplanted monocolonial enclave to a cosmopolitan domain of many cultures and colours, multiculturalism has played a pivotal role in incorporating the symbols of diversity and inclusiveness into the narratives of Canadian "nationhood" (Kymlicka in Gregg, 2006). Many admire its contribution in constructing a social, cultural, and political climate that fosters the principle of inclusion, nurtures diversity, prioritizes tolerance, and promotes equality. Newcomers to Canada are strongly encouraged to participate in and contribute to an inclusive Canada through exemptions from institutional rules to facilitate the process (Heath, 2014).

The worst spin? Critics of an official multiculturalism believe that it fails to deliver on its promise to create a more inclusive Canada, one respectful of differences, responsive to the inequalities of exclusion, and reflective of its pursuit of social justice. Instead, multiculturalism is deployed as a device of control that whitewashes Canada's national narratives and papers over the ongoing coloniality and racialization at the core of Canada building (Dhamoon, 2021). More specifically, a commitment to multiculturalism has proven to be largely ineffective in reducing socio-economic disparities based upon race, gender, and immigrant status (Abu-Laban, 2014; Block & Galabuzi, 2018; Dei, 2011). Racial discrimination persists in the labour market despite the mantra of multicultural inclusion, especially for certain racialized minorities, both Canadian and foreign born (Banerjee et al., 2018). Such an assessment is hardly surprising in view of multiculturalism's symbolic status as inspirational and aspirational, with little in the way of budgetary allocation, implementation protocols, or enforcement powers (Abu-Laban, 2014).

Fifty years of multiculturalism as official policy have made it abundantly clear: we really do not fully understand how, where, or why it "works," whether its impact is direct or indirect, or whether its effects (if any) are short term or long term. Although multiculturalism can be associated with the reconfiguration of Canada along more inclusive lines, its overall impact has been difficult to assess except, perhaps, to make Canadians more self-consciously aware of Canada as multicultural. Societal changes associated with or attributed to an official

multiculturalism might reflect related factors such as (a) the internationalization of a human rights agenda, (b) a highly selective immigration
program that seeks the educated or labour ready, (c) a commitment to
aggressively pursue the settlement and integration of newcomers, and
(d) a relatively open pathway to citizenship through naturalization
(Fleras, 2018; Hansen, 2017). Or, if multiculturalism is acclaimed for
creating a more tolerant, inclusive, and equitable society, then such an
assessment can tap into Canada's prominence as one of the world's most
immigrant-friendly and racially equal countries (MIPEX, 2020; U.S.
News and World Report, 2021). A commitment to multiculturalism
fosters a social climate and national mindset that legitimize a controlled immigration agenda that works to Canada's advantage (Fleras,
2014b; Reitz, 2014). Popular support for multiculturalism also equips
decision makers with considerable wiggle room ("political capital") in
implementing immigration policies and settlement programs without
fear of crippling public criticism or electoral backlash. Hansen (2017)
argues along similar lines. Many of the indicators that multiculturalism is working reflect the success of Canada's controlled immigration
regime that skims off global talent while attracting a steady supply of
temporary workers to do the jobs that the Canadian born disdain. In
short, the working value of multiculturalism is subject to debate and
controversy since its role in and contribution to advancing inclusive
Canada building remain a mystery.

Multiculturalism as an Enigma: Has It Been Worth It?

Does an official multiculturalism matter (a difference that makes a difference)? Have fifty years of official multiculturalism made a difference
in redefining Canada and reshaping Canada building? Half a century
of promises and programs under federal multiculturalism yields a set of
questions that cuts to the core of any assessment. Is Canada still a predominantly monocultural regime, with a few multicultural bits thrown
in to convey the illusion of inclusion? Or should we think of Canada as
having evolved into a robust multicultural domain despite a few pockets of racism that linger as remnants from its White supremacist past?
Can the question be operationalized so that answers are measurable? If
multiculturalism is a causal factor rather than a correlational feature in
creating a new Canada, then how do we disaggregate it from the mix
to determine its potency as a difference maker?

Responses to these questions reinforce the enigma that is multi-culturalism. For example, the following indicators strongly suggest that Canada's multicultural model is working. There is a high level of mutual identification and reciprocal acceptance of immigrants and Canadian-born populations. International studies—including the annual OECD survey involving the Better Life Index (2020)—consistently rank Canada as one of the world's most tolerant countries. In turn, immigrants display high levels of pride in Canada (Adams, 2007), with the vast majority of newcomers acquiring citizenship within ten years (Bloemraad, 2006). Compared with other countries, in Canada naturalized immigrants are more likely to be involved politically as voters, party members, and candidates actively recruited by political parties. Children of immigrants in Canada attain better educational outcomes than those in any other Western democracy, and many second-generation Canadian youth outperform children of Canadian-born parents. The absence of immigrant ghettos in Canada (despite the presence of ethnic enclaves, which generally are about choice or convenience rather than imposed) points to a healthy level of social integration. And increasing rates of interracial marriage and mixed-race offspring suggest that multiculturalism is working (Kymlicka, 2012). Yet these positive changes might reflect factors related to human rights legislation, a progressive immigration program, a focus on the settlement and citizenship of newcomers, and anti-racism interventions. Any indicator of success associated with multiculturalism might be spurious and correlational rather than causal and direct. Achievements under multiculturalism can also be difficult to measure or quantify except through assertions so vague as to be baseless (Hansen, 2014, 2017; Reitz, 2014).

Consensus is divided in assessing the effects of multiculturalism at fifty (Kymlicka, 2021). For the optimists, a multicultural Canada is fundamentally and positively different from the Canada that prevailed in the decades prior to the introduction of the policy in 1971. Open expressions of racism are no longer socially acceptable, Canada no longer claims to be a White supremacist regime, diversity is now prioritized as Canada's strength and a defining feature of national identity, migrants and minorities are touted as integral to Canada and Canada building, and mainstream institutions increasingly accept a duty to accommodate (Adams, 2021; Cardozo, 2021; Fleras & Spoonley, 1999). No less impressive under the sway of multiculturalism are demographic changes.

In a relatively short period of time and without catastrophic incidents, Toronto evolved from a staid and monocultural provincial city (a strong Orange Order agenda dubbed it the Belfast of Canada) into one of the world's most successful and cosmopolitan cities whose official motto, "diversity our strength," captures the ethos of a multicultural ethic (Ruble, 2018).

For the pessimists, half a century of multiculturalizing Canada has been an enigma in the making. Canada might be more multicultural in principle and profile, yet it remains a deeply monocultural regime rooted in the founding assumptions of White supremacy and the foundational principles of an unspoken yet racialized constitutional order (Fleras, 2014a). As proof, consider how the transformation of Canada's political landscape under a multicultural rule has proven to be mixed. Of the 338 seats in Parliament prior to the federal election in 2021, racialized minorities filled 51 and Indigenous people 10, for a combined total of about 16 percent of the seats—a percentage that nearly reflects their proportion of citizens who are eligible voters (Griffith, 2019). A diversity of MPs aside, the political leadership remains resolutely colour coded. Fifty years ago Canada's prime minister and all ten premiers were White and male; at present, with the defeat of Heather Stefanson in Manitoba in October 2023, only Danielle Smith of Alberta and Wabanakwut "Wab" Kinew of Manitoba remain as the exception to this pattern of political leadership at both federal and provincial levels.

A reality gap prevails. Multiculturalism as a framework for governance might commit to a rethinking of what Canada is and what it means to be Canadian. Yet the monoculturality of a sedimented Whiteness continues to suffuse the national agenda in defining what is normal, good, and desirable. Even a commitment to diversity is less than it seems. An official multiculturalism might endorse a Canada of many cultures; nevertheless, it continues to draw the line by monopolizing the right to define what counts as differences and which differences count. With multiculturalism, one can be different but not too different; differences must fall into an acceptable range as tolerated by the mainstream; cultural practices cannot break the law or violate individual rights; and differences should be parlayed into advancing integration, settlement, and participation rather than becoming a stepping stone into siloed communities. Finally, though many regard multiculturalism as a catalyst in advancing a tolerant, inclusive, and equitable Canada, in

reality many racialized minorities continue to struggle with the inequalities of exclusion related to income, employment, and poverty against
a backdrop of pandemic-linked anti-Asian harassment, anti-Black
racism, Islamophobic violence, and continuing antisemitism (Block &
Galabuzi, 2018; Fleras, 2017).

Conclusion: A Reckoning with Multiculturalism

Let us problematize fifty years of Canadian multiculturalism as diversity
discourse and governance model. Championed yet maligned, idealized
as well as demonized, official multiculturalism simultaneously evokes
a multi-edged preference for consensus as well as division; of change
yet stasis; of conformity yet diversity; of control yet emancipation; of
exclusion yet participation; of compliance yet creativity (Fleras, 2020).
To one side, Canada's multiculturalism constitutes a cleverly disguised
discourse in defence of a racialized status quo and monocultural regime;
to the other side, it finds itself on the right side of history in presiding
over a transformational shift in the art of cooperative coexistence. The
interplay of these oppositional dynamics generates yet more uncertainty
and confusion. Of particular note is the looming prospect of formulat-
ing a minority governance that redefines identity and belonging against
the backdrop of an emergent post-multicultural world of splintered
loyalties, multiple identities, and fragmented affiliations (Fleras, 2019).
The challenge of living together differently in a post-multicultural world
is further complicated by the following conflicts of interest: (a) the
relevance of a place-based framework of governance in a transmigrant
and diasporic world of "here," "there," and "everywhere"; (b) the risk
of endorsing a spatialized multiculturalism when people's notions of
identity and belonging are uncoupled from place ("despatialized"); (c)
the dilemmas of a cosmopolitan mindset that encompasses the principle
of universal personhood, though the ideals of fluid crossings and flexible
connections are offset by stricter citizenship protocols and ramped-
up border controls (Geislerova, 2007); and (d) the creation of a new
agenda of governance for engaging complex diversities across a local/
national/global nexus without skittering off on dangerous tangents or
imploding from within.

The interplay of these dynamics yields an intriguing conclusion.
Canada's multicultural space has evolved into a contested site of unresolved tensions: *more complexly diverse and increasingly inclusive yet*

*compromised by an official multiculturalism that, in theory, is no longer con-
ceptually attuned to the emergent realities and unconventional demands of a
post-multicultural world* (Fleras, 2021a). Multiculturalism in its current
iteration might be nearing the limit of its relevance in addressing the
post-national sensibilities of a post-multicultural world (Fleras, 2019).
It might also be tottering on the brink of a legitimacy crisis (both a crisis
of identity and a crisis of confidence) in struggling to right itself in terms
of "what it is" and "what it should be doing." In that multicultural references are increasingly disconnected from the real world of accelerated
change and lived (hyper)diversity, an official multiculturalism increasingly resembles a zombie category. Like the "living dead," it continues
to do discursive work even though the world in which it once flourished
and to which it now refers no longer exists (see Beck, 2002; Meer &
Modood, 2014; Sealy, 2018; Shannahan, 2017). Yet efforts to resurrect a
new multiculturalism are unsettled by hidden agendas and blind spots.
No more so, I would argue, than in repositioning the idea of multiculturalism as a victim of its own virtue. Repeated references to Canada's
status as a multicultural success story generate a smug complacency that
makes Canadians bristle at the prospect of any criticism, less willing to
confront inconvenient truths or harsh realities, and disinclined to learn
from the positives of other multicultural models. Or as Kymlicka (2021)
points out, multiculturalism is so fixed in the Canadian policy landscape,
political imaginary, and national identity that most Canadians are unable
or unwilling to reconsider the possibility of doing it differently. Such
bullheadedness does not bode well for reimagining multiculturalism in
a post-multicultural world.

This apparent contradiction—a twentieth-century simplism floating about in the complexities of a twenty-first-century world—makes
it more important than ever to rethink and reframe multiculturalism through a candid assessment of what it means, if it is working,
and whether it makes any difference. Applying the lens of a riddle-
mystery-enigma nexus to analyzing and assessing fifty years of official
multiculturalism offers a promising option. Framing it along the lines
of a riddle-mystery-enigma nexus allows the problematizing of an official multiculturalism as more contested and contradictory than widely
perceived. A commitment to multiculturalism is shown to enhance yet
detract, divide yet unify, ghettoize yet integrate, prove a hoax yet offer
hope, and reflect hegemony yet represent a catalyst for progressive

change. Neither the costs nor the positives of multiculturalism should be discounted in any analysis or assessment, thus reflecting the ability of the powerless to repurpose the very tools of control for resistance and change (Pearson, 1994). As Barrett (2015, p. 9) explains, reframing multiculturalism in terms of its "simultaneously disabling and enabling quality" empowers it with the leverage and the leeway to criticize Canada for not living up to its obligations while legitimizing a rethinking of the Canadian narrative along a different trajectory. By the same token, no one should underestimate how the homogenizing gaze of official multiculturalism can depoliticize diversity by channelling it into a multi-cul-de-sac of disempowerment (see Mistry, 1995). Its homogenizing logic is no less hegemonic in solidifying a racialized distribution of power and privilege behind a fog of confusion.

Such a mixed assessment—multiculturalism in the vanguard of progress as well as an instrument of pacification—ups the ante for a more nuanced analysis of official multiculturalism than many supporters and critics would care to admit or are willing to concede. Canadian multiculturalism as a political project in minority/diversity governance should not be framed discursively as an either/or proposition. More value can be gleaned from framing it as a both/and discourse—namely, as a launch for resistance *and* oppression in addition to a catalyst for reform *and* repression—with a capacity to generate positive social changes that are workable, necessary, and fair yet also reconstituting the very conditions that necessitated its introduction in the first place (see Kaye, 2017). Assessing fifty years of official multiculturalism beyond the binary of these disparate discourses provides a timely reminder. Canadian multiculturalism as an unfinished project will continue to be mined for insights and applications that shed new light on old orthodoxies (Abu-Laban, 2021; Ghosh, 2011; McDonough, 2011). Fifty years of multiculturalism can also provide a platform for innovative possibilities in steering Canada and Canadians along new multicultural pathways.

References

Abu-Laban, Y. (2014). Reform by stealth: The Harper Conservatives and Canadian multiculturalism. In J. Jedwab (Ed.), *The multicultural question* (pp. 149–172). McGill-Queen's University Press.

Abu-Laban, Y. (2021). Multiculturalism: Past, present and future. *Canadian Diversity, 18*(1), 9–12.

Adams, M. (2007). *Unlikely utopia: The surprising triumph of Canadian pluralism.* Viking.

Adams, M. (2021, 7 October). 50 years of official multiculturalism: It's as Canadian as maple syrup. *Canadian Geographic.* https://canadiangeographic.ca/articles/50-years-of-multiculturalism-where-lived-experiences-make-history/

Adams, M., & Neuman, K. (2018). Canadian exceptionalism in attitudes toward immigration. *Policy Options.* https://policyoptions.irpp.org/magazines/april-2018/canadian-exceptionalism-attitudes-toward-immigration/

Ambrosch, G. (2019, November). Making sense of immigration: Why multiculturalism is at odds with integration. *Aero Magazine.* https://areomagazine.com/2018/11/20/making-sense-of-immigration-why-multiculturalism-is-at-odds-with-integration/

Banerjee, R., Reitz, J. G., & Oreopoulos, P. (2018). Do large employers treat racial minorities more fairly? An analysis of Canadian field experiment data. *Canadian Public Policy, 44*(1), 1–14.

Barrett, P. (2015). *Blackening Canada.* University of Toronto Press.

Beck, U. (2002). The cosmopolitan society and its enemies. *Theory, Culture, and Society, 19*(1–2), 17–44.

Block, S., & Galabuzi, G.-E. (2018). *Persistent inequality: Ontario's colour-coded labour market.* Canadian Centre for Policy Alternatives.

Bloemraad, I. (2006). *Becoming a citizen: Incorporating immigrants and refugees in the United States and Canada.* University of California Press.

Cardozo, A. (2021, 12 October). Multiculturalism is working but there is more to be done. *Toronto Star.*

Cowen, T. (1999, 24 April). Cashing in on cultural free trade: Don't give us shelter: A U.S. economist sings the praises of Canadian artists. *National Post.*

de B'béri, B. E., & Mansouri, F. (2014). Contextualising multiculturalism in the 21st century. In F. Mansouri & B. E. de B'béri (Eds.), *Global perspectives on the politics of multiculturalism in the 21st century: A case study analysis* (pp. 1–13). Routledge.

Dei, G. J. S. (2011, Spring). In defense of official multiculturalism and the recognition of the necessity for a critical anti-racism. *Canadian Issues,* 15–19.

Dervin, F. (2017). *Critical interculturality.* UK Cambridge Scholars Press.

Dhamoon, R. K. (2021). Multicultural colonialism. *Canadian Diversity, 18*(1), 46–50.

Fleras, A. (2014a). *Racisms in a multicultural Canada.* Wilfrid Laurier University Press.

Fleras, A. (2014b). *Immigration Canada.* UBC Press.

Fleras, A. (2017). *Social inequality in Canada.* Oxford University Press.

Fleras, A. (2018). *Citizenship in a transnational Canada.* Peter Lang.

Fleras, A. (2019). *Postmulticulturalism.* Peter Lang.

Fleras, A. (2020). 50 years of Canadian multiculturalism: Accounting for its durability, theorizing the crisis, anticipating the future. *Canadian Ethnic Studies, 51*(1–2), 19–59.

Fleras, A. (2021a). *Canadian multiculturalism @ 50.* Brill.

Fleras, A. (2021b). *Rethinking the academy: Beyond Eurocentrism in higher education.* Peter Lang.

Fleras, A., & Spoonley, P. (1999). *Recalling Aotearoa.* Oxford University Press.

Forrest, J., Poulsen, M., & Johnston, R. (2006). A "multicultural model" of the spatial assimilation of ethnic minority groups in Australia's major immigrant-receiving cities. *Urban Geography, 27*(5), 441–463.

Fries, C. J., & Gingrich, P. (2009). A "great" large family: Understandings of multiculturalism among newcomers to Canada. *Refuge: Canada's Journal on Refugees, 27*(1), 36–49.

Geislerova, M. (2007). The role of diasporas in foreign policy: The case of Canada. *Central European Journal of International and Security Studies, 1*(2), 90–108.

Ghosh, R. (2011, Spring). The liberating potential of multiculturalism in Canada: Ideals and realities. *Canadian Issues*, 3–8.

Giddens, A. (2006, 14 October). Misunderstanding multiculturalism. *The Guardian.* https://www.theguardian.com/commentisfree/2006/oct/14/tonygiddens

Gregg, A. (2006, March). Identity crisis: Multiculturalism: A twentieth-century dream becomes a twenty-first century conundrum. *The Walrus.* https://the walrus.ca/identity-crisis

Griffith, A. (2019, 5 November). House of Commons becoming more reflective of diverse population. *Policy Options.* https://policyoptions.irpp.org/magazines/november-2019/house-of-commons-becoming-more-reflective-of-diverse-population/

Hall, S. (2017). *The fateful triangle: Race, ethnicity, nation.* Harvard University Press.

Hansen, R. (2014). Assimilation by stealth: Why Canada's multicultural policy is really a repackaged integration policy. In J. Jedwab (Ed.), *The multiculturalism question: Debating identity in 21st-century Canada* (pp. 73–87). McGill-Queen's University Press.

Hansen, R. (2017). Why both the left and the right are wrong: Immigration and multiculturalism in Canada. *PS: Political Science and Politics, 50*(3), 712–716.

Heath, J. (2014, 24 March). Misunderstanding Canadian multiculturalism. *Global Brief.* https://globalbrief.ca/2014/03/misunderstanding-canadian-multiculturalism/

Jedwab, J. (2021). The "terms" of multiculturalism. *Canadian Diversity, 18*(1), 22–28.

Kaye, J. (2017). *Responding to human trafficking.* University of Toronto Press.

Kymlicka, W. (2012, February). *Multiculturalism: Success, failure, and the future.* Transatlantic Council on Migration: A Project of the Migration Policy Institute.

Kymlicka, W. (2015). The three lives of multiculturalism. In S. Guo & L. Wong (Eds.), *Revisiting multiculturalism* (pp. 17–36). Sense Publishers.

Kymlicka, W. (2021). Promoting progressive change, legitimizing injustice, or both? *Canadian Diversity, 18*(1), 3–5.

Marche, S. (2016, September). Canada in the age of Trump. *The Walrus.* https://thewalrus.ca/canada-in-the-age-of-Donald-Trump

Marche, S. (2018, 13 August). *An apology for multiculturalism.* Open Canada. https://opencanada.org/apology-multiculturism

McDonough, K. (2011, Spring). Multiculturalisms in tension. *Canadian Issues*, 91–95.

Meer, N., & Modood, T. (2014). Cosmopolitanism and integrationism: Is British multiculturalism a "zombie category"? *Identities, 21*(6), 658–674.

(MIPEX) Migration Integration Policy Index. (2020, 8 December). *Canada ranks fourth in world ranking for immigrant-friendly policies.* The Canadian Excellence Research Chair in Migration and Integration, Ryerson University.

Mistry, R. (1995). *A fine balance*. McClelland & Stewart.

Modood, T. (2014). Understanding "death of multiculturalism" discourse means understanding multiculturalism. *Journal of Multicultural Discourses, 9*(3), 201–211.

Nagle, J. (2008). Multiculturalism's double bind. *Ethnicities, 8*(2), 177–198.

OECD (Organization for Economic Cooperation and Development). (2020). *How's life? 2020: Measuring well-being*. OECD Publishing.

Paikin, Z. (2021, 21 January). *Multiculturalism @ 50*. Open Canada. https://opencanada.org/headline-multiculturalism-at-50

Paquet, G. (2008). *Canada's deep diversity: A governance challenge*. University of Ottawa Press.

Pearson, D. G. (1994). *Canada compared: Multiculturalism and biculturalism in settler societies*. Institute of Social and Economic Research, Memorial University of Newfoundland.

Rao, G. (2007, 17 April). *Multiculturalism in Canada and Austria: Paradoxes of assimilation and integration*. Presentation to the Austrian-Canadian Society, Vienna.

Reitz, J. (2014). Multiculturalism policies and popular multiculturalism in the development of Canadian immigration. In J. Jedwab (Ed.), *The multiculturalism question* (pp. 107–126). McGill-Queen's University Press.

Research Co. (2019, 9 February). *Canadians express lukewarm support for multiculturalism*. https://researchco.ca/2019/02/08/multiculturalism

Ruble, B. A. (2018, 28 February). *Opportunity with dignity: Lessons from multiculturalism in Toronto*. Wilson Center.

Salzman, P. C. (2018). *What comes after multiculturalism?* Frontier Centre for Public Policy.

Sandercock, L. (2003). *Cosmopolis 11: Mongrel cities in the 21st century*. Continuum.

Scott, J. C. (1998). *Seeing like a state*. Institution for Social and Policy Studies, Yale University.

Sealy, T. (2018). Multiculturalism, interculturalism, "multiculture" and super-diversity: Of zombies, shadows and other ways of being. *Ethnicities, 18*(5), 692–716.

Sen, A. (2006). *Identity and violence: The illusion of destiny*. W. W. Norton.

Shannahan, C. (2017). Zombie multiculturalism meets liberative difference: Searching for a new discourse of diversity. *Culture and Religion, 17*(4), 409–430.

Smith, S. (2018, 3 May). Canada ranked fourth most accepting country in the world for immigrants. *Canada Immigration Newsletter*.

Thurairajah, K. (2017). The jagged edges of multiculturalism in Canada and the suspect Canadian. *Journal of Multicultural Discourses, 12*(2), 134–148.

Triandafyllidou, A. (2017). Introduction. In A. Triandafyllidou (Ed.), *Multicultural governance in a mobile world* (pp. 1–16). Edinburgh University Press.

U.S. News and World Report. (2021, 19 April). *Canada named best country in the world by U.S. News and World Report*. Colin Singer.

Wood, P. K., & Gilbert, L. (2005). Multiculturalism in Canada: Accidental discourse, alternative vision, urban practice. *International Journal of Urban and Regional Research, 29*(3), 679–691.

2

Refusing Minoritization:

Indigenous People and the Politics of Multiculturalism

JENNIFER ADESE

From the 1990s to the early 2010s, the word *Aboriginal* was omnipresent in Canadian public discourse, appearing in diffuse political, social, cultural, and economic sites. In my book *Aboriginal™: The Cultural and Economic Politics of Recognition* (Adese, 2022), I write that, although Indigenous activists rallied around the word in the struggle for what is often referred to as "rights recognition," the word is perhaps best understood as the calling card of the emergence of neo-liberal colonialism in Canada. As I discuss in the book and elsewhere, by the time that the City of Vancouver (and Canada) hosted the 2010 Winter Olympic Games, neo-liberal colonialism was covered over in a glossy veneer of Aboriginalized liberal multiculturalism, as showcased with great fanfare during the opening ceremony of the games to depict an origin point for Canada's innate diversity. As multiculturalism has become essential to both Canada's carefully crafted national identity and the core of its national *brand* identity (both at home and on the international stage), Indigenous people were engaged to anchor this identity as long-standing and indeed *innate* to Canada. What was lost in such a display, and in the many other ways that Indigenous people have been drawn into Canadian multiculturalism rhetoric, is a precise understanding of the relationship between Indigenous people and Canadian multicultural policy.

Multiculturalism was never intended for Indigenous people. In fact, from its very origin—in the Royal Commission on Bilingualism and Biculturalism of the 1960s, intent on affirming the purportedly dual character of Canada's core national identity—Indigenous people were positioned as internal outsiders. In this chapter, I therefore focus on the exclusion/inclusion of Indigenous people in the context of the commission. In many ways, the connection between Indigenous people and the commission was an early manifestation of the processes that I explore in my book. Through a critical review of primary documents and secondary literature related to the commission, and drawing from Audra Simpson's framework of refusal, I argue that Indigenous people were resolute in their refusal of the depoliticization of their voices during the commission. Attention to the origin of Canadian multiculturalism policy and this particular moment of Indigenous activism highlights the deep contradictions in creating a narrative of cultural inclusion against the backdrop of a colonial project intent on assimilation. It is a tension that has only become more refined over time. As I discuss in *Aboriginal™* (Adese, 2022), during the Vancouver Olympics (and through to today), Indigenous people who refuse to "play the game" of multiculturalism—continuing instead to oppose the very essence of Canada's claims to sovereignty on Indigenous lands—are cast as bad liberal subjects and as the antithesis of the "good" Canadian state, a modern extension of the discursive framing of Indigenous people as savages unable to civilize "properly."

Building a National Identity: The Royal Commission on Bilingualism and Biculturalism

As other contributors to this volume discuss, multiculturalism finds its origin as government policy with the Royal Commission on Bilingualism and Biculturalism in 1963. Convened to address Québécois contributions to Canadian culture and national identity, the commission recommended, among other things, the official declaration of Canada as a bilingual (English and French) nation, resulting in the Official Languages Act of 1969. The federal government soon faced pressure from other European ethnic Canadians (primarily prairie-based Ukrainians, Poles, and Germans and their associated labour unions) to recognize their contributions to Canada; this in turn led to the establishment of multiculturalism policy in 1971 (formalized in 1988 as the Multiculturalism Act), which recast these and other non-British and non-Québécois populations as "diversities" (see Lalande, 2006; Wangenheim, 1968). These and other "ethnic minority" populations fell outside the narrative of the two founding nations but were recognized within the national fabric based upon their having immigrated to the nation post-Confederation.

A closer look at the genesis of multiculturalism, in the form of the commission, is telling with respect to Indigenous people's inclusion/ exclusion and perspectives on attempts to engender a new national identity. In this period, the Canadian government continued to foster the assimilation of Indigenous people via a number of overt policies and coercive socio-economic mechanisms—most notably through the ongoing imposition of the Indian Act, 1876, which legislated nearly all aspects of the lives of Status Indians, and through the continued operation of Indian residential schools. These policies, along with many others geared to the assimilation of Indigenous people, were viewed as distinct from the work undertaken to foment a national identity. As anthropologist Sandra Lambertus (2002, p. 5) writes, multiculturalism developed along a trajectory separate from policies focused on the assimilation of Indigenous people. According to the commission's terms of reference, dated 19 July 1963, its mandate was to examine "the existing state of bilingualism and biculturalism in Canada and to recommend what steps should be taken to develop the Canadian Confederation on the basis of an equal partnership between the two founding races, taking into account the contribution made by the other ethnic groups to the cultural enrichment of Canada and the measures that should be taken to safeguard that contribution" (Royal Commission, 1970, p. 103). Indigenous people were not factored into the terms of reference at all. Any significant consultation with them was outside the scope of the commission from its inception.

Likely because Indigenous people made themselves known at public consultation meetings held across the country, the commissioners later took pains to clarify that obvious exclusion, acknowledging in their final report that "special attention" must be paid to "the problems of the Eskimo and the Indian in our present world" (Royal Commission, 1970, p. 103). The commissioners write that Canada was born "out of warfare" between the English and the French as "two founding peoples," but "it was born also out of the white man's imposition of his culture upon the original Indians and Eskimos. From the Indian point of view, French and English both have the same title to the land—conquest" (Royal Commission, 1970, p. 134). They acknowledge that some measure of force ("imposition") was applied in the creation of Canada and that Indigenous people were unwilling participants in Canada's national project. At the same time, however, they imply that Indigenous people long ago accepted that "conquest" gave the English and the French title to the land (see Haque, 2012, p. 81).

Those referred to as "the Eskimos and the Indians" are cast as the "first Canadians" who made "a prior contribution" to the country before "all the others" who came later (Royal Commission, 1965, p. 187). The Métis Nation is mostly erased in the report, except as a stand-in for French rights in Manitoba, used as a pawn in the centuries-old battle between the French and the English. The execution of Métis Nation leader Louis Riel, for example, is chalked up to being a matter of differing perspectives that only reveals more about national tensions between the English and the French:

> Conflicts since Confederation are well known, although viewed from totally different aspects by the two main participants. Riel, the "murderer," was hanged; Riel, the defender of minority rights, was judicially murdered. Manitoba was endowed at its birth by an English-dominated federal Parliament, with the two official languages and separate schools; but the local Manitobans took away these rights, and when the Government in power at Ottawa proposed to force the schools back on the unwilling Manitobans, the people in Quebec voted solidly for a Laurier who rejected compulsion. Yet to Quebec the Manitoba experience proves that "les Anglais" everywhere are untrustworthy, and that when the chips are down the majority always wins. (Royal Commission, 1965, p. 134)

First Nations, Métis, and Inuit are all drawn into the national narrative in differing ways. For Métis, it occurs mostly through erasure by being figured solely as a voice for French minority rights and by being denied existence both as a people and as a nation. Métis are non-existent in the report and, consistent with the thinking of the Canadian state and many Canadians at the time, will be assimilated inevitably into the broader

(White) society. Even though the existence of the Métis Nation also predates the formation of Canada, and the Métis were a central party in negotiating Manitoba's entry into Confederation, the Métis Nation is not a factor in the report. For First Nations and Inuit, the commission has to disavow the realities of time. Canada as a nation-state did not exist prior to 1867, inasmuch as both the French and the English made claims to Indigenous lands as colonies, settlements, territories, and provinces. Yet the commissioners redraw the boundaries around Canada and Canadianness, projecting them backward into a pre-Confederation past, making the time "before Canada" still something to which Canadians can lay claim.

First Nations and Inuit as "first Canadians" are made Canadian, their sovereignty and autonomy wiped from historical memory, and their only role is paving a path for those called the "new Canadians." The commissioners ultimately imply Indigenous consent to Canada/Canadianness when their consent was never sought. There is internal debate, however, about how to address Indigenous people in the context of the commission. One of the commissioners, F.R. Scott, a Quebec-born English Canadian poet, lawyer, academic, and politician who co-founded the Cooperative Commonwealth Federation, recounts that in a meeting on 4 March 1966

> the question arose, what shall we do with the Eskimos and Indians? Are they just another ethnic group? Most Commissioners felt that within our terms of reference, they were not in the same position as the new Canadians. Then where would we place them? Gagnon said we must speak about the Eskimos and Indians, otherwise we would look ridiculous to the Canadian public. I said we might have to make some comment about them, but we would make ourselves even more ridiculous if we attempted to pretend we knew anything about the situation. We had no research on it, and Gagnon's and my little tourist trip to Baffin Island could scarcely count as research. I feel this is just one example, of which there are many others, of our knowing about the existence of a problem in Canada, not unrelated to our terms of reference, yet, far beyond our possibility of helpful contribution. (qtd. in Fraser, 2021, p. 145)

Their limited mandate, lack of knowledge and experience, and desire to avoid embarrassment kept the commissioners focused in their work on advancing bilingualism within the government, organizations, and media and among the Canadian public.

The commissioners ultimately settle on language that acknowledges Indigenous people but squarely pin responsibility for the lack of more substantive inclusion on the federal government and their terms of reference. In the "General Introduction," the commissioners clarify that they

> will not examine . . . the question of the Indians and the Eskimos. Our terms of reference contain no allusion to Canada's native populations. They speak of "two founding races," namely Canadians of British and French origin, and "other ethnic groups," but mention neither the Indians nor the Eskimos. Since it is obvious that these two groups do not form part of the "founding races," as the phrase is used in the terms of reference, it would logically be necessary to include them under the heading "other ethnic groups." Yet it is clear that the term "other ethnic groups" means those peoples of diverse origins who came to Canada during or after the founding of the Canadian state and that it does not include the first inhabitants of this country. (Royal Commission, 1967, p. xxvi)

From their language, it is clear that the commissioners see Indigenous people as a separate and distinctive category excluded from the articulation of Canadianness outlined here, positioned rather as "first inhabitants" (or, as previously discussed, "first Canadians") and not as contributors to Canada, either as "founding races" or "other ethnic groups." This has the effect of creating a "third space" in relation to developing multicultural policy in which Indigenous people are neither wholly inside nor wholly outside it (see Bhabha, 2012).

The commissioners note that their terms of reference do not include engaging in "long studies on the rightful status of the Indians and the Eskimos within the Canadian Confederation." Instead, "other bodies," either "official or private in nature," that received financial support from the Department of Indian Affairs and Northern Development would be tasked with doing such work as it pertained to government policy (Royal Commission, 1967, p. xxvi). In a retrospective on the commission, Maxwell Yalden also comments on the exclusion of Indigenous people. Yalden (2013, p. 12) reaffirms that the commissioners relied on the terms of reference to explain their rationale for not including Indigenous people in a more significant way. The commissioners nevertheless advocated for some assistance for Indigenous people to "preserve their cultural heritage," and they specifically called for the Canadian government, and the provinces, to work to ensure that Inuktitut and "the most common Indian dialects" survived. The motivation for doing so, however, was based on the belief that the "cultural heritage" of Indigenous people "is an essential part of the patrimony of all Canadians" (Royal Commission, 1967, p. xxvii). Indigenous people's cultures and languages here are therefore construed as worthy of preservation only in relation to what they mean to and for "all Canadians." The commission's report thus undermines Indigenous sovereignty by positioning Indigenous people as mere occupants of the land (rather than as autonomous Indigenous nations) and by painting the long history of Indigenous existence as merely a precursor to Canada's triumphant rise. Irrespective of the facts that Indigenous histories extend back to time immemorial and that Canada is but a sliver of time in Indigenous lives, the commission positions Indigenous people not only as part of the past but also as relevant only as depoliticized, cultural enhancements to Canada's bilingual and bicultural national base.

In spite of Indigenous people's efforts to be heard by the commission, the commissioners repeatedly note that a focused consideration of the relationship between Indigenous people and the commission's work is outside their scope. The "General Introduction" to their report ultimately refers to "the indigenous cultures" as decidedly not part of the founding of Canada. Although the commissioners, paradoxically, were "careful to acknowledge the special, as in exceptional, founding status of Indians and Eskimos," they largely eschewed Indigenous perspectives on what this might mean in favour of careful tap-dancing around where Indigenous people fit within visions of Canada and Canadianness (Haque, 2012, p. 94; see also Royal Commission, 1965, p. 22). Indigenous people were thus simultaneously positioned *outside* and *inside* the commission's focus.

The Canadian government appeared to assume that the process of assimilation would *naturally* resolve the so-called Indian question and subsume Indigenous people within the fabric of Canadian national identity. Yet Indigenous people repeatedly pushed back against the government's attempted erasure of their voices in the structure of the commission, bolstered by commissioners who considered it necessary to report in some way on Indigenous people's relationship to Canada and its cultural identity. So though Indigenous people were never formally part of the commission—and this exclusion continued through the passage of official multicultural policy in 1988—neither were they entirely absent from it.

Writing Erasure: Revisiting Reports

Inasmuch as the commissioners pinned Indigenous exclusion directly on the federal government in the formal text of the report, it is also worth noting that other writing by the individual commissioners is telling with respect to general attitudes among political actors of the time. In an essay for the commission written in 1965, Commissioner Scott contends that there was nothing but "a half continent, much of it bleak and inhospitable, which possessed few original inhabitants and those but little advanced in the civilized arts [and which] has been subdued for human habitation and developed into an ordered system of society, particularly in the period since 1867" (qtd. in Fraser, 2021, p. xxii). In the mid-twentieth century, Indigenous people were still seen by many politicians as little more than "subdued" savages, not human, and not worthy of consultation. As reflected in the words of Scott, the commissioners were no different in their thinking. As Graham Fraser (2021, p. xxii) writes, "the idea of including Indigenous representatives on the commission simply never occurred to anyone."

Although Indigenous people were largely absent from the commission's preliminary and final reports, and altogether absent from formal consultation, at least one notable study was conducted. In 1966, a two-volume unpublished report titled "Indians and Eskimos of Canada: An Overview of Studies of Relevance to the Royal Commission on Bilingualism and Biculturalism" was completed by Commissioner F.G. Vallee and his research team. Vallee does not address why the government excluded Indigenous people from the commission's terms of reference, but he recognizes that the exclusion constituted a notable absence: "Because of the strong Eskimo and Indian claim to original charter-membership in Canadian society as pre-European occupants of its territory, it might have been expected that the Royal Commission of Bilingualism and Biculturalism would program extensive research into the current position and future prospects of these groups" (Vallee, 1966, p. 1). He notes, however, that the commission did not undertake a more comprehensive study of Indigenous people because what would become the far more comprehensive Hawthorn Report (1964–66) was well under way at the time (p. 1). As such, Vallee's report is short, much of it consisting of an annotated bibliography of existing research.

With respect to new research, Vallee (1966, p. 1) focuses most closely on what he refers to as the most significant matters relevant to the commission's work, offering a brief discussion of issues such as language preservation, population growth, culture, economic development, and education. Vallee ultimately states that relations between Indigenous people and Europeans were largely peaceful. He writes that any major changes to Indigenous people's way of life that might negatively affect the issues on which he was focused were simply the result of "unintended and unforeseen consequences of the introduction from outside their own groups of various objects and patterns of livelihood. ... Whatever the motives and purposes of those who introduced such objects and patterns of livelihood, few of the consequences for Indians and Eskimos could have been foreseen" (pp. 3–4, 7). Although Vallee's report, the only broad-scale "expert" report focused on Indigenous people prepared for the commission, appears to excuse colonialism from being a constitutive force in Indigenous people's lives, there is some recognition that such changes were not entirely innocuous: "Of course, not all important changes are to be traced exclusively to such sources. For many generations, persons and agencies, government and non-governmental, have attempted to deliberately introduce and guide planned changes in Eskimo and Indian populations" (p. 7). Furthermore, Vallee suggests that the tendency to engineer "planned change" had peaked because of negative outcomes such as "the vicious spiral of mistrust, low education, unemployment, poverty, discouragement, and the feeling of being pariahs in what was once their own land" (p. 7). Vallee's language is decidedly placid, reifying narratives of conquest that negate the fact that the *land is still Indigenous land*, yet it serves as an important reflection of the tensions highlighted by Indigenous people with respect to the commission's work and the realities of life at the time under Canadian colonialism.

Vallee (1966, p. 7) also refers to what he calls the "special problems" faced by Indigenous people who endeavour to "establish and maintain Indian and Eskimo organizations on regional and national bases." He asserts that there was never a "united Indian 'front' mounted against the outsiders" (p. 4). Yet it was pan-Indigenous organizations that would help to ensure Indigenous voices were presented to the commission. It is important to clarify here that, though Indigenous people and organizations were not intentionally included in consultations, they made themselves present and known at "public hearings and in the briefs submitted to the Commission" (Gagnon and St-Louis, 2013, p. 44).

On Refusal: Indigenous People and the Royal Commission on Bilingualism and Biculturalism

Indigenous people drew from their capacity for political organizing—such as through the National Indian Council and through their participation in the largely non-Indigenous organization the Indian and Eskimo Association (formed in 1951 by non-Indigenous people; at the time of the commission, Indigenous people comprised 25 percent of the board)—and mounted a determined campaign to contest their exclusion. Although ultimately they would not secure an amendment to the terms of reference or the commission's wider focus, by the end of 1963 the commission did invite Indigenous organizations, and other organizations such as the Indian and Eskimo Association, to submit their own briefs (Haque, 2012, p. 95). As Eve Haque writes, in spite of attempts to exclude Indigenous people from meaningful consultation and consideration, they also used "petitions to the commission which attracted considerable media attention" (p. 71). At a preliminary gathering of the commission in 1963, Ethel Brant Monture, speaking on behalf of the National Indian Council, insisted that "Indians possess a culture quite different from the biculturalism of French Canadians through which is woven a pattern of Canadian rights" (qtd. in Fraser, 2021, p. 269; see also Haque, 2012, p. 70). Monture insisted that Canada should be understood as a "tri-lingual country" to which Indigenous people "have added at least the color," and she called attention to the fact that at the first meeting of the commission "we were told . . . we would be a part of it" (qtd. in Haque, 2012, p. 70). Commissioner Scott reports that Brant Monture "was the only person whose presentation was greeted with clapping" (Fraser, 2021, p. 23). She insisted on being *seen* by the commission while also highlighting the divide between what is said and what is done by Canada.

These lobbying efforts at least propelled some change in attitude regarding the measure of consultation among the commissioners. Scott reports that he put forth to his fellow commissioners that, "since the Indians can and will come before us, whereas the Eskimo cannot," some attempt must be made to meet with the Inuit (Fraser, 2021, p. 65). Over the summer of 1964, F.R. Scott and Jean-Louis Gagnon travelled to four communities: Iqaluit (Frobisher), Cape Dorset, Pangnirtung, and Pond Inlet. Fraser writes that Gagnon later opined in his memoir that, "since the mandate made no mention of the Indigenous people, it was felt that comments should be limited to a few pieties. No-one complained, except perhaps those concerned. But thanks to illiteracy, this omission made little noise" (qtd. in Fraser, 2021, p. 284, n. 97). The commissioners appeared to grapple with the exclusion of Indigenous people from their mandate with a public show of (very limited) consultation, yet Gagnon's words reveal the slippery nature of those efforts. Gagnon admits that their trip to Inuit communities was intended to say and do little, and he appears to be grateful that the Inuit were unable to read the commission's mandate. There is a clear sense of relief that Scott and Gagnon did not have to deal with more than "a little noise." The decisive move to offer "a few pieties," rather than to explain to the Inuit the realities of their exclusion, demonstrates the ease with which the commissioners adhered to their mandate and disregarded Indigenous people's place within their vision of Canada's future.

The strategic exclusion of Indigenous people extends to the preliminary report in 1965 of the Royal Commission on Bilingualism and Biculturalism. The commissioners do not refer to Brant Monture's words, nor do they refer to the National Indian Council's calls for accountability. In fact, in the preliminary report, the commissioners state that it is only with the beginning of their Canada-wide consultations between March and June 1964 that they would come "in contact with Canadians of Indian origin" (Royal Commission, 1965, p. 37). At the gathering in Sudbury in 1964, the commissioners were further pressed on the position of Indigenous people within the government's vision of Canadian Confederation. At an evening meeting during that gathering, a First Nations woman asked "why is the Indian always forgotten? This was the first culture and this was the first language in Canada. We are told that the BNA Act was between the French and English—where was the Indian during this time?" (p. 49). It is a powerful statement that, when read in concert with Brant Monture's words, highlights the *visible* presence of Indigenous women both within Indigenous political organizations and within Canadian political debates at the time. The woman's query explicitly draws attention to both culture and language, questioning the dualism inherent in cultural and linguistic conceptualizations of Canadianness. The woman also draws attention to a vital question: how was it that the commission began from a basis that already excluded Indigenous people? Why did it choose to build upon the legacy of the British North America Act as Canada's "founding document" to extend the erasure of Indigenous people in Canada's new articulation of its national identity?

Indigenous people present at public consultations used the commission as an opportunity not only to continue to challenge such erasure but also to highlight contradictions in the commission's approach. At a meeting in Toronto, a representative from the Indian Advisory Committee of the Ontario Department of Public Welfare summarized the situation: "If the French people think that they lost a lot of their rights since Confederation, what should the Indian say? They lost the whole land" (Royal Commission, 1965, p. 49). Another used the forum to criticize persistent racism in education: "Our children learn that Indians are all savages" from school textbooks (p. 49). Embedded in this comment is a direct critique of the commission's emphasis on cultural preservation and the concurrent racist attack against Indigenous people in education. Another participant was highly critical of the pressures that Indigenous people face to assimilate, particularly when leaving reserves, noting that "as soon as an Indian wants to succeed in Canadian life he must assimilate. They [Canadians] call them non-Indian-Indians" (pp. 49–50). Here the participant notes that, even if meeting a government legal standard of assimilation, it does not mean that a person is no longer perceived as, or treated as, an Indigenous person. Assimilation does not mean the end of anti-Indigenous racism. He also draws attention to how colonial policies long preyed on Indigenous people in incredibly difficult economic situations. They speak to a long history of government policies that tied enfranchisement to certain economic choices for survival, such as obtaining postsecondary education. The reprehensible contradiction of the commission's mandate for linguistic and cultural preservation against the backdrop of a colonial nation still invested in the assimilation of Indigenous people is laid bare in the words of those quoted in the preliminary report.

Indigenous attendees at the gathering in Victoria reiterated the impacts of that odious and glaring contradiction. One person referred to in the preliminary report as "an Indian chief" reportedly said that, "after doing everything to cause the extinction of the Indian language in that region by taking drastic steps to exclude it from the schools, Canadians are now asking that it be exhibited for the tourist trade, even though it is hardly spoken now" (Royal Commission, 1965, p. 67). There is a profound tension named here that remains as relevant today as it was then. The "Indian chief" makes a critique that would become more common in the wake of the official multiculturalism policy implemented in the 1980s and with the expansion of the tourism industry. After centuries of attempts to eradicate Indigenous languages (and indeed Indigenous people as such), the twinning of cultural heritage preservation with neo-liberalism means that Indigenous languages in some contexts are considered economic assets.

Assimilationist policy is directly responsible for robbing Indigenous people of our linguistic heritages. Another "Indian chief" at the meeting in Victoria, when asked about his opinion on French Canadian calls for recognition regarding the French language, offered support for its preservation amid his critique: "If another group can succeed in doing something when we have been condemned to death, we will be glad for them. . . . [M]y grandchildren no longer know the language of my people, but can speak French" (Royal Commission, 1965, p. 126). In London, Ontario, some attendees expressed a different set of concerns, reflecting the problems inherent in the lack of dedicated and genuine engagement with Indigenous nations. Participants in London were specifically concerned about the implications of bilingualism (if any) for the treaty relationship: "Our treaty was written in English and was signed under the British flag. If we change the language, the treaty becomes worthless" (p. 126). The speaker raises yet another important tension at the heart of the origin of Canadian multiculturalism. The treaty rights of Indigenous people were largely non-existent for the commission and entirely irrelevant to the terms set by the Canadian government.

It is here that the work of Audra Simpson (2017) sheds light on Indigenous entanglements with early multiculturalism. Simpson utilizes refusal as a "mode of analysis" to refer to how her community of Kahnawà:ke "used every opportunity to remind each other, and especially non-native people, that this is our land, that there are other political orders and possibilities" (p. 21). By refusing to participate in the "'structure' of settler colonialism that was discernible through time," her nation also made palpably clear its refusal to "signal consent and belonging within a settler political system that would move Mohawks out of their sovereignty into an ambit of 'consent' and with that . . . settler citizenship and the promise of whiteness" (p. 21). Simpson's line of analysis here, while speaking specifically to her own Indigenous nation, provides a useful analytical framework within which to think about what it means more generally for Indigenous people to refuse a kind of citizenship that would be depoliticized and packaged in the name of Canada's cultural identity.

In their statements to the commission, it is clear that Indigenous people refused to consent to a form of "just governance" expressed as bilingualism and biculturalism and later as multiculturalism. Although it is outside the scope of this chapter to offer an expansive analysis of the concept of just governance, it bears discussing briefly here. Pierre Trudeau's core governing ethos in his term as prime minister was a devotion to the concept of a "Just Society." Inarguably invoking the theories of political philosopher John Stuart Mill and his use of the term "just society," in the years following the commission Trudeau directly proposed a government platform that emphasized the importance of individual rights and freedoms limited only by those of another—that no one person's rights should infringe those of another person (see English, 2009). For Trudeau, this foundation was essential for fostering a common good and a belief in universal equality within society. Trudeau (1998, p. 19) included Indigenous people in his vision of a Just Society, stating that in such a society "our Indian and Inuit population will be encouraged to assume the full rights of citizenship through policies which will give them both greater responsibility for their own future and more meaningful equality of opportunity."

In the wake of the commission, as Tk'emlúpsemc scholar Sarah Nickel (2019) writes, the Trudeau government tried to abolish what Trudeau himself saw as special rights for Indigenous people through what is known colloquially as the 1969 White Paper. Special rights for Indigenous people, Trudeau asserted, perpetuated a problematic difference between Indigenous people and Canadians, resulting in "continued socio-economic oppression and political marginaliza-tion" (Nickel, 2019, p. 224). This opinion drew harsh criticism from Indigenous people and Indigenous political organizations. Harold Cardinal, then the president of the Indian Association of Alberta, issued a frank rebuke of the White Paper in the form of *The Unjust Society* (1969). In it, he also speaks to the lingering dark shadow of the commission:

> We listen when Canadian political leaders talk endlessly about strength in diversity for Canada, but we understand they are talking primarily about the French Canadian fact in Canada. Canadian Indians feel, along with other minorities, that there is a purpose and a place for us in Canada which accepts and encourages diversified human resources. We like the idea of a Canada where all cultures are encouraged to develop in harmony with one another, to become part of the great mosaic. We are impatient for the day when other Canadians will accord the Indian the recognition implied in this vision of Canada. (p. 10)

Any hope that Indigenous people had from Trudeau's rhetoric of a Just Society "quickly fizzled when Mr. Trudeau publicly announced that the federal government was not prepared to guarantee aboriginal rights and that the Canadian government considered the Indian treaties an anom-aly not to be tolerated in the Just Society" (Cardinal, 1969, pp. 14–15). Born in this era, then, multicultural governance, as a continuation of just governance, demands consent to a pluralistic vision of an inclusive Canada, one that Indigenous people soundly refused to see as separate from a recognition of sovereignty, treaty rights, and the ongoing impacts of colonization (see Fleras, 2015; Chapter 1, this volume).

Simpson (2017) questions whether consent is even possible. She writes that her nation cannot consent to notions of "just law" and "just governance" in light of the ongoing denial in Canada of the fact that theft (of Indigenous lands, waters, resources, etc.) was, and continues to be, foundational to Canada's existence (p. 26). I have argued elsewhere that Indigenous people cannot give consent to systems founded upon a neo-liberal ethos precisely because "the Canadian state occupied, and continues to occupy, a position of domination in relation to Indigenous peoples; even if Indigenous peoples *want* to be neoliberal subjects, the situation is thus that (particularly for those still governed by the Indian Act of 1876) they are not the free actors that the neoliberal ethos is founded upon" (Adese, 2022, pp. 15–16). Indigenous people cannot consent to systems that deny them the very possibility of choice. Where there is coercion, there can be no consent. For Indigenous people, this is plainly the function and experience of colonialism.

In fact, the commissioners were well aware that Simpson's community of Kahnawà:ke regarded both the English and the French as colonizers. Commissioner Scott shared with the other commissioners "a story about my experience in Caughnawaga and the way the Indians there look upon the French and English as equally Imperialist powers. By this time the members of the Commission were feeling more at ease with one another, and the humourous [*sic*] element became a little more frequent, and therefore helpful" (qtd. in Fraser, 2021, p. 5). That Kahnawà:ke's refusal became a source of humour highlights the insidious nature of the disregard for Indigenous sovereignty at the heart of the work of the commission. Simpson's analytical lens draws our attention to the moments when Indigenous people refuse to acquiese to Canadian settler political structures otherwise taken for granted. At the commission, Indigenous people's refusal to submit to a vision of Canadian national identity devoid of a reckoning with Indigenous rights and ongoing settler colonialism revealed then, much as it does today, the contradictions inherent in multiculturalism as a mode of just governance.

Conclusion

The participation of Indigenous people in the work of the Royal Commission on Bilingualism and Biculturalism, as Haque (2012, p. 95) writes, was largely constrained by the fact that the commissioners were striving to achieve "white-settler cohesion based on the two founding races." When Indigenous people were tangibly considered, such as in the report by Vallee (1966), there was an attempt to divorce culture from the legal-political relationship of Indigenous people with the Canadian state. He contends that, inasmuch as "Indians" were a legal category of focus for the Indian Affairs branch of the day, they also existed as an "ethnic group" (p. 13). Vallee attempts to make the case that, even if Indigenous languages have disappeared or Indigenous people have been assimilated, that does not mean that identification as Indigenous has disappeared—that something such as an "ethnic identity" exists among Indigenous people (p. 77). His words reflect, however, how Indigenous people's refusal was discursively managed and ultimately shelved behind platitudes about the scope of the commission's mandate. At the same time, however, Indigenous people and representative organizations frequently enacted a powerful politics of refusal. To consent to multicultural governance as it was then presented—as the guiding political ethos within Canada (and its most powerful national brand)—would have been to accept cultural minoritization and subjugation in place of Indigenous sovereignty. By consistently demanding recognition of sovereignty and by using the commissioners' language that Indigenous people were also *the* "founding race," and at minimum part of a triad of "Canadian founders," they disrupt the commission's attempt to impose a seamless vision for Canada that conceals, rather than contends with, their sovereignty.

As Simpson (2016, p. 330) writes, refusal is also connected intimately with truth. It is refusal that "holds on to a truth, structures this truth as [a] stance . . . , and operates as the revenge of consent." The term "revenge," as Simpson uses it, signals "an act of historical consciousness, of asserting this against the grain and thus, *avenging* the prior wrongdoing. . . . I mean avenging a prior of injustice and pointing to its life in the present" (2017, p. 26). The truth telling of Indigenous people in the context of the commission's work, then, can be read as this act of avenging a prior wrongdoing but also a wrongdoing in process—the effort to foment a Canadian national identity absolved of guilt and responsibility. The refusal of Indigenous people to subscribe to the government's nascent conceptualization of multiculturalism in the 1960s was based in part upon the exclusionary language that it employed and in part upon its very ideological basis, one that fundamentally negated the sovereignty of Indigenous people with whom Canada is legally bound—via Indigenous, Canadian, and international laws and treaties—to negotiate with on a nation-to-nation basis.

By refusing to allow an "inequity of interpretive possibility," Indigenous people and organizations at the commission hearings enacted the revenge of consent in such a manner as to ensure that their erasure can never be read as *acquiescence* (Simpson, 2017, p. 9).

As Cardinal (1969, p. 13) writes, "if we are to be part of the Canadian mosaic, then we want to be colourful red tiles, taking our place where red is both needed and appreciated." To be appreciated in this sense requires reckoning with those things that the nation-state works to conceal, such as "issues of land theft, genocide, sexual conquest, forced assimilation, displacement, the outlawing of religious practices, residential schools, imposed governments and laws, [and] the extreme intrusions on basic human rights" (Johnson, 2011, p. 111). In the long view of the life of multiculturalism, it is clear that these issues have come to be positioned *outside* the nation, occupying a space separate from Canada's multicultural national identity. In fact, as I discuss in *Aboriginal™* (Adese, 2022), in the decades since Indigenous people have been drawn into multiculturalism's mandate and discourse, a wide range of socio-political, -cultural, and -economic processes has driven the production of an "Aboriginal multiculturalism" in which Canadian politicians, institutions, corporations (both non-profit and for profit), and even Indigenous people ourselves have worked to create a configuration of Indigeneity separate from politics and socio-political concerns. The national narrative of the founding of the nation is conceived instead as a peaceful coming together of diverse peoples and cultures working toward a vision of a common good. It elides the weighty reality that multicultural governance is focused—like any other expression of settler governance—on the socio-political assimilation of Indigenous people.

References

Adese, J. (2022). *Aboriginal™: The cultural and economic politics of recognition*. University of Manitoba Press.

Bhabha, H. K. (2012). *The location of culture*. Routledge.

Cardinal, H. (1969). *The unjust society*. M.G. Hurtig.

English, J. (2009). *Just watch me: The life of Pierre Elliott Trudeau: 1968–2000*. Knopf Canada.

Fleras, A. (2015). *The politics of multiculturalism: Multicultural governance in comparative perspective*. Springer.

Fraser, G. (Ed.). (2021). *The fate of Canada: F.R. Scott's journal of the Royal Commission on Bilingualism and Biculturalism, 1963–1971*. McGill-Queen's University Press.

Gagnon, A.-G., & St-Louis, J.-C. (2013, Autumn). The Laurendeau-Dunton Commission and the need to rethink Canadian diversity. *Canadian Issues*, 43–47.

Haque, E. (2012). *Multiculturalism within a bilingual framework: Language, race, and belonging in Canada.* University of Toronto Press.

Johnson, D. M. (2011). From the tomahawk chop to the road block: Discourses of savagism in whitestream media. *American Indian Quarterly, 35*(1), 104–134.

Lalande, J. (2006). The roots of multiculturalism: Ukrainian-Canadian involvement in the multiculturalism discussion of the 1960s as an example of the position of the "Third Force." *Canadian Ethnic Studies, 38*(1), 47–64.

Lambertus, S. (2002). *Canada's Aboriginal peoples and intersecting identity markers* [Seminar paper]. Seminar on Intersections of Diversity, University of Saskatchewan, Saskatoon, SK. https://www.yumpu.com/en/document/view/17230106/canadas-aboriginal-peoples-and-intersecting-identity-markers-

Nickel, S. A. (2019). Reconsidering 1969: The White Paper and the making of the modern Indigenous rights movement. *Canadian Historical Review, 100*(2): 223–238.

Royal Commission on Bilingualism and Biculturalism. (1965). *Preliminary report of the Royal Commission on Bilingualism and Biculturalism.* Roger Duhamel, Queen's Printer.

Royal Commission on Bilingualism and Biculturalism. (1967). *Report. Vol. 1: General introduction: The official languages.* Roger Duhamel, Queen's Printer.

Royal Commission on Bilingualism and Biculturalism. (1970). *Report. Appendix I: Terms of reference.* Queen's Printer.

Simpson, A. (2016). Consent's revenge. *Cultural Anthropology, 31*(3): 326–333. https://doi.org/10.14506/ca31.3.02.

Simpson, A. (2017). The ruse of consent and the anatomy of "refusal": Cases from Indigenous North America and Australia. *Postcolonial Studies, 20*(1): 18–33.

Trudeau, P. E. (1998). *The just society* [Official statement by the prime minister, 10 June 1968.] In R. Graham (Ed.), *The essential Trudeau* (pp. 16–20). McClelland and Stewart. https://www.edu.gov.mb.ca/k12/cur/socstud/foundation_gr6/blms/6-4-4a.pdf

Vallee, F. G. (1966). *Indians and Eskimos of Canada* (Vol. 1) [Report prepared for the Royal Commission on Bilingualism and Biculturalism]. Queen's Printer.

Wangenheim, E. (1968). The Ukrainians: A case study of the "Third Force." In B. R. Blishen et al. (Eds.), *Canadian society: Sociological perspectives* (pp. 648–665). Macmillan.

Yalden, M. (2013, Autumn). Foreword: The B&B Commission—50 years on. *Canadian Issues,* 8–13.

3

Toward an Emotional Geography of Language for Rethinking Canadian Identity in a Transnational World

ANWAR AHMED

A general consensus among contemporary scholars is that identity is a fluid concept (Lawler, 2014; Zenker, 2018). It becomes more fluid when preceded by a contested concept such as nation/al. In this chapter, I take up "Canadian identity"—the topic of the current volume—to mean Canadian national identity. Canadian nationhood has been popularly discussed and understood through the lens of people's attitudes toward national symbols such as the Charter of Rights and Freedoms, the national flag, the national anthem, hockey, people's shared values, and their degree of pride in such symbols and values (e.g., Sinha, 2015). In this chapter, I draw attention to language and its potential connections with Canadian identity in the contemporary time. Although my focus is on language, it is important to keep in mind that constructing any identity and having it recognized by others is a complex process and that one identity might not be neatly isolated from other identities. Identities are often constructed and understood in a cluster. This makes it difficult to isolate a single identity from the rest of the cluster and "objectively" analyze it. In the pages that follow, first I discuss bilingualism and multiculturalism as two of the building blocks of Canadian identity. Then I focus on how bilingual education policies marginalize languages other than English and French. Next I turn to a discussion of the loss of one's mother tongue/heritage language and how this loss can influence identity negotiations in multilingual contexts. Then I describe how the contemporary context of mobility is different from the one that resulted in Canada's official bilingualism. I also make a case for being more attentive to the intersection of identity, language, and mobility in relation to places. Finally, I develop a notion of emotional geography of language and explain how this notion can be a conceptual intervention to understand the emotional closeness and distance of allophone[1] speakers as they undertake their journeys toward official bilingualism and the construction of a Canadian national identity. Thus, I aim to stimulate discussions about how research on identity and national belonging might benefit from paying more attention to language, emotion, and mobility.

Bilingualism and Multiculturalism: Two Important Ingredients of Canadian Identity

A major element of Canadian history is the conflict between English-speaking and French-speaking European settlers. Both groups competed for domination, control, and recognition. With a long history of tension, francophone Canadians have always worried about the preservation of their language and culture. They have also complained about their relative marginalization in economic and political domains. A turning point in this history of tension was the Quiet Revolution (*Révolution tranquille*) in Quebec in the 1960s when the province saw rapid changes in society, such as the Catholic Church's declining power and progressive challenges to traditional values. Perhaps the most significant change was the French-speaking majority's revolt against the English-speaking elite minority. A political desire for Quebec's separation from the rest of Canada grew stronger, and the anglophone political establishment began to pay attention to this challenge from francophone Canadians. As the Quiet Revolution shed light on a crisis of national unity, a long-cherished desire to establish a homogeneous Canadian state based upon the English language and British culture was shattered. In 1963, Prime Minister Lester B. Pearson created the Royal Commission on Bilingualism and Biculturalism (the B&B Commission). It found "that French Canadians were not well represented in the economy or in the decision-making ranks of government" and "that educational opportunities for francophone minorities outside Québec did not equal those provided for the anglophone minority in Québec" (Historica Canada, 2021, p. 2). After analyzing the cultural, educational, and economic gaps between French and English Canadians, the joint chairs of the B&B Commission—André Laurendeau and Davidson Dunton—pointed out that their work was to address "the greatest crisis in Canadian history" (qtd. in Historica Canada, 2021, p. 9).

Based upon the recommendations of the B&B Commission, the federal government under the leadership of Prime Minister Pierre Trudeau passed the Official Languages Act in 1969. This legislation gave equal status to English and French as the two official languages of Canada and provided bilingual access to all federal services. Passage of the Official Languages Act was an important milestone in Canadian linguistic and political history. In many ways, Canada adopted bilingualism to solve a political problem, not to show love and appreciation for linguistic diversity.

The work of the B&B Commission also paved the way for *multiculturalism* as an official policy, adopted in 1971. The stated aim of this policy was to promote cultural diversity and intercultural contact. While the federal government was dealing with the "Quebec crisis," there was an increasing rate of immigration from culturally and linguistically diverse countries. Various ethnic groups of immigrants were struggling to find their place in Canadian society, already marked by tensions among three "founding peoples": Indigenous, French, and English. At that historical moment, it was a strategic move for the federal government to promote the idea of multiculturalism, which would counteract Indigenous and francophone people's claims for inclusion and recognition. Since its introduction in 1971, the multiculturalism policy has gone through some changes. However, "the core ideas have remained fairly stable: the recognition and accommodation of cultural diversity; removing barriers to full participation; promoting interchange between groups; and promoting the acquisition of official languages" (Banting & Kymlicka, 2010, p. 50).

Although Canadian multiculturalism has been hailed by many as a model for the world, critics have blamed it for creating ethnic enclaves and ghettoization and for failing to establish strong social cohesion with a stable national identity. In that sense, we can perhaps agree that Canada "has passed from a pre-national to a post-national phase without ever having become a nation" (Frye, 1982, p. 15). Although much can be said about Canadian nationalism and the strengths and weaknesses of multiculturalism as a policy, as an ideology, and as a social fact, my primary goal is to look at multiculturalism through a linguistic lens. I would like to underline two of the problems that accompany multiculturalism in Canada. First, Pierre Trudeau's formulation of *multi*culturalism within a *bi*lingual framework downplayed the role of linguistic diversity in developing a multicultural identity. The policy not only encouraged the preservation and promotion of multiple cultures but also forced Indigenous peoples and immigrants to learn the official languages of Canada: French and English. From this perspective, there has been an inherent contradiction in the policy of multiculturalism in an officially bilingual—*not multilingual*—country (see Haque, 2012, for a detailed analysis of multiculturalism in a bilingual framework). Second, multiculturalism as a federal policy has done little for Indigenous peoples in Canada and their cultural preservation and prosperity. It is therefore not surprising that Indigenous peoples perceive multiculturalism as more relevant to settlers than to themselves (Berry, 2013). Indigenous peoples have also raised concerns that multiculturalism, as a policy, has not recognized their struggles to find a place in the Canadian nation (Légaré, 1995; for a discussion of how multiculturalism did little to repair the harms inflicted by colonization, see Adams, 1995).

Although there is widespread support for multiculturalism, promoting this policy within the bilingual framework has been challenging for both federal and provincial governments. One area of challenge is promoting "immigrant" languages or heritage languages so that immigrants and their descendants can maintain their cultural heritage and construct a national identity in the spirit of cultural inclusivity and linguistic pluralism. In "superdiverse" places such as Toronto, London, or New York, people should be able to carry their multiple identities with them, not simply a presumed ethnic identity that multiculturalism has traditionally emphasized (Vertovec, 2010). In such complex environments, language deserves critical analyses not only because multilingualism is under attack, and often conceptualized through a monolingual lens, but also because languages bear traces of memory, post-memory, and dis/continuing citizenship. As Blommaert (2013) suggested, because of the indexicality of languages relative to existing norms and power hierarchies in superdiverse ethnolinguistic contexts, we need to explore the polycentricity of linguistic repertoires in terms of identity, citizenship, and communicative competence. Following this line of argument, I respond in this chapter to a recent call to expand our literacy repertoires and pedagogical practices of critical language education to support students' academic success and democratic citizenship in a time of rising right-wing populism and neo-nationalism (Windle & Morgan, 2020).

Bilingual Education and the Marginalization of "Other" Languages

Although bilingualism is an established social fact in Canada, an important question remains unanswered. Who is the "right kind" of bilingual person? A recent incident highlights the importance of this question. Soon after the announcement of Mary Simon as the governor general of Canada, the Office of the Commissioner of Official Languages received hundreds of complaints about her. People complained about her lack of proficiency in French. Although Simon is bilingual—speaking Inuktitut and English—the complainants argued that she is not the right kind of bilingual person to become Canada's governor general. This example illustrates that Canadian language policy has created a hierarchy of English and French above other languages. As Rosen (2021, para. 13) has argued, "when we establish 'official' languages, we demote all other languages to 'unofficial'" status.

The Canadian Charter of Rights and Freedoms stipulates various rights related to education of and in the official languages. For example, parents whose first language is that of the English or French minority population of the province in which they live have the right to have their children educated at the primary and secondary school levels in that language. In Canada's bilingual education policy, students whose first language is one of the official languages are given opportunities to learn the other official language. However, students whose first language is not one of the official languages do not get the same opportunities because they expend most of their time and energy on learning the more dominant official language in their locality as their second/ additional language. In other words, many individuals from Indigenous and immigrant backgrounds encounter various obstacles to developing English or French bilingualism while preserving their mother tongue. Many of these individuals end up choosing one of the official languages.

Thus, they also become bilingual, not in English and French, but in their mother tongue and one of Canada's official languages. Governor General Simon is an example of this kind of bilingualism.

Many groups of the Canadian population face challenges in becoming officially bilingual, but I choose to focus on learners of English as an additional language (EAL). These learners form a sizable population at primary, secondary, and university levels of education in Canada. Their first language can be an Indigenous language or an "immigrant" language such as Arabic, Chinese, or Amharic. Compared with their peers who speak English as a first language, EAL learners do not get an equal opportunity to develop official bilingualism and to maintain their home language. As Kubota and Bale (2020, p. 774) write, "while public education enables Anglophone students to develop their mother tongue (i.e., English) and French, it denies EALs opportunities to develop bi/multilingual competence that includes their mother tongue." This linguistic barrier is clearly a disadvantage for Indigenous and allophone communities not only for holding constitutional positions (as in the example of Mary Simon) but also for developing a Canadian identity that is cosmopolitan and compatible with the contemporary transnational nature of the global order.

In Ontario, where I lived and worked for many years, allophone students display a strong desire to learn English. Although some of them end up learning French, most of them do not get enough support to develop their mother tongue or what is commonly referred to as their heritage language (HL). Ontario's Heritage Languages Policy funds up to two and a half hours of study per week in publicly funded schools. A heritage language can only be a subject of study, not a medium of instruction. Learning a heritage language occurs outside the school day, and it is separate from the formal school curriculum. For example, the Toronto District School Board offers international languages and African heritage programs one day per week, after the regular school day or on Saturdays. Thus, the Heritage Languages Policy "position[s] heritage-language learning at the margins of school life" (Kubota & Bale, 2020, p. 779). In principle, heritage language education in Ontario was designed to promote the linguistic and cultural diversity that the Canadian government had envisioned; however, strong opposition from some powerful groups has prevented its materialization. Opponents often use financial objections to overspending, reverse racism, and feasibility excuses to paralyze the HL education programs in the province (Kim et al., 2020). The marginalization of HL education is part of a greater scheme to devalue languages other than English and French. Although Canada's multiculturalism is often linked to linguistic diversity, HL education programs have never received sufficient financial and legislative support. The position of HL education at the edge of school life, and the view of HL learning as "non-academically recognized add-ons," have "encouraged immigrants, especially children, to forget their mother tongues" (Burnaby, 2008, p. 337). In short, Ontario's language education policies encourage EAL students, in many ways, to become monolingual English speakers (Kubota & Bale, 2020).

Loss of One's Mother Tongue and Construction of Canadian Identity

Now the question that we are confronted with is what does the loss of heritage languages and an instrumental motivation to become officially bilingual mean for the construction of a Canadian identity? It is important to note that 18 percent of Canadians are now English-French bilinguals. This proportion has remained unchanged since the 2016 census, though there has been a rise in Quebec, offset by a decline in the rest of Canada (Statistics Canada, 2022). Most of these English-French bilinguals are anglophones living in Quebec. Thus, Ottawa's bilingualism is not equally targeted to all Canadians, and there are significant regional variations in this regard. Striking a balance between social cohesion and linguistic pluralism has been a key challenge not only for Canada but also for many democratic nation-states. As May (2008) writes, discussions of citizenship in liberal democracies often focus on the significance of language to national identity. One of the key issues here is "whether speaking the state-mandated or national language . . . is, or should be, a requirement of national citizenship and a demonstration of both political and social integration by its members (especially for those who speak other languages as a first language)" (p. 15). This debate about a state-mandated dominant language and the linguistic diversity in multicultural societies has important implications for people's negotiations of identities. Research in applied linguistics has shed light on a close relationship between language and identity (e.g., Ahmed & Morgan, 2021; Norton, 2019). In this relationship, language and identity shape each other as they supply the terms and means with which identities are negotiated and linguistically indexed (Pavlenko & Blackledge, 2004). Research has also shown how speaking a state-mandated language, in which government services such as health care and education are provided, as a second/additional language puts the speaker in a disadvantaged position because the speaker is often interpellated with imposed identities. For example, Miller's study with immigrant students who speak English as a second language in Queensland, Australia, demonstrated that the "voices [of these students] are differentially valued, differentially audible" (2004, p. 312). Similar findings are in Chapters 4 and 5 of this volume (by Vander Tavares and Jacqueline Ng), which signal practices that exclude English as a Second Language (ESL) students while proposing strategies for better integration and inclusion of such learners. Audibility—a Bourdieusian concept—implies "the degree to which speakers sound like, and are legitimated by, users of the dominant discourse" (Miller, 2004, p. 291).

In addition to this relative lack of audibility, ESL/EAL students often carry an extra burden of practising, improving, and preserving their mother tongue. This affects minority language speakers' identity negotiations in multilingual contexts. Despite a strong link between identity and HL maintenance, "cultural distancing and assimilation pressure encourage language loss, as minority languages face stigma and discrimination" (Tseng, 2020, p. 112). Many immigrant parents perceive their home language as "useless" because of a lack of representation in the wider society and systemic discrimination against "immigrant" languages. Although a heritage language can be a source of pride, many parents worry about their children's educational success. Therefore, they focus more on the dominant language of the new context, sometimes at the expense of losing their home language. For these reasons, "symbolic importance [alone of a heritage language] does not guarantee [its] survival, as demonstrated by the worldwide trend toward minority language loss" (Tseng, 2020, p. 112).

In a context like that of Canada, where significant barriers to the achievement of linguistic diversity remain, what does a Canadian identity mean, and how is such an identity constructed? Let us take a moment to think about the concept of "identity." Etymologically, the term suggests sameness (from the Latin *idem*). A familiar denotation of the term is that people are identical to themselves as well as to others who belong to the same category. This also means that we can understand identity in a negative sense: for example, a certain person is *not like* someone else. In both positive and negative senses, the term indicates stability of character and of social identification across time and space. But this static view of identity is not compatible with actual processes of identification that individuals go through in their individual, social, and political lives. As Lawler (2014, p. 10) writes, reducing identities to stable "categories would be to obscure the tensions within and between identities and to see identities as 'finished' products, rather than as active, processual engagements with the social world." Following this line of work, I do not intend to use the term "identity" to suggest a stable socio-culturally and biologically determined essence of a person. Instead, I look at identity as an active force (more a verb than a noun) to suggest the processes of forming complex subjectivities. One way to understand these processes is to situate identities in spatiotemporal contexts so that we can see multiple facets and inherent tensions in identity work. In sum, I like to see identities "in a constant state of flux, varying from one time and one space to another" (Burgess & Ivanič, 2010, p. 232).

If we view identity as fluid and negotiable, then we must pay attention to the discursive nature of identity construction and the role of power relations in the processes of identity negotiation. This kind of attention is particularly important for the linguistic reality of multicultural Canada. As I mentioned above, Canada's official bilingualism—born from four centuries of colonialism, settlement, and governance and a more recent political crisis in the 1960s—has positioned multilingual speakers who are not English-French bilingual in negative and disadvantageous ways. Before delving into this more, I would like to quote Pavlenko and Blackledge (2004, p. 27), at some length, to summarize socio-linguistic understandings of identity negotiations in multilingual contexts:

> (1) that linguistic and identity options are limited within particular sociohistoric contexts, even though continuously contested and reinvented; (2) that diverse identity options and their links to different language varieties are valued differently and that sometimes it is these links rather than the options per se that are contested and subverted; (3) that some identity options may be negotiable, while others are either imposed (and thus non-negotiable) or assumed (and thus

not negotiated); and finally and most importantly, (4) that individuals are agentive beings who are constantly in search of new social and linguistic resources which allow them to resist identities that position them in undesirable ways, produce new identities, and assign alternative meanings to the links between identities and linguistic varieties.

These socio-linguistic understandings emphasize not only the role of language in identity construction but also people's mobilization of discursive resources to resist imposed identities. Loss of the mother tongue of immigrants and their children is an example of how contemporary contexts of mobility and social integration are sites of struggle over conflicting identities.

The 1960s Context of Bilingualism and the Multilingual Reality of Today's Transnational World

The political crisis that gave birth to official English-French bilingualism in Canada occurred within a very different context from that of today. Canada, especially in urban areas, is now increasingly multicultural and multilingual. For example, municipal services are offered in multiple languages—in addition to English and French—that reflect the demographic makeup of particular localities. One way to understand the current linguistic reality is to look at it through the lens of transnationalism. Transnationalism refers to multiple ties and activities that connect people, institutions, and cultural practices across the borders of nation-states (Vertovec, 2009). Transnationalism has been an effective conceptual intervention to counter methodological nationalism that conflated human societies with nation-states and assumed that members of a nation-state share a common history and a stable set of values (Glick Schiller, 2009). Thus, transnationalism has emerged as a necessary corrective to the promise of globalization for a borderless world. Contrary to some critics' claim (e.g., Bommes, 2005; Waldinger, 2015), transnationalism does not ignore or downplay the importance of nation-states. Instead, it sheds light on the complex nature of interconnectivity across national borders. It shows how mobilities of people, ideas, and goods permeate all spheres of people's personal lives and socio-political activities. Thus, transnationalism is a helpful concept in a world that oscillates between globalization and nationalism (Ahmed & Barnawi, 2021).

In fields in which language is a matter of concern, transnationalism underscores how people's mobility, belonging, and processes of identification are mediated by their relationships with places and social conditions that might or might not recognize their linguistic repertoires and *audibility*. Although mobility is now the new normal, people's abilities to move from place to place and from country to country are differentiated by their economic classes and various forms of sociolinguistic capital. Moreover, mobility is not always a pleasant experience, for many people move to flee violence, poverty, and climate change. But we can safely claim that, when people move from one place to another, they do not necessarily cut off all their ties to the places that they leave behind. As De Fina and Perrino (2013, p. 510) explain, "although in the past, dislocations often implied drastic separations from places and cultures of origin, nowadays the diffusion of new globalizing media has resulted in the ability of displaced populations to keep in touch with their home countries and with other, far away interlocutors." This is a remarkable change since the time of Canada's adoption of bilingualism as an official policy. We can understand this change in light of research emerging from the intersection of language, identity, and transnationalism. For example, De Fina and Perrino have identified a number of shifts in this body of research, and two of these shifts are of particular relevance for my work here:

1. The critique of a view of speech communities as relatively homogeneous, sharing in cultural repertoires and beliefs, and bound to specific locations.

2. The critical re-assessment of a default conception of languages as well-defined codes that can be easily separated from each other and that are anchored to distinctive and bounded speech communities. (2013, p. 510)

These shifts indicate that speech communities as well as their locations have become fluid. Here the concept of speech community does not simply refer to a group that uses the same language. Instead, it is concerned with language ideologies and practices that bind a group of people in ways that have both symbolic and material consequences. As people relocate away from their local communities, they use shared language ideologies and signifying practices to recreate new communities in which relationships and identities are (re)negotiated through language practices (Morgan, 2014). In addition to these shifts, we know from migration research that earlier models of acculturation and assimilation are no longer applicable to transnationally mobile individuals. The theory that all immigrants go through a universal psychological process of cultural adaptation and social integration fails to capture the complexities in contemporary social spaces. Today the acculturation experiences of most immigrants are the results of a dynamic, back-and-forth transaction between self and society, between privilege and marginalization (Bhatia & Ram, 2009). Notions of belonging and identity are now conceptualized and practised along geographically discontinuous lines (Fleras, 2019).

The discussion above suggests that fixed identities in the contemporary transnational world are not possible. People construct dynamic, relational, and hybrid identities as they respond to and build relations with various places that they currently occupy, have left, or aspire to occupy in the future. And the languages of these places—both dominant and marginalized—have significant impacts on their identity negotiations. We cannot possibly understand people's relationships with languages without understanding their relationships with places. People were once asked to forget their places. For example, the Industrial Revolution, urbanization, and the consequential displacement resulted in increased levels of workers' alienation from their selves and their environments. Then came the promise of globalization, and people were encouraged to become global citizens without strong attachments to particular places. In response to such tendencies, some social scientists, especially human geographers, underscored people's affective bonds with places. Notably, Tuan (1990) developed the concept of topophilia to illustrate how people's affective bonds with places contribute to the formation of their values, beliefs, motivations, and identities. Today many social scientists agree that identities are "intrinsically tied to place[s]" (Easthope, 2009, p. 71), and people's relationships with places are intensely emotional (Boccagni & Baldassar, 2015).

Toward an Emotional Geography of Language

Based upon my discussions above, I would like to propose an emotional geography of language to reconceptualize Canadian identity after the transnational turn. Historically, Canada has been able to promote an identity as a tolerant, diverse, peace-loving, and multicultural nation.

However, "perceptions of Canadian uniqueness on issues of internal diversity are much exaggerated" (Kymlicka, 2003, p. 357). For a Canadian identity that must be negotiable in relation not only to internal diversity but also to Canada's place in a globalized and transnational world, I propose that we develop awareness of an emotional geography of language. Here the definition of language is broadened to include multimodal and (trans)semiotic practices. This proposal responds to a recent call to explore the role of affect and the non-discursive in the field of research on language and identity (Zenker, 2018). In the context of this chapter, a turn to affect and emotion is important because language and identity have always played pivotal roles in shaping Canada's policies of bilingualism and multiculturalism. However, we have not been able to answer the following questions. Who is the "right kind" of bilingual person in Canada? Does English-French bilingualism support an inclusive Canadian identity? Since emotion, language, place, and identity are interconnected, how can an emotional geography of language be helpful?

The concept of "emotional geography" is generally used to locate and study emotions in bodies and places and to understand people's relationships with their environments. It points to "the patterns of closeness and distance in human interactions that shape the emotions we experience about relationships to ourselves, each other, and the world around us" (Hargreaves, 2001, p. 1056). In contexts of second and heritage language education, the concept can be useful because it provides us with a lens through which to look at closeness and distance in how individuals relate to each other and to their environments through discursive practices and attachments to languages.

I define emotional geography by using the expression *body and/in space*. First, the human body records the history of all its encounters with other bodies. Here I allude to Baruch Spinoza's notion of the body's affective potential: a capacity to affect and be affected. However, "the capacity of a body is never defined by a body alone but is always aided and abetted by, and dovetails with, the field or context of its force-relations" (Seigworth & Gregg, 2010, p. 3). In this sense, "our first and foremost, most immediate and intimately *felt* geography is the body, the site of emotional experience and expression *par excellence*" (Davidson & Milligan, 2004, p. 523). Second, the spaces where we live out our lives have complex and interconnected relationships with how we feel and understand emotions in our bodies. Spaces also afford us interpretive lenses through which to embody and communicate emotional experiences. For example, "in attempts to articulate emotion—to embody it linguistically—we speak of the 'heights' of joy and the 'depths' of despair, significant others are comfortingly *close* or distressingly *distant*. The articulation of emotion is, thus, spatially mediated in a manner that is not simply metaphorical" (Davidson & Milligan, 2004, p. 523). Thus, when allophone speakers are made ashamed of their mother tongue and expected to learn two new languages to become officially bilingual Canadians, analysis of emotional closeness to and distance from these languages and the cultural practices of those who speak them is an important consideration. It is important because emotional dimensions of language-based identities often influence people's civic engagement and socio-political participation.

Although there is a growing body of research on emotional geography in the fields of human geography and migration studies, educational research on place and space has not taken emotionality seriously (Kenway & Youdell, 2011). In educational contexts, the concept of emotional geography can help us to appreciate how places mediate an individual's emotion and agency and which kinds of pedagogical spaces can be produced as a result of such mediation. As Zembylas (2015) has shown, the concept of emotional geography can draw attention to the emotionality of movement and how such emotionality shapes existing and new social relations. I believe that emotional geography can also help us to understand how language learners negotiate their identities through emotional engagements with themselves and others. This is vital because understanding identity requires "a consideration of the reciprocal effects of commitment, identity salience, and role performance on the generation and experience of affect" (Stryker, 2004, p. 11).

In the Canadian context, policies of official bilingualism encourage domestication and containment of first/heritage language maintenance of allophones. Maintenance and promotion of heritage languages are allowed to continue on terms that do not threaten the economic-instrumental superiority of English and French. In such a context, a complex entanglement of emotion, mobility, and identity can stand in the way of developing a Canadian identity that is inclusive, interrogative, and cosmopolitan. If educational policies force allophone learners and "humiliate" their parents or grandparents as a way of supporting official bilingualism, then English and French—learned as second and third languages—can cause emotional distance and detachment for some allophone speakers. Canadian novelist Nancy Huston's account of bilingualism is illustrative[2] since Huston found her second language—French—to be a language of distance and emotional detachment (see Kinginger, 2004, for details). Applied linguistics research on emotion and bilingualism has also revealed that two or more languages that an individual speaks differ in their emotional impacts: the second/additional language is often a language of emotional detachment (Rajagopalan, 2004). Emotional detachment and distance from the official languages can also negatively affect individuals' political engagement and disposition toward and practice of democratic citizenship. Therefore, an emotional geography of language should consist of

(1) awareness of how people's relations to places influence their identity constructions;

(2) attention to how transnationally mobile people carry with them a history of affective encounters with places, languages, and cultures;

(3) understanding of how affect and identity shape each other by enabling social actors to establish, maintain, or dissolve relationships;

(4) appreciation of the fact that people have a strong emotional attachment to their mother tongue; and

(5) interrogation of policies that promote instrumental motivation to learn state-mandated languages at the expense of mother tongues and heritage languages.

It is my hope that an emotional geography of language will encourage policy makers, researchers, and educators to take a geographical approach to understanding language-based identities constructed with people's memories and emotions and the simultaneity and multiplicity of their experiences in social spaces. An emotional geography of language is also expected to provide them with a conceptual framework to analyze stories such as the complaint about Mary Simon's appointment as Canada's governor general and her lack of English-French bilingualism. Critical and deconstructionist analyses of such stories are necessary (a) to understand the struggles of Indigenous and allophone peoples to find their place in multicultural, linguistically diverse, yet officially bilingual Canada; (b) to appreciate multiple and competing meanings of Canadian identity in the contemporary time; and (c) to reimagine what *being a Canadian* ought to mean in a transnationally connected multilingual world.

References

Adams, H. (1995). *A tortured people: The politics of colonization*. Theytus Books.

Ahmed, A., & Barnawi, O. (2021). Introduction: TESOL teacher education: Oscillating between globalization and nationalism. In A. Ahmed and O. Barnawi (Eds.), *Mobility of knowledge, practice and pedagogy in TESOL teacher education* (pp. 1–12). Palgrave Macmillan.

Ahmed, A., & Morgan, B. (2021). Postmemory and multilingual identities in English language teaching: A duoethnography. *The Language Learning Journal, 49*(4), 483–498.

Banting, K., & Kymlicka, W. (2010). Canadian multiculturalism: Global anxieties and local debates. *British Journal of Canadian Studies, 23*(1), 43–72.

Berry, J. W. (2013). Research on multiculturalism in Canada. *International Journal of Intercultural Relations, 37*(6), 663–675.

Bhatia, S., & Ram, A. (2009). Theorizing identity in transnational and diaspora cultures: A critical approach to acculturation. *International Journal of Intercultural Relations, 33*(2), 140–149.

Blommaert, J. (2013). Citizenship, language, and superdiversity: Towards complexity. *Journal of Language, Identity and Education, 12*(3), 193–196.

Boccagni, P., & Baldassar, L. (2015). Emotions on the move: Mapping the emergent field of emotion and migration. *Emotion, Space and Society, 16*, 73–80.

Bommes, M. (2005). Transnationalism or assimilation? *Journal of Social Science Education, 4*(1), 14–30. https://doi.org/10.4119/jsse-338

Burgess, A., & Ivanič, R. (2010). Writing and being written: Issues of identity across timescales. *Written Communication, 27*(2), 228–255.

Burnaby, B. (2008). Language policy and education in Canada. In S. May & N. H. Hornberger (Eds.), *Encyclopedia of language and education* (2nd ed.), *Vol. 1: Language policy and political issues in education* (pp. 331–341). Springer.

Davidson, J., & Milligan, C. (2004). Embodying emotion sensing space: Introducing emotional geographies. *Social and Cultural Geography, 5*(4), 523–532.

De Fina, A., & Perrino, S. (2013). Transnational identities. *Applied Linguistics, 34*(5), 509–515.

Easthope, H. (2009). Fixed identities in a mobile world? The relationship between mobility, place, and identity. *Identities: Global Studies in Culture and Power, 16*(1), 61–82.

Fleras, A. (2019). 50 years of Canadian multiculturalism: Accounting for its durability, theorizing the crisis, anticipating the future. *Canadian Ethnic Studies, 51*(2), 19–59.

Frye, N. (1982). *Divisions on a ground: Essays on Canadian culture* (J. Polk, Ed.). Anansi.

Glick Schiller, N. (2009). A global perspective on migration and development. *Social Analysis, 53*(3), 14–37.

Haque, E. (2012). *Multiculturalism within a bilingual framework: Language, race, and belonging in Canada.* University of Toronto Press.

Hargreaves, A. (2001). Emotional geographies of teaching. *Teachers College Record, 103*(6), 1056–1080.

Historica Canada. (2021). *Official languages act: Education guide.* http://education.historicacanada.ca/en/tools/626

Kenway, J., & Youdell, D. (2011). The emotional geographies of education: Beginning a conversation. *Emotion, Space and Society, 4*(3), 131–136.

Kim, H., Burton, J. L., Ahmed, T., & Bale, J. (2020). Linguistic hierarchisation in education policy development: Ontario's Heritage Languages Program. *Journal of Multilingual and Multicultural Development, 41*(4), 320–332.

Kinginger, C. (2004). Bilingualism and emotion in the autobiographical works of Nancy Huston. *Journal of Multilingual and Multicultural Development, 25*(2–3), 159–178.

Kubota, R., & Bale, J. (2020). Bilingualism—but not plurilingualism—promoted by immersion education in Canada: Questioning equity for students of English as an additional language. *TESOL Quarterly, 54*(3), 773–785.

Kymlicka, W. (2003). Being Canadian. *Government and Opposition, 38*(3), 357–385.

Lawler, S. (2014). *Identity: Sociological perspectives* (2nd ed.). Polity.

Légaré, E. I. (1995). Canadian multiculturalism and Aboriginal people: Negotiating a place in the nation. *Identities: Global Studies in Culture and Power, 1*(4), 347–366.

May, S. (2008). Language education, pluralism and citizenship. In S. May & N. H. Hornberger (Eds.), *Encyclopedia of language and education* (2nd ed.), *Vol. 1: Language policy and political issues in education* (pp. 15–29). Springer.

Miller, J. (2004). Identity and language use: The politics of speaking ESL in schools. In A. Pavlenko & A. Blackledge (Eds.), *Negotiation of identities in multilingual contexts* (pp. 290–315). Multilingual Matters.

Morgan, M. H. (2014). *Speech communities.* Cambridge University Press.

Noakes, T. (2020). Allophone. In *The Canadian encyclopedia.* https://www.thecanadianencyclopedia.ca/en/article/allophone

Norton, B. (2019). Identity and language learning: A 2019 retrospective account. *Canadian Modern Language Review, 75*(4), 299–307.

Pavlenko, A., & Blackledge, A. (2004). Introduction: New theoretical approaches to the study of negotiation of identities in multilingual contexts. In A. Pavlenko & A. Blackledge (Eds.), *Negotiation of identities in multilingual contexts* (pp. 1–33). Multilingual Matters.

Rajagopalan, K. (2004). Emotion and language politics: The Brazilian case. *Journal of Multilingual and Multicultural Development, 25*(2–3), 105–123.

Rosen, N. (2021). Should bilingualism change in Canada? The debate over Gov. Gen. Mary Simon. *The Conversation.* https://theconversation.com/

should-bilingualism-change-in-canada-the-debate-over-gov-gen-mary-simon-164836

Seigworth, G. J., & Gregg, M. (2010). An inventory of shimmers. In M. Gregg & G. J. Seigworth (Eds.), *The affect theory reader* (pp. 1–26). Duke University Press.

Sinha, M. (2015). *Canadian identity, 2013*. Statistics Canada. https://www150.statcan.gc.ca/n1/pub/89-652-x/89-652-x2015005-eng.htm

Statistics Canada. (2022). *While English and French are still the main languages spoken in Canada, the country's linguistic diversity continues to grow.* https://www150.statcan.gc.ca/n1/daily-quotidien/220817/dq220817a-eng.htm

Stryker, S. (2004). Integrating emotion into identity theory. In J. H. Turner (Ed.), *Theory and research on human emotions* (pp. 1–23). Emerald Group Publishing.

Tseng, A. (2020). Identity in home-language maintenance. In A. C. Schalley & S. A. Eisenchlas (Eds.), *Handbook of home language maintenance and development: Social and affective factors* (pp. 109–129). De Gruyter.

Tuan, Y-F. (1990). *Topophilia: A study of environmental perception, attitudes, and values.* Columbia University Press.

Vertovec, S. (2009). *Transnationalism.* Routledge.

Vertovec, S. (2010). Towards post-multiculturalism? Changing communities, conditions and contexts of diversity. *International Social Science Journal, 61*(199), 83–95.

Waldinger, R. (2015). *The cross-border connection: Immigrants, emigrants, and their homelands.* Harvard University Press.

Windle, J., & Morgan, B. (2020). Remix nationalism and critical language education. In K. McIntosh (Ed.), *Applied linguistics and language teaching in the neo-nationalist era* (pp. 267–294). Palgrave Macmillan.

Zembylas, M. (2015). Researching "emotional geographies" in schools: The value of critical ethnography. In H. Flam & J. Kleres (Eds.), *Methods of exploring emotions* (pp. 181–190). Routledge.

Zenker, O. (2018). Language and identity. In H. Callan & S. Coleman (Eds.), *The international encyclopedia of anthropology* (pp. 1–7). Wiley. https://doi.org/10.1002/9781118924396.wbiea2271

Endnotes

1   In Canada, an allophone is defined as a person who has a first language other than English, French, or an Indigenous language. Approximately 22.3 percent of the Canadian population is considered allophone (Noakes, 2020). In another definition, an allophone is a person whose mother tongue is neither French nor English but might be an Indigenous language. According to this definition and the 2021 census data, "one in four Canadians"—that is, 25 percent of the population—is allophone (Statistics Canada, 2022, para. 4).

2   Huston writes primarily in French, her second language. She also translates her own works into English, her first language.

PART 2

REDEFINING IDENTITIES
in
EDUCATIONAL CONTEXTS

Education is always political. From teaching methods to didactic materials and the "hidden curriculum," formal education works as a vehicle for the transmission of ideologies that organize different groups of people, cultures, and languages into hierarchies. Multicultural education emerged as a way to recognize and address issues of discrimination, especially discrimination toward learners of a minoritized racial, ethnic, and linguistic background. Nevertheless, multicultural education has not been immune from ideological capture and the exclusion of Indigenous knowledges. Neo-liberal multiculturalism, in particular, which focuses on the acknowledgement and celebration of diversity without an actual engagement with issues of social justice, has permeated the field in complex yet subtle ways. Despite these challenges, education remains a site where ideologies can also be critically identified, challenged, and destabilized. Chapters in Part 2 embark on a journey of deconstruction and reconstruction of dominant representations of Canadian identity by dealing with ideological issues that have made invisible the experiences of learners of a plurilingual, racialized, and minoritized background in Canada.

In Chapter 4, Vander Tavares describes changes made to the curriculum of an English as a Second Language course aimed at diversifying representations of "Canadian identity." Tavares positions immigrant and Indigenous literature as the place of departure for teaching and learning English for academic purposes and Canadian culture, thereby confronting issues linked to native speakerism and ethnocentrism that have shaped the foundation of second language and higher education in Canada. In Chapter 5, Jacqueline Ng illustrates how educators can create an inclusive, equitable classroom through transformative multi-literacies pedagogy to enhance English language learners' language learning and reaffirm their identities against cultural and linguistic stereotypes. Ng implements an Identity Text Project through which such learners reconstruct their identities, which by extension helps to expand notions of "Canadian identity." In Chapter 6, Judith Patouma investigates issues of inclusion and identity construction faced by teachers and learners in francophone minority communities. Patouma argues that plurilingual pedagogies are also necessary in diverse, multicultural schools where one image of Canadian culture prevails.

This section demonstrates that "Canadian identity" in educational contexts, despite being embodied multiculturally and multilingually, is not necessarily inclusive. At the same time, chapters in this section put forth social-justice-oriented pedagogical engagements through which issues of belonging can be confronted and the voices of students heard.

4

Canadian Identity from a Multicultural Perspective:
Foregrounding Immigrant and Indigenous Voices
in an ESL Course

VANDER TAVARES

Canada is known globally as a multicultural and welcoming society. Indeed, Canada was the first country in the world to adopt multiculturalism as an official state policy in 1971 (Government of Canada, 2012; see also the chapter by Fleras in this volume). Yet culturally and linguistically minoritized groups in the country face issues of representation and inclusion, particularly when it comes to constructions of national identity. The dominance of anglo- and francophone cultures through colonization has displaced Indigenous knowledges and maintained a hierarchy for other cultural groups that have established themselves in Canada through immigration. In higher education, such issues can be intensified on the basis of a predominantly Eurocentric approach to policy, curriculum, and practice (Pidgeon, 2016). This is certainly the case in the discipline of English as a Second Language (ESL), the foundation of which was shaped by a colonial and Western view of language and culture, thereby contributing to the marginalization of other linguistic and cultural identities in the field.

In this chapter, I focus on how such issues of representation are confronted in a course taught to multilingual and multicultural students at a university in Toronto. I begin with an overview of how coloniality has historically affected the field of second language education. Subsequently, I present the context for the course in relation to the lack of diversity within constructions of Canadian identity and move on to discuss international students' experiences in Canada and relate such findings to broader trends in Canada with respect to issues of diversity, despite discourses of multiculturalism and multilingualism. I then lay out a framework for multicultural education, which plays a dual role in this inquiry: confronting the lack of representation in second language education and in contemporary Canadian society. I also focus on describing how the credit-bearing course in question was designed to foreground the experiences of Indigenous and minoritized immigrant groups in Canada. The conclusion is based on my reflection, as the instructor, on the real and perceived impacts of the course.

Coloniality in Second Language Education

In the past two decades, the field of second language education has seen an increasing recognition of coloniality in its research and teaching practices. According to Maldonado-Torres (2010, p. 97), coloniality refers to the "long-standing patterns of power that emerged as a result of colonialism, but that define culture, labour, intersubjective relations, and knowledge production well beyond the strict limits of colonial administration." Critical discussions about the legacy of colonialism in the field have fuelled the emergence of new perspectives for research and teaching that have sought not only to confront coloniality but also to include new ontologies (Kumaravadivelu, 2016). In the context of English as an additional language (EAL), a term that envelops con-texts where English is spoken as both a foreign and second language, coloniality has been maintained through constructs that reflect epis-temologies, values, and representations of the so-called centre or the Global North (Tavares, 2023a). For most of the history of English language education, such aspects have been considered neutral, better, or the standard (Canagarajah, 2012).

The construct of the native speaker as the ideal speaker of a language has powerfully affected every facet of EAL education. Native speaker teachers of English have been considered better teachers in many parts of the non-anglophone world, driving recruitment policies that have consequently displaced local teachers who possess social and cultural knowledge of the local context (Alshammari, 2021). In a similar vein, native speakerism has also overwhelmingly guided the development of EAL teaching practices and materials until recently. As such, the socio-cultural linguistic resources that multilingual students bring into their EAL classes have been traditionally seen as barriers to the development of the students' (native-like) proficiencies in English. Such an approach is rooted in the monolingual mindset to English language learning, which purports that the best way of learning English is through English and English only (Slaughter & Cross, 2021). Multilingual approaches to language learning are not new. However, coloniality has served to delegitimate them.

The "ideal" speaker of English is not simply *any* native speaker of the language. The ideology of native speakerism reflects speakers of a particular socio-linguistic profile whose language, especially in terms of accent, is considered "standard" English. For this reason, race cannot be detached from the construct of the native speaker. Ethnically and racially minoritized native speakers of English have faced issues of representation and exclusion on the basis of language practices reflective of dominant Anglo-Saxon cultures (Ruecker & Ives, 2015). Therefore, the linguistic and cultural construction of the native speaker of English has direct implications for how multilingual, multicultural EAL teachers and students see their place in the classroom and, by extension, in the host society. Academically, professionally, socially, and psychologically, ideologies of native speakerism alone are enough to make multilingual EAL speakers feel inferior and marginal (Tavares, 2022a; Zacharias, 2019).

Although this chapter is situated in the field of English as a Second Language, it is important to critically recognize the political assumptions behind such a term. The "superiority" of English, as Shin (2006) points out, is reflected in the very name of the field, in which ESL stemmed from TESOL: teaching English to speakers of *other* languages. In the context of coloniality in language education, then, "other" does not simply mean different—it is embedded within a hierarchy. As such, naming a course an ESL course or an individual as an "ESL speaker" is not a neutral act as far as the dominance of English prevails (Shin, 2006). "ESL classes" have often held an inferior status historically as remedial classes for "deficient" speakers of the language. "English as an additional language," on the other hand, emerged as a more inclusive term, since English is, for many, not a second but another language within their multilingual repertoire (Webster & Lu, 2012).

Manifestations of Canadian Identity

For many onlookers, the image of Canada is one in which multiple cultural and ethnic groups live together harmoniously. Yet what it means to be Canadian, at a deeper level, still reflects Eurocentric values, behaviours, and languages for a larger group, despite the rich history of Indigenous peoples and non-European groups in the country. Raney (2009) presented an account of research conducted outside Quebec in which the construct of "being Canadian" was critically explored, as elaborated in the introduction to this volume. Characteristics such as being born in Canada, living most of one's life in Canada, having Canadian citizenship, and being a Christian were considered "very important" to being Canadian (Raney, 2009, p. 14). All such expressions of Canadian identity can, and in many instances have, perpetuated the exclusion of various other groups in Canadian society. Since in this chapter I focus on a course that prioritized Indigenous and immigrant perspectives on the concept of Canada as a nation, in the following paragraphs I aim to briefly problematize the four aforementioned facets of Canadian identity in light of the experiences of the two latter groups: Indigenous and immigrant Canadians.

The course discussed in this chapter was taught at York University, situated in Canada's most culturally and linguistically diverse city. The first three expressions of Canadian identity previously mentioned are thus in direct conflict with the multicultural reality and fabric of the university and the city. According to statistics gathered by the city (City of Toronto, 2017), the majority of immigrants tend to come to Toronto at or after the age of twenty-five, with only a small minority of Torontonians being born in the city. In terms of religion, a national survey in 2018 found that among respondents, "a slim majority of Canadian adults (55%) say they are Christian" (Pew Research Center, 2019). The survey also found that, as immigration grows, affiliation with other faiths also increases, whereas identification with Christianity declines. This reality stands in great contrast to the results of the survey.

Such trends reinforce the need for notions of Canadian identity to be expanded, or else the delegitimization of many new Canadians will continue. These concerns around inclusion and recognition align with recent findings on the experiences of immigrants to Canada (Basok & George, 2020). George and Selimos (2019) reported on the difficulties that newcomers experienced as they moved to Canada late in adulthood.

Challenges included systemic exclusion and marginalization based upon the lack of work experience and education in Canada, contributing to feelings of unbelonging. Equally important to this discussion is the recognition of the historical exclusion of Canada's Indigenous peoples from constructions of Canadian identity (Beavon et al., 2005). Although some progress has been made, as Downey (2018, p. 21) has argued, "shifting forms of colonialism" have become ingrained in how Canadian society recognizes Indigenous peoples and their contributions to the country. For example, Indigenous peoples still lack representation at various levels of government despite increased national attention directed toward Indigenous identity in Canada (Heritz, 2018).

Multilingual International Students in Canada

In recent years, Canada has become one of the top destinations for higher education for international students. Canada has been historically considered a welcoming and safe place for international students in light of its political stability. Other contributing factors to the ascension of Canada internationally include the cost of tuition for international students relative to other destinations and the uncomplicated process of obtaining a student visa (Chen, 2008). Nowadays, the majority of international students in Canada come from Asia, particularly China and India (Canadian Bureau for International Education, 2020). According to a survey conducted in 2018 by the Canadian Bureau for International Education (CBIE, 2020), at least 60 percent of international students indicated that they planned to apply for permanent residence in Canada. Despite their desire to stay in the country, research has illustrated that international students encounter a number of structural challenges to their positive socio-cultural adjustment in Canada (see the chapter by Longboat et al. in this volume).

Some of these issues stem from what might be better characterized as neo-racism, based not only upon race but also, and primarily, the hierarchy of cultures and languages (Lee & Rice, 2007). Because neo-racist attitudes consider some cultures better than others, discrimination toward inferiorized and marginalized groups becomes seemingly justified by the goal of "maintaining a good society" (Tavares, 2022a). For instance, in a study by Houshmand et al. (2014, p. 381), international students of a racialized background felt as though "their domestic White peers did not care about or want their presence on campus." Neo-racism can manifest in subtle and overt forms, including exclusion, stereotyping, and avoidance by local students (Tavares, 2021b, 2023b). Fu (2021) encountered similar experiences with the students in her study. The international students, also of a racialized background, explained that despite weeks of working together with local students, they felt deliberately ignored by the same local students when they met by chance outside the classroom.

Many of the issues that international students continue to collectively encounter reveal that efforts to promote equity, diversity, and inclusion are lacking. Experiences of marginalization affect not only the academic outcomes of international students but also their mental health and well-being (Tavares, 2022b). Equally concerning is the fact that these issues are not confined to the academic setting (Tavares, 2023c; Wei & Bunjun, 2021). In the workplace as well as in Canadian society at large, international students are affected by discrimination despite public discourses that recognize cultural and linguistic diversity in Canada as one of its strengths (Reichert & Bouajram, 2021) and the need for skilled labour. It is not uncommon that international students who speak English with a (racialized) accent feel discriminated against and have their international work experience disregarded by employers (Nunes & Arthur, 2013). Such experiences provide a glimpse of the boundaries of monolingual and monocultural constructions of Canadian identity in the context of the experience of international students in Canada.

Multiculturalism and Multicultural Education

Multicultural education recognizes education as a product of political and cultural influences. Jehangir (2010, p. 537) explains that multicultural education critically considers "the impact of historic and institutional racism, classism, and mainstream cultural capital on the educational experience of students, particularly those who have been historically absent from higher education." Indeed, though multiple cultural communities might live together, not all cultural knowledges are included equally in the curriculum, with some not being included at all. Diversity in relation not only to *what* is taught but also to *how* it is taught has direct implications for the academic experiences and outcomes of under-represented groups and for the image of society as supportive of all learners (Gay, 2004). For this reason, (critical) multicultural education approaches should not be reduced only to content—they must be embedded at every level of the educational experience, from the classroom to administration and governance (Gay, 2004).

Multicultural education has comprehensive and holistic aims for institutions of education. Van Garderen and Whittaker (2006) proposed five guiding dimensions for implementing multicultural education, though primarily in the classroom. The five proposed dimensions are distinct yet still interrelated within the framework: content integration, the knowledge construction process, an equity pedagogy, prejudice reduction, and an empowering school culture and social structure.

The first dimension—content integration—relates to "the extent to which teachers use examples and content from a variety of cultures and groups" to teach discipline-specific content (p. 16). This dimension is directly relevant to my inquiry in this chapter since the representation of non-anglophone cultures has been an issue in second language education and, to a different degree, in Canadian education more generally. In the Canadian context, under-represented groups may include people of colour, Indigenous peoples, Acadians, and particular immigrant groups (e.g., Gallop & Bastien, 2016).

The second dimension involves teachers' roles in equipping students to identify and confront the influence of discipline-specific biases and assumptions. In other words, it relates, on one hand, to what counts for knowledge that has been linked to dominant modes of thinking and seeing the world, and on the other, to the empowerment of students to reconceptualize epistemological processes in education.

The third dimension—an equity pedagogy—relies on teachers' modifications to their pedagogies to include teaching approaches that will improve all students' chances of success. Such modifications will reflect teaching and learning styles consistent with those of all groups represented in the classroom (Van Garderen & Whittaker, 2006). This dimension intertwines precisely with what Jehangir (2010) proposed in terms of drawing on students' lived experiences and perspectives to shape pedagogy. An equity pedagogy can help to foster a sense of belonging and respect while involving the student socially and academically (Jehangir, 2010).

The fourth dimension deals with identifying and changing students' racial attitudes. As the name suggests, educational attempts to reduce rather than eliminate prejudice might be more effective and realistic (Beelmann & Lutterbach, 2020). Van Garderen and Whittaker (2006) recommend implementing educational approaches that deconstruct concepts and behaviours that reinforce negative racial attitudes. Abacioglu et al. (2019, p. 7) found that teachers who "not only talk about multiculturalism as an abstract ideal, but also enact it in the classroom by being aware of issues around diversity and acting on it" contribute significantly to improving student engagement through prejudice reduction. Based on this, teachers can draw from their own as well as their students' lived experiences to exemplify manifestations of racial, ethnic, and linguistic discrimination, while also discussing ways to confront them. In doing so, sensitivity to and awareness of "matters of cultural pluralism" may be cultivated in the classroom community as a whole (Abacioglu et al., 2019, p. 7).

The fifth dimension is about creating an empowering school culture and social structure. This dimension considers potentially fundamental changes across and within the socio-cultural fabric of schools and the communities within which they are embedded. Nevertheless, there are initiatives specifically for the classroom which teachers can work with to support and empower minoritized groups. These initiatives can include changes at a deeper level, such as co-constructing teaching and learning expectations, developing opportunities for which the heritage languages and cultures of students and minoritized groups are repositioned as assets, as well as more surface-level changes, as in displaying flags and increasing visual cultural representations that can become the object of study in class (Van Garderen & Whittaker, 2006). Despite these suggestions, the potential of multicultural education has been increasingly undermined by a neo-liberal approach to cultural and linguistic diversity in Canada. For instance, Miled (2019) has called attention to the issue of "tokenism" within multicultural education and to the neglect of other expressions of diversity beyond culture, race, and ethnicity.

ESL 1450: Thinking about Contemporary Canada

From January to April 2020, I designed parts of the curriculum for a course titled Thinking about Contemporary Canada at York University. The course (henceforth ESL 1450) was cross-listed between the disciplines of ESL and humanities since it incorporated the development of academic and linguistic skills while introducing students to social and cultural themes related to contemporary Canada. ESL 1450 was intended for local and international students of multilingual backgrounds who spoke English as an additional language. The academic skills to be developed included critical thinking, reading comprehension, research and assessment of secondary literature, and citation and referencing in accordance with academic conventions. Conversely, linguistic skills included quoting, paraphrasing, summarizing, constructing evidence-based supporting and refuting arguments, and developing oral and listening skills individually and through group-based presentations (Tavares, 2020).

Social and cultural themes were introduced through course readings and videos. These materials emphasized a range of perspectives and experiences rooted in Canada, voiced by groups and individuals of different social, political, linguistic, ethnic, and cultural backgrounds but especially by those of minoritized and immigrant ones. The course readings focused on issues critical to arrival, belonging, and the idea of (de)constructing Canada as a nation by drawing from seminal and emerging readings of an academic and journalistic nature (Tavares, 2020). ESL 1450 was guided by the following areas of inquiry: Canadian culture, issues and trends in Canadian society, lived experiences of minority groups in Canada, and the languages of Canada. In this iteration of the course, the student body consisted of eleven multilingual students from China, Turkey, Iran, Pakistan, and Canada. The students' majors included business, economics, kinesiology, computer science, and general social sciences.

As a class, we met twice a week for six hours of instruction. The course relied heavily on social interaction as a means of teaching and learning, grounded in a social approach to learning in which knowledge is constructed in collaboration (Kumpulainen & Wray, 2003). Learning through social interaction was significant in the course since it afforded the students the space to contribute to the topics being discussed from a first-person, subjective perspective. Since the students had lived through different experiences of transnationalism, multiculturalism, and multilingualism prior to joining the course, their contributions were also pedagogical. Many of the themes discussed were new for the students, such as the cultural identity of Indigenous peoples in Canada, Indigenous languages, and the current political relationship between Indigenous peoples and the Canadian government. However, other themes reflected aspects of the students' individual trajectories to and within Canada and were therefore more familiar.

Throughout the course, many of the students' assumptions about Canada as a country were challenged, some with great surprise. In conversations with the students, I came to learn that many of their assumptions about Canada and Canadians were rooted in stereotypes presented in their former English language learning classes and materials in their countries of origin as well as in representations of Canada in media, such as films and TV series, both in Canada and abroad. Overall, such representations lacked diversity and advanced a primarily European/Anglo-Saxon image of Canada and Canadians. In the course, the process of confronting the prevalence of such images began within the first dimension of Van Garderen and Whittaker's (2006) framework for multicultural education: content integration. The course kit, which contained the course readings, was organized into five sections: government and politics; nation: identity and conflict; economic and social issues; the arts; and fiction. Some of the required readings were government policies and documents presented for context and later critically discussed in juxtaposition with content from journalistic and scholarly pieces.

The Canadian Multiculturalism Act, the Charter of Rights and Freedoms, and some of the Truth and Reconciliation reports were used as foundational texts in the course. Readings about or by members of minoritized groups, such as immigrants and Indigenous Canadians, were reviewed in light of the foundational texts. For instance, Abdulhamid Hathiyani's (2007) research article was used to illustrate the marginalization and exclusion of educated immigrants from the Canadian labour market, and modernist painter Daphne Odjig's works were shown and discussed in relation to their contributions to representations of Canadian identity through the arts. Neil Bissoondath's (1994, p. 83) article "The Simplification of Culture" was examined to draw attention to the complex ways in which multiculturalism can be experienced by minoritized groups—in this case, issues of heritage culture commodification were identified in how the author's culture was "displayed, performed, admired, bought, sold or forgotten." Issues of racialization and bilingualism were also explored through the same text.

Readings, videos, and discussions were conceptualized as sites of critical thinking for the purpose of de- and reconstructing general and scholarly knowledge. Course materials and activities were not used only for diversifying or recreating the teaching and learning content. They also sought to demonstrate what the dominant mechanisms of knowledge production are and how they operate in terms of preventing other forms of thinking about Canadian identity in the humanities and second language education. Students were introduced to discussions of Indigenous English (Fadden & LaFrance, 2010) and other varieties considered less prestigious or marginalized. The idea of language, specifically spoken and written Canadian English, was problematized since the students were encouraged to critically consider whose identity "standard" English reflects and whether "different" ways of speaking English in Canada are accepted in higher education. Such engagement represented the dimension of knowledge production (Van Garderen & Whittaker, 2006).

· The students' lived experiences of transnationalism were also pedagogical since they helped to foreground diverse constructions of Canadian identity. In reading and discussing the materials, the students were able to relate to some of the challenges and successes identified by Canadians of a minoritized group. The course content seemed viscerally relatable rather than abstract, impersonal, or disconnected from the students' realities. Informal conversations were important because some of the students had already settled in Canada as new residents, whereas others were planning to do so upon graduation. By problematizing their own experiences with education, language, ethnicity, race, age, and gender, the students were able to develop an understanding of how their multiple identities were under-/mis/represented in Canadian society. Reaching this level of comfort took time since many of the students initially thought that they should not critique Canada given their position as "foreigners" (see Tavares, 2021a).

In fact, to critically understand how Canadian identity is traditionally represented, the students needed to deconstruct their own racial attitudes, evoking experiences cultivated within the fourth dimension of Van Garderen and Whittaker's (2006) multicultural education framework. In the course, deconstructing racial attitudes unfolded on two levels. First, the students had to confront their own assumptions that French and English Canadians were the only "real" Canadians. This meant confronting subtle or ingrained forms of coloniality and actively expanding the image of Canadians to include the excluded or minoritized. Second, the students had to challenge their own perspectives on *their* places in Canadian society: for instance, resisting the inferior positioning of themselves as speakers of English as a "second language" in light of native speaker Canadians or their national status as international students or permanent residents in light of Canadians born in the country. Such emotional and intellectual labour was both a product and a process of critical multicultural education (Jehangir, 2010).

Concluding Thoughts

In this chapter, I reflected on an attempt to diversify representations of Canadian identity in a credit-bearing university course. As argued initially, dominant constructions of Canadian identity reflect certain patterns of colonialism and coloniality in intersecting sociological domains. Considering the course in focus, the domains of language, culture, and ethnicity emerged as the most relevant ones for discussion and analysis, as the unmarked Canadian identity is generally representative of a native speaker of English of anglophone ancestry. Drawing on a multicultural education framework, I outlined how the course was designed to challenge dominant constructions of Canadian identity by including perspectives on and by historically minoritized, excluded, or othered Canadians in the curriculum. In problematizing Canadian identity, this chapter makes a contribution to recent trends in second language education and (Canadian) cultural studies in which language, identity, and ethnicity are approached from a critical multicultural and decolonial perspective.

Confronting coloniality in education is a challenging and complex undertaking because it requires an epistemological and emotional shift (with)in those involved. As the instructor, I learned that the students in ESL 1450 had not expected to learn about Canadian culture from such a critical perspective that, at times, was uncomfortable for them. Indeed, many of the students had anticipated coming into the course only to have their own understandings reaffirmed. A critical, multicultural education perspective requires that students (and teachers) confront their own assumptions and, by extension, take part in a collective effort to change the status quo. Despite the apprehension that some of the students might have felt in the early days of the course, their later engagement with pedagogical activities in the course suggested that they had developed a willingness to approach social, cultural, and linguistic issues from a more critical perspective, in addition to an understanding of the importance of doing so.

It was evident to me, as the instructor, that the students concluded the course with a more multifaceted understanding of multiculturalism in Canada. On the most basic level, for instance, most of the students had never heard of some of the issues faced by Indigenous Canadians. Additionally, many mentioned that they were unaware, prior to taking ESL 1450, of the structural challenges that immigrants and minoritized Canadians can encounter in the domains of employment and education. Essentially, the "lessons learned" by the students may be viewed as having the potential to meet the outcome aimed for within the last dimension of Van Garderen and Whittaker's (2006) multicultural education framework: promoting change in society. However, since efforts to bring about social change are continuous and need to be cultivated within a supportive space, it is of central importance that a comparable educational experience is available across all of the courses that comprise the students' academic education. Without such continuity, critical engagement will remain discrete and optional, thus undermining the broader goals of a social-justice-oriented multicultural education.

References

Abacioglu, C. S., Zee, M., Hanna, F., Soeterik, I. M., Fischer, A. H., & Volman, M. (2019). Practice what you preach: The moderating role of teacher attitudes on the relationship between prejudice reduction and student engagement. *Teaching and Teacher Education, 86,* 1–10.

Alshammari, A. (2021). Job advertisements for English teachers in the Saudi Arabian context: Discourses of discrimination and inequity. *TESOL Journal, 12*(2), 1–13.

Basok, T., & George, G. (2020). "We are part of this place, but I do not think I belong." Temporariness, social inclusion and belonging among migrant farmworkers in southwestern Ontario. *International Migration, 59*(5), 1–14.

Beavon, D. J., Voyageur, C. J., & Newhouse, D. (Eds.). (2005). *Hidden in plain sight: Contributions of Aboriginal peoples to Canadian identity and culture* (Vol. 1). University of Toronto Press.

Beelmann, A., & Lutterbach, S. (2020). Preventing prejudice and promoting intergroup relations. In L. Benuto, M. Duckworth, A. Masuda, & W. O'Donohue (Eds.), *Prejudice, stigma, privilege, and oppression: A behavioral health handbook* (pp. 309–326). Springer.

Bissoondath, N. (1994). *Selling illusions: The cult of multiculturalism in Canada.* Penguin.

Canadian Bureau for International Education (CBIE). (2020). *Media: Facts and figures.* https://cbie.ca/infographic/

Canagarajah, A. S. (2012). Teacher development in a global profession: An autoethnography. *TESOL Quarterly, 46*(2), 258–279.

Chen, L. H. (2008). Internationalization or international marketing? Two frameworks for understanding international students' choice of Canadian universities. *Journal of Marketing for Higher Education, 18*(1), 1–33.

City of Toronto. (2017). *2016 Census: Housing, immigration and ethnocultural diversity, Aboriginal peoples.* https://www.toronto.ca/wp-content/uploads/2017/12/9282-2016-Census-Backgrounder-Immigration-Ethnicity-Housing-Aboriginal.docx

Downey, A. (2018). *The creator's game: Lacrosse, identity, and Indigenous nationhood.* UBC Press.

Fadden, L., & LaFrance, J. (2010). Advancing Aboriginal English. *Canadian Journal of Native Education, 32*, 143–153.

Fu, J. (2021). The role of two extracurricular programs in international students' informal learning experiences in Atlantic Canada. In V. Tavares (Ed.), *Multidisciplinary perspectives on international student experience in Canadian higher education* (pp. 156–176). IGI Global.

Gallop, C. J., & Bastien, N. (2016). Supporting success: Aboriginal students in higher education. *Canadian Journal of Higher Education, 46*(2), 206–224.

Gay, G. (2004). The importance of multicultural education. *Educational Leadership, 61*(4), 30–35.

George, G., & Selimos, E. D. (2019). Searching for belonging and confronting exclusion: A person-centred approach to immigrant settlement experiences in Canada. *Social Identities, 25*(2), 125–140.

Government of Canada. (2012, 19 October). *Canadian multiculturalism: An inclusive citizenship.* https://web.archive.org/web/20140312210113/http://www.cic.gc.ca/english/multiculturalism/citizenship.asp

Hathiyani, A. (2007). Professional immigrants on a road to driving taxis in Toronto. *Our Diverse Cities, 4*, 128–133.

Heritz, J. (2018). From self-determination to service delivery: Assessing Indigenous inclusion in municipal governance in Canada. *Canadian Public Administration, 61*(4), 596–615.

Houshmand, S., Spanierman, L. B., & Tafarodi, R. W. (2014). Excluded and avoided: Racial microaggressions targeting Asian international students in Canada. *Cultural Diversity and Ethnic Minority Psychology, 20*(3), 377–388.

Jehangir, R. (2010). Stories as knowledge: Bringing the lived experience of first-generation college students into the academy. *Urban Education, 45*(4), 533–553.

Kumaravadivelu, B. (2016). The decolonial option in English teaching: Can the subaltern act? *TESOL Quarterly, 50*(1), 66–85.

Kumpulainen, K., & Wray, D. (Eds.). (2003). *Classroom interactions and social learning: From theory to practice.* Routledge.

Lee, J. J., & Rice, C. (2007). Welcome to America? International student perceptions of discrimination. *Higher Education, 53*(3), 381–409.

Maldonado-Torres, N. (2010). On the coloniality of being: Contributions to the development of a concept. In W. Mignolo & A. Escobar (Eds.), *Globalization and the decolonial option* (pp. 94–124). Routledge.

Miled, N. (2019). Educational leaders' perceptions of multicultural education in teachers' professional development: A case study from a Canadian school district. *Multicultural Education Review, 11*(2), 79–95.

Nunes, S., & Arthur, N. (2013). International students' experiences of integrating into the workforce. *Journal of Employment Counseling, 50* (1), 34–45.

Pew Research Center. (2019, 1 July). *5 facts about religion in Canada*. https://www.pewresearch.org/fact-tank/2019/07/01/5-facts-about-religion-in-canada/

Pidgeon, M. (2016). More than a checklist: Meaningful Indigenous inclusion in higher education. *Social Inclusion, 4*(1), 77–91.

Raney, T. (2009). As Canadian as possible . . . under what circumstances? Public opinion on national identity in Canada outside Quebec. *Journal of Canadian Studies, 43*(3), 5–29.

Reichert, P. N., & Bouajram, R. (2021). Beyond recruitment: Career navigation and support of international students in Canada. In V. Tavares (Ed.), *Multidisciplinary perspectives on international student experience in Canadian higher education* (pp. 308–327). IGI Global.

Ruecker, T., & Ives, L. (2015). White native English speakers needed: The rhetorical construction of privilege in online teacher recruitment spaces. *TESOL Quarterly, 49*, 733–756.

Shin, H. (2006). Rethinking TESOL from a SOL's perspective: Indigenous epistemology and decolonizing praxis in TESOL. *Critical Inquiry in Language Studies, 3*(2–3), 147–167.

Slaughter, Y., & Cross, R. (2021). Challenging the monolingual mindset: Understanding plurilingual pedagogies in English as an additional language (EAL) classrooms. *Language Teaching Research, 25*(1), 39–60.

Tavares, V. (2020). *Thinking about contemporary Canada* [Syllabus]. Department of Languages, Literatures and Linguistics, York University.

Tavares, V. (2021a). *International students in higher education: Language, identity, and experience from a holistic perspective*. Lexington Books.

Tavares, V. (2021b). Feeling excluded: International students experience equity, diversity and inclusion. *International Journal of Inclusive Education*, 1–18.

Tavares, V. (2022a). Neoliberalism, native-speakerism and the displacement of international students' languages and cultures. *Journal of Multilingual and Multicultural Development*, 1–14. https://doi.10.1080/01434632.2022.2084547

Tavares, V. (2022b). From Macau to the United States and Canada: A transnational journey of longing for belonging. *Comparative and International Education, 51*(1), 92–108.

Tavares, V. (Ed.). (2023a). *Social justice, decoloniality, and southern epistemologies within language education: Theories, knowledges, and practices on TESOL from Brazil*. Routledge.

Tavares, V. (2023b). Pushed to the periphery: Understanding the multiple forms of exclusion experienced by international students from Asia. In A. Kim, E.

Buckner, & J. M. Montsion (Eds.), *International Students from Asia in Canadian Universities* (pp. 144–156). Routledge.

Tavares, V. (2023c). Take it or leave it: The employment-related experiences of an international student prior to academic studies. In J. K. N. Singh, R. L. Raby, & K. Bista (Eds.), *International Student Employability: Narratives of Strengths, Challenges, and Strategies about Global South Students* (pp. 159–171). Springer International Publishing.

van Garderen, D., & Whittaker, C. (2006). Planning differentiated, multicultural instruction for secondary inclusive classrooms. *Teaching Exceptional Children, 38*(3), 12–21.

Webster, N. L., & Lu, C. (2012). "English language learners": An analysis of perplexing ESL-related terminology. *Language and Literacy, 14*(3), 83–94.

Wei, M. L., & Bunjun, B. (2021). "We don't need another one in our group": Racism and interventions to promote the mental health and well-being of racialized international students in business schools. *Journal of Management Education, 45*(1), 65–85.

Zacharias, N. T. (2019). The ghost of native speakerism: The case of teacher classroom introductions in transnational contexts. *TESOL Journal, 10*(4), 1–14.

5

Reconstruction of Canadian Identity in Second Language Education:
Creating an Inclusive Classroom for English Language Learners

JACQUELINE NG

Global connectedness and global engagement have become the norm in the school system in Canada and have built an increasingly heterogeneous linguistic and cultural landscape (Kubota, 2016). Canadian identity is expected to be shaped by the values of diversity in this multilingual, multicultural country. However, the hegemonic power of English and French and the resulting White supremacist complacency have caused stresses and tensions with Canadian multiculturalism (Banting & Kymlicka, 2010) and constrained the construction of Canadian identity to a narrow path. The problematic definition of Canadian identity divides Anglo-Saxon Canadians dominating the mainstream from those "ethnic" Canadians being excluded in a "marginal third space" (Tavares & Maciel Jorge, this volume). This misleading dichotomy has been evident in second language education that streams native English speakers and English language learners (ELL) in contradictory directions and stereotypes them from biased perspectives. Whereas the former learners are perceived as socially privileged in the mainstream, the latter learners are regarded as low achievers or "so-called others" (Li, 2019, p. 6) who face social disadvantages such as stereotype threat and social discrimination in the paradox of Canadian multiculturalism (Bannerji, 2000).

To challenge the current operation of coercive relations of power (Cummins, 2009a) in the third space, educators need to address a central question in language classrooms and communities. Which instructional approaches and strategies should be adopted to promote academic achievement and identity construction of marginalized students? In this chapter, I discuss how ELL students in a Canadian university can be supported to rethink and negotiate their hyphenated or diasporic identities (Li, 2019) during their transnationalism in Canada and how educators can create an inclusive, equitable classroom through transformative multiliteracy pedagogy (Cummins, 2009b) to facilitate ELL students' language learning and positively reaffirm their identities. I further explore how ELL students can embrace the beauty of their heritage and share their voices by constructing an Identity Text Project in which they can invest their cultural knowledge, linguistic repertoire, and self- and socially assigned identities. I conclude that turning ELL students' linguistic and cultural knowledge into effective educational resources can empower these marginalized students to learn and relearn certain cultural expectations, position and reposition themselves in a multifaceted society, and shape and reshape their Canadian identities to achieve educational and social success.

Teaching and Research Context

Framed within critical action research (Burns, 2019; Kemmis et al., 2014), this study is intended to provide a holistic view of collaborative pedagogical design of a creation-action-reflection cyclical process to improve teaching practices with critical orientation (Song et al., 2023). The study is conducted in an English for Academic Purposes (EAP) course offered by a large Canadian university serving over 50,000 students. The course is designed to help ELL students from diverse linguistic and cultural backgrounds to build content knowledge of Canadian language, culture, and identity and to develop academic literacy skills through discussions of different academic genres. It aims to support ELL students to explore multimodality-enhanced and experiential education tasks for effective academic learning and social connections in Canadian society. Many ELL students, however, struggle with their academic status and social identities when they are advised to enrol in an EAP course to improve their academic English literacy, usually considered the key to success in postsecondary education. The

EAP classroom can be regarded as both a third space and a comfort zone for marginalized students. Some ELL students are disappointed to be streamed into a remedial-structured EAP class that seems to exclude them from the mainstream program, and therefore they might self-identify as incapable or incompetent learners regardless of whether the EAP course can contribute academic credits to their university programs and prepare them for their future careers and social participation in this English-dominated country. Yet these students can feel safe and relieved in the EAP classroom without worrying that their non-native accents or English skills will interrupt their intercultural communications. These mixed feelings tend to keep ELL learners in the third space, both voluntarily and reluctantly, rather than moving them forward to develop their transnational identities in the new country.

Transformative Multiliteracies Pedagogy

The process of identity negotiation is the core component and major determinant of ELL students' cognitive engagement and learning success (Cummins, 2001) but has not received much attention in second language education research. Creating an inviting classroom with ample opportunities for ELL students to express their voices, co-construct knowledge with teachers and peers, and actively engage in the community is an urgent educational need in most multilingual and multicultural societies. Second language education is welcoming new waves of diversified values and technological expertise that students can bring into the classroom in the globalized, digital age. The New London Group (2000) introduces the timely, prominent construct "multiliteracies" promoting the growing importance of students' linguistic and cultural diversity and the multiplicity of information and communication technologies to encourage students to use multiple literacy practices to make meaning in the learning process. The four major components of the multiliteracies framework offer instructional guidelines for teachers to support ELL students: (1) situated practice suggests that students should be provided with opportunities to scaffold their prior knowledge and be immersed in meaningful, experiential learning; (2) overt instruction involves explicit instructions of key concepts and theories that explain underlying learning processes; (3) critical framing asserts that teachers need to guide students to critically reflect on their learning and interpret concepts or ideologies in relation to their cultural and social relevance; (4) transformed practice advises teachers to ensure that students transfer their learned knowledge from school to social situations. In short, teachers need to understand the significance of the languages and cultural resources of ELL students in promoting their self-esteem, learning motivation, school performance, and identity development. Literacy education therefore needs to transform from traditional mere literacy pedagogy, which focuses on a single cultural form of language, to multiliteracies pedagogy, which acknowledges all cultures, languages, and multimodalities as dynamic representational resources (Cazden et al., 1996) and powerful learning tools in the twenty-first century.

Building upon the conceptual lenses of the multiliteracies framework, Cummins (2009b) proposes transformative multiliteracies pedagogy to raise the learning attainment of ELL students through the process of identity negotiation and collaborative power relations in the classroom. Transformative multiliteracies pedagogy primarily aims to prepare ELL learners for full participation in school and society by valuing their linguistic, cultural, and intellectual properties, increasing their social awareness of social justice, and offering them empowering educational opportunities. It incorporates critical inquiry into the curriculum by guiding students to challenge social inequity, react to social realities, and develop critical thinking skills necessary for academic and social success. This new pedagogy equally emphasizes the importance of integrating innovative teaching strategies and instructional designs to empower ELL students to actively immerse themselves in dialogic learning and reflect on their learning experiences (Ukpokodu, 2009).

Extensive research (e.g., Rajendram, 2015; Skourtou et al., 2006) shows that transformative multiliteracies pedagogy can reinforce higher-order cognitive and academic skills as a result of intercultural communications and critical inquiry. Designing a culturally sensitive learning environment for ELL students can engage them in active, meaningful learning (Willis, 2000). Meskill (2005), in her research project Triadic Scaffolds, found that the dynamic, productive communications generated by ELL students with multimodal tools can help them better position and affirm their identities relative to using computers in a traditional classroom. The study concluded that an inviting classroom is important for healthy and prosperous academic development of minoritized students: "As active participants, they are positioned to construct their contexts of being and learning, a process that benefits from inclusion as opposed to exclusion" (Meskill, 2005, p. 56). In a similar vein, Harrell-Levy and Kerpelman (2010, p. 77) claim that teachers can be reliable facilitators in constructing students' identities when they employ a transformative teaching approach that "involves fostering collaborative learning and empowering students to think creatively and critically." Prioritizing students' diversity in transformative multiliteracies pedagogy, Ntelioglou (2012) asserts that ELL students can utilize their home languages and cultures as powerful capital to learn the target language and thereby validate and affirm their identities (Rajendram, 2015). Other research studies (e.g., Koga, 2006; Nguyen & Kellogg, 2005; Vyas, 2004) report that global learning networks can enable teachers to understand ELL students' language socialization and identity-building processes. In this regard, teachers can positively engage ELL students in a transformative classroom if they can recognize global diversities and work closely with all students to transform social realities.

Although more research findings are needed to prove the correlation between transformative multiliteracies pedagogy and identity construction of ELL students, the educational values of this pedagogy should not be overlooked. Transformative multiliteracies pedagogy is an attempt to establish collaborative power relations and provide inclusive learning opportunities for ELL students to reduce their chances of discriminatory experiences and therefore empower them in the academic and social contexts. This pedagogy offers practical suggestions for educators and researchers to support ELL students with the effective use of multilingual, multicultural, and multimodal practices. For example, teachers can motivate ELL students to use their language and cultural experience to share their autobiographies in class. Teachers can also design student-controlled activities to connect their pre-existing knowledge with course materials. Teachers are advised to implement peer inquiry tasks such as online discussions, partner readings, group research inquiry projects, and panel presentations to create a peer-supportive learning environment for ELL students. To sum up, educators need to devote themselves to a promising instructional approach by incorporating ELL students' previous experiences in the learning process and to creating a context of learning empowerment in which all students' identities can be recognized and appreciated.

Transformative multiliteracies pedagogy attempts to free marginalized students from coercive power relations by advocating that power should be shared equally among students in the school and social members in the community (Ng, 2018). Understanding the ideologies and potential benefits of such pedagogy is therefore a crucial step toward informing the classroom practice and pedagogical design of language instructors.

Classroom Practice: Creating Identity Texts

In terms of practising transformative multiliteracies pedagogy in an EAP classroom, this study is designed to incorporate multimodal tasks and assignments in the curriculum to facilitate ELL students in understanding the target language and reflecting on how they perceive their self-assigned and socially assigned identities in Canada. In their groundbreaking work examining the efficacy of such a pedagogy, Cummins and Early (2011) introduced the making of an identity text as a powerful pedagogical tool to maximize academic engagement among ELL students by recognizing their linguistic and cultural assets and asserting their identities in the learning process. Identity texts refer to students' production of linguistic, cultural, artistic, and academic works that can be displayed or performed within "the pedagogical space orchestrated by the class teacher.... [The teacher holds] a mirror up to students in which their identities are reflected back in a positive light" (Cummins et al., 2005, p. 40). With the support of multiliteracies resources, ELL students can produce their identity texts in written, auditory, spoken, visual, spatial, gestural, artistic, musical, digital, and/or multimodal forms. Identity texts can be used as an effective tool to promote learning motivation and learning equity for those marginalized ELL students when teachers are committed to creating an open learning space in which all students can scaffold their learning experiences, share their language and cultural resources, expand their imaginations, showcase their personal strengths and talents, and take full control of their learning (Ng, 2018). In light of the positive outcome of students' self-image and the improved quality of their learning, identity texts can empower ELL students by reducing the social gap between majority and minority groups in school and supporting them to perform more confidently and successfully than in a top-down, strictly controlled classroom.

The pedagogical value of identity texts is further acknowledged by researchers and educators since this emerging literacy practice can serve multiple purposes in three major learning spaces. The *narrative space* created by teachers in a multilingual and multicultural classroom views identity texts as socio-cultural artifacts in which students can tell personal stories that provide cultural insights or describe their transformations in identity that involve the impacts of family, culture, race, religion, and so on. The *reflective space* enables students to critically reflect on their struggles, power dynamics, reconciliations, and negotiations in their identification processes (Zaidi et al., 2016). The *creative space* encourages students to create original, innovative identity texts in multimodal forms to demonstrate their special skills, talents, expertise, imaginations, and valuable insights.

The EAP course documented in this study examines the interrelationship among Canadian culture, language, and identity pertaining to founding nations in Canada, social integration of immigrants, diversity and inclusion, and reconceptualization of Canadian identities. Most ELL students in the course identify themselves as marginalized immigrants, international students, or racialized or minoritized members of Canada. To facilitate the identity formation and academic engagement of these marginalized students, they were invited to produce an Identity Text Project in which they could share their personal experiences, journeys to Canada, acculturation, and identity transition. They were inspired to integrate multiliteracies resources and multimodal elements of digital design, photography, artwork, or any form of performance to tell a story of who they are and how they construct their transnational identities. The students could produce their identity texts in various forms, including infographic posters, self-portraits, galleries, poetries, photo journals, illustrations, digital stories, recorded videos, podcasts, dance performances, music productions, and so forth. They could, for instance, write multilingual poems to express their multicultural identities through "translanguaging": that is, using a variety of language practices in their linguistic repertoires or in their new communities (García & Kleyn, 2016). They could also design layered symbols, colours, texts, images, and animations in their identity texts, attached to their recorded videos and multimodal reflections, that could be published in the digital gallery of the class. This practice of multiliteracies, supported through digital media and multimodal devices, can be used to enrich ELL students' literacy development and identity construction.

Showcasing the Identity Text Project

As the focus of the transformative multiliteracies pedagogy, identity texts are employed to offer marginalized students educational support to succeed in school and social support to integrate into the new society by (re)affirming their identities and social status (Cummins & Early, 2011). In our EAP course, we read Bannerji's (2003) short story "The Other Family" to discuss concepts such as social marginalization, power relations, domination and oppression, assimilation, intersectionality, identity positioning, and so on. The protagonists, a mother and her daughter, belong to a Black family and are new immigrants to Canada. Bannerji describes prominent features of the young girl—her dark skin, dark eyes, and black hair—in contrast to the White skin, blue eyes, and blond hair of the majority in the mainstream. After moving to Canada, this immigrant family lives in a White-dominated society. The school to which the girl goes is a White supremacist institution in which the teachers, school leaders, and teaching materials represent the hegemony of the White model that all students are expected to learn and follow. The girl is directed by a teacher to draw a picture of her family by copy-ing the image of a White "Canadian family" from a textbook, making her mother anxious and distraught because she thinks that her daughter is about to forget her own culture, family heritage, and original identity. The girl finally becomes aware that she is "the other" and different from the majority in both the class and the community. Throughout the story, the protagonists are not given names, and they are regarded as "nobod-ies" because they seem to fail in their assimilation and struggle with their transnationalism. Based upon our textual analysis of the story, I asked my students to reflect on their self-identification and social positioning in the Identity Text Project. I attempted to establish rapport with the students by sharing my personal and professional trajectories through my own identity texts in the form of a digital language autobiography:

> Being born, raised and educated in the British colonial Hong Kong (HK), I have been exposed to the language, traditions, customs, values and educational models of both the Chinese and British cultures. Realizing the hegemonic power of

English and having an innate attachment to my mother tongue, Cantonese, I was pleased and thankful to grow bilingually in HK. . . . The political disturbances and unrests that took place in Mainland China around the 90s made many HK people like me feel hesitant to learn Mandarin as my L3 [third language], and more importantly, confused of my new socially-assigned identity.

My family's decision to immigrate to Canada further complicated my identity positioning. Upon my arrival, I was fascinated by the mosaic multicultural values of Canada. But then when I received such questions as: "Where are you from?" "How do you say this in Mandarin?", I started to realize that my social identity is somehow constructed by people's assumptions and perceptions of my outlook, cultural background, origin, and accent. Despite the fact that Hong Kong is now part of China, I still affirm that I am a Hong Konger when answering those questions. . . . Am I trying to correct people's misunderstanding of my outer identity, or am I making a claim of my inner identity? I know I may be seen as "the other" in people's eyes, but I appreciate every opportunity that shapes me as a unique person. I am becoming more aware of my self-assigned identity and developing a stronger attachment to my HK cultural roots after moving to Canada. I am more interested in relearning my first language in the new country and rebuilding a hyphenated identity in my transnational journey.

Most ELL students were captivated by my identity text, which inspired them to respect others' distinctive experiences while strengthening their inner identities, often disregarded or unnoticed in English-dominated schools in which the main focus is on accelerating their proficiency in English (Gallagher, 2011). In producing their identity texts, the students were encouraged to draw from their distinctive linguistic and cultural features that represent their personal qualities in a diversified community. They prepared their storytelling by connecting their previous experiences with the textual meanings of the course readings through guiding questions such as the following. What can you tell us about your background and journey to Canada?

How did you find Canadian cultural practices and values similar to or different from your own culture? Did you try to assimilate into a melting pot or integrate into a mosaic model in the new country? What does it mean to be "Canadian" to you? Have you encountered any challenges adapting to the new culture? Have you ever found yourself losing your native identity and becoming "the other" when you failed to assimilate to the majority group (Bannerji, 2003)? Have you made any effort to make yourself a "Canadian"? How would you comment on your existing identity in Canada? Do you think you are struggling with a "hyphenated identity" with "splitting personalities" (Yi, 2002) or enjoying an "integrating identity" with privileges from both cultures? The students were invited to create bi- or multilingual identity texts, then narrate their personal stories in class or in recorded presentations with their plurilingual or translanguaging practices (García & Otheguy, 2020), and finally showcase their innovative, multimodal Identity Text Project on the class website.

Upon approval from the Research Ethics Committee and formal consent from the students, I discuss in this chapter the making of identity texts in 2021 by two students who came from different socio-cultural backgrounds but constructed and shaped their transnational identities with similar positive attitudes. The first example showcases an ELL student's identity portraits (Figure 5.1 and Figure 5.2) and self-reflections in his Identity Text Project. This student, Daniel, identified himself as an international student from China and a newcomer to Canada. He appreciated the chance to make oil paintings to "narrate" his journey to Canada. As the artist of his identity portraits and the author of his digital story, he portrayed the boat in Figure 5.1 as a representation of himself sailing on the ocean. The boat is covered by black and white shredded paper, impeding the student in identifying his direction and destination. Daniel expressed that he was travelling with a "vacant inner heart" given all the uncertainties, fears, anxieties, and confusions in his journey. His feelings of panic and worries were intensified when he started his academic program, in which he encountered the acute challenges of language barrier, culture shock, and social integration. Daniel felt as if he was sailing alone on the empty ocean. In contrast to the monochromatic colour scheme in the initial stage of his transnational journey, the warm tones in Figure 5.2 represent his stage of cultural adjustment and identity transformation. Daniel was grateful for the consistent support that he

Figure 5.1. Student sample of identity portrait—transnational identity (2021). Courtesy of the student.

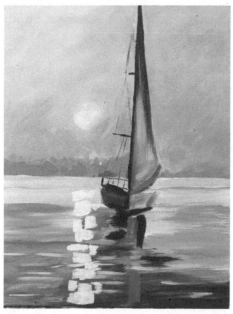

Figure 5.2. Student sample of identity portrait—journey to Canada (2021). Courtesy of the student.

received from his teachers, academic advisers, friends, neighbours, and community members who genuinely welcomed him in the multicultural society. He reflected on the symbolic meaning of his oil painting by associating his past experience with the key concept of "transnational identity" discussed throughout the course. To Daniel, the sun in his identity portrait symbolizes vitality and a hopeful future if he can be equally accepted and respected by others in Canada:

> The boat is traveling on the beautiful ocean with the colorful waves that represent my transnational journey. The waves keep moving, evolving, and transforming from time to time. I myself have gone through ups and downs in this process, and luckily, I am seeing these warm ocean currents in my trip and new chapter of life. The boat at the end finds the right path and direction and is moving towards the sunlight which represents [the] light of hope.... Cultural acceptance is one of the best features of the Canadian culture. We came together to learn from each other's life experience, cultural heritage, and cultural behavior, and in return we could re-think ours in the new country. Although I cannot foresee any obstacles before I reach my destination, I am hopeful that my transnational identity will be accepted by others in the new culture. I am proud to be who I am!

Although Daniel described himself as a silent, passive learner in the past, he was excited to take the lead in the process of inquiry by exchanging cultural experiences with peers from diverse backgrounds. When presenting his Identity Text Project in class, Daniel employed translanguaging practice to discuss the representational meanings of his favourite cultural rituals, such as decorating Chinese lanterns and preparing cultural foods for special occasions. Such cultural topics activated the prior experiences of other students keen to share their cultural traditions and cuisines. This ELL student, who self-identified and was socially identified as a marginal learner at the outset, was finally able to engage his peers in productive intercultural dialogue and knowledge building in the transformative learning space.

The second example exhibits another powerful Identity Text Project featuring a digital bilingual book comprising an Infographic poster and canvas paintings by a student, Julia, who came to Canada as a

Figure 5.3. Student sample of Identity Text Project—hyphenated identities (2021). Courtesy of the student.

Syrian refugee. Julia realized that her refugee status would assign her a marginalized identity, so she devoted her best efforts to fulfilling her learning goals in the educational context and to surviving socially in the community. In her canvas paintings illustrating her Syrian Canadian identity (Figure 5.3), Julia expressed her "inner turmoil" by contrasting her views of Syria and Canada:

> The past in my hometown, Lattakia, was associated with massive wildfires caused by airstrikes, bombs and military helicopters. The situation in Syria had put me in a live or die situation since 2011 when the Syrian Civil [W]ar broke out. My only hope of living a decent and safe life was fully attached to the idea of immigrating to another country. My present time in Canada is impacting me positively with its breath-taking natural sceneries. I feel the need to reflect my sense of security and serenity of Canada through the image of the blue peaceful sky in my portrait, which was very unusual in my home country.

In spite of the indescribable hardships, dangers, and disputes that Julia endured in her home country, she did not reject her cultural identity; rather, she was motivated and determined to explore more of her cultural roots after relocating to Canada. In her multimodal identity text, Julia narrated her story with her bilingual skills, making her voice more intriguing and striking her audience in a powerful manner:

Moving to Canada did not take away my memories back in Syria where I was raised by my beloved family and met my best friends in life. I am still maintaining my native language, culture and family heritage that have shaped me as a special person. I really like the *Identity Text Project* because it helps me dig deeper into my root[s] and reflect on my experience as a newcomer in Canada. This project inspires and reminds me that I am not forgetting my home country while I am also proud of my Canadian identity. I think this is the greatest gift in my transnational process.

In the Undergraduate Research Fair of York University in 2021, Julia was invited to display and present her Identity Text Project. Her academic excellence, cultural pride, and social success were acknowledged by a wide audience. Many participants across the university mentioned that they were impressed and moved by Julia's story of transnationalism from Syria to Canada, from a desperate war zone to a peaceful country, and from an initial marginalized identity to an accepting Canadian identity.

In their transnational identity search through digital storytelling, these ELL students were pleased to narrate their stories with their plurilingual skills, reflect on their cultural adjustment and acceptance, and engage in critical inquiry and knowledge generation with their peers, instructor, and community members. They were also able to overcome the uneasiness, uncertainties, and challenges that they encounter at first in the new culture and consequently reassure and reconstruct their identities.

Implications and Conclusion

Maximizing the cognitive engagement and learning potential of ELL students, identity texts can lead to valuable pedagogical outcomes in three learning spaces. In the narrative space, identity texts connect the past and the present of ELL students when they are provided with equal opportunities and a comfortable platform in which they can activate their prior knowledge, immerse themselves in meaningful experiences through situated practice, tie their personal experiences to the crucial concepts or theories learned through overt instruction, and narrate their stories in their own voices. In the reflective space, identity texts connect intercultural groups when ELL students are motivated to utilize their linguistic repertoires and exchange cultural experiences with others. Doing so allows them to further reflect on their social positions through critical framing and critical lenses. In the creative space, identity texts enable ELL students to make use of innovative practices and multiple resources to learn the target language and apply the learned knowledge in social settings. They can become the designers and owners of their learning and academic products in this transformed practice.

Many ELL learners are marginalized in Canada with overflowing impediments such as emergent English proficiency, non-native English accent, social isolation, exclusion, power imbalance, and discrimination. Their self-assigned and socially assigned positions in the marginal third space make it difficult for them to achieve educational success, cultural adaptation, and social integration. To correct the stereotypical misconception that ELL learners are low achievers in the school system or leftover in the larger society, educators should see the urgency of implementing transformative multiliteracies pedagogy to open up new pedagogical possibilities to foster ELL students' meaning-making processes, make full use of their experiences to generate new knowledge, redefine and reshape their identities, and get their voices heard through the creation of identity texts in order to empower these students linguistically, culturally, intellectually, and socially. Learning can take place outside a structured classroom and be made meaningful by supporting learners to transform their knowledge and skills in real-world contexts. Designing student-led, holistic activities such as identity texts can serve to "humanize" students. Such activities gesture toward decentralizing the hegemonic power of the majority language and culture and deinstitutionalizing the traditional classroom to make the transformative classroom more creative, healthy, and engaging (Alber, 2017).

In the pursuit of educational and social justice, the inclusive value of identity texts can be expanded from a classroom to a broader social context by equally respecting and appreciating marginalized members' prior experience, cultural knowledge, linguistic resources, personal perspectives, and new insights. Establishing collaborative relations of power in Canadian society can turn the marginal third space into an optimal interpersonal space where minoritized members can construct and negotiate their Canadian identities in positive ways, and all social members can celebrate cultural and linguistic diversity in a truly multicultural nation.

References

Alber, R. (2017, 16 March). *Updating an age-old class activity.* Edutopia. https://www.edutopia.org/blog/updating-age-old-class-activity-rebecca-alber

Bannerji, H. (2000). The paradox of diversity: The construction of a multicultural Canada and "women of color." *Women's Studies International Forum, 23*(5), 537–560. Pergamon.

Bannerji, H. (2003). The other family. In E. C. Karpinski (Ed.), *Pens of many colours: A Canadian reader* (pp. 182–187). Harcourt Brace Canada.

Banting, K., & Kymlicka, W. (2010). Canadian multiculturalism: Global anxieties and local debates. *British Journal of Canadian Studies, 23*(1), 43–72.

Burns, A. (2019). Action research in English language teaching: Contributions and recent developments. In G. Xuesong (Ed.), *Second handbook of English language teaching* (pp. 991–1005). Springer.

Cazden, C., Cope, B., Fairclough, N., Gee, J., Kalantzis, M., Kress, G., Luke, A., Luke, C., Michaels, S., & Nakata, M. (1996). A pedagogy of multiliteracies: Designing social futures. *Harvard Educational Review, 66*(1), 60–92.

Cummins, J. (2001). *Negotiating identities: Education for empowerment in a diverse society* (2nd ed.). California Association for Bilingual Education.

Cummins, J. (2009a). Pedagogies of choice: Challenging coercive relations of power in classrooms and communities. *International Journal of Bilingual Education and Bilingualism, 12*(3), 261–271.

Cummins, J. (2009b). Transformative multiliteracies pedagogy: School-based strategies for closing the achievement gap. *Multiple Voices for Ethnically Diverse Exceptional Learners, 11*(2), 38–56.

Cummins, J., Bismilla, V., Chow, P., Cohen, S., Giampapa, F., Leoni, L., Sandhu, P., & Sastri, P. (2005). Affirming identity in multilingual classrooms. *Educational Leadership, 63*(1), 38–43.

Cummins, J., & Early, M. (2011). *Identity texts: The collaborative creation of power in multilingual schools.* Trentham Books.

Gallagher, E. (2011). Weaving other languages and cultures into the curriculum in international primary schools. In J. Cummins & M. Early (Eds.), *Identity texts: The collaborative creation of power in multilingual schools* (pp. 78–84). Trentham Books.

García, O., & Kleyn, T. (2016). *Translanguaging with multilingual students: Learning from classroom moments.* Routledge.

García, O., & Otheguy, R. (2020). Plurilingualism and translanguaging: Commonalities and divergences. *International Journal of Bilingual Education and Bilingualism, 23*(1), 17–35.

Harrell-Levy, M. K., & Kerpelman, J. L. (2010). Identity process and transformative pedagogy: Teachers as agents of identity formation. *Identity: An International Journal of Theory and Research, 10*(2), 76–91.

Kemmis, S., McTaggart, R., & Nixon, R. (2014). *The action research planner: Doing critical participatory action research.* Springer.

Koga, N. (2006). *Incorporating the idea of social identity into English language education* [Conference paper]. APERA Conference, Hong Kong. http://edisdat.ied.edu.hk/pubarch/b15907314/full_paper/1167645159.pdf

Kubota, R. (2016). The multi/plural turn, postcolonial theory, and neoliberal multiculturalism: Complicities and implications for applied linguistics. *Applied Linguistics, 37*(4), 474–494.

Li, J. (2019). *The transcultural streams of Chinese Canadian identities.* McGill-Queen's University Press.

Meskill, C. (2005). Triadic scaffolds: Tools for teaching English language learners with computers. *Language Learning and Technology, 9*(1), 46–59.

New London Group. (2000). A pedagogy of multiliteracies: Designing social futures. In B. Cope & M. Kalantzis (Eds.), *Multiliteracies: Literacy, learning and the design of social futures* (pp. 9–37). Routledge.

Ng, J. (2018). *Multiliteracies in the context of a sister class project: Pursuing new possibilities in second language education* [Doctoral dissertation, University of Toronto]. TSpace. https://tspace.library.utoronto.ca/handle/1807/89879

Nguyen, H. T., & Kellogg, G. (2005). Emergent identities in on-line discussions for second language learning. *The Canadian Modern Language Review, 62*(1), 111–136.

Ntelioglou, B. Y. (2012). *Drama pedagogies, multiliteracies and embodied learning: Urban teachers and linguistically diverse students make meaning* [Doctoral dissertation, University of Toronto]. TSpace. https://tspace.library.utoronto.ca/handle/1807/43403

Rajendram, S. (2015). Potentials of the multiliteracies pedagogy for teaching English language learners (ELLs): A review of the literature. *Critical Intersections in Education, 3*, 1–18.

Skourtou, E., Kourtis-Kazoullis, V., & Cummins, J. (2006). Designing virtual learning environments for academic language development. In J. Weiss, J. Nolan, J. Hunsinger, & P. Trifonas (Eds.), *The international handbook of virtual learning environments* (pp. 441–467). Springer.

Song, H., Makinina, O., & Ng, J. (2023). Multiliteracies-enhanced practices as empowerment pedagogy for teaching transnational English language learners in a CLIL-based EAP course in Canada. *English Teaching & Learning*, 1–25.

Ukpokodu, O. (2009). The practice of transformative pedagogy. *Journal on Excellence in College Teaching, 20*(2), 43–67.

Vyas, S. (2004). Exploring bicultural identities of Asian high school students through the analytic window of a literature club. *Journal of Adolescent and Adult Literacy, 48*(1), 12–23.

Willis, A. I. (2000). *Critical issue: Addressing literacy needs in culturally and linguistically diverse classrooms.* ERIC. https://eric.ed.gov/?id=ED480228

Yi, S. K. (2002). An immigrant's split personality. In E. C. Karpinski (Ed.), *Pens of many colours: A Canadian reader* (pp. 406–409). Harcourt Brace Canada.

Zaidi, Z., Verstegen, D., Naqvi, R., Dornan, T., & Morahan, P. (2016). Identity text: An educational intervention to foster cultural interaction. *Medical Education Online, 21*(1), Article 33135. https://doi.org/10.3402/meo.v21.33135

6

Les enjeux du plurilinguisme en milieu scolaire francophone minoritaire :
Inclusion et construction identitaire polymorphe

JUDITH PATOUMA

Bien que la francophonie soit importante au Canada, il n'en reste pas moins que le français est la langue d'une minorité dans le contexte actuel. Le Québec a une majorité de francophones et dans les autres provinces, majoritairement anglophones, les francophones sont dits en situation minoritaire. Selon Statistique Canada, en 2021 la population de langue maternelle française à l'extérieur du Québec représentait 3,3 % de la population totale. Cependant, ces chiffres, comme le souligne Remysen, sont sujets à interprétation puisqu'ils varient selon la « façon dont l'étiquette francophone est définie » (2019, p. 17). Cette étiquette sert soit à désigner les Canadiens dont le français est la langue maternelle (« excluant les Canadiens anglophones ou les nouveaux arrivants qui adoptent le français ») sans cibler leur utilisation de la langue dans différents contextes, soit les Canadiens qui s'expriment dans la langue sans viser leurs compétences et le contexte d'utilisation de celle-ci.

En dehors du Québec, les Canadiens francophones se situent majoritairement dans les provinces de l'Atlantique (le Nouveau-Brunswick, la Nouvelle-Écosse, l'Île-du-Prince-Édouard) et en Ontario. Selon Remysen, « La francophonie canadienne constitue [...] une communauté plurielle qui comprend des systèmes écolinguistiques singuliers, marqués par différentes manières d'être francophones »

(2019, p. 15). Cette caractéristique va être d'autant plus accentuée avec l'apport des réfugiés et de l'immigration.

Effectivement, dans les contextes minoritaires francophones au Canada, la vitalité linguistique est fortement reliée aux tendances démographiques des différentes communautés francophones (Landry, Allard et Deveau, 2010) ; les populations immigrantes ont un impact notable sur cette vitalité dans notre société canadienne multiculturelle et dans ses communautés francophones. Ainsi, les réflexions s'orientent de plus en plus sur la manière d'accueillir la diversité et l'ouverture sur les cultures du monde (Pilote, 2014). Les enjeux de l'immigration demandent des aménagements dans différents espaces dont celui du milieu éducatif. Pour cela, le rôle de l'école francophone (au niveau linguistique et culturel) doit se redéfinir (Gérin-Lajoie, 2008). La mission de l'école francophone en milieu minoritaire est double : la réussite éducative des élèves et la construction identitaire. L'apport du plurilinguisme et du pluriculturalisme, à travers l'immigration, est un élément supplémentaire à considérer de plus qu'il est reconnu que l'école joue un rôle dans les mécanismes de reproduction sociale (Farmer et Heller, 2008).

D'après l'Association canadienne d'éducation de langue française (ACELF), la construction identitaire est « un processus hautement dynamique au cours duquel la personne se définit et se reconnaît par sa façon de réfléchir, d'agir et de vouloir dans les contextes sociaux et l'environnement naturel où elle évolue. » (2006, p. 4) Nous pouvons alors nous demander quelles sont les pédagogies mises en place pour l'inclusion des différentes cultures en contact et quel impact cela va avoir sur la construction identitaire des apprenants et des enseignants. Après avoir fait un état des lieux des enjeux de l'immigration en milieu francophone minoritaire, nous aborderons le nouveau paradigme adopté dans l'institution scolaire pour l'accueil de la diversité, pour ensuite nous intéresser aux questions de la construction identitaire des apprenants. Nous terminerons par une proposition de pistes pédagogiques.

I- État des lieux des enjeux de l'immigration en milieu francophone minoritaire

Bien que majoritairement anglophone, 75,5 % en 2021 selon les données de Statistique Canada (2022), le Canada est un pays à deux langues officielles, l'anglais et le français. Ce statut juridique permet de desservir la population dans les deux langues, ce qui est important notamment en ce qui concerne les milieux minoritaires francophones. Selon l'Article 23 de la Charte canadienne des droits et libertés, les communautés linguistiques minoritaires (francophones ou anglophone) ont droit a une éducation dans leur langue. Les conseils scolaires francophones ont le droit de gestion et de contrôle de leurs écoles (affaire Mahé), entre autres des programmes d'étude et des aspects linguistiques et culturels de l'enseignement. Il est à constater que les écoles francophones en milieu minoritaire ont un rôle différent des écoles en milieu majoritaire. En effet, elles doivent non seulement amener les apprenants à développer des savoirs, des savoir-faire, des savoir-être et des savoir-vivre ensemble, mais elles ont aussi un rôle important à jouer dans la construction identitaire des apprenants. Dans un contexte où nous observons l'augmentation du nombre de familles exogames, l'école est souvent le lieu où les apprenants vont le plus souvent parler en français. En 2021, selon la Fédération nationale des conseils scolaires francophones (2021), on compte 28 conseils scolaires francophones et acadiens en contexte minoritaire au Canada. Ces conseils scolaires offrent des services éducatifs en français à près de 173 000 élèves rassemblés dans plus de 700 établissements scolaires élémentaires et secondaires (Maternelle à la 12ᵉ année).

En 2000, la Fédération des communautés francophones et acadienne du Canada (FCFA) (2021, p. 3) a identifié l'immigration comme « principal enjeu pour le développement des communautés francophones et acadienne » et ses membres s'engagent depuis à accueillir des immigrants de divers horizons culturels. Cette volonté d'intégration vient du fait que la population des communautés francophones et acadienne est déficitaire. Selon le Commissariat aux langues officielles du Canada (CLO) (2021), divers facteurs sont liés à ce déficit : une chute marquée de la fécondité ; une transmission intergénérationnelle incomplète de la langue maternelle française des parents aux enfants ; des transferts linguistiques intergénérationnels vers l'anglais comme langue d'usage au foyer parmi la population de langue maternelle française ; un vieillissement accru de la population d'expression française ; des tendances à la mobilité interprovinciale suivant la conjoncture notamment économique. En plus de ces facteurs, dont certains représentent des tendances lourdes, l'immigration représente un facteur clé (Houle et Corbeil, 2017). Selon Statistique Canada, « Grâce à sa forte fécondité, la population de langue maternelle française [en particulier au Canada hors Québec] a pu se maintenir jusque dans les années 1950, malgré un contexte où l'immigration ne lui était pas favorable. Toutefois, depuis le recensement de 1951, le pourcentage que représente cette population au sein du Canada est en baisse constante » (Statistique Canada, 2018, p. 3).

Pour toutes ces raisons, l'immigration est une solution appuyée par la FCFA : « l'inclusion de la diversité culturelle est particulièrement importante dans un contexte minoritaire, car elle permet l'élargissement de l'espace francophone et le renforcement de la langue française tout en assurant la pérennité des communautés. » (FCFA, 2021, p. 3) Cependant, les populations immigrantes ne sont pas majoritairement francophones et même si plusieurs s'expriment en anglais, force est de constater que certaines populations n'ont ni le français ni l'anglais comme langue première (CLO, 2021, p. 15). Selon Marcoux et Richard (2018), le Canada doit rechercher de nouveaux bassins de recrutement

Figure 6.1. Tableau sommaire des régions et principaux pays d'origine des résidents permanents d'expression française admis selon la définition de 2006 (données pour la période de 2001 à 2020 et de 2016 à 2020) et selon la définition de 2016 (donnés pour 2019), Canada hors Québec.

Top 10 pays d'origine des résidents permanents d'expression française admis hors Québec selon la définition de 2006 (Période de 2001 à 2020)	Top 10 pays d'origine des résidents permanents d'expression française admis hors Québec selon la définition de 2006 (Période de 2016 à 2020)	Top 10 pays d'origine des résidents permanents d'expression française admis hors Québec selon la définition de 2016 (Période de 2019)
1. France (22,9%)	1. France (32,9%)	1. France (22,1%)
2. Congo (RDC) (12,5%)	2. Congo (RDC) (10,5%)	2. Maroc (13,2%)
3. Haïti (8,6%)	3. Cameroun (6,2%)	3. Algérie (11,4%)
4. Cameroun (5,6%)	4. Maroc (5,7%)	4. Burundi (6,6%)
5. Maroc (5,2%)	5. Algérie (5,4%)	5. Cameroun (6,4%)
6. Burundi (4,3%)	6. Burundi (4,7%)	6. Congo (RDC) (5,8%)
7. Algérie (3,8%)	7. Haïti (4,6%)	7. Tunisie (5,8%)
8. Côte d'Ivoire (2,7%)	8. Côte d'Ivoire (2,9%)	8. Haïti (3%)
9. Liban (2,3%)	9. Belgique (2,7%)	9. Liban (2,4%)
10. Île Maurice (2,1%)	10. Djibouti (2,1%)	10. Île Maurice (2,3%)

Source : *Commissariat aux langues officielles, Étude d'analyse de la cible de 4,4 % d'immigration d'expression française au sein des communautés francophones en situation minoriraire : près de 20 ans après son adoption, il est temps de faire mieux et d'en faire plus,* 2021.

de la population pour augmenter la population francophone hors Québec. Ces bassins sont notamment l'Europe et le continent africain.

Le tableau ci-dessus indique les différentes populations immigrantes d'expression française qui se trouvent hors Québec. Cette diversité reflète la variété de cultures et de langues qui pourraient se trouver en milieu scolaire dans la francophonie minoritaire. Quelles sont les stratégies mises en place pour l'inclusion ? Les documents de la FCFA indiquent clairement qu'elle prône une politique d'inclusion de la diversité culturelle dans les organismes de langue française. En ce qui concerne les institutions scolaires, comment les écoles de langue française en milieu minoritaire vont-elles accueillir cette diversité ?

II- Un nouveau paradigme pour accueillir la diversité

L'immigration a amené les différentes instances fédérales et provinciales à s'interroger sur l'accueil de la diversité ; il va de soi que l'école tient une place clé dans les processus d'accueil, d'intégration et de valorisation ethnoculturelle. L'augmentation de l'immigration et sa diversification se font dans toutes les provinces et territoires, mais le Québec, où le français est la langue officielle majoritaire, accueille le plus d'immigrants francophones. Bien que ce chapitre traite de la francophonie hors Québec, il est nécessaire de faire un point sur les structures d'accueil que cette province a mis en place afin d'avoir une idée de ce qui existe.

L'éducation interculturelle

Au Québec, dès 1998, le ministère de l'Éducation met en place une Politique d'intégration scolaire et d'éducation interculturelle (Québec, ministère de l'Éducation, 1998). Sur le plan de l'intégration, le document mentionne un rapport de réciprocité dans la connaissance des cultures :

> Il importe de souligner que l'intégration est un processus qui va dans les deux sens. Elle exige des efforts d'adaptation et d'adhésion aux valeurs communes de la part des élèves immigrants et immigrantes, mais aussi une ouverture à la diversité et la mise en œuvre de moyens précis de la part du milieu social et scolaire qui les accueille. La spécificité du milieu scolaire et celle des besoins des élèves nouvellement arrivés doivent être reconnues de part et d'autre. Cette relation de réciprocité faite du respect mutuel des obligations est essentielle à la réussite de l'intégration. (Québec, 1998, p. 2)

Cette formulation est importante notamment en ce qui concerne la construction identitaire de nos apprenants que nous allons discuter dans la partie III.

En 2015, Grégoire-Labrecque s'est interrogée sur l'impact des formations interculturelles du ministère de l'Éducation du Québec que cette politique suggérait afin de renouveler « la réflexion et les pratiques sur les enjeux de la diversité ethnoculturelle dans les établissements scolaires » (Grégoire-Labrèque, 2015, p. 39). De cette étude il est ressorti l'importance de la formation interculturelle et le développement des compétences interculturelles des enseignants. La formation interculturelle (qui découle de l'approche interculturelle) est un processus dynamique de la compréhension de l'Autre et de Soi. Il est donc nécessaire que la formation interculturelle et la mise en place d'appui pédagogique ainsi que l'apprentissage « de résolutions de conflits en contexte de diversité ethnoculturelle et religieuse » (2015, p. 60) fassent partie de l'éducation permanente.

La formation interculturelle s'inspirant des écrits de Abdallah-Pretceille (2003) comme elle est abordée dans le plan du ministère est une démarche réflexive de l'enseignant, mais qu'en est-il du point de vue pédagogique ? Comment les enseignants acquièrent-ils des outils pour enseigner à un public diversifié puisque ce que l'on vise est la réussite scolaire des élèves dans le respect de leur identité culturelle ?

La diversité et l'inclusion scolaire

Plusieurs chercheurs se sont penchés sur les notions de diversité et d'inclusion scolaire, dont Prud'homme, Ramel et Vienneau en 2011. Il semble que la formation de base concernant la diversité ethnoculturelle, religieuse et linguistique dans les universités du Québec soit insuffisante (Larochelle-Audet, Borri-Anadon, et Potuin, 2016). Bien qu'il y ait plusieurs spécialistes en pluriculturalisme et en plurilinguisme, très peu d'enseignants ont reçu « une formation relative à la diversité ethnoculturelle, à l'immigration ou encore au racisme » (2016, p. 176). Il semblerait que la problématique de l'inclusion doit être considérée dans un paradigme holistique en consultant toutes les instances concernées (sociales, politiques, etc.). L'éducation inclusive, telle que décrite dans ce chapitre, est fondée sur des principes démocratiques et humanistes (Prud'homme, Ramel et Vienneau, 2011) ainsi que sur des valeurs d'équité et de justice sociale (Barton, 2010 ; Mittler, 2000 ; Potvin, 2013).

Dans un article intitulé « Assimilation, intégration ou inclusion : quelle vision pour l'éducation de langue française en contexte minoritaire ? », Dalley (2014) mentionne que « l'inclusion exige un engagement de la part de tous dans la construction d'un espace continuellement en mouvance. Cette co-construction ne peut avoir lieu que dans une relation d'interdépendance entre partenaires égaux qui y proposent légitimement leurs langues, leurs cultures et leurs savoirs au projet commun. Finalement, ce n'est que l'inclusion qui peut faire profiter l'ensemble de la francophonie et la richesse de sa diversité » (Dalley, 2014, p. 32). Ainsi cela ne vient que confirmer qu'au niveau conceptuel, que cela vienne d'un milieu majoritaire ou minoritaire francophone, nous nous rejoignons dans cette définition qui vise la valorisation de Soi et de l'Autre dans toute sa complexité.

L'hétérogénéité et la différenciation : des richesses pour la salle de classe

Toute classe est nécessairement hétérogène. Dans les salles de classe, des apprenants de cultures et de langues différentes, issus de trajectoires différentes se côtoient. La prise en compte de la singularité de chacun, et donc de l'hétérogénéité, va permettre d'influencer la motivation des apprenants. Alors que pendant longtemps les politiques éducatives mettaient plus l'emphase sur l'uniformisation de la salle de classe, ce changement de paradigme va permettre de développer une pédagogie plus humaniste axée sur les besoins de l'apprenant. Une des orientations du Conseil supérieur de l'éducation du Québec est la mise en place d'une éducation inclusive (2017, p. 5). Il propose de mettre en place un continuum (voir Figure 6.2). La diversité dans les salles de classe est vécue aussi de manière différente du fait de l'apport de l'immigration. L'hétérogénéité se caractérise par différents aspects qui sont, pour ne citer que quelques-uns : la structure des familles, les conditions de vie, la culture et les langues dans le milieu familial.

III- La construction identitaire, la langue et l'équité

Dans les milieux francophones minoritaires, les écoles ont plusieurs mandats : la réussite scolaire des apprenants et la construction langagière, culturelle et identitaire. Toutes ces dimensions sont liées de manière intrinsèque. Dans un contexte minoritaire, l'apprenant arrive à l'école avec un bagage langagier et culturel de sa communauté

Figure 6.2. Le Continuum vers une éducation inclusive pour tous

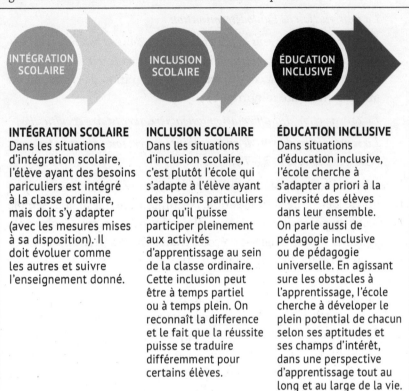

INTÉGRATION SCOLAIRE
Dans les situations d'intégration scolaire, l'élève ayant des besoins pariculiers est intégré à la classe ordinaire, mais doit s'y adapter (avec les mesures mises à sa disposition). Il doit évoluer comme les autres et suivre l'enseignement donné.

INCLUSION SCOLAIRE
Dans les situations d'inclusion scolaire, c'est plutôt l'école qui s'adapte à l'élève ayant des besoins particuliers pour qu'il puisse participer pleinement aux activités d'apprentissage au sein de la classe ordinaire. Cette inclusion peut être à temps partiel ou à temps plein. On reconnaît la difference et le fait que la réussite puisse se traduire différemment pour certains élèves.

ÉDUCATION INCLUSIVE
Dans situations d'éducation inclusive, l'école cherche à s'adapter a priori à la diversité des élèves dans leur ensemble. On parle aussi de pédagogie inclusive ou de pédagogie universelle. En agissant sure les obstacles à l'apprentissage, l'école cherche à développer le plein potentiel de chacun selon ses aptitudes et ses champs d'intérêt, dans une perspective d'apprentissage tout au long et au large de la vie.

Source : Québec, Conseil supérieur de l'éducation. *Pour une école riche de tous ses élèves : S'adapter à la diversité des élèves, de la maternelle à la 5ᵉ année du secondaire*, 2017.

minoritaire, de sa communauté majoritaire ou des deux. Maintenant avec l'apport de l'immigration, les apprenants se retrouvent dans des situations de contact de langues diverses alors que la langue d'enseignement est le français. Gauvin proposa un outil conceptuel qui s'intitule CLIC : Construction langagière, identitaire et culturelle (Figure 6.3). Cet outil a permis de voir différentes composantes qui entrent en jeu dans les différentes constructions susmentionnées. L'auteure s'est inspirée des six dimensions identitaires de l'école orientante de Bégin, Bleau et Landry (2000) :

- *La construction du sens de sa réalité langagière, identitaire et culturelle minoritaire ;*

- *La construction de la littératie minoritaire ;*
- *La construction de l'autodétermination ;*
- *La construction du sens de soi et de l'autre dans sa communauté minoritaire et dans la communauté majoritaire ou face à elle.* (Ici, nous pourrions ajouter la communauté d'immigration d'origine qui est une communauté minoritaire) ;
- *La construction de l'affirmation langagière, identitaire et culturelle ;*
- *La construction du sens de responsabilité envers son vécu et en français.* (Gauvin, 2009b, p. 71-72)

Il semble évident que la recherche de Gauvin n'avait pas pour but d'introduire le facteur de l'immigration. Néanmoins, ce travail nous semble pertinent du point de vue conceptuel de plus qu'il a servi a évaluer des programmes d'études dans des écoles francophones (fransaskoises) en milieu minoritaire. L'étude datant de 2009, il serait intéressant d'évaluer la composante de la construction identitaire aujourd'hui.

S'appuyant sur les recherches de Marianne Cormier (2005), un cadre de la pédagogie en milieu minoritaire a été dressé ; encore une fois, le but était de conscientiser les apprenants à la problématique de l'assimilation par la communauté anglophone et de les sensibiliser à l'impact de cette présence majoritaire puisque cela avait une incidence sur la langue d'usage au foyer et à l'école ainsi que sur la construction identitaire. Le document de Cormier est fondateur et n'avait pas pour but de discuter la sensibilisation aux nouveaux arrivants dans le système scolaire. L'ACELF (2006) s'est inspirée de ces principes et a aussi élargi son impact.

Figure 6.3. Les composantes de la construction langagière, identitaire et culturelle (CLIC) en milieu francophone minoritaire : une dynamique intégrative.

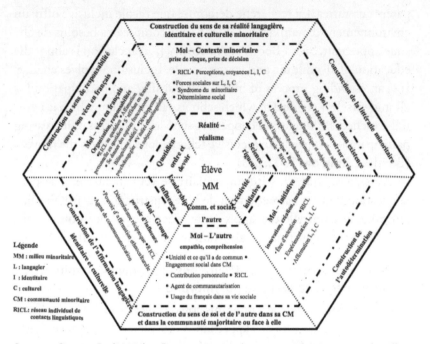

Source : Gauvin, L. (2009a). « La construction langagière, identitaire et culturelle : un cadre conceptuel pour l'école francophone en milieu minoritaire », *Cahiers franco-canadiens de l'Ouest*, vol. 21, n° 1/2, p. 119, utilisée avec permission.

L'ACELF propose 8 principes directeurs dans la construction identitaire :

1. S'inscrire dans la francophonie contemporaine ;
2. Miser sur la créativité et l'innovation ;
3. Valoriser la diversité ;
4. Favoriser l'action concertée de la famille, de la communauté et de l'école ;
5. Développer un rapport positif à la langue française ;
6. Créer des liens au sein de la francophonie ;
7. Encourager la mobilisation ;
8. Viser les effets durables.

Les programmes d'études intègrent ces principes dans leur contenu et il est donc un document directeur pour les enseignants, apprenants, parents et autres. La recherche démontre que l'école inclusive offre un environnement dynamique où il faut tenir compte des besoins de chaque apprenant. Selon Booth et Ainscow, « [...] inclusion is about the education of all children and young people. Inclusion involves change. It is an unending process of increasing learning and participation for all students. It is an ideal to which schools can aspire but which is never fully reached. But inclusion happens as soon as the process of increasing participation is started. An inclusive school is one that is on the move. » (Booth et Ainscow, 2002, p. 3)

Ainsi, alors que l'institution scolaire se veut inclusive, il se pose la question de la construction ou de la reconstruction identitaire linguistique et culturelle des apprenants avec l'accueil des immigrants. Comment cette construction s'opérationnalise-t-elle en salle de classe ?

IV- La (re)construction identitaire des apprenants en milieu scolaire : vers une identité polymorphe ?

Nous avons vu que l'école a pour mission de créer un cadre inclusif afin de favoriser le bien-être de l'apprenant sur le plan émotionnel et identitaire. Cependant, l'expression d'une identité culturelle homogène peut être complexe étant donné que nous sommes une minorité linguistique et de plus, que les immigrants représentent une minorité, voire des minorités, dans la minorité (Gallant, 2007, p. 93) puisqu'ils peuvent être d'origines ethnoculturelles diverses.

Dans l'espace de la salle de classe, l'apprenant est dans une situation de co-construction avec les autres. Au-delà des contenus notionnels, il doit apprendre le vivre ensemble, valoriser la diversité identitaire/culturelle et se construire de façon holistique. Quelles sont les dynamiques qui se mettent en place ? La notion d'identité est un concept qui se nourrit de différents courants de pensée. Apparue en psychologie sociale avec Erickson, elle a aussi des racines dans l'anthropologie, la psychanalyse, la sociologie, la linguistique, la didactique des langues-cultures ... et aujourd'hui dans le champ des neurosciences. Ainsi le concept est très dynamique et cela contribue à sa richesse.

Suivant une perspective interactionniste, pour nous l'individu (et dans notre cas particulier l'apprenant) se construit dans et par différentes situations d'interactions. « Le Soi, en tant qu'objet pour soi, est essentiellement une structure sociale et naît dans l'expérience sociale » affirme Mead (1963, p. 115). L'école étant un microsystème de la société, nous pouvons conclure que c'est un lieu de construction identitaire. L'approche dominante dans les contextes scolaires actuels est la pédagogie du socioconstructivisme (Vygotski, 1985). C'est une théorie de l'apprentissage qui montre l'importance des interactions sociales et de la culture dans les situations d'enseignement-apprentissage et dans la création des connaissances. Selon Vygotski, les savoirs et les disciplines scolaires ont un impact sur les structures mentales et contribuent à la construction de la personnalité de l'apprenant. Alors, quels sont les concepts identitaires qui entrent en jeu dans ce contexte pluriel concernant l'apprenant et l'enseignant ? Dans le but de mieux comprendre ce qui est en jeu, nous retiendrons ici les notions de catégorisation et d'identification, les sentiments d'appartenance, les crises et les stratégies identitaires.

La catégorisation et l'identification

Ces deux notions vont de pair. L'individu vit dans un système complexe et pour trouver toute la cohérence de son monde, il « l'ordonne, le systématise et le simplifie » (Tajfel, 1982, p. 21). Cette catégorisation peut concerner l'âge, le groupe social, les valeurs et la culture, parmi d'autres. De même que pour pouvoir se construire, il devra emprunter (s'identifier) à des connaissances, des cultures, etc. Pour de nombreux chercheurs, l'identification est un processus actif. D'après Mucchielli, l'identification consiste à « reconnaître quelque chose à certains signes pour pouvoir le ranger dans une catégorie de connaissance » (1986, p. 31) ; ainsi, les individus choisissent de s'identifier à un groupe à un moment donné de leur évolution personnelle. Si nous prenons l'exemple de la salle de classe, la catégorisation et l'identification vont dans les deux sens : celui de l'apprenant et de l'enseignant. Comment l'apprenant va-t-il catégoriser les différentes personnes dans la salle de classe et à qui va-t-il s'identifier ? Sera-t-il en mesure de s'identifier à la culture de l'école, de sa communauté d'adoption ? L'enseignant pourra-t-il s'identifier à certaines valeurs des apprenants de sa classe ? Lesquelles ? Pourront-ils développer un sentiment d'appartenance au groupe ?

Les sentiments d'appartenance

Les sentiments d'appartenance sont en lien avec les notions précitées. Selon Blanchet et Francard (2003, p. 19), « il ne suffit pas d'éprouver un sentiment d'appartenance pour que cette identité soit effective (ce sentiment ne peut pas se former isolément chez l'individu) : elle n'est effective que si elle est perçue et reconnue par autrui. » Ainsi le sentiment d'appartenance est relié de manière intrinsèque à la perception et à la volonté de l'Autre. Dans le cas des écoles, et plus particulièrement en milieu minoritaire, comment est créé ce sentiment d'appartenance ? Comment l'institution scolaire fait-elle appartenir ses apprenants ? Cela est un critère encore plus important concernant les apprenants immigrants ou réfugiés puisqu'ils viennent de contextes différents et que le sentiment d'appartenance est signe d'une intégration réussie. C'est aussi une compétence socioaffective à développer pour que les apprenants se construisent sur des bases saines de l'estime de soi et peut-être un moyen de renforcer le sentiment de sécurité linguistique.

Les crises identitaires et les stratégies identitaires

Puisque les apprenants (issus de l'immigration) arrivent dans une structure scolaire nouvelle, il serait intéressant de réfléchir à la notion de l'identité sous l'angle de la crise, dans le sens de rupture avec un système connu. Selon Kasterztein, « L'analyse des travaux sur les 'crises identitaires' nous mène à penser que lorsque l'élasticité maximale des systèmes est atteinte, en particulier lorsque l'univers relationnel se transforme radicalement et que l'existence même de l'acteur comme être séparé et valorisé est mise en cause, une rupture se produit qui nécessite l'élaboration d'une nouvelle structure […] l'importance du phénomène étant encore plus grande pour les adolescents immigrés. » (1998, p. 30) Comment accompagner les apprenants de manière efficace dans ces situations de ruptures ? L'auteur ajoute que les individus vont être dans une double tension psychologique venant de l'intérieur (endogène) et de l'extérieur (exogène). Cette tension les poussera à mettre en place des stratégies identitaires qui auront pour but de leur permettre d'exister.

Ainsi, Kasterztein définit l'identité comme « une structure polymorphe dynamique, dont les éléments constitutifs sont les aspects psychologiques et sociaux en rapport à la situation relationnelle à un moment donné d'un agent social (individu ou groupe) comme acteur social. » (1998, p. 28) L'identité linguistique aura, donc, différents aspects selon les situations de communications (salle de classe, famille, communauté, etc.) et il en sera de même pour les identités culturelles. Cependant, polymorphe ne veut pas dire dissolution identitaire, mais ce serait un indice d'adaptabilité.

V- Le plurilinguisme et le pluriculturalisme

Comme nous l'avons mentionné précédemment, l'école inclusive semble le nouveau cadre à établir pour l'accueil de la diversité (le terme ici principalement consacré à la diversité issue de l'immigration ou des migrants d'origines diverses). Bien que nous pouvons trouver beaucoup d'informations au plan conceptuel, il reste néanmoins que l'opérationnalisation de l'inclusion de la diversité dans les écoles n'est pas toujours évidente. C'est dans cette optique que Bergeron, Rousseau et Leclerc proposent l'utilisation de la pédagogie universelle (en anglais *universal pedagogy*). Ce concept, qui vient de l'architecture (Bernacchio et Mullen, 2007 ; Renzaglia et coll., 2003), permet d'examiner le contexte en profondeur et, au plan pédagogique, les besoins différenciés des apprenants. Cela pourrait être un cadre intéressant pour tous les élèves. Voici les différentes étapes mentionnées par Bergeron, Rousseau et Leclerc (2011, p. 98-99) :

1. Établir des buts : quelles sont les cibles à atteindre afin de proposer un défi important à la hauteur des capacités de chacun des apprenants ?

2. Analyser la situation actuelle : quel est le profil de la classe ? Comment est-elle diverse ?

3. Appliquer la pédagogie universelle pour bonifier la situation actuelle : planifier diverses situations d'enseignement.

4. Mettre en œuvre la situation d'enseignement-apprentissage selon les principes de la pédagogie universelle : faire vivre aux élèves différentes situations d'enseignement-apprentissage planifiées au préalable.

À l'ère de la mondialisation et de l'intégration des langues et cultures en salle de classe, les apprenants doivent, comme nous l'avons mentionné, développer des compétences dans la langue de l'école, des savoir-faire, des savoir-être et le savoir-vivre ensemble. Beacco et ses collègues ont préparé un *Guide pour le développement et la mise en œuvre de curriculums pour une éducation plurilingue et interculturelle* et le Centre européen pour les langues vivantes (CELV), dans son Cadre de référence pour les approches plurielles des langues et des cultures (CARAP), propose un référentiel afin de guider les enseignants dans l'évaluation des compétences des apprenants. Plusieurs travaux et programmes existent pour soutenir les conseils scolaires et le personnel enseignant dans l'appropriation et la diffusion de contenus pédagogiques. Pour en citer quelques-uns :

Evlang : L'éveil aux langues

En 1984, Hawkins définit pour la première fois la notion de l'éveil aux langues, *language awareness* ou la sensibilisation aux langues. L'éveil aux langues, la découverte active de plusieurs langues, se développe dans des sociétés multiculturelles. Les apprenants sont mis en contact avec différents corpus, oraux et écrits, pour découvrir (s'éveiller) à différentes langues du monde. Il ne concerne pas l'enseignement-apprentissage d'une langue en particulier, mais le développement des compétences métalinguistiques et plurilingues : les cultures langagières, des attitudes positives face aux langues en contact dans l'environnement de l'apprenant. Celui-ci sera mis dans une posture d'observateur d'où il pourra réfléchir sur les langues, les comparer, etc. Selon Candelier (2003, p. 20), « L'éveil aux langues se détache de l'enseignement précoce des langues dans le sens où il fait de la 'diversité des langues et des cultures un objet d'activités à l'école'. »

L'intercompréhension des langues

« L'intercompréhension entre les langues parentes propose un travail parallèle sur plusieurs langues d'une même famille, qu'il s'agisse de la famille à laquelle appartient la langue maternelle de l'apprenant (ou la langue de l'école) ou de la famille d'une langue dont il a effectué l'apprentissage. On tire parti des atouts les plus tangibles de l'appartenance à une même famille – ceux relatifs à la compréhension – qu'on cherche à cultiver systématiquement. » (CELV, 2007, p. 8)

La didactique intégrée

« Ce type de modalité s'inscrit dans une double perspective, visant à la fois et de manière conjointe l'appui sur les savoirs et savoir-faire antérieurs et une meilleure appropriation des langues de l'école. La dimension réflexive explicite, associée à ces activités, contribue grandement à faire travailler les enfants sur leurs représentations de la différence. » (Castellotti et Moore, 2011b, p. 31)

La pédagogie sensible à la culture (culturally responsive teaching)

Gay (2000) et Villegas et Lucas (2001) qualifient d'« enseignement sensible à la culture » ou « pédagogie sensible à la culture » un enseignement « qui reconnaît que les modes d'apprentissage des élèves sont différents et parfois associés au milieu d'origine, à la langue, à la structure familiale et à l'identité sociale ou culturelle. » (Centre franco, 2019) Cette pédagogie a pour volonté d'utiliser la diversité comme un outil efficace pour s'approprier les cultures en salle de classe. Le Centre franco, avec l'appui financier du ministère de l'Éducation de l'Ontario et du gouvernement du Canada, a développé un site web afin de soutenir le personnel enseignant dans leur enseignement-apprentissage.

Conclusion

Nous avons vu que les missions de l'école en milieu minoritaire sont nombreuses. Non seulement vise-t-elle la réussite scolaire des apprenants, mais aussi leur construction identitaire et de fait leur bien-être. La pédagogie en milieu minoritaire s'est longtemps focalisée sur la sensibilisation des apprenants (francophones et acadiens) aux cultures francophones et aux dangers de la culture anglicisante du milieu. Mais aujourd'hui, l'apport de la diversité demande que les pédagogies soient plus ouvertes et inclusives pour aller vers la connaissance de l'Autre et la construction de Soi. L'éducation plurielle semble une solution puisqu'elle cible la population immigrante, mais pas seulement. Tout apprenant peut bénéficier des avantages d'une éducation qui amène à la découverte de soi et à la compréhension de l'autre dans des dimensions systémiques. Ce déplacement de regard vers un paradigme plurilingue semble modifier les fondements de l'éducation en milieu minoritaire. Plusieurs études ont mentionné la nécessité du partenariat famille-école-communauté, mais très peu de recherche se fait au niveau des pédagogies intégratives dans la salle de classe. Il est nécessaire de comprendre non seulement les trajectoires des apprenants et la dynamique de leur construction identitaire, mais aussi il semble important de mettre en place une éducation au pluriculturalisme pour les enseignants afin de leur donner les outils nécessaires à leur enseignement.

Le pluralisme linguistique et culturel est maintenant une réalité dans nos écoles. Il faut ainsi repenser le rôle de l'école pour qu'il y ait une meilleure compréhension et un meilleur rapport aux langues, aux cultures et aux identités.

D'un autre côté, comme nous l'avons vu, il y a des défis à surmonter puisque les classes peuvent être très hétérogènes tant dans la diversité des apprenants que dans la gestion des compétences non homogènes. Et qu'en est-il de la relation famille-école ? Quelles sont les conséquences du changement culturel et linguistique à l'intérieur des familles ? Peuvent-elles soutenir l'apprentissage de leurs enfants ? De quelle manière leur identité personnelle, familiale, sociale va-t-elle être affectée ? Quelles seront les nouvelles réflexions et les nouveaux cadres à mettre en place qui prendront en compte la complexité et les singularités des apprenants et des enseignants ? Voici quelques problématiques et pas des moindres sur lesquelles il faudrait une réflexion profonde dans le souci du développement holistique de l'apprenant et de l'enseignant.

References

ABDALLAH-PRETCEILLE, Martine (2003). *Former et éduquer en contexte hétérogène : pour un humanisme du divers,* Paris, Anthropos, 226 p.

ASSOCIATION CANADIENNE D'ÉDUCATION DE LANGUE FRANÇAISE (ACELF) (2006). *Cadre d'orientation en construction identitaire,* Québec, 35 p. [https://numerique.banq.qc.ca/patrimoine/details/52327/60812].

BARTON, Len (2010). « The politics of education for all », dans RIX, Jonathan et coll., *Equality, Participation and Inclusion: Diverse Perspectives,* 2ᵉ éd., New York, Routledge, p. 90-98.

BEACCO, Jean-Claude et coll. (2016). *Guide pour le développement et la mise en œuvre de curriculums pour une éducation plurilingue et interculturelle,* Strasbourg, Conseil de l'Europe, 179 p.

BÉGIN, Luc, Michel BLEAU et Louise LANDRY (2000). *L'école orientante : la formation de l'identité à l'école,* Outremont, Éditions Logiques, 112 p.

BERGERON, Léna, Nadia ROUSSEAU et Martine LECLERC (2011). « La pédagogie universelle : au cœur de la planification de l'inclusion scolaire », *Éducation et francophonie,* vol. 39, n° 2, p. 87-104. [https://doi.org/10.7202/1007729ar]

BERNACCHIO, Charles et Michelle MULLEN (2007). « Universal design for learning », *Psychiatric Rehabilitation Journal,* vol. 31, n° 2, p. 167-169. [https://psycnet.apa.org/record/2007-17828-012]

BLANCHET, Philippe et Michel FRANCARD (2003). « Appartenance (sentiment, d') », dans FERRÉOL, Gilles et Guy JUCQUOIS (dir.), *Dictionnaire de l'altérité et des relations interculturelles,* Paris, Armand Colin, p. 18-25. (collection Dictionnaire)

BOOTH, Tony et Mel AINSCOW (2002). *Index for Inclusion: Developing Learning and Participation in Schools,* Centre for Studies on Inclusive Education (CSIE), Bristol, 102 p.

CANDELIER, Michel (dir.) (2003). *L'éveil aux langues à l'école primaire – Evlang : bilan d'une innovation européenne,* Louvain-la-Neuve, De Boeck Supérieur, 384 p.

CASTELLOTTI, Véronique et Danièle MOORE (2011a). « Répertoires plurilingues et pluriculturels : leur valorisation pour une meilleure intégration scolaire », *Babylonia,* 1/11, p. 29-33.

CASTELLOTTI, Véronique et Danièle MOORE (2011b). « La compétence plurilingue et pluriculturelle. Genèses et évolutions d'une notion-concept. » Éditions des Archives contemporaines. *Guide pour la recherche en didactique des langues et des cultures. Approches contextualisées,* p. 241-252. (hal-01295032)

CENTRE EUROPÉEN POUR LES LANGUES VIVANTES (2007). *Cadre de référence pour les approches plurielles des langues et des cultures – À travers les langues et les cultures, Version 2,* Graz, Autriche [https://carap.ecml.at/Accueil/tabid/3577/language/fr-FR/Default.aspx]

CENTRE FRANCO (2019). *Pour une pédagogie sensible et adaptée à la culture* [https://psac.lecentrefranco.ca/index.html]

COMMISSARIAT AUX LANGUES OFFICIELLES DU CANADA (2021). *Étude d'analyse statistique de la cible de 4,4 % d'immigration d'expression française au sein des communautés francophones en situation minoritaire : près de 20 ans après son adoption, il est temps de faire mieux et d'en faire plus. Rapport final,* Ottawa, Ontario, 87 p. [https://www.clo-ocol.gc.ca/sites/default/files/2023-06/etude-analyse-immigration-expression-francaise.pdf]

CORMIER, Marianne (2005). « La pédagogie en milieu minoritaire francophone : une recension des écrits », Moncton, Fédération canadienne des enseignantes et des enseignants / Institut canadien de recherche sur les minorités linguistiques, 39 p. [http://icrml.ca/images/stories/documents/fr/cormier_marianne_recension.pdf]

DALLEY, Phyllis (2014). « Assimilation, intégration ou inclusion : quelle vision pour l'éducation de langue française en contexte minoritaire ? », dans BERG, Carlson et coll., *La francophonie canadienne dans toutes ses couleurs et le défi de l'inclusion,* Quebec, Presses de l'Université Laval, p. 13-33.

DUBAR, Claude. (2000). *La crise des identités : l'interpretation d'une mutation,* Paris, Presses universitaires de France, 239 p.

FARMER, Diane et Monica HELLER (2008). « La sociologie de l'éducation », dans LAFLAMME, Simon et Jean LAFONTANT (dir.), *Initiation thématique à la sociologie,* 2e édition, Sudbury, Éditions Prise de Parole, p. 123-158.

FÉDÉRATION DES COMMUNAUTÉS FRANCOPHONES ET ACADIENNE (2021). *Guide sur l'inclusion des personnes issues de la diversité culturelle dans les communautés francophones et acadiennes du Canada,* Ottawa, Fédération des communautés francophones et acadienne, 18 p. [https://www.immigrationfrancophone.ca/images/Bibliotheque/Guide_Inclusion_Final.pdf]

FÉDÉRATION NATIONALE DES CONSEILS SCOLAIRES FRANCOPHONES (2021). *Bâtir notre avenir au présent,* Ottawa, Fédération nationale des conseils scolaires francophones. [https://fncsf.ca/wp-content/uploads/2023/06/Offre_de_services_2023.pdf]

GALLANT, Nicole (2007). « Ouverture et inclusion identitaire en milieu francophone minoritaire : quand les immigrants sont la minorité dans une minorité », *Nos diverses cités*, vol. et n° 3, p. 93-97.

GAUVIN, Lucie (2009a). « La construction langagière, identitaire et culturelle (CLIC) en milieu francophone minoritaire : une dynamique intégrative », *Cahiers franco-canadiens de l'Ouest*, vol. 21, n° 1-2, p. 87-126.

GAUVIN, Lucie (2009b). *La construction langagière, identitaire et culturelle en milieu minoritaire et les programmes d'études fransaskois pour la quatrième année*. Mémoire, Université du Manitoba, 179 p.

GAY, Geneva (2000). *Culturally Responsive Teaching: Theory, Research, and Practice*, New York, Teachers College Press, 2000, 251 p.

GÉRIN-LAJOIE, Diane (2008). « Le travail enseignant en milieu minoritaire », dans DALLEY, Phyllis et Sylvie ROY (dir.), *Francophonie, minorités et pédagogie*, Ottawa, Les Presses de l'Université d'Ottawa, p. 65-84.

GRÉGOIRE-LABRECQUE, Geneviève (2015). « La pertinence de l'étude des formations interculturelles dans l'approfondissement des enjeux de la diversité ethnoculturelle dans les établissements scolaires », *Approches inductives en anthropologie*, vol. 2, n° 2, automne, p. 39-66. [https://doi.org/10.7202/1032606ar]

HAWKINS, Eric (1984). *Awareness of Language: An Introduction*, Cambridge, Cambridge University Press, 223 p.

HOULE, René et Jean-Pierre CORBEIL (2017). *Projections linguistiques pour le Canada 2011-2036. Série thématique sur l'ethnicité, la langue et l'immigration*, Ottawa, Statistique Canada, 140 p.

KASTERZTEIN, Joseph (1999). « Les stratégies identitaires des acteurs sociaux : approche dynamique des finalités », dans CAMILLERI, Carmel, *Stratégies identitaires*, Paris, Presses universitaires de France, p. 27-41.

LANDRY, Rodrigue, Réal ALLARD et Kenneth DEVEAU (2010). *École et autonomie culturelle. Enquête pancanadienne en milieu scolaire francophone minoritaire*, Gatineau, Patrimoine canadien et Institut canadien de recherche sur les minorités linguistiques (ICRML) (collection Nouvelles perspectives canadiennes).

LAROCHELLE-AUDET, Julie, Corina BORRI-ANADON et Maryse POTVIN (2016). « La formation interculturelle et inclusive du personnel enseignant : conceptualisation et opérationnalisation de compétences professionnelles », *Éducation et franco-phonie*, vol. 44, n° 2, automne, p. 172–195. [https://doi.org/10.7202/1039027ar]

MAGNAN, Marie-Odile et coll. (2021). « Édito - L'éducation inclusive en contexte de diversité ethnoculturelle : comprendre les processus d'exclusion pour agir sur le terrain de l'école », *Recherches en éducation*, vol. 44, p. 2-15.

MARCOUX, Richard et Laurent RICHARD (2018). « Les dynamiques démographiques dans l'espace francophone face aux enjeux de l'immigration internationale de langue française au Québec et au Canada », *Francophonies d'Amérique*, n° 46-47, automne 2018, hiver 2019, p. 73-96.

MEAD, George Herbert (1963). *L'esprit, le soi et la société*, Paris, Presses universitaires de France, 332 p.

MITTLER, Peter (2000). *Working Towards Inclusive Education*, London, David Fulton Publishers, 222 p.

MUCCHIELLI, Alex (1986). *L'Identité*, Paris, Presses universitaires de France, 127 p. (collection Que Sais-je ?).

PILOTE, Annie (dir.) (2014). *Francophones et citoyens du monde : éducation, identités et engagement*, Québec, Presses de l'Université Laval, 292 p. (collection Culture française d'Amérique).

POTVIN, Maryse (2013). « L'éducation inclusive et antidiscriminatoire : fondements et perspectives », dans Mc ANDREW, Marie, Maryse POTVIN et Corina BORRI-ANADON (dir.), *Le développement d'institutions inclusives en contexte de diversité*, Québec, Presses de l'Université du Québec, p. 25-42.

PRUD'HOMME, Luc, Serge RAMEL et Raymond VIENNEAU (2011). « Valorisation de la diversité en éducation : défis contemporains et pistes d'action », *Éducation et francophonie*, vol. 39, n° 2, automne, p. 1-5. [https://doi.org/10.7202/1007724ar]

QUÉBEC. CONSEIL SUPÉRIEUR DE L'ÉDUCATION (2017). *Pour une école riche de tous ses élèves : s'adapter à la diversité des élèves, de la maternelle à la 5ᵉ année du secondaire*, Conseil supérieur de l'éducation, 155 p. [https://www.cse.gouv.qc.ca/wp-content/uploads/2017/10/50-0500-AV-ecole-riche-eleves.pdf]

QUÉBEC. MINISTÈRE DE L'ÉDUCATION (1998). *Une école d'avenir : politique d'intégration scolaire et d'éducation interculturelle*, Québec, Ministère de l'Éducation, 42 p. [http://www.education.gouv.qc.ca/fileadmin/site_web/documents/education/adaptation-scolaire-services-comp/PolitiqueMatiereIntegrationScolEducInterculturelle_UneEcoleAvenir_f.pdf].

REMYSEN, Wim (2019). « Les communautés francophones dans les provinces majoritairement anglophones du Canada : aperçu et enjeux », *Travaux de linguistique*, n° 78, p. 15-45. [https://doi.org/10.3917/tl.078.0015]

RENZAGLIA, Adelle et coll. (2003). « Promoting a Lifetime of Inclusion », *Focus on Autism and Other Developmental Disabilities*, vol. 18, n° 3, p. 140-149.

STATISTIQUE CANADA (2022) *Alors que le français et l'anglais demeurent les principales langues parlées au Canada, la diversité linguistique continue de s'accroître au pays : Le Quotidien* diffusion 2022-08-17 [https://www150.statcan.gc.ca/n1/daily-quotidien/220817/dq220817a-fra.htm#:~:text=Faits%20saillants,75%2C5%20%25%20en%202021]

STATISTIQUE CANADA (2018). *Mégatendances canadiennes : l'évolution des populations de langue maternelle au Canada, de 1901 à 2016.* [https://www150.statcan.gc.ca/n1/fr/pub/11-630-x/11-630-x2018001-fra.pdf?st=keJrgGla]

TAJFEL, Henri (1982). *Social Identity and Intergroup Relations*, Cambridge, Cambridge University Press, 528 p.

VILLEGAS, Ana Maria et Tamara LUCAS (2001). *Educating Culturally Responsive Teachers: A Coherent Approach*, Albany, SUNY Press, 272 p.

VYGOTSKY, Lev. S. (1985). *Pensée et langage*, traduction de Françoise Sève, Paris, Editions Sociales, 419 p.

PART 3

BEYOND MARKED IDENTITIES
in
LITERATURE

Literature offers a window into the cultural traditions and practices of different communities around the world. As such, literature helps not only to create but also shape the visions of the society that we live in for those who look in from the outside. In Canada, despite its praised multicultural fabric, works of literature, especially fictional works, have played a major role in elevating the anglophone literary tradition and, to a lesser extent, the francophone literary tradition while neglecting Indigenous and immigrant works, which embody diversity in terms of knowing, telling, feeling, and existing. In this section, the anglophone ontology of Canadian literature is confronted from within. Both chapters in this section bring bicultural experiences and bilingual perspectives, primarily from an immigrant Portuguese Canadian position, to critically explore the practices of the literary field and publishing industry in Canada. These chapters demonstrate that reconceptualizing Canadian literature is essential for cultural and linguistic inclusivity.

In Chapter 7, Irene Marques problematizes the predominance of English as a global and literary language that makes us prone to internalizing the Anglo-Saxon ethic and aesthetic in the Canadian literary landscape. In particular, Marques argues that Canadian literature continues to privilege the Anglo-Saxon ethic and aesthetic, thereby controlling *how* one tells one's story and *what* story one tells. However, the *how* seems to be more contentious than the *what*: even if there is currently encouragement from the Canadian literary establishment for writers from different backgrounds to write and publish their own stories, they are still asked to write in line with the Anglo-Saxon aesthetic. In response, Marques presents some strategies that would generate a shift toward more inclusion within the Canadian literary scene, and a move away from the predominant Anglo-Saxon literary paradigm, so that our multicultural theoretical proclamations become a practice that validates and includes plural identities and literary voices.

In Chapter 8, Maria João Maciel Jorge argues that labels of ethnic, minority, and immigrant writing are often used pejoratively to limit or exclude the contributions of culturally minoritized writers. A cultural and linguistic monoculture prevails that privileges English despite the historical marginality of Canadian literature and its potential to accommodate cultures in inclusive ways. Maciel Jorge addresses such issues by confronting the exclusion of Portuguese Canadian writers and focuses on the works of bilingual and bicultural Portuguese Canadian writers, such as Irene Marques and Paulo da Costa, who not only point out these pitfalls but also interrogate, challenge, and destabilize established models. Inspired by cultural difference, Marques's and da Costa's fictional and scholarly works subvert immigrant communities' ghettoization, praise bilingualism, and promote other literary influences and styles.

7

The Case for Literary Extroversion and Human Consciousness Expansion in Canadian Literature:
Writing, Identity, and Belonging beyond the Anglo-Saxon Ethic and Aesthetic

IRENE MARQUES

In this chapter, I argue that the advancement of literature in general (literature written in different languages), transpersonal consciousness, and the forging of a more transcultural society in Canada—one that reflects a multitude of ethics and aesthetics and will pave the way for an expanded collective human consciousness—are highly dependent on access to different literatures and languages, directly or indirectly through translation. The predominance in Canada of English as a global and literary language makes us prone to internalize what I term the "Anglo-Saxon ethic and aesthetic," engendering a monocultural and incestuous literary landscape that feeds on itself. To counteract that phenomenon, I present language and literary diversity as fundamental not only to the creative process but also to fostering transcultural learning, "beingness," and affiliation, allowing us to move from "introversion" to "extroversion," consequently paving the way for a more transnational citizenry whose consciousness steps outside the single (monocultural) lens. I examine the prevalence of the noted Anglo-Saxon ethic and aesthetic and related issues in the context of Canada, officially a bilingual country with a colonial past—with speakers, writers, and readers in many other tongues—that proclaims to follow a brand of multiculturalism that allows all voices to be heard and to contribute to Canadian identity. Yet, as I argue, Canadian literature continues to privilege the Anglo-Saxon ethic and aesthetic on different levels, controlling *how* one tells one's story and *what* story one tells. However, my argument is that the *how* seems to be more contentious than the *what*. If there is currently encouragement from the Canadian literary establishment for writers from different backgrounds (who have been traditionally marginalized or overlooked, such as racialized minorities or non-binary groups) to write and publish their own stories, in my experience we are still asked to write very much in line with the Anglo-Saxon aesthetic. Based upon my own experience as a bilingual writer in Canada and established postulations related to the links among literature, development of cognition and production of knowledge, emotional maturity, expansion of consciousness, and theories of linguistic relativism and translation, I present some strategies to generate a shift toward more inclusion within the Canadian literary scene and a move away from the predominant Anglo-Saxon literary paradigm so that our multicultural theoretical proclamations become a practice that validates and includes plural identities and literary voices. My writing style sometimes becomes more creative, mixing academic discourses with creative ones. Given my subject matter, I find this style more suited to articulate my visions.

Building upon Aristotle's (1954; original ca. 367–322 BCE) claims in *Rhetoric* and *Poetics* as they pertain to the link between our interest in literature and our passion for learning, and approximating literature to philosophy (the word *philosophy* literally means "love for learning"), American philosopher Martha Nussbaum (1990, p. 47) states the following in her book *Love's Knowledge: Essays on Philosophy and Literature*: "We have never lived enough. Our experience is, without fiction, too confined and too parochial. Literature extends it, making us reflect and feel about what might otherwise be too distant for feeling." This assertion speaks to us about the fundamental value of reading literature, moreover literature from worlds different from our own, to go beyond the scantiness and brevity of our lives. We might travel a lot, live in different places, and die at the age of 100, yet our grasp of reality will remain narrow, centred on our dominant cultural environment and the language that we speak. Literature offers us that wonderful gift of being able to go outside ourselves, seeing beyond what our immediate "eye" can catch, and connecting us with people who are vastly different from us and otherwise inaccessible. In books, we have space within which to connect with characters, unlike or like us, and in that process learn more about ourselves and others. In books, we enter that silent time and space full of voices, and in that accompanied solitude we reflect on how others live, what makes them happy and unhappy, vulnerable, wise. Such reflection enlarges our own paradigms, allowing us to envisage new possibilities for our lives, opening us up ontologically and epistemologically, leading to consciousness expansion and collective merging. Literary critic Harold Bloom (2001, pp. 28–29) argues many of these points in his own way: "We read Shakespeare, Dante, Chaucer, Cervantes, Dickens, Proust, and all their peers because they more than enlarge life. . . . We read deeply for varied reasons, most of them familiar: that we cannot know enough people profoundly enough; that we need to know ourselves better; that we require knowledge, not just of self and others, but of the way things are."

Now let us suppose that we read only novels written in English by contemporary American writers that offer recipes on how to be happy, and being happy involves being able to make a lot of money and buy a lot of things—the staple of capitalism. Or that we read only the male masters of the Western canon noted above by Bloom (2001). What happens to our selves when we live on this literary staple food alone? Given that literature (and art in general) functions as knowledge production—in other words, literature teaches and promotes ideology (either directly or indirectly through *what* it says, *how* it says it, and even *who* says it)—if we read only the first type of writers, then we might come to believe that there is only one way to be happy: through money and capitalism. Conversely, if we read only the second kind of writers, then we might think that all masters of literature and storytelling are European men.

Contemporary Nigerian writer Chimamanda Adichie argues in her speeches *The Danger of a Single Story* (2009) and *To Instruct and Delight: A Case for Realist Literature* (2012) that literature produces knowledge, ways of seeing and being in the world. Literature produces knowledge about peoples and cultures, and it transmits that knowledge to those who read it. It transmits an ethic and aesthetic particular to a culture at a certain time in history. In her words, "literature is never just words. When I read Graham Greene and Virginia Woolf, I am being delighted and entertained, but I am also learning of a certain sensibility, a certain

Englishness" (Adichie, 2012, 34:55). Adichie notes that, when she was young, she only read novels (mostly English novels) with White characters in them, so she thought that Black people could not be characters in novels, much less good (moral/ethical/civilized) ones. But then she discovered African writers such as Chinua Achebe and Camara Laye who had Black characters in their novels, multidimensional and positively depicted characters, and she thought that Black people too were worthy novel material. This is especially important because Black people and the African continent have often been written about by Western (White) writers in negative or stereotypical ways—creating what Adichie calls "a single story" about Africans and Africa. She quotes the African American sociologist W. E. B. Du Bois (1926/2008), who affirms that all art is propaganda in the sense of putting forward a certain culture, its ethics and aesthetics.

The issues raised by Adichie are applicable to Canada or the world at large, given that English is the predominant Canadian and global (transnational) language. In *Born Translated: The Contemporary Novel in an Age of World Literature* Rebecca Walkowitz (2015, pp. 10–11) asserts that "English is the dominant language of commerce and technology, at least for the moment, and it has the greatest number of readers, once we include second- and third- as well as first-language users throughout the world. Those who write in English can therefore expect their works to be published in the original and to reach many audiences in English-language editions." Moreover, only about 3 to 6 percent of literatures (depending on whose statistics one consults) written in languages other than English are translated into English, whereas 50 percent of literatures in English are translated into other languages, and non-English-speaking countries translate widely from other languages. As Hephzibah Anderson (2014) notes, "literature—fiction especially— offers a crucial window into the lives of others, promoting empathy and understanding in a way that travelling somewhere rarely does. By not translating more widely, publishers are denying us greater exposure to one of reading's most vital functions. Compare that Anglophone two or three per cent to figures in France, where 27% of books published are in translation. And if that sounds a lot, you might care to know that in Spain it's 28%, Turkey 40%, and Slovenia a whopping 70%."[1]

This imbalance in translation and the predominance of English in Canada and globally generate a Canadian (and global) monocultural and incestuous literary landscape that feeds on itself and is charac-terized by the predominance of what I term here the "Anglo-Saxon ethic and aesthetic." Anglo-Saxon literatures (or literatures written in English from the former British Empire, which, to be fair, differ from the Anglo-Saxon ethic and aesthetic though are still in English—albeit often a new English infused with other languages) enter the world's *consciousness*, making it the norm, the mirror in which one sees oneself, erasing or pushing aside other languages, stories, and worldviews. We thus have an unbalanced act of assimilation, reminiscent of colonial times when Africans were taught in English (or other European languages) and had English (or, e.g., French or Portuguese) works translated into African languages *to teach them the way, the civilized way*, as it was called in those days. Language and literature were then and continue to be today powerful mechanisms to colonize the mind, to borrow from the well-known book *Decolonizing the Mind: The Language of African Literature*, by Kenyan scholar and writer Ngũgĩ wa Thiong'o (1986).

In her essay "On Some Recent Worrying over World Literature's Commodity Status," Sarah Brouillette (2014)—quoting theorists such as Emily Apter and Rebecca Walkowitz and the anti-establishment literary magazine *n+1*—argues that there is currently a global literary elite (composed of writers, agents, university creative writing programs, etc.) generating a monoculture in writing. This elite often values the same type of writing (literal, plot-driven, minimalist, etc.) that erases differences and privileges certain global languages, mostly English but also Mandarin, Spanish, and French (see also Pariat, 2021). Brouillette adds that this writing is often "born translated" or uses simplistic style and language with the aim of being adapted to film and reaching the Hollywood world.

When I send my manuscripts to publishers in Canada, I frequently receive comments echoing what Brouillette (2014) refers to: they want shorter sentences, less flowery or metaphorical language, more plot-driven narratives, and a style that employs the "show, don't tell," rule *ad nauseum*. They also ask about my specific audience, which might indicate that they have a narrow idea about reading audiences in Canada and think that there isn't one for the kind of writing that I undertake. Given that about 51 percent of the population in Toronto alone was born outside Canada (Surman, 2015) and therefore exposed to other languages and literatures, Canadian writers from these groups possess an ethic and aesthetic that come from their mother tongue and from being exposed to literature in that tongue, which they then (naturally) inject into their writing. We carry within us things from the past, those sacred stamps that cannot and should not be erased, forgotten, or suppressed: things of the mind, things of the soul, things of the body. We would think, then, that we do indeed have varied audiences in Canada who would welcome varied types of fiction that follow different ways of "telling" (different aesthetics). Paulo da Costa and I, for instance, are both bilingual writers writing in English and Portuguese. When we write in English, there is often a specific ethic and aesthetic that can be perceived in our work that come, at least partly, from the Portuguese language and the type of literatures to which we were exposed, which tend to value the lyric, the metaphorical, the philosophical, the emotional, the magic-realist, and so on. I argue that such literary ethic and aesthetic are different from much of the Anglo-Saxon ones, which tend to value realism, minimalism, pragmatism, materialism, and a certain type of rationalism. That ethic and aesthetic dominate much of the current Canadian literary scene as I see it, and there is an unwillingness to discuss these issues. I have written some pieces on this matter and tried to publish them in national newspapers such as the *National Post* and the *Globe and Mail* or the literary journal *Canadian Literature*, but they were rejected or altogether ignored. Moreover, in 2018, I sent an abstract on this topic to the Canadian Literary Symposium scheduled to take place in May 2019 at the University of Ottawa, the themes being diversity and structural inequality in the Canadian literary scene. The abstract was rejected on the ground that the organizers were accepting only abstracts that dealt more directly with the conference themes. I do understand, of course, that they had to make choices based upon the themes of the conference, but I argue that their understanding of diversity was based principally upon under-representation or inequality related to race, gender, and other "visible" differences reflected in literary institutions whose ethos reflects and benefits mainly White, hetero, and other mainstream groups. That makes it difficult for racialized groups, visible minorities, Indigenous peoples, and women to be represented in (or thrive within) the Canadian literary scene. Although these are pressing and important issues that for the past few years have been given quite a bit of attention by literary and academic institutions, I argue that currently there is insufficient attention given to diversity in terms of the literary aesthetic and ethic of the different ethnicities in the sense that I have been discussing here. This is a fundamental aspect to be considered in a country of immigrants like Canada, where the "minds" coming in are accustomed to other ways of writing, have read widely outside the Anglo canon, and thus bring with them literary traditions and tastes that differ from the dominant Anglo-Saxon ones.[2]

The fact that I, as a Canadian of Portuguese descent, may be considered White does not mean that I share the same aesthetic sensibilities as Anglo-Saxon Canadians. There are many "Whites" in the pool of "Whites" in Canada, just as there are many "Blacks" in the pool of "Blacks." Different ethnic groups have different aesthetics, different ways of "telling" stories based upon the languages and literatures to which they have been exposed in their countries of origin, so insisting that we write in the same way isn't conducive to the implementation of a truly multicultural and diverse landscape in Canada. Although there is currently an interest in and a push toward accepting diverse literary voices in Canada, I argue that there is still a preference for a certain way of "telling" stories. In other words, the literary establishment seems to be more willing to publish books by diverse groups, but it still favours the Anglo-Saxon aesthetic that I note above. "Yes, tell us your stories, but tell them through an aesthetic that we understand, one that follows what we consider good writing." But isn't the medium the message? Isn't the *how* a fundamental part of the *what*? The Canadian literary industry needs to expand its horizons by valuing literatures that fall outside the predominant Anglo-Saxon ideals so that our cultural diversities can manifest in the books that we write.

I argue that writers who have access to more than one language or are bilingual can create unique works of fiction in both languages because each language that they know is fertilized by the other—each is pushed beyond its own limits, generating new ways of writing, seeing, and understanding. Linguists and language theoreticians such as Alexander von Humboldt (1997), Edward Sapir (1986), Ngũgĩ wa Thiong'o (1986), and Benjamin Lee Whorf (1964) have defended, to different degrees, the thesis of linguistic relativity, positing that each language creates a certain view of reality. In generic terms, this means that each language is born from a specific socio-political and physical environment and that human thought is influenced (made even) by language, so it follows that each language, to a certain extent, creates a specific reality for its speaker, a particular view of the world. Each language "makes up" a different world. Such linguistic relativity, one can argue, can imprison monolingual writers and readers in a single (or at least a more isolated) worldview, making them less able to transmit trans-cultural perspectives through their writing or to learn through other human collectivities, less equipped to tap into diversity of thought and belief, more prone to fall into a single, self-referential, epistemological view, especially if they do not read in translation abundantly. Reading in translation can attenuate what I designate here as literary "introversion" and move us toward literary "extroversion." Although translation does not constitute direct access to other languages and their worldviews, it allows us to experience other ways of being and seeing. Translation, in some ways, is a new type of language between the original language and the target language—a *língua* born from the need to understand the original *língua* and its world. This might be why translation should be less about using a purist approach (less concerned with literalness) and more about finding the best way to capture the reality of the orig-inal language. The result is a new language that in fact can reveal even more than what was revealed (or intended to be revealed) in the original language. Not only does the target language learn from the original one, but also it can push the revelations of that language into another realm, revealing new nuances in meaning that could not be found (detected) in the original work but now appear in the translation. This process of translation allows each language to grow, to minimize its shortcomings, its incompletion. Walter Benjamin (2002) argues these points well in his well-known essay "The Task of the Translator."

As with writers who write and read in more than one language, we have multiple signifiers and signifieds from two languages (and the many that they already contain in them since no pure language exists) interacting with one another and engaging in an obsessive quest to find light. These signifiers and signifieds act like tricksters, pushing, provoking, teasing, stimulating each other, constantly calling for more meaning, marvelling and awakening our minds, bodies, souls, senses, and rational and non-rational intelligences—bringing us closer to a larger truth. This is an extraordinary abracadabra in which words do make things happen. Thus, translation develops language, literature, and knowledge. In her aforementioned book, Walkowitz (2015) refers to this phenomenon by noting that writers who write and are fluent in more than one language use their multilinguistic knowledge to create innovative works of fiction in their own ways. In *Why Translation Matters*, and drawing from Benjamin's and Goethe's views on the importance of translation, Edith Grossman (2010) states that "translation infuses a language with influences, alterations, and combinations that would not have been possible without the presence of translated foreign literary styles and perceptions, the material significance and heft of literature that lies outside the territory of the purely monolingual. In other words, the influence of translated literature has a revivifying and expansive effect on what is hideously called the 'target language'" (see the section "Introduction: Why Translation Matters").

Considering what I discuss above related to how literature and language carry aesthetic thought and cultural identity and form and expand consciousness, and the importance of reading in translation to exit monocultural views, I now focus on some specific aspects that could contribute to creating a more inclusive and multicultural Canadian literary scene reflective of the many peoples who call this country their physical home yet have difficulty finding themselves reflected in its cultural landscape. How can we then create a literary culture in Canada more reflective of the many peoples who make up our country, peoples who have within them a multitude of languages and literary aesthetics informing their views of the world? How can we create a culture of writing, reading, thinking, and seeing that allows these different ethics and aesthetics to enter the Canadian imaginary? One way in which this can be implemented is not only to have those who control the literary industry (agents, publishers, editors, jury members of literary prizes, etc.) come from the different groups that compose our society in terms of ethnicity, race, gender, sexual orientation, and so on but also to include a greater diversity of aesthetics. As I argue above, it is not sufficient to allow or encourage those groups whose stories have been kept on the margins historically or altogether excluded from the Canadian literary canon to write their stories but still favour the Anglo-Saxon aesthetic, for the *what* is highly related to the *how*. It is therefore vital that literary institutions are run by people who represent a wide variety of ethics and aesthetics. And what would be some of the ways to accomplish that? We should first make a serious effort to have agents, publishers, editors, and jury members of literary prizes who read outside the anglophone canon and are familiar with a wide variety of literary trends. This can be accomplished by ensuring that they read sufficient literature in translation or in other languages if they can do so. As discussed above, given the low number of books written in other languages and translated into English, it would also be necessary to increase the number of translations into English from other languages. This increase would allow schools in Canada, from kindergarten to postsecondary levels, to increase the number of books in translation in their curriculums so that students can learn from this multicultural pedagogy that deviates from Anglo-Saxon models and expand their consciousness and imaginary about what it means to be Canadian.

Moreover, we should aim to choose people born outside Canada and educated in other languages/cultures and thus exposed to other literary aesthetics, other ideas of what literature is or should be—*how* and *what* it should tell/teach. It would also be important to have representatives with substantial knowledge of literature. Do they have some formal training in literary studies? What makes them qualified to be judges for literary prizes or to appraise a manuscript and deem it worthy of literary quality and therefore publication? I frequently see judges on literary panels who have published very little themselves or do not seem to have any special qualifications that should be required for such a task or are mostly monolingual. In addition, writers who have won prestigious prizes routinely become jury members for literary competitions immediately after, suggesting that winning automatically makes one the ideal person to be a judge. Although I am not arguing that the winner does not know anything about literature or did not write an outstanding book that merited the accolade, this system of appointing judges can be counterproductive because it creates a vicious cycle: one wins a prize because he/she/they wrote something that appealed to the predominantly Anglo-Saxon literary establishment, and that person then goes on to be a judge for another literary competition, and the same process is repeated again and again.

Furthermore, though I currently see representatives of different visible minorities or even sexual orientations on many literary panels, I do not see enough representatives of groups who do not come from former British colonies or whose first language is not English. Again this suggests a concern for diversity related to racialized or even non-binary persons, who traditionally have not been able to tell their stories or be part of literary circles, not a concern for diversity in terms of literary aesthetic or people born outside Canada. Iranian Canadian Bänoo Zan, a well-known literary activist and poet in Toronto, and the organizer of the poetry reading series of Shab-e She'r, described as "Toronto's most diverse & brave poetry & open mic" on her Instagram, has voiced these concerns recently when speaking about her experience as a judge for the Guernica Prize for Literary Fiction:

> This doesn't happen in Canada as often as it should but the three of us together—Danila Botha Vernon, Kevin Wilson, and I—members of the jury for The Guernica Prize for Literary Fiction, awarded a significant Canadian literary prize (worth $1000) to an immigrant writer from outside North America, Europe, and (former) English-speaking colonies. Literary recognition, in the form of prizes or other accolades, is not usually granted to non-native speaker immigrant writers from regions other than Europe or (former) European and North American colonies. Immigrant writers from countries that have not been linguistically colonized have been left out of the literary mainstream because of their cultural, political, and linguistic accents. This has been a loss to literature in Canada: of vision, perspective, and urgency. It is when you lose your accent, your access to the language of your ancestors, that you are deemed worth attention by those who can write only in the dominant language. It is when you are assimilated, when you have erased the traces of who you are, that you are acknowledged. We, the jury, took the step to redress this erasure. (Zan, 2021b)

Although I agree with Zan that there is a preference in the Anglo-Saxon tradition in Canada for writers from former English colonies, I would not say that Canadian writers of European descent outside England, who speak and often also write in other languages (and there are so many, including me), are necessarily better off in Canada. It is not merely a matter of accent but also a matter of ethic and aesthetic, what Zan seems to be referring to when she speaks of "cultural, political, and linguistic accents."[3] It is also a matter of how other languages can inform Canadian writers who are not from Anglo traditions when they write in English, thus pushing English beyond its capacities, bringing in innovations of all sorts that monolingual English speakers who barely read in translation fail to understand. They thus become stuck in an incestuous/self-referential circle of writing and reading that does not feed off other traditions, bringing in little innovation, to recall my previous arguments about the importance of translation in order to advance individual literatures and languages. The literary ethic and aesthetic in Canada are Anglo based when they come from former British colonies since colonized peoples have also internalized and developed what Adichie has called a "certain sensibility, a certain Englishness" (2012, 34:55). This occurs through the reading of English literature, which causes a mental colonization, as wa Thiong'o noted (1986), even if, of course, and as pointed out earlier, literatures in English from former British colonies are often new English(es) infused with local languages, and represent a vast array of cultural traditions different from that of the colonizing nation (England).

It would also enhance the Canadian literary scene to have publishing houses with enough financial resources and interested in publishing books in translation. Additionally, for bilingual writers in Canada (beyond French), there should be specific programs that help these writers in terms of translating their books into English.

One last point that I would like to make is that in my experience we have many small publishers in Canada that often specialize in specific types of literature (gay, women, Caribbean, Jewish, Italian, African, Indian, etc.) and are interested in publishing only or mostly literature from specific groups. Although these publishing houses exist to allow minorities to publish their books, which might not be published by more traditional (mainstream) publishers, this also creates ghettoization, further dividing Canadians by placing them into specific ethnic, racial, and other categories and not necessarily encouraging different groups to commingle and learn from one another. In fact, many publishers also ask writers who are considering submitting their work to them to read the books that they publish and to indicate in their submissions why they think they would be good fits—thus creating more silos and ghettoization in the publishing industry and making writers do extra work that in reality should belong to publishers. These small publishing houses also depend mostly on funding from Canadian arts institutions and have little interest in promoting the books that they publish, choosing just a few and expecting authors to do a lot of the promotion and selling of their books.[4] These publishers often also ask writers to procure reviews of their books or ask friends and acquaintances in the literary community to write blurbs and accolades, which I consider unethical, to say the least—thus engendering and perpetuating incestuous circles in the Canadian literary industry. For people who dislike such self-promotion and selling, who are reserved and introverted (as many writers are), this means that their books often fall into oblivion. There is also another negative consequence. I have been told by publishers that, if books by a particular writer do not sell (or sell sufficiently), then that writer might have difficulty publishing again, because publishers have access to sales lists and might not want to publish another book by that writer; in fact, they likely look at previous sales by the author before even reading a submitted manuscript. It might well be a masterpiece, but who cares? In my view, it would be more productive to have fewer publishing houses with more capacities in terms of finances and staff widely familiar with literature who can evaluate and promote books from a variety of writers with the same interest and investment.

Canada is a vast country with many stories pulsating in it, from west to east, from south to north, a land with multifaceted physical, mental, and cultural geographies. Let our literature reflect that stunning wealth. It is this writing that will make us bigger, more relatable to one another, and minimize divisions between groups, ethnicities, and races, creating a literary imaginary in which all Canadians see themselves reflected. It is this writing, open to others and otherness, their sounds and sentences, their strangeness and familiarity, their sorrow and gayness, this inking unsure of its own isolated capacities yet always relentless in its journey toward the light, that will bring wonder, magic, wisdom, and greater fulfillment and consciousness expansion to us. *Us*—sons and daughters of words, made of and out of words, beings in search of ourselves, each other, and the reality of the world, the universe.

We are a country of others among others, constantly striving to become the same. The term "same" here implies reaching a stage where peoples of different backgrounds see each other not in terms of being less or more than the others because they are not comparing themselves to model citizens associated with the ethnicities and cultures of the founding nations (England and France) but as beings vis-à-vis other beings of equal merit and capacity. Those others remind them of themselves (of their own differences) and in that sense help them to find (and expand) their sense of self. This implies entering a realm of transdialectical, transpersonal learning in which one group allows another group to be itself and comes to adjust to and learn from that group. This does not mean losing our differences and becoming alike; rather, it means inhabiting more fluid identities, getting into and out of our selfhood to reach a greater (and more Canadian) selfhood. A literature that allows the many others to tell their stories through their own aesthetic is fundamental to this process of growing and widening the Canadian imaginary. By opening itself to the literatures of the many others of this nation, the Canadian literary industry will aid in the concretization of our multicultural agenda, allowing for a vortex of converging ideas, views, and aesthetics to cover the pages of the books that we read, books that then enter us and expand our consciousness. I end with the pertinent question posed in the title of Edward Chamberlin's (2003) groundbreaking book, in which Chamberlin discusses the importance of story, belief, truth, history, Indigenous ways of viewing the world and the self, and how we can all cohabit in Canada and give voices to our own stories while fundamentally respecting Indigenous land, culture, story, and history: *If This Is Your Land, Where Are Your Stories?* He answers with *Finding Common Ground.* "Common ground" here implies a respect for all stories, all histories, all ways of viewing the world and the self, and mostly an understanding that all stories and histories are relative, made up by arbitrary linguistic systems that give sense to the senseless but are fundamental for humans to inhabit this world (and dream of the ones beyond it).

References

Adichie, N. C. (2009). *The danger of a single story* [Video]. TED. https://www.ted.com/talks/chimamanda_ngozi_adichie_the_danger_of_a_single_story?language=en

Adichie, N. C. (2012). *To instruct and delight: A case for realist literature* [Video]. YouTube. https://www.youtube.com/watch?v=vmsYJDP8g2U

Anderson, H. (2014, 21 October). Why won't English speakers read books in translation? BBC. http://www.bbc.com/culture/story/20140909-why-so-few-books-in-translation

Aristotle. (1954). *The rhetoric and the poetics of Aristotle.* Random House. (Original ca. 367–322 BCE.)

Benjamin, W. (2002). The task of the translator. In M. Bullock & M. W. Jennings (Eds.), *Walter Benjamin: Selected writings: Volume 1, 1923–26* (pp. 253–263). Belknap Press of Harvard University Press.

Bloom, H. (2001). *How to read and why.* Touchstone Books.

Boyd, M. (2016, 9 April). *The infamous three percent.* Diálogos: Intercultural Services. https://dialogos.ca/2016/04/the-infamous-three-percent/

Brouillette, S. (2014). On some recent worrying over world literature's commodity status. *Maple Tree Literary Supplement, 18.* https://www.mtls.ca/issue18/impressions/

Castaldo, J. (2022, 19 August). Publishing in Canada is broken. Will the pending Simon and Schuster–Penguin Random House merger make it worse? *The Globe and Mail.* https://www.theglobeandmail.com/arts/books/article-canada-publishing-industry/

Chamberlin, E. J. (2003). *If this is your land, where are your stories? Finding common ground.* Alfred A. Knopf Canada.

Du Bois, W. E. B. (2008). *Criteria of negro art.* http://www.webdubois.org/dbCriteriaNArt.html. (Original work published 1926.)

Grossman, E. (2010). *Why translation matters* [Kindle version]. Yale University Press.

Humboldt, W. von. (1997). *Essays on language.* J. Wieczorek & I. Roe (Trans.). T. Harden & D. Farrely (Eds.). Peter Lang.

Marques, I. (2016). Notes on the incestuous and monocultural nexus of the literati. *Maple Tree Literary Supplement, 21.* https://www.mtls.ca/issue21/irene-marques

Marques, I. (2017). Canada's literary mono-culture and its 'politics' of separation. *Maple Tree Literary Supplement, 22.* https://www.mtls.ca/issue22/round-table/

Nussbaum, M. (1990). *Love's knowledge: Essays on philosophy and literature.* Oxford University Press.

Page-Fort, G. (2018, 3 August). Why do Americans read so few books in translation? *Literary Hub.* https://lithub.com/why-do-americans-read-so-few-books-in-translation/

Pariat, J. (2021, 4 July). Decolonising creative writing: It's about not conforming to techniques of the Western canon. *Scroll.in.* https://scroll.in/article/999215/decolonising-creative-writing-its-about-not-conforming-to-techniques-of-the-western-canon

Sapir, E. (1986). *Selected writings of Edward Sapir in language, culture, and personality.* D. G. Mandelbaum (Ed.). University of California Press.

Surman, R. (2015, 24 January). A snapshot of Toronto: 51% of residents were born outside Canada, Vital Signs Report finds. *National Post.* https://nationalpost.com/news/toronto/a-snapshot-of-toronto-51-of-residents-were-born-outside-canada-vital-signs-report-finds

wa Thiong'o, N. (1986). *Decolonizing the mind: The language of African literature.* James Currey.

Walkowitz, R. L. (2015). *Born translated: The contemporary novel in an age of world literature* [Kindle version]. Columbia University Press.

Whorf, B. L. (1964). *Language, thought, and reality: Selected writings.* MIT Press.

Zan, B. (2021a, 3 December). Snapshots of an outsider. *The hyphenated generation anthology*. Facebook. https://www.facebook.com/banoo.zan

Zan, B. (2021b, 7 December). *This doesn't happen in Canada as often as it should but the three of us together. . . .* Facebook. https://www.facebook.com/banoo.zan

Endnotes

1   See also Boyd (2016); Page-Fort (2018).

2   For further discussions on these issues, see Marques (2016); Marques (2017).

3   Zan has also indicated that, even though she organizes poetry events and invites many poets to participate in them, she has often felt that many of the poets invited have ostracized her and would not invite her to join them in social events after readings. This sentiment is relayed in one of her poems, "Snapshots of an Outsider," recently published in an anthology titled *The Hyphenated Generation* (2021a).

4   According to a *Globe and Mail* article (Castaldo, 2022), "in 2021, independent publishers in Canada accounted for 5.3 per cent of English-language physical book sales, according to BookNet Canada, a non-profit. This is despite the fact that these publishers, buoyed by government funding, put out most new Canadian books every year, between 75 per cent and 80 per cent. It's a bizarre situation, where titles are effectively lost in a void, outsold by books from foreign-owned multinationals such as Penguin Random House (PRH), HarperCollins and Simon & Schuster (S&S), which also distribute large numbers of imported works."

8

Confronting Exclusion in English Canadian Literature:
Portuguese Canadian Hybrid and Hyphenated Voices and Identities

MARIA JOÃO MACIEL JORGE

In this chapter, I examine the role and the positionality of Portuguese Canadian writers within the field of English Canadian literature. I consider that mainstream literature, originally driven by British tradition, perceived market tastes, and imagined audiences, maintains and perpetuates a colonial and divisive attitude toward the country's multicultural diversity and the nation's official commitment to multiculturalism. For instance, labels of ethnic, minority, and immigrant writing are often used pejoratively to limit and exclude the contributions of culturally minoritized writers. As such, a cultural and linguistic monoculture prevails that privileges English despite the historical marginality of Canadian English and its potential to accommodate cultures in inclusive ways. I address such issues in this chapter by confronting the exclusion of Portuguese Canadian writers and focusing on the works of bilingual and bicultural Portuguese Canadian writers, such as Irene Marques and Paulo da Costa, who have pointed out these pitfalls and whose approaches interrogate, challenge, and destabilize established models. Inspired by cultural difference, fictional and scholarly works, Marques and da Costa subvert immigrant communities' ghettoization, praise bilingualism, promote other literary influences and styles, and endorse in particular a hybrid, in-between, or hyphenated identity, best suited to an affirmative and complete ethnic experience. In doing so,

Marques and da Costa elevate transnational, hybrid, and hyphenated identities as models for inclusion and belonging, both in the imagined world and in the real world of North America's most diverse nation.

Mainstream Literature, Portuguese Immigration, and Exclusion of Portuguese Canadian Writers

Canadians of Portuguese background, such as Irene Marques and Paulo da Costa, have found and established their literary voices as bilingual and bicultural.[1] Writing in English and Portuguese, they, like Canadian writers of other ethnically minoritized origins, have not only destabilized notions that define English Canadian literature but also set forth important discussions regarding labels of minority and ethnic writing and the value of hybrid and hyphenated identities that call for inclusion and belonging. Often writing from a "third space," in the words of Homi Bhabha (1994), these hybrid writers are reshaping and redefining English Canadian literature by questioning the legitimacy of a literature anchored in a colonial, monocultural past while promoting a multiplicity of literary and historical multicultural identities that align with the nation's actual diversity.

The exclusion of ethnically diverse writers is as old as the notion of Canadian literature itself, ironically also born out of exclusion. Critics have considered the Canadian short story, for instance, at least until recently, a marginal genre that has systematically excluded Canada's first (Indigenous) inhabitants and their histories. In this vein, what has been traditionally defined as Canadian literature reflected the contributions of the country's first European settlers: the French and the British. In its beginning, much of the literature produced by English-speaking writers was driven by British tradition; thus, it did not foster a so-called Canadian identity but positioned itself, as critics have noted, in "an unfortunate colonial position" (MacLeod, 1999, p. 162). Early English writers were also subjected to several issues that hindered their production. MacLeod identifies, for instance, matters of audience and identity, in which Canada stands apart as a peripheral country whose literature would not have the same appeal to readers in the United States or Britain. Yet, and despite a shift to privilege novel writing in the 1980s, the short story as a genre is used by Canadian writers "perhaps all unconsciously, as a kind of cultural-political protest, subversively, and with a sophisticated irony that remains mostly lost upon the central, dominant, financially rewarding, self-regarding cultures in which they need to succeed, America's" (Lynch & Robbeson, 1999, p. 8).

In terms of the contributions of Portuguese Canadians, and in particular the works of Marques and da Costa, it is also crucial to understand the trajectory of the Portuguese in Canada and this community's historical and current challenges. The Canadian mosaic grew considerably with mass migrations that continue to shape Canada as a multicultural, visibly diverse country. Although the presence of the Portuguese in Canada dates back to the fifteenth century, their migration in substantial numbers took place only in the 1950s. The large exodus was driven by Canada's promotion of immigration designed to meet demands in agriculture and railway construction. Those who immigrated were from rural environments, for the most part, victims of extreme poverty, and they looked at Canada as a country that would lead to a secure financial future. The Portuguese have settled in many areas of Canada, but most reside in Ontario.[2] Today they have a thriving community that has left its unique imprint on the cultural diversity of the country. In addition, certain community enclaves, such as the large one in Toronto, are self-contained and self-sufficient, according to the findings of geographer Carlos Teixeira (2000, pp. 215–216): "In the last four decades they have constructed a thriving, complex community, setting up organizations, businesses, and communication-information services in their own language. The high level of institutional completeness is well demonstrated by the appreciable number of ethnic businesses."

Yet the Portuguese are often still viewed as a ghettoized community, and despite their successes in some areas they struggle with issues of academic underperformance and lack visibility in several other realms. Mainstream media tend to focus on the community's deficiencies and offer recurring publications on the academic struggles.[3] And, though one can find references to the dictatorship, ironically named New State (Estado Novo, 1933–1974), as one of the root causes of this problem, the media have failed to recognize the cultural impacts and scars left by the longest dictatorship in Western Europe. Values of Catholic humility and simplicity coupled with systemic fear and a high level of illiteracy are key considerations in understanding the long dictatorship under the powerful and authoritarian rule of Antonio de Oliveira Salazar and its repercussions on the collective identity.[4] Perhaps, then, it should not come as a surprise that a community with a majority of illiterate blue-collar workers has had difficulty in acquiring visibility in the area of literature.

In 2000, António Augusto Joel published a chapter in *The Portuguese in Canada* in which he states that literature of Portuguese background has failed "to achieve the status of mainstream literature" and identifies content based upon ethnographic exercises of memory and nostalgia, along with language, as major barriers to Portuguese Canadian literary success. Joel gives much relevance to the work of Erika de Vasconcelos, not just because she writes in English, but also, and according to Joel, primarily because, like the American Katherine Vaz, they "reject self-imposed segregation, [and] their work is clearly and consciously intended to be mainstream literature" (p. 224). Although what Joel means by "mainstream literature" is never fully addressed, there are moments when we might interpret it to stand for works that do not deal with the immigrant experience. In fact, Joel views Vasconcelos's *My Darling Dead Ones* (1997) not as an immigrant book but as a book "about a Canadian woman discovering who she is by understanding the lives of her ancestors" (p. 233). Joel attempts to explain the "mainstream" nature of the novel by citing the author's words on the role of memory and cultural heritage: "I haven't read anything Canadian that was written about Portugal. I mean I'm sure there are articles and stuff like that, but certainly not in mainstream fiction, so it's kind of nice to be the first to do it" (p. 233).

Ultimately, what Joel deems immigrant experience and "mainstream" literature appear not as opposite concepts but as different ways to address culture and memory, or, in the case of Vasconcelos, they are differentiated only by use of the English language. In the most recent edition of *The Portuguese in Canada* (2009), Isabel Nena Patim's chapter "Literature of Portuguese Background in the Context of Literature in Canada" replaces Joel's earlier chapter. Patim's findings add considerably to Joel's chapter by including, as the author states in her introduction, "an analysis of LPBC[5] within the broader context of literature written and published in Canada" (p. 270). This section, arguably Patim's most innovative, speaks to the contributions of writers within the context of Canadian literature written in English. Patim brings forth the plurality of voices and the concept of hyphenated identity, and she laments that, though several anthologies of the sort have been published, none exists regarding Portuguese Canadians. She points out the possibility of approaching contemporary LPBC as postmodern Canadian literary texts because "postmodern literature shapes cultural anxieties, fragmented structures, divided and undermined selves. These selves are confronted with realities that co-exist in a space and time, in a global sphere, at a speed never experienced before. Canada somehow contains the particular conditions needed to produce the postmodern text: a multicultural population, a decentralized geography, and a cultural ambivalence toward the English and the Americans" (pp. 276–277). Yet, despite her efforts, Patim does not include any authors other than those already explored by Joel. Thus, though acknowledging the lack of Portuguese Canadian writers, she makes no reference to other hyphenated voices, nor does she illustrate how such hyphenated voices are producing postmodern texts that focus on other cultural realities.[6]

Labels of Exclusion

It is important to this discussion to consider also the place of what has been traditionally deemed ethnic, immigrant, or multicultural literature. Perhaps the least problematic aspect of Joel's article is that it reveals two types of literature at play, one considered Canadian mainstream, the other considered ethnic and by default marginal. In fact, in *Other Solitudes: Canadian Multicultural Fictions*, Linda Hutcheon (1990) avoids using the term "ethnic" altogether because of its negative connotations. On the one hand, and though the Greek *ethnos* signifies "nation" or "people," meaning that the two dominant cultures—French and English—should also be ethnic, this term is not applied to them; thus, as Hutcheon notes, "the fact that the word is not used points to a hierarchy of social and cultural privilege" (p. 2). On the other hand, given earlier associations of the word *ethnic* with pagan and heathen "or in its more recent ones with 'foreign', the word ... always has to do with the social positioning of the 'other', and it is thus never free of relations of power and value" (p. 2). Viewed in this light, Joel's article does appear to express a strong desire to move away from such negativity associated with ethnic writers and thus position the English work of Vasconcelos as an attempt to be mainstream through the adoption of English as the socially and culturally privileged language. However, Patim's and Joel's contributions—much like those of the majority of literary critics—fall short and therefore fail to explore other literary voices and experiences.

For instance, Albert Braz (2011) focuses solely on the immigrant experience in Anthony de Sa's fiction and offers only this additional minor observation: "The one other well-known English-Canadian writer is Paulo da Costa, the author of the 2002 short-story collection *The Scent of a Lie*. However, da Costa writes mainly about Portugal, rather than the Portuguese-Canadian experience" (p. 72). Thus, critics have been slow to recognize writers who pursue other interests and literary devices that serve to capture a multitude of cultural identities and experiences. In this manner, critics have also contributed to further ghettoization.

From Exclusion to Inclusion and the Potential of Multiculturalism

In the past twenty years, there have been a substantial number of anthologies that not only deal with ethnic literature but also signal the growing popularity of such literature in North American contexts as well as the potential shift from the margin to the centre. *Adjacencies: Minority Writing in Canada* (Beneventi et al., 2004), *Making a Difference: Canadian Multicultural Literature* (Kamboureli, 1996), and *Writing Canadians: The Literary Construction of Ethnic Identities* (Keller & Kuester, 2002) are just a few examples that signal this shift and illustrate its potential. As Sherry Simon (2004, p. 10) writes, "minority writing is no longer to be automatically equated with marginality. In fact, as this specific anthology [*Adjacencies*] demonstrates, 'the writing of difference' is moving closer to the centre of the literary landscape. These shifts emphasize the need to re-explore the tensions pulsing through conceptions of literary difference, to re-examine the minor." According to Simon, such writers are pioneering new paths in literature, not only in the manner "in which identity issues are stimulating the invention of new forms" (p. 10) but also in "the capacity of difference to inspire innovative thought, to use uncertainty as a level to provide new understandings" (p. 19). Amaryll Chanady (2004, p. 24) speaks to the growing popularity of ethnic writers now visible in the "creation of academic programmes, special issues of learned journals, collective volumes and conferences on ethnicity, as well as a better understanding of the effects of discrimination and a greater visibility of literature by authors perceived as ethnic." Arun Mukherjee (1994, p. xiii) also points out the value of small presses, in particular how they "and their authors have brought down the fortifications erected by the Canadian literary establishment and changed the face of the Canadian literary landscape. Both the entity called 'Canadian literature,' and the essentialized Canadian identity it was premised on[, have] ... been seriously eroded." Yet, despite this positive renewal and shift regarding ethnic writers, those of Portuguese background are still, for the most part, absent in contemporary anthologies.[7]

Much of the discussion regarding the Canadian literary landscape hinges on the official policy of multiculturalism, its advantages and its disadvantages. Chanady (2004, p. 25) notes the criticism of multiculturalism by those who argue that "ethnic labelling contributes to ghettoization, but also by cultural critics such as Mireille Rosello, who denounces all forms of classification (especially those based on ethnicity or race) as exclusionary." Also acknowledging the pitfalls, Hutcheon (1990, p. 15) nonetheless suggests that multiculturalism can serve as "an innovative model for civic tolerance and the acceptance of diversity that is appropriate for our democratic pluralist society."

In fact, both authors whom I focus on in this chapter consider multiculturalism an important facet of their lives and creative works. In "Beyond Bullfights and Ice Hockey—An Architecture of Multicultural Identity," da Costa (2015, p. 15) speaks of his desire to live in Canada since it is "a society where cultural diversity is encouraged." He speaks of diversity "as important in the construct of an individual identity, as in the larger society, impl[ying] a vision of multiculturalism beyond clustered and isolated cultural islands dotting a country" (p. 16). He adds that multiculturalism needs to occur at the individual level, thus "allowing you and me to interweave and belong to a complex hive of cultural heritages, languages and relationships" (p. 16). More recently, da Costa (2021) reasserted the value of multiculturalism as a way to experience different perspectives of seeing and living for personal enrichment and growth. Marques (2008, p. 195) also speaks of the value of multiculturalism by defining herself as a "divided self, a product of Canadian multiculturalism, and its tolerances, values and opportunities."

Confronting Exclusion with Inclusive Cultural and Linguistic Narratives of Belonging

Since both Marques and da Costa spent their childhood and adolescent years in Portugal, Portuguese language and culture are important aspects that inspire and guide their creativity. In an interview with Millicent

Borges Accardi (2014), Marques states that, "because my formative years were spent in Portugal, my writing is very much influenced by it and not just in terms of the themes related to ways of life there, like social class, gender issues, poverty, hard work on the land, . . . but also in terms of the aesthetic guiding it." As Marques (2017) elaborates in conversation with Amatoritsero Ede in "Canada's Literary Mono-Culture and Its 'Politics' of Separation,"

> Canadians do come from many places around the world where English is not the lingua franca and they come with the ethic and aesthetic of their languages and literatures. If we are to become diverse artistically, we need to allow the many ethics and aesthetics of the people who make up Canada to "write themselves" in Canada so that the country can reflect its real inhabitants. This means that even if the writing medium is English, that English will be injected with the "otherness" of all those people who live here, their ethic and aesthetic. That "otherness" will create innovative and powerful literature. We must remember that language and literature grow the best when in contact with other languages and literatures, other ethics and aesthetics, and not in isolation.

Da Costa (2015, p. 16) affirms that "I write in either English or Portuguese, as my mind travels in two linguistic landscapes." And Marques (2016, para. 9) believes "that writers who have access to two languages and are fully bilingual can create more unique works of fiction in both languages, for each language they know feeds the other, pushing it beyond its own limits, making it find novel ways of saying."

Da Costa's collection of short stories, *The Scent of a Lie* (2002), recognized as the first in Canadian literature to hail from Portuguese villages, is distinctive because of the "in-between," both culturally and linguistically, that da Costa weaves throughout as a sort of homage to hyphenated identity and its benefits. As da Costa (2012) explains in an interview, "writing in a second language I feel freer from its rules and limitations. A native speaker absorbs a language's inherent syntax and semantics by osmosis. One's relationship to its mechanics and foundations is often an unconscious one. Second language speakers enter the language from both directions, consciously and unconsciously."

The often pejoratively assigned ethnic identity, according to da Costa, does not limit writers. On the contrary, it provides them with a considerable degree of freedom: "While growing up in Europe I only wrote in Portuguese and I felt constrained in my approach to writing. Now, feeling linguistically ambidextrous, I have learned to take my new risk-taking, playful mind—cultivated in my relationship to the English—and apply it to my mother tongue. Now my Portuguese writing shows more vitality and playfulness than when I first began writing from within its invisible constraints. I can now work simultaneously on projects in either English or Portuguese shifting easily from one language to another" (da Costa, 2012).

Da Costa (2015, pp. 16–17) considers unfamiliar sounds and sights important in order to experience other tongues or, as he puts it, "to embrace the experience of not knowing. I trust that meanings will surface as you observe the unfamiliar words of Portuguese. We can practice not understanding another and still be present for the experience."

Marques likewise acknowledges the creative potential that derives from a different language. The preference for open vowels, as in her most recent novel, *Daria*, is an aspect that the author claims to be an influence from Portuguese (2021a). The power of sound, for instance, is also relevant. Marques (2017, para. 7) remarks that

> it induces a dwelling of sorts that makes me feel extended, travelling between timeframes or suspending the notion of present, past and future—enter a holistic sphere that is timeless. Of course, that I would also say that writing in general (and especially literary writing) in either language induces this similar feeling of wholeness or dwelling. I will also say that one language feeds the other, makes it better: knowing and writing in Portuguese enhances my literary writing in English and vice-versa. This relates to the importance of how literatures and languages actually feed off each other and constitutes a very important reason why writers should try and read in different languages, if they can, and if they can't, they should at least read books in translation.

The richness of another language and the ability to write in more than one language can serve the writer well in terms of enhanced creativity, for "one is pushed to see the world in another way" (Marques, 2021, 10:10).

As da Costa explores his cultural makeup, he asserts that belonging to two cultures—Portuguese and Canadian—does not mean that he shares all traits of both cultures. On the contrary, he is "atypical," participating only in experiences that he finds link to his being, without the need to "prescribe … clichés of identity" (da Costa, 2015, p. 18). In fact, his biculturalism resides at the margin, where "one finds room to grow" (p. 18). As such, da Costa can enter what he calls a "third dimension that encompasses both identities" (p. 19). This third dimension, or a "third space" in the words of Bhabha (1994), offers the bicultural and bilingual writer a privileged position. According to Bhabha, these "in-between spaces provide the terrain for elaborating strategies of selfhood—singular or communal—that initiate new signs of identity, and innovative sites of collaboration, and contestation, in the act of defining the idea of society itself" (pp. 1–2). As Bhabha explains, these new signs of identity challenge the concept of homogeneous "'national' cultures," which increasingly "are being produced from the perspective of disenfranchised minorities" (pp. 5–6). Da Costa (2015) posits multicultural individuals not as "a handicap [but] rather a gift to ourselves and to society" (p. 21). Most of the themes in his writing are driven, in fact, by an interest in understanding "how we can live together in community, respecting and encouraging differences. I'm interested in exploring the limitations of our linguistics codes in intrapersonal communication, in the search of who we are and where we came from" (da Costa, 2021; my translation).

Marques notes additional concerns with the limitations faced by writers threatened by what she deems the Anglo-Saxon ethic and aesthetic that privileges sameness and monoculture, thus impoverishing and erasing diversity in writing. In "Notes on the Incestuous and Monocultural Nexus of the Literati," Marques (2016) expands on this issue. She suggests the existence of incestuous tendencies in Canada's literary world, an issue, according to her, present in much of the literature being produced around the world as well. Citing other authors, such as Sarah Brouillette, Marques claims the existence of a literary elite—made up of publishing houses, university creative writing programs, editors, agents, and the like—who determine "what good literature is" (para. 4). In doing so, they establish a monoculture with a type of writing that is "(literal, plot-driven, minimalist, etc) [and] that tends to erase difference and privileges certain global languages (mostly

English though languages like Mandarin, Spanish, and French … are also important)" (para. 5). Yet, though many works in English are translated into other languages, "only about 2 to 3% of works written in other languages are translated into English" (para. 6). The preference for and predominance of English affect writers of other cultural and linguistic backgrounds, such as Marques, for "we carry in us things from the past, those sacred stamps that cannot and should not be erased, forgotten or suppressed: things of the mind, things of the soul, things of the body" (para. 7). Addressing the Portuguese heritage that she shares with da Costa, Marques explains that the connection to Portuguese culture is present even when writing in English, "a specific ethic and aesthetic that can be perceived in our work which comes from the Portuguese language and the type of literatures we were exposed to, which tend to value the lyric, the metaphoric, the philosophical, the emotional, the magic-realist, etc. This ethic and aesthetic [are] … quite different from the Anglo-Saxon one which tends to value realism, minimalism, pragmatism, materialism and a certain type of rationalism" (para. 7). However, as Marques elaborates, the Anglo-Saxon monoculture pervades and prevails; from agents, to publishing houses, to jury panels, and even in matters of audience, the "imagined literary audience" is also presumed to be Anglo-Saxon. This issue was signalled by Mukherjee (1994, p. xiii) in the introduction to *Oppositional Aesthetics: Readings from a Hyphenated Space*: "The literary institution does not provide equal access to all points of view. If one does not write in sanctioned ways, one does not get published in the right places."

Toward Inclusion and Belonging:
Transcultural and Transnational Narratives

Although da Costa's (2002) short stories in *The Scent of a Lie* capture the author's desire for vitality and playfulness, the collection also appropriates the true potential of multiculturalism to expose the many human facets of living (da Costa, 2021) through its use of Portuguese words, landscapes, and cultural expressions that pepper the English discourse with cultural difference. From the *Senhores* to Padre Lucas's customary *sesta* to a selection of maize bread, salted olives, and lupini beans in "Roses for the Dead," da Costa (2002) reminds us of the lives of those explored in a climate in which Catholic ideology and class rigidity do little to lessen the burden of the peasantry. His collection of short stories as a whole explores themes relevant to a construction of Canadian identity, as Gerald Lynch (2001, p. 190) points out: "The self may be a constructed identity that can blossom in an interdependent relationship with the natural world; individual rituals, symbols, and memories are necessary to cultural continuity; . . . self-identity and the process of self-realization may be connected forever to [the] place of origin as home. Such lessons are reasonably humanist, broadly conservative, and distinctly, identifiably Canadian."

In the last story of *The Scent of a Lie*, for instance, and perhaps most notably, it is in immersion in the natural world where the lessons mentioned above by Lynch are negotiated. Old man Prudêncio Casmurro makes peace with an increasingly unnatural world by unchaining "his world. [He offers] freshly harvested strawberries, and invited them inside" (da Costa, 2002, p. 129). The value of community and respect for nature are evident in this story, and da Costa closes the collection with the positive message that Prudêncio's garden can serve as a model for populating an otherwise bare and concrete city.

The fictional worlds of Marques that include rural and urban Portugal, colonial and postcolonial Portugal and Africa, as well as Toronto, the home of well-established immigrant communities from Portuguese-speaking countries, also pay homage to the formation of multicultural identity through their themes, Portuguese ethic and aesthetic, and bicultural and bilingual inclusions. Much like the Canadian immigrant experience, Marques's characters appear across times and continents. Pires Laranjeira (2009, p. 6), in his introduction to Marques's *Habitando na metáfora do tempo*, notes the importance of interculturality or cultural reciprocity in Marques's narratives, "of learning of the fundamental differences that sustain the sameness of the world, . . . the memory of a woman looking at the world, . . . or poetic chronicles of a migratory bird." As a result, "miscegenation [becomes] praise for interculturality, a curse against xenophobia" (my translation). In fact, in *My House Is a Mansion* (Marques, 2015), Amélia, the main protagonist, leaves her Portuguese village to travel the world. Yet these travels, which transcend time and space, also include the author's homage to interculturality through her frequent incursions into other languages or in-between spaces. In her most recent novel, *Daria* (2021a), the multicultural scene of Toronto is an important aspect of the narrative, in which a multitude of stories and characters gather in the multicultural city. As Marques (2021, 3:15) claims, "we are all connected to one another and I like to bring the world to the page when I'm writing." Daria, a young Portuguese immigrant in Toronto, much like the author herself, has a special bond to her country of origin, revealing what Lynch (2001, p. 189) has observed: "Canadian writing advises that you must return, in order to place the past apart, to read its other-centred rules in a fresh way, and to make the present and future home, whatever its relationship with a distant childhood, your own."

Conclusion

Portuguese Canadian writers, like all other ethnically diverse Canadian writers, find themselves at a crossroads. Marques and da Costa matured as writers in Canada, a once peripheral country, with added prejudice and exclusion, as traditional labels of ethnic writing or other similar markers have ironically excluded them from mainstream literature in a country widely praised for its immigrant multiculturalism. Nevertheless, both Marques and da Costa, while occupying a hybrid space, the in-between of multiculturalism, have claimed a different position, one not limited to the Portuguese Canadian experience but transnational and in constant negotiation with their many lived and imagined cultures. Canadian literature must divest itself from any and all exclusionary labels and embrace such writers beyond the boundaries of immigration and/or emigration.

References

Andrew-Gee, E. (2013, 7 January). What's eating Little Portugal? *Maisonneuve: A Quarterly of Arts, Opinion & Ideas*. https://maisonneuve.org/article/2013/01/7/whats-eating-little-portugal/

Azevedo, M. (2022, 20 February). What's eating Little Portugal?, a riposte, or "The chickens come home to roost." *Academia*. https://www.academia.edu/4594117/Education_and_the_Portuguese_Inquisition

Beneventi, D. A., Canton, L., & Moyes, L. (Eds.). (2004). *Adjacencies: Minority writing in Canada*. Guernica.

Bhabha, H. K. (1994). *The location of culture*. Routledge.

Borges Accardi, M. (2014, 2 April). Irene Marques: On women's voices and cultural identity—Interview. *Portuguese American Journal*. https://portuguese-american-journal.com/irene-marqueson-womens-voices-and-cultural-identity-interview/

Braz, A. (2011). The homeless patriot: Anthony de Sa and the paradoxes of immigration. In T. F. A. Alves, I. M. F. Blayer, & F. C. Fagundes (Eds.), *Narrating the Portuguese diaspora: Piecing things together* (pp. 63–76). Peter Lang.

Chanady, A. (2004). The construction of minority subjectivities at the end of the twentieth century. In D. A. Beneventi, L. Canton, & L. Moyes (Eds.), *Adjacencies: Minority writing in Canada* (pp. 21–37). Guernica.

da Costa, P. (2002). *The scent of a lie*. Ekstasis Editions.

da Costa, Paulo (2005). *Notas-de-rodapé—Portuguese poems*. Livros Pé d'Orelha.

da Costa, P. (2012, 18 November). At home in two cultures: In conversation with Paulo da Costa. http://www.paulodacosta.ca/at-home-in-two-cultures/

da Costa, Paulo (2012). *O perfume da mentira*. Livros Pé d'Orelha.

da Costa, Paulo (2013). *The green and purple skin of the world*. Freehand books.

da Costa, P. (2015). *Beyond bullfights and ice hockey: Essays on identity, language and writing culture*. Boavista Press.

da Costa, P. (2021, 1 November). Paulo da Costa. https://descendencias.pt/paulo-da-costa/

Goncalves, L., & Matos, T. C. (Eds.). (2015). *Writers of the Portuguese diaspora in the United States and Canada: An anthology*. Boavista Press.

Hutcheon, L. (1990). Introduction. In L. Hutcheon & M. Richmond (Eds.), *Other solitudes: Canadian multicultural fictions* (pp. 1–16). Oxford University Press.

Joel, A. A. (2000). Literature of Portuguese background in Canada. In V. M. P. da Rosa & C. Teixeira (Eds.), *The Portuguese in Canada: From the sea to the city* (pp. 223–235). University of Toronto Press.

Kamboureli, S. (Ed.). (1996). *Making a difference: Canadian multicultural literature*. Oxford University Press.

Keller, W. R., & Kuester, M. (Eds.). (2002). *Writing Canadians: The literary construction of ethnic identities*. Universitätsbibliothek Marburg.

Laranjeira, P. (2009). Introduction. In I. Marques, *Habitando na metáfora do tempo: Crónicas desejadas* (pp. 5–8). Edium Editores.

Lynch, G. (2001). *The one and the many: English-Canadian short story cycle*. University of Toronto Press.

Lynch, G., & Robbeson, A. A. (Eds.). (1999). *Dominant impressions: Essays on the Canadian short story*. University of Ottawa Press.

MacLeod, A. (1999). The Canadian short story. In G. Lynch & A. A. Robbeson (Eds.), *Dominant impressions: Essays on the Canadian short story* (pp. 161–166). University of Ottawa Press.

Marques, Irene (2007). *Wearing glasses of water*. Mawenzi.

Marques, I. (2008). Poetry, culture and the states of being. Literary Forum with International Research Confederacy on African Literature and Culture. http://www.africaresearch.org/Papers/Np05Ltct.pdf

Marques, Irene (2012). *The perfect unravelling of the spirit*. Mawenzi.

Marques, Irene (2013). *An exercise in loss and findings*. Guernica.

Marques, I. (2015). *My house is a mansion*. Leaping Lion Books.

Marques, I. (2016, August–December). Notes on the incestuous and monocultural nexus of the literati. *Maple Tree Literary Supplement, 21*. https://www.mtls.ca/issue21/irene-marques

Marques, I. (2017). Canada's literary mono-culture and its 'politics' of separation [Interview with Amatoritsero Ede]. *Maple Tree Literary Supplement, 22*. https://www.mtls.ca/issue22/round-table

Marques, I. (2021, 9 November). *Interview with Crystal Fletcher, all about Canadian books* [Video]. YouTube. https://www.youtube.com/watch?v=repC1nfiNbY

Marques, Irene (2021a). *Daria*. Inanna Publications.

Marques, Irene (2021b). *Uma casa no mundo*. Imprensa Nacional–Casa da Moed.

Miska, J. (1990). *Ethnic and native Canadian literature: A bibliography*. University of Toronto Press.

Monteiro, G. (2015). Preface. In L. Goncalves & T. C. Matos (Eds.), *Writers of the Portuguese diaspora in the United States and Canada: An anthology* (pp. 11–13). Boavista Press.

Mukherjee, A. (1994). *Oppositional aesthetics: Readings from a hyphenated space*. TSAR Publications.

Patim, I. N. (2009). Literature of Portuguese background in the context of literature in Canada. In V. M. P. da Rosa & C. Teixeira (Eds.), *The Portuguese in Canada: Diasporic challenges and adjustment* (2nd ed.) (pp. 269–280). University of Toronto Press.

Simon, S. (2004). Introduction: "Land to light on?" In D. A. Beneventi, L. Canton, & L. Moyes (Eds.), *Adjacencies: Minority writing in Canada* (pp. 9–20). Guernica.

Teixeira, C. (2000). On the move: Portuguese in Toronto. In V. M. P. da Rosa & C. Teixeira (Eds.), *The Portuguese in Canada: From the sea to the city* (pp. 207–220). University of Toronto Press.

Teixeira, C., & da Rosa, V. M. P. (2000). Introduction: A historical and geographical perspective. In V. M. P. da Rosa & C. Teixeira (Eds.), *The Portuguese in Canada: From the sea to the city* (pp. 3–17). University of Toronto Press.

Viveiros, F. (Ed.). (2013). *Memória: An anthology of Portuguese Canadian writers*. Fidalgo Books.

Endnotes

1   Paulo da Costa and Irene Marques are prolific writers within a variety of genres. They have published several works in English and Portuguese. Da Costa is the author of *The Green and Purple Skin of the World* (Freehand Books, 2013), *The Scent of a Lie* (LPO, 2012, 2nd ed.), *O perfume da mentira* (Livros Pé d'Orelha, 2012), *Notas-de-rodapé—Portuguese poems* (Livros Pé d'Orelha, 2005), and *Beyond Bullfights and Ice Hockey* (Boavista Press, 2015). His works also appear in audio chapbooks and several anthologies. Da Costa is also an award-winning writer who has earned, for instance, the Commonwealth Prize for Best First Book (Canada and Caribbean regions, 2003), the City of Calgary W. O. Mitchell Book Prize (2002), and the recent

James H. Gray Award for Short Non-Fiction (2020). Marques is the author of three poetry collections, *Wearing Glasses of Water* (Mawenzi, 2007), *The Perfect Unravelling of the Spirit* (Mawenzi, 2012), and *An Exercise in Loss and Findings* (Guernica, 2013). She is also the author of the short-story collection *Habitando na metáfora do tempo: Crónicas desejadas* (Edium Editores, 2009) and three novels: *My House Is a Mansion* (Leaping Lion Books, 2015), *Uma casa no mundo* (Imprensa Nacional–Casa da Moeda, 2021), and *Daria* (Inanna Publications, 2021). *Uma casa no mundo* received the inaugural Prémio Imprensa Nacional/Ferreira de Castro.

2   In a census in 1991, there were over 200,000 people of Portuguese ethnic origin living in Ontario alone (see Teixeira & da Rosa, 2000, p. 7).

3   See, for instance, Andrew-Gee (2013).

4   Manuel Azevedo (2022) offers an interesting view of the matter.

5   The initialism stands for literature of Portuguese background in Canada.

6   Patim (2009, p. 278) also acknowledges such a shift by pointing out current studies of Canadian literature "that include works and voices traditionally excluded or marginalized. More relevant than applying traditional thematic approaches to Canadian literature is simply to identify issues shared by Canadian literary texts written by authors of different origins. Canada's multicultural identity has been expressed through numerous authors of numerous backgrounds."

7   To my knowledge, there are only two anthologies that include Portuguese Canadian writers: *Memória: An Anthology of Portuguese Canadian Writers* (Viveiros, 2013) and *Writers of the Portuguese Diaspora in the United States and Canada: An Anthology* (Goncalves & Matos, 2015). Both feature works by da Costa and Marques and several other established and emerging writers, and both are the results of efforts by small presses to "find a place in the sun for what until recently was an exercise" (Monteiro, 2015, p. 11). There are no Portuguese Canadian writers included in the other aforementioned anthologies (*Adjacencies* [Beneventi et al., 2004], *Making a Difference* [Kamboureli, 1996], and *Writing Canadians* [Keller & Kuester, 2002]). They are also absent in bibliographies (e.g., Miska, 1990).

PART 4

ELEVATING TRANSCULTURAL IDENTITIES
in
NATIONAL SPACES

The chapters in this section examine how both immigrant and First Nations Canadians contest and recreate "Canadian identity" from a transcultural perspective. The section offers insights into "Canadian identity" from multiple perspectives, some of which have not been part of the conversation on national multiculturalism thus far: older Cambodian Canadians, a First Nations university professor, a former refugee from Serbia, two international students from Kenya and India, and youth of Guatemalan, El Salvadoran, and Nicaraguan backgrounds.

In Chapter 9, Shamette Hepburn explores the complicated and multilayered contexts of Cambodian Canadian identity formation and expression. Hepburn foregrounds the protracted process of resettlement and integration of Cambodian Canadians since their initial entry into Canada. The research presented in this chapter brings into focus little-known ways in which first-generation Cambodian Canadians, who represent a small percentage of the general population, navigate issues of inclusion and exclusion in this cultural milieu. Hepburn discusses Cambodian Canadians' conceptions of identity and belonging vis-à-vis mechanisms that have been designed to support the integration of resettled populations but that simultaneously stabilize an "objective" Canadian national identity. Given that these two functions appear to be in apposition, critical transnationalism is employed to highlight typologies of Cambodian Canadians' identity that exist within and beyond frameworks of acculturation and adjustment. Cambodian Canadians deploy a transcultural understanding of identity and inclusion that weaves together Western values of self-knowledge, materialism, and individualism and the cooperative ethos of Khmer-Buddhist traditions within the Canadian body politic. Importantly, facets of their transcultural identity pry away the apparent monocultural fixity of the Canadian national identity, expand it, and generate new thematics for understanding inclusion and the long-term outcomes of resettlement processes.

In Chapter 10, Catherine Longboat, Snežana Obradović-Ratković, Esther Wainaina, and Reshma Rose Tom discuss their commonalities and differences in understanding "Canadian identity" through their connections to land, language, and education. As a diverse group of women—one born on the Canadian territory of Turtle Island/North America and three coming from Serbia, Kenya, and India—the authors reflect on their experiences in Canada, which has a history of welcoming settlers with promises of land free for the taking. Longboat and her colleagues problematize the approach to reconstructing "Canadian identity" before centring the intention of original peoples to coexist with settler nations. In these times of truth and reconciliation, COVID-19, and recently discovered graves of missing residential school children, the authors challenge the symbolic references to Canada as a country of compassion, freedom, and good education through the Two-Row Wampum Belt story, a lens of coexistence. By weaving together multiple voices, this chapter invites educators, scholars, and policy makers to understand the complexities of settler relationships with original peoples before considering a reconstruction of "Canadian identity."

In Chapter 11, Veronica Escobar Olivo employs narrative inquiry to understand and document the experiences of twenty first-and-a-half-generation and second-generation Central Americans (ages twenty to twenty-nine) living in Toronto. Central American migration to Canada grew exponentially during the mid-1980s to early 1990s because of the civil wars in Guatemala, El Salvador, and Nicaragua. With many migrants now having lived in Canada for several decades, there are also many first-and-a-half-generation and second-generation Central Americans who have settled and grown up in Canada. The violence from which most of them living in Canada fled played a vital role in their migration and subsequent settlement experiences. The chapter is therefore informed by the following question: how has this history affected the experiences of first-and-a-half-generation and second-generation Central Americans in Canada? Escobar Olivo explains that both the former, who spent most of their lives in Canada, and the latter, born in Canada, experienced ongoing difficulties rooting themselves as Canadians. Existing as racialized bodies, the youth struggled to navigate ethnicity since they could not relate to their parents' experiences or be accepted as wholly Canadian. Enduring discriminatory encounters and being treated as the "other" made these Canadians feel as if they were not entitled to claim their Canadian identities. This chapter provides insights into the experiences of hybrid-identity Canadians in one of the world's most diverse cities, where a monocultural vision of identity nonetheless prevails.

9

A Transcultural Reconstruction
of Identity and Inclusion:
The Cambodian Canadian Experience

SHAMETTE HEPBURN

Migration constitutes a disruptive cultural force within
globalization. Unlike earlier phases, where the problems of
religious, social, and cultural difference were held at a safe
distance from metropolitan homelands, contemporary migration
intrudes directly into, disturbs, challenges, and subverts,
metropolitan cultural space. It projects the vexed issue of
pluralism and difference into the settled monocultural spaces of
the Western metropolis. It has produced an epistemic rupture,
generating the thematics of a new problematic—that of the
postcolonial moment.

—Stuart Hall (2003, p. 196)

This passage, written by cultural theorist Stuart Hall, an authority on identity formation among migrant populations, highlights the tensions and possibilities that accompany contemporary mobilities as they penetrate relatively stable cultural spaces. Hall (1992, 2003) suggests that transcultural identities emerge from antagonistic and fractured historical ideas and practices. Consequently, the process of identification through which we project ourselves into cultural identities has become more capacious and complex. Postmodernity, through the prism of globalization and international migration, has resulted in the mobile life course now "understood as a panorama of cultures [and identities]" (Freidman, 1987, p. 35). Transcultural identities are therefore forged through interactions between different groups of people and the integration of "new discourses and knowledge systems into new forms of cultures situated within specific temporal and spatial spectrums" (Li, 2019, p. 3).

My main preoccupation with identity in this chapter is its performance within a transcultural context and its nature as lived among former Cambodian refugees in a transnational social field.[1] Specifically, I explore their contemporary later life adaptations associated with their resettlement experiences. This is an important and timely exercise because "it is how the contrived necessity of identity-building and re-building feels, how it is perceived from inside and how it is lived through that [really] matters" (Bauman, 2000, p. 87). Moreover, as Cambodian Canadian transnationals, they have now entered the distal phase of their resettlement process, yet little is known about how they assert their expansile transcultural identities, navigate later life trajectories, and/ or cultivate a sense of belonging in Canada. I preface my discussion by outlining that my insights have been gleaned from my community-based research, which examined the livelihood strategies of aging Cambodian Canadians and other aging transmigrant populations in northwest Toronto.[2] The grounded theory study examined the narratives of fifteen Cambodian Canadian older adults (aged fifty-five and older) among participants in an adult day program. All participants were born in Cambodia and entered Canada as refugees after living in refugee camps in Thailand or Vietnam. Within the sample, there were fourteen women and one man, typical of the adult day program participants, the majority of whom are women. Purposive and theoretical sampling strategies were utilized to recruit potential participants. Data collection occurred on site at the Jane and Finch Community and Family Centre over a five-month period between November 2019 and March 2020. Although I am a gerontological social worker and an interpretive gerontologist with extensive practical experience engaging with aging transmigrant populations in Toronto, I am not a member of the Cambodian Canadian community. Throughout the process of engagement with members of the community, I fostered a dialogical space that foregrounded Cambodian Canadians' epistemologies and constantly questioned the bearing of my location through critical reflection and reflexivity.

Critical Transnationalism and Multiculturalism: A Conceptual Framework

Cambodian Canadian transnationals are among increasing cohorts of racialized diasporic older adults in Canada. Critical transnationalism supports an analysis of Cambodian Canadians' negotiation with the national, such as policies flowing from the multiculturalism of difference, and the transnational, such as mobile itineraries and minutiae of everyday lives within their communities and the wider transnational social field. The perspective is attentive to questions of politics and power and how, in turn, such questions can uncover new forms of neo-colonialist practices of settlement and individual or collective responses to these practices. For example, among refugees and newcomers, language acquisition has been associated with fostering positive resettlement outcomes, such as "community, self- and socioeconomic worth, mobility, access to information and knowledge," and of course adaptation and integration (Graff, 1979, p. xv). However, there are incongruities associated with the process. Migration regimes are inherently political and can be tools of oppression when they foster deficit perspectives and engage in social control (Lankshear & Knobel, 2006; Luke, 2003; Wickens & Sandlin, 2007). As former refugees, Cambodian Canadian transnationals contend with globalizing processes that have implications for democracy, citizenship, and nationalism (Anthias, 2012). Thus, they interface with national borders, policed formally and informally as barriers against undesirable others. This policing is done through "migration controls, racism and the desire for the integration and management of minorities within, while excluding others on the outside and the inside" (Anthias, 2012, p. 103).

Everyday border systems devise and utilize processes and practices for sorting and excluding migrants (Morrice, 2019). Within the settlement process, literacy and language education are often positioned to facilitate and manage the liminal integration of particular immigrants and refugees in Canada. Racialized and diasporic subjects, such as Cambodian Canadians, continually seek to resist the marginalization ascribed to migration. They do so by asserting their presence in the metropolitan body politic, and they resist oppression by seeking to generate critical, transformative knowledge of their own communities. For example, they form community-based organizations focused on mutual aid, civic engagement, advocacy, and cultural preservation, such as the

Canadian Cambodian Association or the Association of Meatophum Khmer of Canada, based in Toronto. Coloma (2017, p. 100) states that, "for racialized minority, diasporic, and colonized subjects and for those in solidarity with them, to work against epistemicide is to generate and enact a paradigmatic shift in the curriculum of empire and global migration. It is fundamentally a critical project that calls into question received ideas, destabilizes interpretations, imagines other possibilities, and struggles for ... societal transformation." Contemporary migration inserts positional differences and disjunctions within relatively stable national imaginaries. As a result, the differential distribution of life chances is "grounded in the spatial dichotomy of what is identified as centre and periphery" and in questions of identity, belonging, and citizenship (Kunow, 2016, p. 101).

Policies and practices associated with multiculturalism have been central to the initial resettlement and integration of Cambodian refugees in Canada. When presented to Cabinet in 1971, the policy of multiculturalism was justified as a new understanding of Canadianism, with one of its several citizenship objectives being the stimulation of a meaningful Canadian consciousness (Uberoi, 2018). Key to this process was the promotion of social inclusion, whereby members of ethnocultural groups could participate in the institutional life of the nation (Kymlicka, 2012). Clause 31b of the Multiculturalism Act outlines, *inter alia*, the aim "to convey a strong sense of legitimacy to those individuals and communities who feel and/or understand that either their culture or their race has limited their role and acceptance in Canadian society" (Government of Canada, 2021). Despite criticism that multiculturalism is divisive and marginalizing, many Canadians are proudly multicultural, and multiculturalism has been widely accepted as part of the Canadian national identity. The Environics Institute (Adams, 2021) indicates that ordinary Canadians increasingly identify multiculturalism and diversity as the most important attributes of Canada's national identity.

An examination of Cambodian Canadians' integration into Canadian society is illustrative of the layered nature of multiculturalism as a public policy (official state policy) and as a practice in terms of how it permeates the quotidian experiences and political struggles of ethnocultural individuals and communities (Wong & Guo, 2015). As the introduction to this volume shows, a more expansive discussion of multiculturalism is long overdue. Fleras (this volume) and Fleras and Kunz (2001) contend that multiculturalism is a social fact, an ideology, a policy, a practice, and a critical discourse. However, the concept demarcates the normative framework for society building and national identity through which Cambodian Canadian transnationals are incorporated into Canada (Kymlicka, 2012). They largely conceive of multiculturalism not only within the normative framework of the wider Canadian society but also as a demographic and social fact of their everyday life experiences as aging transnationals and former refugees still in an ongoing process of integration. In the transnational social field, they contend with transmigratory mobilities and translocal linkages that extend well beyond the territorial boundaries of Canada.

Cambodians in Canada: Protracted Resettlement

Following the fall of the Khmer Rouge regime in 1979, thousands of Cambodians fled to Vietnam and Thailand. Over time, some 300,000 resettled in the United States, the United Kingdom, New Zealand, and Australia; Canada accepted 18,602 refugees between 1980 and 1992 (McLellan, 1995, 2004). The latest Canadian census indicates that the total population of Cambodian Canadians is approximately 38,490, with the majority living in Quebec and Ontario (Statistics Canada, 2017). Approximately 6,000 Cambodian Canadians (2,740 males and 3,205 females) live in Toronto. There is a lack, however, of adequate census data on aging Cambodian Canadians, many of whom have been in Canada for almost forty years. Oblique census data are attributed to the population's language barriers, difficulty understanding and completing census forms, and reticence in disclosing personal information (McLellan, 2009).

Prior to resettlement in Canada, Cambodians living in the United Nations High Commission on Refugees camps in Thailand and Vietnam faced numerous barriers to opportunities for selection for entry: "[Since] most Khmer refugees came from rural cultural settings, it was assumed that Western foods, technology, values, and styles of personal interaction would be too overwhelming for them" (McLellan, 2009, p. 32). Approximately 55 percent of Cambodian refugees accepted by Canada were government sponsored, and 45 percent were privately sponsored through religious organizations. Most of these refugees were rural people with little or no primary education (84 percent).

Only 2 percent stated that they had finished high school and had some postsecondary education. Upon their arrival in Canada, more than 90 percent could not speak French or English, the country's official languages (McLellan, 1995).

The majority of Cambodian refugees initially settled in larger urban areas such as Montreal and Toronto. Refugees typically preferred smaller cities, which they believed would be more conducive to acquiring language skills, finding employment, and integrating into communities (McLellan, 1995, 2004, 2009). Refugees who settled in cities in Ontario—such as Hamilton, Kingston, London, Ottawa, Toronto, and Windsor—were affected by the limited availability of Khmer translators. Given that language support was essential for their engagement in routine activities such as communicating with medical professionals or school staff, limited support would have a far-reaching impact on their everyday lives and overall social participation (McLellan, 2009). Furthermore, barriers to English as a Second Language (ESL) training resulted in resettlement challenges, such as social isolation.

McLellan (2009) observes that barriers to English language acquisition were a significant impediment to resettlement. As an earlier life course trajectory, such acquisition would function to restrict refugees' abilities to build the social capital required for integration and inclusion. Overall, inadequate social service provision to Cambodian refugees in Ontario resulted in "low levels of advocacy and cultural brokering for specialized resettlement" (McLellan, 2009, p. 52) and later resulted in Cambodian Canadians having limited social capital, which might have slowed their integration into Canadian society (Hepburn, 2021).

Inadequate language support was one of many issues faced by refugees and might have been symptomatic of a general lack of coordination of support services. Once refugees addressed survival issues during their initial relocation, they were left to contend with managing life on their own in a challenging and confusing resettlement process. As "victims of war and political violence, their memories of terror and cruelty, although receded, still lingered on and remained locked in their psyche" (Das et al., 2013, p. 330). Historically, social services providers displayed a significant lack of understanding of the needs of Cambodian refugees (Ostrander et al., 2017). Given social workers' position in Canada's resettlement bureaucracy, questions have emerged about whether a displayed lack of understanding of refugees' needs was indicative of the refugee-host tensions that flowed from social categories such as race, class, and gender, further compounding the resettlement process. Despite their length of time in Canada, Cambodian Canadians experience a protracted resettlement process further complicated by the exigencies of aging.

Navigating the Resettlement Bureaucracy

In Canada, the educational needs of adult newcomers and refugees are typically addressed by programs that provide basic language, literacy, skills, and professional training (Guo, 2015). Programs are typically offered by school boards, postsecondary institutions, non-governmental organizations, and the private sector. ESL programs were first offered by the federal government in 1947 (Guo, 2015; McDonald et al., 2008). In 1978, the Canada Employment and Immigration Commission, under the auspices of the federal government, rolled out a national language training project that complemented the Canadian Job Strategies program. This program targeted newcomers and Indigenous people who lacked proficiency in English or French, which presented a barrier to their employment. The program offered a training allowance to heads of households, typically male (Guo, 2015). The assimilationist ethos flowing from the Citizenship Act in 1947 sought to replace newcomers' languages and cultures with English and French and to facilitate Anglo-Saxon acculturation.

In 1986, after a legal challenge and complaints of gender discrimination, the federal government created the Settlement Language Training Program, which did not focus on newcomers' preparations for the labour market. It provided access to 500 hours of basic English training, daycare funding, and transportation support, mainly to women (Guo, 2015). In the early 1990s, a shift in ESL program objectives occurred. Once overtly focused on assimilation and nation building, objectives were now attuned to integration. In 1992, the Language Instruction for Newcomers (LINC) program was created as a key element of the Immigration Plan for 1991 to 1995 under a federal integration strategy. LINC programs marked a shift in language training, from programs based upon increasing employability to those focused on integration (Guo, 2015). The programs provide access to 900 hours of instruction and focus more on the functions of language, such as survival-level skills. Program participants are taught and evaluated in a framework of task-based assessments and twelve Canadian Language Benchmarks measuring proficiency.

LINC certification is a standardized measure for employers in Canada. However, it has been criticized for separating language from literacy. For example, in its delivery, instructors separate learners' process of learning to read from their process of learning a second language (Duguay, 2012). Another program, Enhanced Language Training (ELT), which started in 2003, provides language training geared to specific professional fields such as nursing and engineering (Boyd & Cao, 2009). It also focuses on interpersonal skill development and cross-cultural communication in order to support the maintenance of employment. ELT programs offer in-class instruction, support job searches, and provide unpaid work placements (Guo, 2015). The relationship between language training and employment represents a contemporary shift in government focus from assimilation to employability and integration. This might have accounted for the truncated language support that first-generation Cambodian Canadians received, for they were in the cross-currents of varying education policies and program changes during their early resettlement period. Among Cambodian refugees arriving in Canada in the 1980s and 1990s, over 50 percent were functionally illiterate in the Khmer language (McLellan, 2009).

In an analysis of Employment and Immigration Canada data, McLellan (2009) explains that, among the 18,602 Cambodian refugees resettled in Canada between 1980 and 1992, only 8 percent reported either French or English fluency. Of the entire group, 31 percent (or 5,678) had no formal education, and 54 percent (or 9,980) had received some primary education in Cambodia; 3 percent (or 624) reported completing education levels equivalent to Grade 9. The number reporting completion of some secondary school was 1,513 (or 8 percent), only 393 (or 2 percent) had completed secondary school, and 488 (or 3 percent) had some postsecondary education (McLellan, 2009). These significant language and educational needs and challenges should have signalled to social workers and other members of Canada's resettlement bureaucracy the need for highly specialized service provision and long-term support.

McLellan (2009, p. 46) observes that "low educational and literacy statistics clearly demonstrated the Cambodians' need for extensive language and job skills training to facilitate secure employment and adaptation." Yet, despite their pre-migration and settlement challenges, refugees were provided ESL training for the first six months after their arrival in Canada, and it was offered to the heads of households and then discontinued after they found employment. Agencies providing services to Cambodian refugees in the 1980s reported serving refugee households typically led by women. These households were in distress and experiencing family isolation with no access to ESL and other supports. Many refugees had already been in Canada for almost a decade before ever coming in contact with a service worker (McLellan, 2009). Difficulty with second language acquisition has persisted among aging cohorts of Cambodian Canadians over the long term.

Critical ethnic scholars such as Sunera Thobani (2007, p. 3) discuss the treatment of refugees in relation to the positioning and over-representation of the national subject as embodying "the quintessential characteristics of the nation and the personification of its values, ethics, and civilizational mores." Thobani explains that, in the master narrative of the nation, "exalted subjects" are at the centre, whereas others, especially those who are racialized, such as refugees, are relegated to the margins. Refugees unfortunately have been seen as drawing upon the nation's resources instead of being seen as contributing members of society. Limited English proficiency is synonymous with limited integration into the community and society. This is significant given the length of time since first-generation Cambodian Canadians were initially resettled. More so, language proficiency is central to the economic integration of newcomers in Canada and bolsters their ability to access higher education and labour market opportunities. Research has shown that immigrants who do not have proficiency in one of Canada's official languages in the workplace lag in earnings, with gaps more significant for women than men (Aydemir & Skuterud, 2005).

Community-Based Support, Resilience, and Integration

Now in the latter stages of the migratory life course, Cambodian Canadian transnationals have been shown to have limited English-language proficiency. Factors internal and external to them as learners appear to have affected their attainment of the language proficiency levels required for acceptable degrees of social participation and inclusion in their communities (Duguay, 2012). However, to compensate, Cambodian Canadian transnationals have high levels of community-based service utilization and participation in social service programs that support their independent living within their communities. For example, the adult day program at the Jane and Finch Community and Family Centre's Unity in Diversity: Aging at Home Program in northwest Toronto is extremely popular with Cambodian Canadians. The program is situated within a continuum of support services for older adult immigrants and refugees intended to foster resilience and later-life learning (Hepburn, 2021). It serves as a gateway for older adults to access appropriate health-care information and services through links with local health-care and allied providers. Importantly, as service users, they are encouraged to engage collaboratively with staff in program development in order to ensure that services are relevant and sensitive to their needs. Scheduled activities include dances, luncheons, trips, and workshops.

At the centre, aging Cambodian Canadians receive social service support in an ethnocultural framework from bilingual Khmer staff who facilitate community-based education and access to mainstream services. In this setting, they are able to mobilize cultural capital, build community, and engage in cooperative learning activities focused on group learning, sharing, and interdependence and aligned with and affirming their Khmer-Buddhist traditions. For example, program staff observe the age-based social hierarchy and adhere to traditional expectations of respect and courtesy when engaging participants. Learning activities are designed in a manner that requires working toward group goals even if individual understanding (or mastery) is also an outcome.

Program staff explain that, given the varying levels of literacy and cognition among Cambodian Canadians, as service users they feel comfortable learning in Khmer and believe that they are respected despite their challenges. Their curiosity and excitement when learning new things and participating in activities are indicative of their level of comfort, safety, and trust. Learning in a group setting has increased their motivation and willingness to take risks. For example, when presented with an opportunity to learn about communication technology and how to use computer equipment safely, program participants are eager to take advantage of the opportunity because the new knowledge will increase their ability to communicate with their local and transnational social networks. The day program also provides a safe space in which Cambodian Canadians can take into account past events and build shared memories in a process of cultural recovery and well-being. This is possible because many participants have been accessing the service for many years and have formed bonds with other members who share similar experiences of past trauma and resilience (Hepburn, 2021).

Study participants reflected on their time in Canada, with many commenting on their experiences just before their arrival, their first impressions of the country, and the ensuing years. One participant who arrived in Canada in 1991 explained that, "when I came, there were a lot of obstacles, but thank goodness there was ESL support so that I could understand how the society works." Another participant explained that, while in a refugee camp in Thailand, she understood that getting an early grasp of English would help her to adjust to life in Canada. Therefore, she started learning English before being resettled in Canada. Her prior exposure to English aided her in a comparatively smoother transition than those of other refugees who were functionally illiterate, had no prior education in English, or knew very little about Canada or Canadian society. As she commented, "I did some English in Thailand. I didn't come here to learn 'ABC.' I had that already, so when I came and got the ESL I could just laugh because I had my English in Thailand. Some people waited to get the English here, but I knew it was better to start learning once we knew we would get the chance to come to Canada. When they interviewed me in Thailand, I even did it in English, and they were saying 'Wow, you are ready for Canada!'" This participant displayed significant agency in trying to learn English before arriving in Canada in preparation for her resettlement. Moreover, she gathered information about Canada and what was involved in successfully resettling and integrating into Canadian society. The ability to understand a society's mores is integral both to social inclusion and participation and to the functioning of multiculturalism, in which members of the population learn about what it takes to be multicultural citizens and agree to participate (Kymlicka, 2012). One participant commented on her first impressions of Canada soon after her arrival: "When I came, it was so cold, but it was beautiful. I had my children with me. I said to myself that I am going to be happy here. I didn't have the language, and I was scared, but I knew I was going to be okay."

Participants explained that over time their utilization of local programs stimulated a desire to learn more about Canadian society, which in turn helped them to develop a Canadian consciousness and integrate into the society to varying degrees. One participant explained that "I come to the program often because I get to learn new things and know what is happening in the community and meet with my friends. The staff help to look after my health and dental [care] and tell me where to go. I know more about staying healthy here [in Canada]. I would not have these things in Cambodia." Another participant stated that "education is the way to the community and support. It is the way to get ahead. . . . I am a Canadian now, and I have been away from Cambodia for a long time. [I am] an old woman, [and] Cambodia is no longer for me because there is no medical support. It is easier to have a life here." By increasing their knowledge of Canada and understanding how to navigate their local communities and the wider society, Cambodian Canadians are steadily increasing their levels of integration into and sense of belonging in Canada. They also have the benefit of comparison because of their routine travels between Cambodia and Canada and communication with friends and family members via social media. This is especially important for aging members of the community now more rooted in Canada.

Cambodian Canadians' Transcultural Identities

Cambodian Canadians have a "unique constellation of characteristics, including their ancient history, their traditional culture and unfamiliarity with Western urban culture, and the traumatic circumstances of their flight" (Hopkins, 1996, p. 3), rendering their patterns of adjustment and integration unlike those of other East Asian populations usually studied, such as Vietnamese. For example, distress among resettled Cambodian refugees, referred to as "cultural bereavement," has been most pronounced in North America, where Cambodian Canadians have been pressured to abandon their cultural practices (Eisenbruch, 1991; Hepburn, 2021). In a study of grief and mourning among Cambodian refugees, Boehnlein (1987, p. 765) indicates that many individuals have lost family members, savings, and possessions, and "others lost their means of livelihood, previous social status or social role. In addition, all Cambodian refugees have literally lost their homeland and many aspects of their rich and centuries-old cultural traditions." Given these circumstances, how do Cambodian Canadians express their transcultural identities? An analysis of their adaptation to or adjustment in multicultural Canada is really an examination of their learning practical livelihood strategies while developing a Canadian and translocal consciousness. As refugees, they have had to learn a new culture and way of life. This learning entails material, social, and ideological transformations that affect their routines of everyday life and shape their worldviews and behaviours (Li, 2019).

A critical transnational approach to an exploration of how Cambodian Canadians participate in the co-construction of the Canadian multicultural mosaic and adapt to Canadian society highlights their constant negotiation of socio-cultural ideologies and practices. For example, all participants in the study reported that they have entered old age in Canada and thus view themselves as deeply embedded in Canadian society, so much so that they do not envision ever moving back to Cambodia permanently. This signifies the acceptance of a transcultural identity made possible by their multicultural identity.

Cambodian Canadian transnationals' sense of belonging in Canada is also linked to the concept of elective belonging, which refers to personal biographies and identities attached to specific locales. Their increasing attachment to Canada indicates a correlation between place and identity as well as the performance of identity itself (Savage et al., 2005). Arguably, a sense of belonging is not solely applicable to a fixed community, with the implications of closed boundaries, but more fluid, seeing places as sites for performing identities and trying to avoid the precarity that has accompanied globalization (Hepburn, 2020). Transnationalism and globalization have created new opportunities for reimagining later life attachments to space and place. The transnationals' connection to and identification with Cambodia remain strong, however, but run in tandem with the deployment of a transcultural identity that reflects an expedient and practical negotiation of belonging. Canada over time has become their home, where they feel most safe and cared for.

This process of negotiation shapes their identities, but it also highlights possibilities and limitations associated with "self-perception, self-expression, and self-projection in relation to others and to their positions in Canada and in the world" (Li, 2019, p. 3). Cambodian Canadians create and constantly redefine their transcultural identities, which emerge within modalities of power on both personal and collective scales. Through culture, mobility, and transnational exchanges, Cambodian Canadians constantly reproduce themselves as new kinds of subjects and, as they age, continually respond or adapt to life course trajectories within the cultural and political streams of Canada and Cambodia (Li, 2019).

A Diasporic Aesthetic: Western Values and Khmer-Buddhist Traditions

Cambodians' resettlement in Canada presents marked distinctions between their lives under the Khmer Rouge and in the refugee camps in Thailand and Vietnam. Although the former refugees have shown flexibility and willingness to adapt to life in Canada, many barriers have hindered their access to Canadian culture and social participation. These barriers include physical and mental health, trauma, loss of kin, loss of personal autonomy, the chaotic circumstances under which they fled Cambodia, and the enduring impacts of these experiences (Hopkins, 1996). The conditions in refugee camps in Thailand also compounded these issues.

In their resettlement away from repressive regimes, which enforced both collective survival and barriers to knowledge, Cambodian refugees began adapting to a society that differed from Khmer-Buddhist traditions, which emphasized extended-family dependency and fostered an ethics-regulated social hierarchy (McLellan, 2004; Ong, 2003). In Canada, they are navigating a multicultural society based upon Western social ethics that celebrate self-knowledge, materialism, and individualism. In the initial phases of resettlement, refugees faced "pressures to perform as knowing subjects who are 'free' to refuse or accept rules, 'free' to govern themselves" (Ong, 2003, p. 18). This transition has affected all aspects of Cambodian Canadians' lives, permeating social networks, identities, community social cohesion, and family dynamics in resettlement (McLellan, 2004).

Yet, within this new cultural milieu, Cambodian Canadians have also had to adapt to life within the transnational social field by bridging Western values and Khmer-Buddhist traditions on multiple scales, nationally and transnationally. It is from this negotiation with the national and the transnational that varying typologies of their transcultural identities emanate and are deployed in everyday life circumstances and as livelihood strategies. A Cambodian Canadian diasporic aesthetic can account for this bridging because it is a discursive, transcultural phenomenon that promotes social cohesion (Wynter, 1992). And it does so within the context of a Western cultural imaginary. The diasporic aesthetic is "a 'syncretic' dynamic, which critically appropriates elements from master-codes of the dominant culture and 'creolizes' them, disarticulating given signs and re-articulating their symbolic meaning" (Hall, 1992, p. 235).

In the transnational spaces of the diaspora, individuals and communities construct narratives of the past to explain their current situations, both to others and to themselves, from particular vantage points. Thus, the diasporic aesthetic serves as a conduit for facilitating Cambodian Canadians' critical engagement with the quotidian while preventing an evanescing of cultural memory. It articulates what it means to be Cambodian and Canadian within the transnational social field, the nuanced ways in which structural resources are accessed, how social systems are navigated, and how cultural and religious traditions are utilized to configure their life chances. Fundamentally, the diasporic aesthetic fosters cultural certitude and self-definition despite physical separation from Cambodia or ongoing integration in Canada. For example, Cambodian Canadians' transnational religious practices, which encompass connections to the performing arts, dance, and music, direct the navigation and expression of transcultural identities among Cambodians living in Cambodia and those living in the diaspora. Theravada Buddhism is the primary way in which the Cambodian way of life is expressed and practised in Canada. Some of these forms of expression flow from family-focused rituals such as the *Pchum Ben* festival, which honours ancestors (September), and weddings, blessings, funerals, traditional cuisine, language, and social hierarchies. Other forms flow from life rituals or from what McLellan (2004, p. 8) describes as "the ceremonial cycle of commemorations" such as the *Visak Bocie*, which celebrates the birth, death, and enlightenment of the Buddha (May), the *Kathin* festival, during which gifts are presented to monks (October), and the Cambodian new year (April). Other rituals include those associated with merit making, healings, memorials, and exorcisms. Cultural and religious institutions and the routine visits of monks from Cambodia also support the development and maintenance of transnational and diasporic identities. The symbolic and institutional power of artistic and religious practices serves to strengthen cultural bonds between Canada and Cambodia and recreates and redefines Khmer culture in the diaspora and transnational social field.

Transcultural identities are also deployed as livelihood strategies in response to declining welfare state provisions and changing needs. Western socio-political thought presents ideological barriers that Cambodian Canadians have had to push against in drawing from their traditions and new (formal and informal) learning. The underlying myths associated with "'bootstrap success' and the efficacy of individual effort" convey the idea that, over time, refugees will integrate into Canadian society (Hopkins, 1996, p. 155). These myths leave little room in social and ideological structures for refugees to be considered as being in transition or even in a phase of protracted transition given their unique and challenging circumstances.

Cambodian Canadian transnationals' appropriation and rearticulation of cultural codes are also shown in their self-directed approach to their health and well-being as they age. For example, self-directed approaches to lifelong learning have emerged as an important consideration of how Cambodian Canadian transnationals are able to contend with the exigencies of aging and ongoing integration into Canadian society. Within their communities, they display a keen awareness of community-based resources, engage in information-seeking behaviour in order to manage their incomes, utilize health and social services, and actively maintain their local and transnational social networks (Hepburn, 2021).[3]

Collective resilience is also an important aspect of their later life adaptations, and it is connected to a practical application of their transcultural identities. The engagement in community-based learning activities (e.g., psychogeriatric education modules focused on nutrition, financial literacy, and access to health-care and social services) has emerged as an essential and transformative livelihood strategy among Cambodian Canadians. This is exemplified in their high levels of participation in individual and cooperative learning activities that allow them to live independently in their communities and participate in civic and community life. They have focused their learning on maintaining their quality of life and collective wisdom. Although they value traditional practices, they are also interested in the practical ways in which they can maintain their well-being in Canada in a manner that affirms their cultural values.

Importantly, Cambodian Canadians utilize social media platforms to maintain cross-border social ties, a defining feature of a transnational and transcultural lifestyle. Remarkably, they do so despite low levels of literacy. These activities reveal their ability to learn new skills and compensate for language deficits (Hepburn, 2021). Communication technologies such as video calling and voice messaging have expanded their social fields and revealed their daily literacy and language practices within their local and transnational communities. These practices also open up opportunities for service providers to recognize their individual and collective resilience mechanisms, build upon them, and support their independence and social inclusion.

Conclusion: Possibilities and Limitations

Cambodian Canadians' transcultural identities and lifestyles are indicative of forms of differentiated citizenship that allow seemingly peripheral populations not only to express their distinct practices but also to highlight occluded aspects of nation building unexplored within the Canadian multicultural mosaic. Within the transnational social field, their status as a resettled population circumscribes their identities and subjectivities. Cambodian Canadians' transcultural identities can be framed within a dynamic and processual frame "that recognizes the interconnectedness of different identities and hierarchical structures relating to gender, ethnicity, race, class, and other social divisions at local, national, transnational and global levels" (Anthias, 2012, p. 102). This approach allows for the traditionally undifferentiated, fixed, and often stereotypical subject of the "refugee" to be considered through multilayered forms of human mobility and/or movement. Thus, the aging Cambodian Canadian transmigrant subject and the varying identities and social structures that they mobilize and contend with in later life are illuminated with attendant limitations and possibilities within multicultural Canada and the wider transnational social field.

Through this framing, we can account for the various locations and dislocations with which they contend at various scales. National boundaries, with affective, experiential, and discursive properties, are recast onto a global imaginary fraught with inequality. As shown in their navigation of the resettlement bureaucracy, Cambodian Canadians' experiences are permeated by power relations. In this context, these relations provide the framework that apportions the varying amounts of social, economic, and cultural capital available to Cambodian Canadians and how and where they perform and narrate their identities. Location and the movement and mobilization of social, cultural, and political capital are essential considerations for Cambodian Canadians' transcultural identity formation and expression.

Identity is an ongoing project or task and the name given to what is really an escape from uncertainty (Bauman, 2000). This is also true for

Cambodian refugees who were initially resettled in Canada almost four decades ago and have now entered the latter stages of the migratory life course. As Cambodian Canadians, they have developed transcultural identities that have flowed from the multicultural ideals and complex diversities that circumscribe yet simultaneously expand the Canadian national identity.

Transcultural identities, expressed spatially and temporally, are transformed constantly in how individuals and groups are represented or constructed in the cultural systems in which they live. Through their articulation of multiple ways of being and engaging in their social spaces, aging Cambodian Canadian transnationals embody a new world archetypal subject who reconstructs home, everyday life, and identity within the context of a complex and layered migratory life course. Cambodian Canadians' transcultural identities support the development of cultural certitude and self-definition, enabling them to navigate power dynamics and layered cultural exchanges from interstitial and marginal spaces toward inclusion and the co-construction of a culturally diverse Canadian society.

References

Adams, Michael. (2021). 50 years of multiculturalism. Environics Institute. https://www.environicsinstitute.org/insights/insight-details/50-years-of-multiculturalism

Anthias, F. (2012). Transnational mobilities, migration research and intersectionality: Towards a translocational frame. *Nordic Journal of Migration Research, 2*(2), 102–110. https://doi.org/10.2478/v10202-011-0032-y

Aydemir, A., & Skuterud, M. (2005). Explaining the deteriorating entry earnings of Canada's immigrant cohorts, 1966–2000. *Canadian Journal of Economics, 38*(2), 641–672. https://doi.org/10.1111/j.0008-4085.2005.00297.x

Bauman, Z. (2000). *Liquid modernity*. Polity.

Boehnlein, J. K. (1987). Clinical relevance of grief and mourning among Cambodian refugees. *Social Science and Medicine, 25*(7), 765–772.

Boyd, M., & Cao, X. (2009). Immigrant language proficiency, earnings, and language policies. *Canadian Studies in Population, 36*(1), 63–86. https://doi.org/10.25336/P6NP62

Coloma, R. S. (2017). We are here because you were there: On curriculum, empire, and global migration. *Curriculum Inquiry, 47*(1), 92–102.

Das, M., Dubus, N., & Silka, L. (2013). Decades after resettlement: Later life experiences of Cambodian refugees. *Humanity and Society, 37*(4), 327–345. https://doi.org/10.1177/0160597613510705

Duguay, A. L. (2012). The school of life: Differences in U.S. and Canadian settlement policies and their effect on individual Haitian immigrants' language learning. *TESOL Quarterly, 46*(2), 306–333. https://doi.org/10.1002/tesq.23

Eisenbruch, M. (1991). From post-traumatic stress disorder to cultural bereavement: Diagnosis of southeast Asian refugees. *Social Science and Medicine, 33*(6), 673–680.

Fleras, A., & Kunz, J. (2001). *Media and minorities: Representing diversity in a multicultural Canada.* Thompson Education Publishing.

Freidman, J. (1987). Prolegomena to the adventures of Phallus in Blunderland: An anti-anti-discourse. *Culture and History, 1*(1), 31–49.

Government of Canada. (2021). Canadian Multiculturalism Act. https://laws-lois.justice.gc.ca/PDF/C-18.7.pdf

Graff, H. J. (1979). *The literacy myth: Literacy and social structure in the nineteenth-century city.* Academic Press.

Guo, Y. (2015). Language policies and programs for adult immigrants in Canada: Deconstructing discourses of integration. In S. Guo & E. Lange (Eds.), *Transnational migration, social inclusion and adult education* [Special Issue]. *New Diections for Adult & Continuouss Education 146,* 41–51. https://doi.org/10.1002/ace.20130

Hall, S. (1992). Cultural identity and cinematic representation. In M. B. Cham (Ed.), *Ex-iles: Essays on Caribbean cinema* (pp. 220–236). Africa World.

Hall, S. (2003). Creolization, diaspora, and hybridity in the context of globalization. In O. Enwezor, C. Basualdo, U. M. Bauer, S. Ghez, S. Maharaj, M. Nash, & O. Zaya (Eds.), *Creolite and creolization: Documenta 11 platform 3* (pp. 180–198). Hatje Cantz.

Hepburn, S. (2020). Signalling the end of the migration journey: Exploring transnational ageing narratives on residential selection. *Journal of International Migration and Integration, 21*(4), 1263–1278.

Hepburn, S. (2021). Adult day support and community resilience: An analysis of the experiences of ageing Cambodian Canadians. *SN Social Sciences, 1*(1), 1–23. https://doi.org/10.1007/s43545-020-00015-3

Hopkins, M. (1996). *Braving a new world: Cambodian (Khmer) refugees in an American city.* Bergin & Garvey.

Kunow, R. (2016). Postcolonial theory and old age: An explorative essay. *Journal of Aging Studies, 39,* 101–108. https://doi.org/10.1016/j.jaging.2016.06.004

Kymlicka, W. (2012). *Multiculturalism: Success, failure, and the future.* Migration Policy Institute.

Lankshear, C., & Knobel, M. (2006). *New literacies: Everyday practices and classroom learning* (2nd ed.). Open University Press.

Li, J. T. (Ed.) (2019). *The transcultural streams of Chinese Canadian identities.* McGill-Queen's University Press.

Luke, A. (2003). Literacy and the other: A sociological approach to literacy research and policy in multilingual societies. *Reading Research Quarterly, 38*(1), 132–141.

McDonald, L., George, U., Cleghorn, L., & Karenova, K. (2008). *An analysis of second language training programs for older adults across Canada.* University of Toronto Press.

McLellan, J. (1995). *Cambodian refugees in Ontario: An evaluation of resettlement and adaptation.* York Lanes Press.

McLellan, J. (2004). Cambodian refugees in Ontario: Religious identities, social cohesion and transnational linkages. *Canadian Ethnic Studies, 36*(2), 101–118.

McLellan, J. (2009). *Cambodian refugees in Ontario: Resettlement, religion, and identity.* University of Toronto Press. https://doi.org/10.3138/9781442697713

Morrice, L. (2019). Abyssal lines and cartographies of exclusion in migration and education: Towards a reimagining. *International Journal of Lifelong Education, 38*(1), 20–33. https://doi.org/10.1080/02601370.2018.1489425

Ong, A. (2003). *Buddha is hiding.* University of California Press.

Ostrander, J., Melville, A., & Berthold, S. M. (2017). Working with refugees in the U.S.: Trauma-informed and structurally competent social work approaches. *Advances in Social Work, 18*(1), 66–79. https://doi.org/10.18060/21282

Savage, M., Bagnall, G., & Longhurst, B. (2005). *Globalization and belonging.* SAGE.

Statistics Canada. (2017). *Immigration and ethnocultural diversity highlight tables, 2016 Census.* (Catalogue No. 98-402-X2016007). https://www12.statcan.gc.ca/census-recensement/2016/dp-pd/hlt-fst/imm/index-eng.cfm

Thobani, S. (2007). *Exalted subjects: Studies in the making of race and nation in Canada.* University of Toronto Press.

Uberoi, V. (2018). National identity: A multiculturalist approach. *Critical Review of International Social and Political Philosophy, 21*, 46–64.

Wickens, C. M., & Sandlin, J. A. (2007). Literacy for what? Literacy for whom? The politics of literacy education and neocolonialism in UNESCO and World Bank–sponsored literacy programs. *Adult Education Quarterly, 57*(4), 275–292. https://doi.org/10.1177/0741713607302364

Wong, L., & Guo, S. (2015). Revisiting multiculturalism in Canada: An introduction. In S. Guo & L. Wong (Eds.), *Revisiting multiculturalism in Canada: Theories, policies and debates* (pp. 1–14). Birkhäuser Boston.

Wynter, S. (1992). Rethinking "aesthetics": Notes towards a deciphering practice. In M. B. Cham (Ed.), *Ex-iles: Essays on Caribbean cinema* (pp. 237–279). Africa World.

Endnotes

1   Transnational social fields refer to cross-border practices and ways of being and belonging that circumscribe migrants' personal networks or social ties.

2   Transmigrants are immigrants who develop and sustain cross-border familial, social, organizational, religious, and political relationships. They are therefore rooted simultaneously in more than one locale, typically between host and home countries.

3   Social service utilization among Cambodian Canadian older adults is exceptionally high at the Unity in Diversity: Aging at Home Program, the sole adult day program supporting the community in northwest Toronto.

10

The Conundrum of Reconstructing Canada's Identity without Reconciliation

CATHERINE LONGBOAT, SNEŽANA OBRADOVIĆ-RATKOVIĆ,
ESTHER WAINAINA, AND RESHMA ROSE TOM

In Canada, a capitalistic society that practises neo-liberalism, the steps required for building relationships that include the earth's offerings are ignored. As we write, we are aware that we live in the Anthropocene age of discomfort and fear. Amid COVID-19, the public gaze was on media that highlighted the grounds of residential schools because "remote sensors picked up 'anomalies' and what are called 'reflections' that indicate the remains of children may be buried at the site" (Kennedy, 2022, para. 2) while the Canadian government challenged the process of reconciliation concerning the compensation of Indigenous children involved in the Sixties Scoop (Gilmore, 2021).

To understand the process of reconciliation, it is critical to "sideline both white supremacy and the settler superiority complex by putting Indigeneity at the centre of a revised constitution" (Clarke, 2021, para. 1). In the words of Justice Murray Sinclair, reconciliation "is not an act of forgiving past wrongs but a process of dismantling the ongoing colonial relationship that treats Indigenous Peoples as less than human. Reconciliation is not a matter of benevolence or charity. It is a matter of respect and rights" (qtd. in Braga, 2021, para. 1). With such a revised Constitution, the voices of Indigenous peoples will strongly advocate for truth and the health of North America. This document will address the continent as Turtle Island through the voices of woodland Indigenous peoples such as Lenape, Iroquois/Haudenosaunee, and Anishinaabe/ Ojibwa. As sovereign peoples, Indigenous peoples are committed to the earth given obligations and responsibilities such as Haudenosaunee concepts entrenched in the story of a Great Law (Wallace, 1946; Williams, 2018) indicative of balance and harmony among all animate and inanimate beings for earthly sustainability. This commitment is in their languages, their lifestyles, and their education systems.

As Indigenous scholars in Turtle Island/North America, Africa, Asia, and Europe, we scrutinize the commonly known, assumed, and imposed identity of Canada as a country of choice and opportunity. We explore the concept and the reality of identity in the contexts of colonization and reconciliation. During the past two years, we wrestled with the following question. How can we conceptualize a Canadian identity that includes both Indigenous and settler cultures, lifestyles, and histories? We agreed that our indigeneity and identity are rooted in the land, our ancestral languages, and our education. We are aware that education can be a tool not only of colonization but also of reconciliation. To conceptualize education as a tool of reconciliation, we explored the truths around the meaning of coexistence as encapsulated within the Great Law and the Two-Row Wampum Belt stories.

In this chapter, we challenge the call to reconstruct a young country's identity, for Canada's identity has yet to be constructed through the reconciliation of White settlers' colonial lifestyles with original peoples' stories. We wrote this chapter to disrupt the notion of Canada's identity as a country of "democracy, peace, and kindness throughout the world" (Truth and Reconciliation Commission, 2015, p. vi).

Conceptual Framework

We reflected on our relationships with land, language, and education through storytelling and the Two-Row Wampum Belt story. Indigenous storytelling is oral but often accompanied by mnemonic symbols to aid the memories of tellers over generations. A wampum bead is held as sacred by Haudenosaunee people with a story connected to healing and wellness, predating the Six Nations/Haudenosaunee Confederacy (Wallace, 1946; Williams, 2018). These tubular shell beads of purple and white (Figure 10.1) have been designed into a sequence of rows to tell a story about the first treaty relationship in 1612 (Williams, 2018), between the Haudenosaunee people of Turtle Island and the Dutch

Figure 10.1. Dr. Catherine Longboat holding her Two-Row Wampum teaching tool. Photo taken by Nicole Owl @mslocosmemories. Courtesy of Catherine Longboat.

and English colonial settlers, symbolizing an Indigenous canoe and a White settlers' ship travelling down the same river together as two sovereign nations. Through storytelling and a Two-Row Wampum Belt lens of coexistence, we explored our commonalities and differences, negotiated our vulnerabilities and strengths, and learned each other's stories. We deepened our sense of belonging to our group as scholars and allies, reclaiming our commitment to Mother Earth, deepening our roots in the lands of our birth, and declaring our love for the land that we currently inhabit.

Methodological Approach: Writing as Nomadic Inquiry

Over the course of a year, until COVID-19 prevented us from meeting face to face, we initially met biweekly to puzzle over, write about, and investigate Canadian history and the meaning of our words, our education, and our origins. We agreed that we are indigenous to the land of our ancestors with our own history and current collective struggle on Turtle Island and that we differ, yet seem to be similar, in our struggles and our strengths. We have struggled for being Indigenous (Catherine), refugee (Snežana), and international students (Esther and Reshma) in Canada because our education is discarded, our identities are racialized, and our needs and rights are ignored or marginalized. We are strong because we honour our cultural backgrounds and build relationships and alliances. We kept meeting notes and identified the dominant stories emerging from our conversations and reflections.

Writing can be considered a method of nomadic inquiry (St. Pierre, 1997a) and storytelling (St. Pierre, 1997b). For us, writing is representation, simulation (Baudrillard, 1988), subversion (Butler, 1990), analysis, and method of discovery. Our writing is personal, political, and cross-cultural. As soon as we started writing this chapter, we scheduled monthly meetings to write and reflect on the writing process and content. Over a year, we reflected on our readings, biweekly and monthly meeting discussions, and personal and professional experiences to engage with the concepts of decolonization, reconciliation, and coexistence. Throughout the process of researching and writing, we shared our cultural and professional knowledge as writers, educators, colleagues, and allies. During each monthly conversation, we took turns keeping notes to document our oral contemplative ideas, questions, concerns, and learning. We started writing this chapter by developing a literature review on Indigenous and immigrant voices in graduate education. Next we wrote our individual stories to position ourselves as scholars, researchers, and people indigenous to our ancestral lands. Throughout our collaborative writing, we continued reflecting, discussing, questioning, and revising our collective story of struggle, resilience, and coexistence. With each meeting, Snežana, Esther, and Reshma first learned the stories of Catherine's people and, through a steep learning curve, the stories of the original peoples who remained hidden from first contacts with settlers, wondering who we (and Canada) might become if those stories were shared and honoured. "Onkwehonwe (Mohawk language) or Ögwë̀ö:weh (Cayuga language) means 'original people,' and is used by Hodinöhsö:ni' (Haudenosaunee) people to refer to Indigenous peoples in general, not only members of the Six Nations Confederacy" (Hill & Coleman, 2019, p. 356).

Our Individual Stories

Catherine

Catherine is a person of mixed Indigenous descent, a learned member of two clan families (Wolf and Golden Eagle) and two nations (Haudenosaunee/Iroquois/Six Nations/Mohawk and Anishinaabe/Ojibwe). She is a Turtle Island/North American Indigenous person born and raised in Canada. Turtle Island exists geographically as a large land mass surrounded by large bodies of water in the northern hemisphere, the Atlantic Ocean to its right and the Pacific Ocean to its left; Canada is the northern colonized division of Turtle Island/North America.

Catherine has an Indigenous spirit name that indicates her roles and responsibilities among her parents' people. They include her studies of ethical space theory (Poole, 1972), the space between the two purple rows of the Two-Row Wampum Belt that signifies two solitudes and a cultural divide symbolized by three white rows in which cultural differences can be addressed with peace, friendship, and respect (Longboat, 2008a, 2008b). She carries a Two-Row Wampum Belt as a teaching tool. Her second identity is that she has a doctoral degree in policy and leadership in education. She is an assistant professor in the Inaugural Program of Indigenous Educational Studies, Faculty of Education, at Brock University. Her work involves transforming leadership and educational approaches in higher education with Indigenous and non-Indigenous faculty and students.

Catherine asserts that Indigenous identities are connected to the land. The Onondaga story outlines the oral storytelling of Sky Woman and how the birds, animals, and water creatures determined to catch her so that she could safely land on the volunteer turtle's back (Onondaga Historical Association, n.d.). Kimmerer (2013) determines the identity of Sky Woman as the first immigrant to Turtle Island. Therefore, the story of Haudenosaunee peoples is that of being Turtle Island/North American Indigenous peoples rather than Canadians.

Snežana

Snežana was born and raised in socialist Yugoslavia. Her mother had four grades of elementary school education and her father a high school diploma. Her parents did not study *Pedagogy of the Oppressed* (Freire,

1968), but they believed in the power of education. At that time, education in Yugoslavia was free, and Snežana and her brother obtained teaching degrees. Educated in the spirit of social justice, equity, and solidarity, Snežana believes in humanity, respect, and coexistence rather than oppression, domination, and hierarchy.

In Canada, her teaching credentials and experiences from Yugoslavia were dismissed. Snežana was without English, credentials, and land. Since 1998, she held fifteen low-wage jobs, such as cleaning hotel rooms and delivering newspapers. From 2000 to 2014, Snežana worked full time, studied full time, and took care of her family. She is now a research officer and instructor in the Faculty of Education, Brock University.

In her doctoral dissertation (Ratković, 2014), Snežana explored the experiences and identities of ten refugee women teachers from the former Yugoslavia who immigrated to Canada during or after the Yugoslav wars that raged from 1991 to 1995 and split the country into seven new political entities. She honoured participant voices through bilingual stories, poems, a play, and a film entitled *InTercultural WORKS* (Ratković et al., 2018). The play and the film offered open and safe spaces in which Indigenous peoples, newcomers to Canada, and White settlers' descendants educated one another. Snežana is committed to building bridges toward reconciliation by learning Indigenous peoples' stories and by creating scholarly communities with diverse Indigenous and settler groups.

Esther

Esther came to Canada from Kenya as an international student and a mother of three. She is a graduate student and a teaching assistant in the Faculty of Education at Brock University. In her master's thesis, Esther explored internationalization at higher education institutions in Western, English-speaking countries by centring the experiences of graduate students in a segregated, international program. She problematizes the dominant and neo-liberal approaches to internationalization in higher education and advocates for the decolonization of education in Canada and beyond.

Esther is committed to anti-racism and coexistence, recognizing that imperialist strategies feed on the principle of "divide and conquer." Aware that colonization and suffering are happening all around the world, she believes that separation of Indigenous peoples and recent settlers on Canadian soil is unnatural and dangerous. Esther contemplates her initial assumptions about having the same colonizing experiences as Indigenous peoples in Canada: "I shared my initial questioning of the 'place' of a newcomer in Canada such as myself. Having come from a country with colonial history, I assumed that I naturally shared the experience of colonization with Indigenous people in Canada." In one of her master's classes, Esther realized that her colonial experiences differed from those of Indigenous peoples in Canada: "I gradually found that my understanding was, at best, very limited. My first awakening from this false sense of commonality came when an Indigenous student in one of my graduate courses explained the continuing oppression in relation to land and self-determination. I was horrified to learn that immigrant communities (of which I am a part ... as an international student looking to remain in Canada), whether knowingly or unknowingly, can contribute to continued oppression through 'settler identities'" (Lowman & Barker, 2015) on Turtle Island.

Esther learned from Métis writer and educator Chelsea Vowel (2016) the difference between the privileges of original and recent settlers in Canada. Recent settlers, especially non-European peoples, are pulled into the settlement process, but often they are denied the social privileges of bringing their laws and customs into Canada. Integrating Indigenous storytelling in education, such as the Two-Row Wampum Belt, and encouraging alliances with Indigenous peoples would assist recent settlers in understanding and connecting with indigeneity on Turtle Island.

Reshma

Reshma is an international student from India, a graduate of the Master of Education program, Faculty of Education, Brock University. She experienced a series of difficulties while trying to understand her location within Canadian society. Reshma faced identity confusion, which happens when a host society offers international students a myriad of culturally unfamiliar choices, such as diverse ideologies, lifestyles, and job opportunities, resulting in a culture shock, cross-cultural identity reconstruction, and "a potentially confusing, challenging, and even painful journey" (Liu & Rathbone, 2021, p. 44). To make informed choices in Canada, Reshma required a perspective different from her original cultural lens based upon her upbringing in India. An international student is expected to choose roles and adjust for successful integration into Canadian society. However, Reshma found it difficult to reconcile her new and diverse roles, such as graduate student, research assistant, and newcomer to Canada, with her cultural pre-migration identity to create a meaningful and unified sense of belonging in Canada. She lacked an immediate, approachable, and emotional support system. She struggled to accept the role of an immigrant and faced the challenges of being homesick and finding a stable part-time income to support herself.

Unlike the original peoples of Canada, Reshma was welcomed to integrate into the Canadian education system and society as an international graduate student. She came to Canada expecting safety, belonging, and self-actualization. However, Reshma did not experience immediate self-actualization. Before coming to Canada, she lived with her prosperous, upper-middle-class parents in their ancestral home in India, and enjoyed her own home space for rest and play, a good income with an accommodating schedule, and dining predilections. In Canada, she was eager to find accommodations near Niagara Falls, an affluent location within the tourist industry and advertised on the Brock University website. However, because of the lack of funds, Reshma had to share a room with another student rooted in Muslim culture. Cultural differences disrupted her daily schedule and need for privacy to rest, study, work, and prepare meals. Reshma struggled to collaborate with her roommate toward an agreeable schedule and combined budget to allow for savings.

Reshma was enticed to participate in the Canadian dream of diversity, equity, and inclusion, but she was not aware of how such a promising outcome could be fulfilled. Although she was able to work to pay for her shared accommodations, she was offered only the manual labour of cleaning hotel rooms. She experienced a myriad of culturally related issues (e.g., displacement, identity confusion, and language differences) within Canadian multiculturalism. Although Reshma experienced colonial upper-class status in India, she could not reclaim such status in Canada.

Our Conversations

Catherine brought her knowledge of the past from an Indigenous oral perspective. She guided Snežana, Esther, and Reshma through the process of understanding the lens through which Indigenous peoples see themselves as an integral part of the "web of life" among nature and in relation to all that exists on the land and in the water and sky. She brought to the group understandings of the tools used to teach, such as the Great Law and Sky Woman. The introduction of Haudenosaunee stories is a prelude to other Indigenous stories. Latimer (2020) investigates Indigenous cultural groups such as Pacific Northwest Indigenous peoples who have stories of beings called "transformers" who become the spirits of the land: "The transformer Q!a'neqe lak married the daughter of Gwa' nalalis at Whulk, and Gwa' nalalis was later transformed into the river gwa' ne [the Nimpkish River]" (Government of British Columbia, n.d.). In Inuit culture, they live and interact with not only humans but also animals. So intimate is the relationship between human and animal that Inuit mythology tells of a time when a human could become an animal and an animal could become a human. The Inuit stories of Sedna explain the reason for her insistence on protocols and processes for hunters to demonstrate respect for Inua, the soul (Google Art and Culture, n.d.). If the sky world also had these beliefs, then Sky Woman brought understandings with her. In this place that we identify as earth today, it is these beings who saw the first newcomer: a pregnant Sky Woman. These beings strategized for her safe landing from the sky and then accommodated her needs by offering their knowledge and resources for her well-being and sustenance. The ensuing relationship demanded understandings of collaborative living under the Great Law that existed prior to the arrival of Sky Woman. The Great Law is the ecological and cosmological adherence to, respect for, and living with systems that are non-human, both animate and inanimate. The Great Law champions balance and harmony. When one subscribes to it, the return to a good life, or *mino-bimaadisiwin* (an Ojibwe word), extends to future generations, with land, water, and air maintained in their purest states without human interference.

Original peoples extended their knowledge of the Great Law to newly arrived White settlers, who came after the Doctrine of Discovery of 1493 (Wolfchild & Newcombe, 2015). Seeing the distress of these newly arrived settlers, the original peoples living on the eastern coast of Turtle Island rose to offer them their knowledge of how to live on the land. Eventually, however, these original peoples realized the intentions of the newcomers to claim the land and its resources without collaboration. The realization of the newcomers' intentions moved slowly westward across the Canadian Shield, through the Prairies, and across the Rocky Mountains to reach the tribes of the West Coast. The newcomers applied their knowledge from the lands that they came from and had no regard for the Great Law. They brought colonialism, oppression, and individual proprietary notions of land, and exploitation began. This was evident in the fences built to set colonial boundaries across territories and in foreign plants and animals infiltrating the land along with the newcomers.

The instructions for living on the land are found in the Haudenosaunee Great Law for peaceful coexistence, balance, and harmony among all animate and inanimate beings for earthly sustainability and sharing— never taking more than needed and always giving back for equilibrium. The Haudenosaunee organize themselves as a confederacy of Mohawk, Cayuga, Onondaga, Seneca, Oneida, and Tuscarora tribal groups. Other tribal groups organize themselves into confederacies that address their own realities for sovereignty, internal community disputes, and territorial regulations for resources and food, such as the Three Fires Confederacy of the Ojibwe, Potawatomi, and Odawa. The prospect of a changing landscape upon the arrival of settlers signalled the need to design a series of symbolic references that would be easy to understand across different nations. At first, an iron covenant chain of three rings representing peace, friendship, and respect formalized a collaborative relationship between the settlers and the Haudenosaunee peoples living on the East Coast of Turtle Island. Later these three rings became silver rings that could be polished and were longer lasting than iron.

In 1613, the creation of a Two-Row Wampum Belt constructed an oral story of the first relationship between the first settlers and the Mohawk peoples on the eastern shores of Turtle Island/North America. The original peoples offered their understanding to the settlers that both nations, despite their different lifestyles, would travel side by side in peace, friendship, and respect. However, the two nations travelled the same route in different boats—each with its different laws and realities on how to pursue a good life.

The three silver rings are further represented within the Two-Row Wampum Belt as the three white beads separating the two rows of purple beads sitting on a matte of white beads. The two purple rows equally represent the settlers and the original peoples and their vehicles at the time. The settlers arrived in their cumbersome ship with their hierarchy of labourers and passengers, whereas the original peoples could easily manoeuvre in their canoe, guided by the ancestral knowledge of each person within that canoe. The design of the belt allowed respect equally between humans rather than scrutiny and labelling of differences.

Land

As women and scholars, we are sensitive to variations of the White settlers' initial representations of Turtle Island as an empty, open, and barren land free for the taking of rich resources or prime lands for settlement, including justifying acts of genocide (Loomba, 2015). Canada's neo-liberal identity is built upon this legacy. We watched the documentary film *The Doctrine of Discovery: Unmasking the Domination Code*, which presents the Papal Bull by Pope Alexander VI of 1493 (Wolfchild & Newcombe, 2015). The foreign code of domination sanctified the dehumanization of the original inhabitants with violent intrusion upon and possession of lands, resources, and labour of those who lacked European Christian faith. The original peoples lived on their lands striving to attain a good life through mutual trading and leading peaceful, sovereign lives according to the Great Law. They were unprepared for the alternative worldview forcefully imposed on them by the newcomers. After a period of coming to know the land, the colonial settlers devised the heinous plan to take away all resources from the original peoples.

Snežana felt appalled, but not surprised, by the dehumanizing and genocidal nature of colonization in North America. She described her participation in the KAIROS Blanket, an experiential and teaching exercise in Toronto, developed by KAIROS Canada to educate participants about the history of colonization, genocide, and Indigenous peoples' displacement on Turtle Island (KAIROS Canada, 2020). Participants step on blankets representing the land as guided by the scripts read by trained facilitators. Snežana shared this emotional experience: "The land originally inhabited by Indigenous original peoples shrank to patches. After the exercise, participants sat in a circle and reflected on the experience. I was unable to speak. I was overwhelmed by deep sadness, bursting into tears." The taking of land by the Canadian government is a continuing and complicated strategy.

Rather than admitting that the land belongs to the original inhabitants, the federal government has determined an ongoing process of delays and avoidance in honouring treaty agreements (Parliament of

Canada, 2018). As of 1 December 2022, there were "about 407 accepted for negotiation, 61 claims before the Specific Claims Tribunal and about 177 specific claims . . . currently under review or assessment" (Crown-Indigenous Relations and Northern Relations, 2022).

In Canada, Christian newcomers and the federal government imposed a 150-year scheme of assimilation through residential schools. The last school, the Gordon Reserve Indian Residential School, was closed and demolished in 1996 (Hanson et al., 2020). Assimilation included attempts to remove the identities of Indigenous peoples through the power of the Indian Agent and, subsequently, the Indian Act. Irwin (2018) indicates Indian Agents as representatives of the Canadian government's enforced oppressive acts from 1830 to 1960. The Indian Act was first passed in 1876 and has been revised many times. It still exists today (Justice Laws, 2023). During the late nineteenth century and early twentieth century, immigrants and Indigenous peoples were targeted for overt assimilation. It was no coincidence that in 1947 the Canadian Citizenship Act combined its management of Indian Affairs, immigration, naturalization, and citizenship services under a new department, Citizenship and Immigration (MacDonald, 2014). The rights of the original peoples, their identities, and their "blood quantum" are controlled by Indian Affairs to differentiate First Nations, Métis, and Inuit and to determine who might qualify under the terms of treaty benefits. The treaties were agreements for the future of original peoples that included monetary assistance, gifts, security for health and wellness, and continuance of good living achieved prior to the arrival of the settlers in return for sharing their territories with them. However, the colonizers imposed the ways of their original lands on Indigenous peoples. Today the Canadian population lacks knowledge of how the government avoids its legal obligations to compensate Indigenous peoples in ways outlined in the treaties for the exchange of peace and land. Thus, Indigenous peoples are portrayed as enemies of the Crown rather than as sovereign benefactors of lands and resources with original rights and inheritance.

As an international student from India, Reshma dug deeper to relate stages of psychological identity development in a new land. Ethnic minority graduate students, including international graduate students, try to blend in, but elements of racism and other societal ills become obstacles as they seek inclusion in the host society (Clark et al., 2012; Everall, 2018). Snežana argues for coexistence: "We should move away from the concept of 'inclusion' because inclusion implies that some people have the power to include while others are waiting to be included. We should replace inclusion with non-hierarchical co-existence, and this goal can be achieved only by dismantling the linear and hierarchical colonial structures we currently inhabit." Efforts at decolonization can reveal this conundrum of inclusion in a society that identifies itself as multicultural. Iseke-Barnes (2008) argued that this process of decolonization can be achieved by unpacking and disrupting colonizing agendas in the university classroom; reclaiming Indigenous peoples' governance, spirituality, and ceremony; and reconnecting to land, history, and education while addressing community-based issues and needs. This process must start with individuals who understand "themselves as culturally located and affected by cultural influences that have taught them to accept biased accounts of history, misinformation, and miseducation" (Iseke-Barnes, 2008, p. 145). There is a lot of work to do in, around, and outside the classroom to achieve true decolonization and understand inclusion as a hierarchical, colonial concept.

Reshma contemplated her cross-cultural immigrant location as that of coexistence: "Each one of us carries the values, views, and identities of our ancestors. Sky Woman fell from the sky knowing that there was no going back home. She knew that her future lay here. The animals, birds, and nature came together to protect and accommodate her. She was an outsider but became one with the land. I believe that, even today, there can be a safe, comfortable space for international and immigrant students to coexist with the unfamiliar socio-cultural fabric of Canada." We unpacked the dilemmas of newcomers/settlers, discerning that the original peoples welcomed the newcomers just as the first beings welcomed the original peoples.

Esther kept our conversations in the present by arguing that the division of Indigenous and settler peoples on Turtle Island is an imperialist invention. Stanley et al. (2014) argue that immigration to Canada creates colonizers. In the same vein, Chatterjee (2019) warns that "the very process of becoming a good, successful, moral, and respectable citizen with access to the resources of the state transforms newcomers into colonialists" (para. 6). Viewing Canada through a postcolonial, liberal lens, Esther argues that the "separation of Indigenous and immigrant peoples is unnatural and constitutes a racialized and colonial state," and she advocates for integration and alliance—rather than segregation and hostility—between Indigenous peoples and settlers. The connection between Indigenous peoples' and recent settlers' stories of displacement in Canada's capitalist society centres on colonialism, resources, economics, education, and "politics of accountability for immigrant settlement on Indigenous land" (Chatterjee, 2019, p. 645). Chatterjee argues that the effects of settler colonialism on Indigenous peoples and immigrants intersect and inform each other. As of 21 June 2021, the Canadian government addressed Truth and Reconciliation Commission (TRC) Call to Action 94 with Bill C-8 to help ensure that newcomers to Canada learn more about Indigenous history and rights as indicated in the new Citizenship Oath: "I swear (or affirm) that I will be faithful and bear true allegiance to Her Majesty Queen Elizabeth the Second, Queen of Canada, Her Heirs and Successors, and that I will faithfully observe the laws of Canada, including the Constitution, which recognizes and affirms the Aboriginal and treaty rights of First Nations, Inuit and Métis Peoples, and fulfill my duties as a Canadian citizen" (Senate GRO, 2021, para. 6). The current allegiance is to King Charles the Third (Government of Canada, 2022).

Recognizing imperialist strategies that thrive on pitting disposssessed people against each other is important in the anti-racist movements of Indigenous peoples' self-determination and immigrants' civil rights in Canada. Sharing historical experiences (both oral and written) of colonization and displacement can build alliances between Indigenous peoples and newcomers, but there is concern that Indigenous peoples and newcomers demonstrate little interaction and cross-cultural understanding (Vols, 2020). Therefore, it is critical that Indigenous peoples and newcomers acknowledge the intersections of oppression for both groups, identify the dominant source of oppression, and build alliances for decolonization, healing, and wellness (Battiste et al., 2002). The future of all peoples depends on the land, and it is at risk.

Language

As a diverse group of women scholars, we speak English—the language of the colonizer—in our public interactions and within the university, but we speak our ancestral languages in our homes and ethnic communities. Language is an integral part of every culture and identity development since it defines relationships with the land. Therefore, how language is addressed within an education system determines coexisting relationships with the land.

Language contributes to Canadians' sense of pride and shapes their identities (Canadian Heritage, 2019). Canada is a bilingual country, with English and French as its official languages. Canadian leaders are encouraged to speak these two languages to reach most of the population and immigrants. MacDonald (2014, p. 66) asserts that "dominant views often hold that multiculturalism as 'unity in diversity' has successfully integrated newcomers into mainstream Canadian society." Equality presents itself through proficiency in either English or French or both. Equity would embrace the languages of the first peoples on Turtle Island.

The Canadian K–12 curriculum is written in English or French, imposing the subtleties of colonial thoughts, values, and behaviours as well as the denial of a privileged hierarchy. The Canadian education system exposes and punishes resistant students who choose to live within the ideals of their Indigenous original languages and cultures. The resistant student objects to the multicultural illusion of successfully identifying as Canadian. Posing Turtle Island's Indigenous peoples as first peoples with their own languages, cultures, and systems of governance prior to White settlement is a political agenda that juxtaposes Indigenous peoples as a threat, segregating them from Canada's social fabric and the potential allyship of immigrant Indigenous peoples from other places in the world.

Brian Francis (2021) of the Mi'kmaq Nation voiced language and culture loss of Indigenous peoples in his post on Facebook in response to the discovery of Indigenous children buried on residential school grounds in Kamloops, British Columbia: "Try to understand the generations of our ancestors who were stripped of their songs, their language, their prayers, and their spirituality. We will never get that back, but tomorrow you can return to the normalcy and beauty of being 'Canadian.'" The loss of language, however, is of no concern to those who speak French or English since either language signals the identity of being Canadian. Indigenous peoples' languages are relegated to the margins of the Canadian education system and society, an indication of racism and inequality within a country where the languages of Indigenous peoples once flourished.

Indigenous peoples' languages are a powerful tool for creating and conveying geopolitical-based knowledge. Colonial treaty makers presented documents solely in the subtleties of written English to their own advantage. The terms in the treaties, written in English, obscured the contents of bi/multilingual negotiations and denied Indigenous peoples the opportunity to contribute their own understandings of what the future of Canada should be. The Aboriginal Justice Implementation Commission (1999, para. 2) provides a deeper understanding of the vision and importance of what a treaty meant for original peoples and future generations: "They have argued for a conceptual interpretation of the treaties, one reflecting their spirit and intent, which is more in line with what the original signatories believed the agreements entailed. To Indian leaders, the treaties are a recognition of Indian sovereignty. As long as the treaties continue in existence—despite their flaws—they serve as a continuing recognition of the Indian right to autonomy and self-government." Such subtleties are found in the words as written on a blackboard in the media strategy of the 1950s to promote residential schools: *desire, wealthy, grateful.* These words were the backdrop for children well dressed in European clothing along with their smiling faces, presenting an elusive picture for the Canadian gaze (CBC, 1955, 1:19) and erasing Indigenous peoples' identities (Francis, 2011). We agreed that the English language institutionalized structural oppression in different domains of life, including religion, law, media, health care, and education.

Language also plays a large part in racism (Alim et al., 2016). Reshma found it difficult to find a suitable place in Canadian society as an outsider who speaks English with an accent. However, she realized that her life in Canada was challenging and uncomfortable but still more privileged than the lives of original peoples forced into residential schools, non-voluntary and non-compensatory manual labour, and an abusive, isolating educational experience. Racism and exclusion through the use of language must be scrutinized in the current Canadian education system to engage in truth telling and reconciliation. For students and educators who come from a settler-privileged location, "the confrontation and elimination of racism can be very challenging, because . . . [they question] the national image that they have built as Canadians" (Battiste, 2013, p. 125). This image of Canadian identity must be questioned because it validates the colonial violence toward and exploitation of Indigenous peoples and their lands and resources (Fast & Drouin-Gagné, 2019). The struggle, resistance, and guilt that truth telling might provoke cannot be an excuse to delay the responsibilities and narratives of reconciliation (Craft & Regan, 2020; Regan, 2011).

Education

For more than 150 years, Indigenous peoples suffered injustice in their education. They were victims of experimental environments of assimilation. The grand plan forced Indigenous children into residential schools and ripped them from their culturally caring, nurturing parents, families, communities, and relations. They were transported by plane, train, or other vehicle and dispersed to unfamiliar geographical locations. They faced enduring pain, defeat, shame, guilt, and most of all confusion about who they were. They were not released until they reached eighteen years of age or close to it. If kindness was afforded, then children were sent home to die when afflicted with pneumonia, tuberculosis, or other life-threatening diseases. One of Catherine's grandfathers and many of her uncles attended residential schools and came home without language, culture, or educational certification.

Catherine talked about how some non-Indigenous students in her undergraduate classes shared their feelings of guilt, shame, and anger upon learning the stories of colonization that caused intergenerational trauma for Indigenous peoples. Other students were shocked that such atrocities would occur against anyone. At this point, they considered allyship. These reactions are familiar to us as students, instructors, and authors. We encounter this dilemma among students and others learning the truths of Canada's past (Siemens & Neufeld, 2022).

The TRC Calls to Action 62–65 suggest a plan for education reform, funding, and culturally age-appropriate course content. "Reconciliation is about respect. That includes both self-respect for Aboriginal people and mutual respect among all Canadians" (TRC, 2015, p. 185). We wondered who would take responsibility for the many inequalities imposed on original peoples. For example, though clean drinking water is a right of non-Indigenous Canadians, there is a water crisis in many First Nations communities. Kirlew (as cited in Goldfinger, 2021, para. 36) argues that "Canadians need to challenge their colonial belief systems and ask themselves why it's acceptable for First Nations communities not to have access to clean, running water." Contemplating the Canadian government's resistance to providing infrastructure and clean water in Indigenous reserves should be part of classroom discussions on issues of equity, restorative social justice, and values across cultures. A resource for such contemplations might be Perry (2016).

Why did all this extreme mistreatment of another culture happen? What did educators do to address it in the past, and what is being done today? We agreed that it is a settler problem rather than an Indigenous problem. We also recognized that for newcomers "it is easier to say I am a newcomer. I have no past or part in it." We acknowledged the importance of taking on responsibility for the past so that healing can happen.

Esther noted that our understanding of social justice in Canada is "rooted in how we see our place in the world." The next step toward social justice is to acknowledge the historical claims on land and self-determination of Indigenous communities as "respectful spaces of knowing" (Lowman & Barker, 2015, p. 20) where settlers learn truths and understand Indigenous worldviews on coexistence in an ethical space. Osmond-Johnson and Turner (2020, p. 54) describe ethical space as "a new theoretical space from which to explore the practices of non-Indigenous leaders who are attempting to navigate these complexities." They acknowledge that "navigating the ethical space between Indigenous and non-Indigenous world views is indeed complex and complicated work" (p. 74).

Tanaka (2017) suggests education and indigenization as a solution for coexistence: "Our way forward invites educators towards being-becoming indigenist. . . . [T]o connect deeply with and embody soul, place, and relational accountability" (p. 210). The Two-Row Wampum Belt story conveys two solitudes, and this separation requires conversations on issues of sovereignty, self-determination, self-governance, language, education, allyship, and coexistence on the land, reminding us that, in Canada, we are all treaty people.

Canada's Identity

The inequalities between Indigenous peoples and recent settlers are rooted in colonial multiculturalism (MacDonald, 2014). It is obvious to Reshma that "the quest for Canadian identity . . . is to assimilate peoples into one diversified, multicultural bowl." Esther articulates a similar position: "I would envision [that] the first step for immigrant peoples is recognizing the falsehood of the multicultural 'salad bowl' or 'cultural mosaic' metaphors that present Canada as the mix of coexisting nations, languages, and cultures because the multicultural Canadian identity is, rather, a structure of hidden identities."Thobani (2007, p. 29) also argued that within multicultural Canada "beats the heart of a stubbornly colonial national-formation, sharing a common imaginary with other white settler societies." Similarly, Day (2000, p. 197) described Canada's policy of multiculturalism as the "creative reproduction of the colonial method of strategic assimilation."Furthermore, Thobani (2007, p. 18) claimed that a ranking of Canadian citizens creates the categories of dignified (nationals), marked for physical and cultural extinction ("Indians"), and conditionally included (immigrants, migrants, and refugees): "The racial configurations of subject formation within settler societies are thus triangulated: the national remains at the centre of the state's (stated) commitment to enhance national well being; the immigrant receives a tenuous and conditional inclusion; and the Aboriginal [Indigenous peoples of Turtle Island] continues to be marked for loss of sovereignty." MacDonald (2014, p. 82) also acknowledged this triangulated construction of Canadian identity by concluding that Indigenous peoples of Turtle Island have often been disregarded for failing to integrate as well as immigrants: "Multiculturalism elides the distinct historical, legal, and constitutional aspects of Aboriginal rights, as well as Aboriginal languages, values, governance traditions, and other aspects of Aboriginal ways of knowing and being." Acknowledging this triangulated construct of Canadian identity, we concluded that Indigenous peoples, non-Indigenous Canadians, and recent settlers in Canada are related not only to each other but also to animate and non-animate beings, reconnecting our discussions and our identities to the land.

Final Reflections

A lack of compassion for the land allows racism, inequality, and inequity to thrive. In Canada, there is little to no effort to understand the ways that language connects people to or disconnects them from the land. The ways of Indigenous peoples were not to mix and meld to become a subjugated population through treaty or adoption but to live with newcomers in friendship, peace, and respect. However, through colonial language, education, and interpretation of "power" over the land, Indigenous peoples on Turtle Island are segregated, whereas newly arrived peoples—culturally, racially, and ethnically diverse—comply with settler rule through the ceremony of becoming Canadian citizens. TRC

(2015) Call to Action 94 recently passed as Bill C-8, which requests a change in Canada's oath of citizenship to affirm newcomers' commitments to Canadian law, the Constitution, and Indigenous and treaty rights of First Nations, Inuit, and Métis peoples. The new citizenship guide incorporates a section on treaties, the Indian Act, and residential schools, including the physical and sexual abuse of residential school students (Johnson, 2021).

Indigenous peoples born on Turtle Island and peoples indigenous to other lands are two segregated populations under colonial agency that continues to control and hinder Indigenous and newcomer relationships and identities. Yet there is a way forward. Linking Indigenous peoples' knowledge, original oral stories, and languages to education systems in Canada might begin with understanding how coexistence works for the benefit of the land and the peoples on it, leading to good living, health, and peace. Such understanding germinates from the Haudenosaunee Two-Row Wampum Belt story. Early settlers, immigrants, refugees, and international students who landed on the turtle's back during the previous century can make lives for themselves and connect to this land with love, compassion, and responsibility. Canada must be transformed through language, education, and Indigenous-settler alliances "so that our children and grandchildren can live together in dignity, peace, . . . reconciliation, equity, and co-existence" (TRC, 2015, p. 8).

A true Canadian identity cannot be reconstructed without a deep understanding of the need to offer compensation—respectful recognition of Indigenous peoples' territories, lands, languages, and exchanges—as reconciliatory justice for original peoples. To entrench such recognition, Canada must abolish its colonial lens and structures. Only then can it truly become a place of compassion, freedom, and good education. On this journey of Canadian identity re/construction, we invite educators, scholars, policy makers, government officials, and the Canadian and global public to engage with the following question. How can the process of reconciliation in ethical space and Canadian identity re/construction be understood in relation to land, language, education, and the Two-Row Wampum Belt story?

References

Aboriginal Justice Implementation Commission. (1999). *The justice system and Aboriginal people volume 1—chapter 5, Aboriginal and treaty rights: Problems with the validity and text of treaties.* Manitoba Government. http://www.ajic.mb.ca/volume1/chapter5.html#17

Alim, H. S., Rickford, J. R., & Bali, A. F. (Eds.). (2016). *Raciolinguistics: How language shapes our ideas about race.* Oxford University Press.

Battiste, M. (2013). *Decolonizing education: Nourishing the learning spirit.* Purich Publishing.

Battiste, M., Bell, L., & Findlay, L. M. (2002). Decolonizing education in Canadian universities: An interdisciplinary, international, Indigenous research project. *Canadian Journal of Native Education, 26*(2), 82–95. https://www.proquest.com/docview/230305394

Baudrillard, J. (1988). *Jean Baudrillard: Selected writings* (M. Poster, Ed.). Stanford University Press.

Braga, J. (2021, 12 July). *Human rights, equity and inclusion: Reflections from National Indigenous History Month at Waterloo.* University of Waterloo. https://uwaterloo.ca/indigenous/news/reflections-national-indigenous-history-month-waterloo

Butler, J. (1990). *Gender trouble: Feminism and the subversion of identity.* Routledge.

Canadian Heritage. (2019, 26 November). *Statistics on official languages in Canada.* Government of Canada. https://www.canada.ca/en/canadian-heritage/services/official-languages-bilingualism/publications/statistics.html

CBC. (1955). CBC-TV visits a residential school in 1955: Broadcast claimed residential school offered 'chance at a new future' for Indigenous children. *CBC.* https://www.cbc.ca/archives/cbc-tv-visits-a-residential-school-in-1955-1.4667021

Chatterjee, S. (2019). Immigration, anti-racism, and Indigenous self-determination: Towards a comprehensive analysis of the contemporary settler colonial. *Social Identities, 25*(5), 644–661. https://doi.org/10.1080/13504630.2018.1473154

Clark, C. R., Mercer, S. H., Zeigler-Hill, V., & Dufrene, B. A. (2012). Barriers to the success of ethnic minority students in school psychology graduate programs. *School Psychology Review, 41*(2), 176–192. https://doi.org/10.1080/02796015.2012.12087519

Clarke, G. E. (2021, 10 July). July 10: "Let us sideline both white supremacy and the settler superiority complex by putting indigeneity at the centre of a revised Constitution." What does reconciliation look like? Plus other letters to the editor. *The Globe and Mail.* https://www.theglobeandmail.com/opinion/letters/article-july-10-let-us-sideline-both-white-supremacy-and-the-settler/

Craft, A., & Regan, P. (2020). *Pathways of reconciliation: Indigenous and settler approaches to implementing the TRC's Calls to Action.* University of Manitoba Press.

Crown-Indigenous Relations and Northern Relations. (2022). *Specific Claims Branch national status report on specific claims.* Government of Canada. https://services.aadnc-aandc.gc.ca/SCBRI_E/Main/ReportingCentre/External/externalreporting.aspx

Day, R. J. F. (2000). *Multiculturalism and the history of Canadian diversity.* University of Toronto Press.

Everall, R. (2018). *Graduate student mental health and wellness report.* University of Alberta Faculty of Graduate Studies and Research. https://www.ualberta.ca/graduate-studies/media-library/about/faculty-and-staff/resources-for-supervisors-and-graduate-coordinators/20181128_graduate-student-mental-health-wellness-report.pdf

Fast, E., & Drouin-Gagné, M-È. (2019). We need to get better at this! Pedagogies for truth telling about colonial violence. *International Journal of Child, Youth and Family Studies, 10*(1), 95–118. https://doi.org/10.18357/ijcyfs101201918808

Francis, B. (2021, 1 June). Grassroots NB [Facebook page]. Facebook. https://www.facebook.com/grassrootsnb/posts/332467758585243

Francis, D. (2011). *The imaginary Indian: The image of the Indian in Canadian culture.* Arsenal Pulp Press.

Freire, P. (1968). *Pedagogy of the oppressed.* Bloomsbury Academic.

Gilmore, R. (2021, 27 October). Ottawa should not appeal tribunal order to pay Indigenous kids: Advocates. *Global News.* https://globalnews.ca/news/8329247/indigenous-children-court-appeal-compensation-canada/

Goldfinger, D. (2021, 30 September). "An ongoing symbol of colonization": How bad water affects First Nations' health. *Global News.* https://globalnews.ca/news/8199988/first-nations-water-crisis-health-effects/

Google Art and Culture. (n.d.). *Inua: The soul. Human, animal and spirit in Inuit culture.* https://artsandculture.google.com/usergallery/ZQLSgp4T9xozIw

Government of British Columbia. (n.d.). Whulk. *BC Geographical Names.* https://apps.gov.bc.ca/pub/bcgnws/names/54929.html

Government of Canada. (2022, 20 September). *Discover Canada: The Oath of Citizenship.* https://www.canada.ca/en/immigration-refugees-citizenship/corporate/publications-manuals/discover-canada/read-online/oath-citizenship.html

Hanson, E., Gamez, D., & Manuel, A. (2020, September). *The residential school system.* Indigenous Foundations: First Nations and Indigenous Studies University of British Columbia. https://indigenousfoundations.arts.ubc.ca/residential-school-system-2020/

Hill, R., & Coleman, D. (2019). The Two Row Wampum–Covenant Chain tradition as a guide for Indigenous-university research partnerships. *Cultural Studies, Critical Methodologies, 19*(5), 339–359. https://doi.org/10.1177/1532708618809138

Irwin, R. (2018, 25 October). Indian Agents in Canada. *The Canadian encyclopedia.* https://www.thecanadianencyclopedia.ca/en/article/indian-agents-in-canada

Iseke-Barnes, J. M. (2008). Pedagogies for decolonizing. *Canadian Journal of Native Education, 31*(1), 123–148. https://www.proquest.com/docview/230303573

Johnson, R. (2021, 29 June). Citizenship oath sworn by new Canadians now recognizes Indigenous rights. *CBC.* https://www.cbc.ca/news/indigenous/new-citizenship-oath-ndigenous-rights-1.6080274

Justice Laws. (2023, 11 January). Indian Act (R.S.C., 1985, c. I-5). https://laws-lois.justice.gc.ca/eng/acts/i-5/

KAIROS Canada. (2020). *Blanket exercise.* https://www.kairosblanketexercise.org/programs/

Kennedy, D. (2022, 27 May). "Biggest fake news story in Canada": Kamloops mass grave debunked by academics. *New York Post*. https://nypost.com/2022/05/27/kamloops-mass-grave-debunked-biggest-fake-news-in-canada/

Kimmerer, R. W. (2013). *Braiding sweetgrass: Indigenous wisdom, scientific knowledge and the teachings of plants*. Milkweed Editions.

Latimer, A. (2020). Encoded knowledge in oral traditions: Skwxwú7mesh transformer sites and their relationship with landscape perception and use [Unpublished master's thesis]. Simon Fraser University. https://summit.sfu.ca/item/20812

Liu, W., & Rathbone, A. (2021). The complexity of international student identity. *Journal of Belonging, Identity, Language, and Diversity (J-BILD), 5*(2), 42–58. https://bild-lid.a.ca/journal/volume-5_2-2021/j-bild_5-2_liu_rathbone/

Longboat, C. (2008a). Ethical space in the intellectual terrain: A cultural perspective. *Theme Issue—Canadian Journal of Native Education, 31*(1), 72–83. https://www.proquest.com/docview/230303160

Longboat, C. (2008b). Ethical space in a secondary school: A case study [Unpublished master's thesis]. Brock University. Brock University Digital Repository. http://hdl.handle.net/10464/1522

Loomba, A. (2015). *Colonialism/postcolonialism*. Routledge.

Lowman, E., & Barker, A. (2015). *Settler identity and colonialism in 21st century Canada*. Fernwood Publishing.

MacDonald, D. B. (2014). Aboriginal peoples and multiculturalism reform in Canada: Prospects for a new bi-national society. *Canadian Journal of Sociology, 39*(1), 65–86.

Onondaga Historical Association. (n.d.). *The creation story* [Video]. YouTube. https://www.youtube.com/watch?v=WSzDM7Jmg94man

Osmond-Johnson, P., & Turner, P. (2020). Navigating the "ethical space" of truth and reconciliation: Non-Indigenous school principals in Saskatchewan. *Curriculum Inquiry, 50*(1), 54–77. https://doi.org/10.1080/03626784.2020.1715205

Parliament of Canada, House of Commons. (2018, February, 42nd Parliament, 1st Session). *INAN Committee report no. 12—Indigenous land rights: Towards respect and implementation: Report of the Standing Committee on Indigenous and Northern Affairs*. https://www.ourcommons.ca/DocumentViewer/en/42-1/INAN/report-12/page-5

Perry, A. (2016). *Aqueduct: Colonialism, resources, and the histories we remember*. ARP Books.

Poole, R. (1972). *Towards deep subjectivities*. Allen Lane/Penguin.

Ratković, S. (2014). Teachers without borders: Exploring experiences, transitions, and identities of refugee women teachers from Yugoslavia [Unpublished doctoral dissertation]. Brock University. Brock University Digital Repository. http://hdl.handle.net/10464/5243

Ratković, S., & Winters, K-L. (Directors), with Heryka, M., Dénommé-Welch, S., Longboat, C., Spratt, B., Vinod, S., Rana, B., Ahmed, N., Yang, S., Varghese, A., Scott-England, S., Sault, V., Ahmed, A., Ahmed, S., Kitchings, S., Taylor, M., Magowan, C., Di Cesare, D. M., & Ratković, I. (2018). *InTercultural WORKS* [Video]. YouTube. https://www.youtube.com/watch?v=aUM3sHdBzr8

Regan, P. (2011). *Unsettling the settler within: Indian residential schools, truth telling and reconciliation in Canada.* UBC Press.

Senate GRO. (2021, 21 June). Indigenous rights now included in Canada's citizenship oath: Bill C-8 has received royal assent. *News.* https://senate-gro.ca/news/c8-citizenship-oath-indigenous/

Siemens, J., & Neufeld, K. H. S. (2022). Disruptive knowledge in education for reconciliation: The effects of Indigenous course requirements on non-Indigenous students' attitudes. *Canadian Journal of Education, 45*(2), 375–399. https://doi.org/10.53967/cje-rce.v45i2.4867

Stanley, A., Arat-Koç, S., Bertram, L. K., & King, H. (2014, 18 June). Intervention—"Addressing the Indigenous-immigration 'parallax gap.'" *Antipode Online.* https://antipodeonline.org/2014/06/18/addressing-the-indigenous-immigration-parallax-gap/

St. Pierre, E. A. (1997a). Circling the text: Nomadic writing practices. *Qualitative Inquiry, 3*(4), 403–417. https://doi.org/10.1177/107780049700300403

St. Pierre, E. A. (1997b). Nomadic inquiry in the smooth spaces of the field: A preface. *International Journal of Qualitative Studies in Education, 10*(3), 365–383. https://doi.org/10.1080/095183997237179

Tanaka, M. T. D. (2017). *Learning and teaching together: Weaving Indigenous ways of knowing into education.* UBC Press.

Thobani, S. (2007). *Exalted subjects: Studies in the making of race and nation in Canada.* University of Toronto Press.

Truth and Reconciliation Commission of Canada (TRC). (2015). *Final report of the Truth and Reconciliation Commission of Canada—Volume one: Summary, honoring the truth, reconciling for the future.* James Lorimer & Company.

Vols, A. (2020). The call for critical multiculturalism: Indigenous and newcomer relationships in the context of the Canadian settler state. *University of Saskatchewan Undergraduate Research Journal, 6*(3), 1–10. https://doi.org/10.32396/usurj.v6i3.469

Vowel, C. (2016). *Indigenous writes: A guide to First Nations, Métis, and Inuit issues in Canada.* HighWater Press.

Wallace, P. A. W. (1946). *White roots of peace: The Iroquois book of life.* Clear Light Publishers.

Williams, P. (2018). *The Great Law of Peace—Kayanerenkó:wa.* University of Manitoba Press.

Wolfchild, S. P. (Director), & Newcombe S. T. (Co-Producer). (2015). *The doctrine of discovery: Unmasking the domination code* [Video]. 38 Plus 2 Productions. https://doctrineofdiscovery.org/the-doctrine-of-discovery-unmasking-the-domination-code/

11

"Que Soy Yo?":
Identity and Belonging among Central Americans in Canada

VERONICA ESCOBAR OLIVO

Central American migration to Canada dates back to the 1980s. Many Central Americans migrated with young children or have had children since settling. Drawing from twenty individual interviews and eight photovoice projects with first-and-a-half-generation and second-generation Central Americans in the Greater Toronto Area (GTA), I explore in this chapter how complex migration histories and processes and encounters of racialization shape the identities and feelings of belonging of Central Americans growing up in Canada. An abundant literature focuses on refugees' settlement experiences and those of children of immigrants (Ansion & Merali, 2018; Carranza, 2007, 2012; Creese, 2019; Riaño-Alcalá, 2008), but less explored are the impacts of migration and settlement on the children of refugees. In the case of first-and-a-half-generation and second-generation Central American Canadians, the combination of complex migration history, racism, and ongoing practices of othering have resulted in complex identity formation and belonging. Central American Canadians are constantly negotiating where—and if—they belong.

Central Americans in Canada

Latin Americans in Canada are a relatively small and new community, though in recent years migration from this region has steadily increased, contributing markedly to the foreign-born population of Canada. From

2005 to 2014, Latin Americans accounted for 10 percent of all newcomers each year (Ansion & Merali, 2018). Latin Americans or Latino/a/x comprise a diverse group with varied national, class, racial, cultural, political, regional, and religious attributes (Veronis, 2010). Although Latin Americans are frequently considered a single, monolithic group in the Canadian context, there are meaningful differences among those identified as Latin American, especially in terms of their reasons for migration, periods of migration, and settlement experiences in Canada. According to the 2021 census, the largest group of Latin Americans in Canada resides in Ontario (42.9 percent) (Statistics Canada, 2022).

Although migration from Latin America remains relatively consistent, migration from the Central American region dates mainly to the mid-1980s and early 1990s (Carranza, 2007; Poteet & Simmons, 2014; Simmons, 1993). The Central American region is made up of the countries El Salvador, Guatemala, Honduras, Nicaragua, and Costa Rica. According to Simmons (1993), migration from Central America to Canada was virtually non-existent until 1979, when, following civil unrest in Guatemala, El Salvador, and Nicaragua, migration began in earnest. Between 1980 and 2000, an estimated 90,000 Central Americans sought refuge in Canada, settling in major metropolitan areas such as Montreal, Vancouver, and Toronto (García, 2006; Poteet & Simmons, 2014). The majority of Central Americans living in Canada have come from El Salvador and Guatemala (Poteet & Simmons, 2016).

Literature specific to the Central American community in Canada is limited. Following the initial settlement of Central Americans in the 1990s, most studies focused on incoming refugees and their ability to "integrate" given the circumstances of their arrival (Pottie et al., 2005). Poteet and Simmons (2014) discuss the difficulties faced by early groups of Central Americans who arrived in Canada, noting the traumatic circumstances of departure and the decline of economic opportunities during the period of migration. Most Central Americans settled in multi-ethnic residential areas that offered affordable housing, where average incomes are low and new immigrants are concentrated (Poteet & Simmons, 2014). However, because of low numbers, Latin Americans in general, and Central Americans specifically, have not successfully formed ethnic enclaves popular with other ethnic groups (Poteet & Simmons, 2014; Veronis, 2007).

Central American Youth: Growing Up in Canada and Belonging

Prior to the arrival of Central Americans, in 1971, Canada became the first country in the world to adopt an official policy of multiculturalism (Ali, 2008). The Canadian Multiculturalism Act (1985) recognizes cultural pluralism as the essence of Canadian identity. However, scholars have pointed out that the formalization of multiculturalism in law has given way to the normalization of colour-blind logic (Galabuzi, 2011). Rather than eliminating racial disparities, the policy functions to mask the reality that Whiteness remains the cultural norm and that Canadian society unavoidably continues to reflect White culture, norms, and values (Akuoko-Barfi et al., 2021). Discourses of multiculturalism undermine claims of racism by veiling the reality that Whiteness remains the benchmark and that other cultures, particularly of racialized and ethnicized groups, are perceived as "different." The obscurity of discrimination reflects the deep entrenchment and normalization of othering practices and contributes to the belief that racism does not exist in Canada (Nichols, 2019). In many ways, the pervading narrative of multiculturalism in Canada works to decentre and dismiss the experiences of racialized youth.

For such youth, struggling to root themselves in their Canadian identity stems from these continuous othering practices. Discourses about what constitutes the other are central to defining who belongs in a given space (Creese, 2019; Parada et al., 2021). Signs of unbelonging can include language, accent, age, gender, clothing, religion, and skin colour; those perceived as possessing the wrong attributes are subject to discourses and practices of othering (Creese, 2019; Escobar Olivo et al., 2022; Parada et al., 2021). Other studies (Ali, 2008; Creese, 2019) have found that racialized youth are presumed to be immigrants, even if born in Canada, and are thus perceived as not belonging. Youth are subject to standardized mechanisms of othering and discourses surrounding their belonging in Canada (James, 2019; Parada et al., 2021). Socially, racialized youth are constantly rejected and prohibited from the right to claim a Canadian identity. Questions such as "Where are you from?" and similar micro-aggressions function to remind youth that they are perceived as not belonging (Ali, 2008; Creese, 2019; Escobar Olivo et al., 2022). In her study of the identity-building process of second-generation African Canadian youth, Creese (2019) found that youth who perceive higher levels of racism are more likely to reject a Canadian identity. Tairo (2013) describes the phenomenon of Latin American youth living in a state of in-betweenness as they struggle to manoeuvre through both Latin American and Canadian cultures. In-betweenness leaves them feeling insecure and inadequate and leads overall to difficult experiences of fitting in (Tairo, 2013).

Various studies have explored the experiences of children of immigrants and belonging. Simmons and Plaza (2006), for example, explored the "marginal" position of those either born to Caribbean parents or born in the Caribbean but schooled in Canada. They argued that youth in the Caribbean form segmented identities in which they attempt to navigate two cultures by alternating between Canadian and Caribbean cultural values. Similarly, Wilkinson (2018) found that racialized youth who experience processes of othering and must balance competing cultural values develop a sense of uncertainty and placelessness. Uncertainty arises from the inability to identify entirely with a single culture, be it their mainstream Canadian culture or their heritage culture (Woodgate & Busolo, 2021).

Studies focused on Central American youth specifically have explored themes like the process of acculturation of Central American families, focusing primarily on the generational differences between parents and their children (Carranza, 2007, 2012). Findings from a study by Carranza (2007) indicate that Central American daughters must learn to navigate two cultures simultaneously, influenced by their mothers' culture and the broader Canadian culture. Participants in the study struggled to make sense of the sometimes contradictory values presented between cultures (Carranza, 2007). Similarly, in their study with Central American male youth, Poteet and Simmons (2016) found that they struggled to integrate into and develop strong ties to the larger Canadian culture. Both participants who were born in Canada and those who had migrated at a young age were deeply affected by the circumstances of their families' migration to Canada, which created barriers to their settlement in Canada.

Methodology

The present study of Central American youth in the GTA used a qualitative approach involving narrative interviews and photovoice. The interviews enable participants to recount their narratives so that, though the researcher attempts to recount them, the participants remain active in terms of how they wish to represent themselves (Menard-Warwick, 2011). Similar to narrative design, photovoice makes participants who have been traditionally represented as silent subjects active participants who share their visions and participate actively in their social worlds (Kia-Keating et al., 2017). Photovoice as a data collection method asks participants to use pictures and written narratives to reflect on their surroundings, showing the researcher the world through their eyes (Castleden et al., 2016).

The present study explored how migration histories and racialization processes shape the identities and feelings of belonging of Central Americans growing up in Canada. The findings of this study were collected in two phases. Twenty first-and-a-half-generation and second-generation Central Americans (aged twenty to forty-five) living in Toronto participated in semi-structured interviews in the first phase. Eligibility requirements in the first stage included participants older than sixteen who had either been born in a Central American country and migrated to Canada with their parents or been born and raised in Canada but whose parents had migrated from Central America. In-depth, semi-structured interviews were conducted in this phase. Participants were asked open-ended questions to allow for narrative construction. This method allowed them to claim identities for themselves (Menard-Warwick, 2011). Questions centred on participants' experiences growing up and living in the GTA; their experiences of various elements of day-to-day life; and their understandings of community, belonging, and identity. Each interview ranged from one hour to two hours. Interviews were conducted in either English or Spanish depending on participant preference. The interviews were then transcribed and analyzed for general themes regarding place making, identity, and belonging. In total, twenty-one participants were interviewed. The analysis presented in this chapter is based upon a sample of twenty participants. One participant's narrative has been excluded because the participant migrated to Canada on their own as a teenager. Of the twenty participants in the sample, eight self-identified as male, and twelve self-identified as female.

The first interviews were analyzed and followed by photovoice workshops designed for Central American youth (sixteen to twenty-five). Eight second-generation Salvadoran youth participated and created their photovoice projects centred on themes of exclusion and belonging. In the second stage, to engage with Central American youth in a relevant way that centred their voices, photovoice workshops were organized. Participants were asked to explore the themes of belonging, identity, and community through photographs, taking pictures of what they thought represented the concepts in their lives and accompanying each picture with a personal narrative. The second stage was intended to explore the experiences of participants in the first stage who identified as second generation. Eight youth between the ages of sixteen and twenty-five participated in this stage; three youth self-identified as male, and five youth self-identified as female.

Prospective participants were recruited through purposive and snowball sampling methods. One of the team members, a community worker, contacted either first-and-a-half-generation or second-generation Central Americans living in Canada, and members of the research team—the majority of whom were part of the Central American community—reached out to existing contacts who fit the criteria. Participants were also asked to share the study with eligible contacts in their networks. The twenty participants from the interview stage and the eight participants from the photovoice stage have been given pseudonyms.

Findings

This section is organized around four identified themes. The four themes are impact of migratory history, (lack of) belonging in Canada, competing cultures, and making sense of identity.

Impact of Migratory History

The context of migration and seeking refuge in Canada during the civil war was a recurring theme in the interviews and photovoice projects. The majority of the participants had family members who had migrated because of civil unrest. For some, the impact of being descended from parents who had endured violence was a veil of silence in their families. Carmen noted that her family rarely discussed the reason for migrating, and though she had many questions her father simply would not speak about his past. She said that "my dad, he never talked to me personally about why he came, but my mom told me that it was because of the war. So there isn't a lot of detail—it isn't something that we—it isn't something that we talk about much in my family. . . . My dad is very quiet; he doesn't talk much about the past." Sandra described how the unwillingness to discuss the migration trauma affected her ability to form a complete sense of self. She did not ask questions out of respect for her family's wishes, but the silence resulted in endless questions about her own identity: "But I felt that they didn't really want to talk about it, especially [because] a lot of family members that were killed in the war. So you know I try not to ask many questions, but I really wanted to know. What's my background, what was the reason, why are you Salvadoran, and why am I Mexican? What kind of mess happened in there, right?"

Most participants were aware that migratory trauma affected their parents' mental health, which in turn affected how they were raised. The strained level of communication rendered it difficult for the participants to connect to their parents and, by extension, their cultures. Debra indicated how later in life migration negatively affected her parents' mental health and ability to connect to her and her siblings: "You know that we never spoke about mental health. Like now that I am an adult now, I see that what we went through was a mental health issue. Again, coming from—you leave your country, and you leave your family, and try to raise one on your own, and you have no support system. I understand now why they did the things that they did."

Others had vague ideas why their parents had opted to flee. Alex described the general sense of fear that she carried as a child; although at the time she did not fully comprehend what was happening with the civil war, she remained aware that death was a constant possibility. This deeply increased her anxiety:

> We came directly to Toronto. To Scarborough. And at that age I just remember feeling very confused. It could be because we took up and left from completely different places and because we left my great-grandmother behind, with whom I had been since I was born. My mom says that I kept on saying "She died right? She died?" Because I thought that is what happened; we just didn't see her anymore. So it was just a lot of confusion. I remember starting, I am not sure if it was preschool or daycare, but I didn't want to be separated from my parents. I had this constant fear that I was going to be left. And that lasted a couple of years until I got into grade school.

(Lack of) Belonging in Canada

For many of the participants, knowledge of the difficult circumstances that their families had left and the difficult experiences of migration affected their sense of belonging. When asked if she felt as if she belonged in Canada, Diana answered that she never felt as if she did; growing up surrounded by immigrants, she noted that all of them felt the same way: "Growing up, I knew why we were here, I knew why my parents came, so it was hard in that there were hard experiences, seeing my parents struggle so much, seeing the people I knew struggle so much, and having these issues with the migration process and all that came with [it]. . . . I wouldn't say [that I felt as if I belonged] in Canada, growing up with a lot of immigrants you knew that you didn't fully belong here, but you also knew that there were people who also didn't belong here."

The participants identified many discriminatory or othering practices encountered during their experiences growing up in Canada. For some, discrimination began as early as school age. In schools, participants encountered micro-aggressions from authority figures who instilled in them a sense of unbelonging. Sam described situations in which she felt as if she was being singled out in the classroom, such as when all the students spoke in their cultural languages. As Spanish speakers, she and her friends were constantly getting into trouble: "When I was in high school, I would also have another Spanish-speaking friend, we would speak Spanish, and then we would get into trouble for speaking Spanish, and then other people would be like talking in their languages, and they would never get in trouble, and I would be like, what?"

Other participants shared similar experiences. Emily described similar micro-aggressions during her schooling. She felt actively excluded, so much so that she came to hate school since she received different treatment based upon her background: "My teachers, definitely their favourites were *los blanquitos*, you know what I mean, whenever there were arguments between me and my friends, and to be honest with you they were predominantly Italian and Portuguese. When I used to have arguments with them, it used to be me who would get into trouble. And me who was in the corner and me who was . . . separated from the group. I was very excluded. And I remember crying, and I hated school."

Outside education, youth also described experiencing discrimination from other state actors, including the police. Mark described generally feeling uneasy around the police. He'd had a handful of harmful run-ins with the police from a young age. Mark thought that police officers treated him differently because of his ethnicity, and he felt as if he were constantly being targeted. The negative perceptions and stereotypes of the Latin American community created interactions of hostility: "So I was this little kid fighting with authority, and I felt the way they handled me was not right, and it might have been different for someone like a Canadian. And that situation just opened my eyes of like, you know, how, a Latino, you're always a target."

Gloria explained that stereotypes surrounding the Salvadoran community were present in Toronto. Often, when sharing that she was Salvadoran, the automatic connection made was related to gang activity. When asked what she would like to change about the experiences of Central Americans living in Toronto, she shared that she would like to get rid of stereotypes that made her feel othered and misunderstood: "I'd like to change the stigma, it's kind of hard especially like Salvadorans, a lot of what you hear especially when I say that I am Salvadoran, is some reference to MS-13, or Salvatruchas,[1] or some ridiculous reference, it's so automatic, and that is all that is really seen."

For Linda, the complete understanding of feeling othered occurred in university. It was not that she experienced it more or less as a grown-up but that she began to understand that she was perceived as different in Canadian society. The treatment that she experienced as the "norm" growing up was not the standard that others experienced, and she realized that she had internalized and normalized othering practices: "I think in university you start seeing [or] … understand[ing] more of those pieces and how you are perceived in society as an immigrant, as a person of colour, as a woman, and adding all those intersectionalities. I think it makes you realize a lot of the things that you probably didn't when you were growing up because you thought that it was the norm."

Competing Cultures

As a result of the othering and discriminatory practices encountered by first-and-a-half-generation and second-generation Central Americans in Canada, participants often described the complex nature of attempting to identify as belonging in the country. Carmen described feeling rejected by Canadian society since people often perceived her as not belonging and made her feel othered through questions such as "Where are you from?" At the same time, she felt rejected by her Salvadoran culture because she had been born and raised in Canada, leading to an identity crisis: "I'm not Canadian because people are constantly sending me somewhere else, and I'm not Salvadoran because I wasn't born there; I wasn't raised there. I'm familiar with the culture, but it isn't mine. So it's difficult for me to understand that. What am I? Am I Canadian? Am I Salvadoran?"

Similarly, in his photovoice project, Simon expressed that balancing two heritages was a struggle for himself and others because of the processes of ousting in school and society: "All my life I'd considered myself half Salvadoran and Canadian. I could never abandon one or the other, yet in some cases people find it a struggle with both. They feel ousted by this sort of mixed heritage, be it in school or in society. I myself have come across said situation."

For another participant, growing up in Canada as a racialized person meant always being aware of her double identity. The impact of growing up Central American in Canada meant that Joanna was constantly aware of and surrounded by stories of racism and realities such as deportation: "I was raised—unfortunately—watching families get separated through deportation. I was raised watching individuals struggle to assimilate in a new country. See, I was born with a double identity. I was raised aware of race relations."

Making Sense of Identity

Younger participants (ages sixteen to twenty-six) shared the processes of negotiation that they undertook to understand their identities. The youth participants in the photovoice projects described a process of gradually embracing the duality of their identities by accepting their differences and developing new, hybrid identities. In his photovoice project, Diego featured a tattoo that he had designed as a reminder not to forget his roots: "This design [has] ... various symbols that I associate with Latin America, intertwined with some abstract/geometric artistry, and will be placed prominently on my arm. For me, this tattoo is my way to remember where I come from no matter where I go, to remember who I am and who I am proud to be."

Like Diego, all participants noted that they were proud of their heritage despite the difficulties growing up as Central Americans in

Canada. Melanie, for example, reflected that, through the migration history, parental trauma, and system biases that she faced growing up Salvadoran in Canada, she was proud of her heritage: "I am proud to be Salvadoran regardless of all the systemic problems I had to face growing up in Canada. I am not ashamed to be who I am today. . . . If I am alive today, [it] is because I want to embrace my Salvadoran community, and I want them to know that we have so much to contribute to our Canadian society."

When asked what she wanted other Central Americans growing up in Canada to know, Carmen urged them to know that they did not have to choose: "[I want others to know] that they don't have to define themselves in just one way. Because it would freak me out a lot, because I was like 'Am I from here, or am I from there?' But it isn't necessary to put labels on it and define yourself just one way." After having grown up worried about how to identify and feeling othered in Canada, Carmen learned that identity is fluid and that the ability to take the best of both worlds is a benefit.

Discussion

The testimonies reveal how first-and-a-half generation and second-generation Central Americans have struggled to establish a sense of belonging in Canada. Caught between two cultures, the participants described the hardships that come from addressing an identity rooted in historical trauma, coupled with the ongoing discrimination that they encounter in Canadian society.

Many of the participants interviewed expressed a lack of understanding of their cultural roots. The violent and abrupt uprooting of their families from Central America often led to a veil of silence in families who attempted to re-establish themselves in the new country. For parents who had fled because of violence and insecurity, there persisted a sense of suddenness rooted in their abrupt departures. Suddenly leaving a country profoundly affects the sensory experiences of a refugee who attempts to navigate the present and make sense of the past (Parada, 2012; Riaño-Alcalá, 2008). Parada (2012) discusses the reality of his existence as a Salvadoran refugee, describing a sense of negotiation and mistrust that results from his dichotomous existence. No longer completely Salvadoran but encountering forms of oppression in Canada, some refugees feel that they are unable to live fully accepted in either context or community (Parada, 2012). This process and its impacts extend beyond refugee parents who make the initial decision to migrate, with significant effects for their children (Escobar Olivo et al., 2023). Participants echoed similar impacts as they attempted to navigate and understand their experiences growing up in Canada and their roots in Central America. Despite either being born or experiencing the majority of their childhoods in Canada, participants described ongoing feelings of displacement that they inherited from their parents.

In her study of relationship building between Salvadoran mothers and daughters, Carranza (2007) found that the mothers employ strategies of *no pensar*, in which they put negative experiences out of their minds and make conscious choices to carry on as if their traumatic experiences had never happened. A similar phenomenon occurred for several participants. For those raised with *no pensar*, the veil of silence presented them with questions regarding their identities as they attempted to understand their family dynamics without any concrete explanation of who they were and how it affected them. Most of the participants interviewed knew the reasons for their parents' initial migrations; however, the degree to which the context was spoken about varied. Regardless of the level of openness in families, participants noted that the reasons for their parents' migrations negatively affected their ability to establish a strong sense of belonging. Although *no pensar* as a strategy of survival aided parents in carrying on, it prevented their children from fully understanding who they were and how their families' migrations affected them.

No pensar was not the case for all participants; for some, the context in which their parents had chosen to leave had a direct impact on their childhood. Similar to the findings of Carranza (2007) and Poteet and Simmons (2016), the study in the GTA found that Central American youth continue to be affected by their families' migration histories. The difficult circumstances of migration and the ongoing difficulties of settlement shaped the experiences of most participants. Many discussed how seeing their family members struggle to adapt following experiences of violence and discrimination affected their own perceptions of belonging. Notably, when parents faced discrimination based upon language and accent, participants perceived this as an affront to their own belonging. As one participant observed, being in a community surrounded by people who "did not belong" made her feel as if she too did not belong.

The questions of who they were or the memories of trauma were exacerbated by their ongoing experiences of discrimination in Canada. Most of the participants described at least one instance of discrimination that made them feel as if they did not belong in Canada. Often they cited micro-aggressions that caused them to question their place in Canada, whether or not they had been born in the country. Participants also described encountering practices of othering in different realms of their daily lives, including schooling.

The findings indicate that key institutions such as schools do not foster environments in which Central Americans feel safe or as if they belong. As Tairo (2013) posits, Latin American youth are constantly under scrutiny in educational institutions that influence how they perform being good students and Latin Americans. Despite the presentation of multiculturalism, Whiteness remains embedded in Canadian educational institutions and othering practices by educators and peers that serve to remind first-and-a-half-generation and second-generation Central Americans that they do not belong. Participants consistently encountered messaging that they were not wholly accepted, and most shared encounters of discrimination within educational institutions. The possibility that Central Americans might encounter discrimination in their everyday lives created a general sense of unbelonging, negatively affecting their ability to feel Canadian.

Experiencing two cultures at once further affected the identity building of Central Americans. Individuals grew up with Central American cultural practices, norms, and values in their homes but encountered contradictory counterparts in school, media, and broader Canadian society (Carranza, 2015; Escobar Olivo et al., 2023). When navigating Latin American identity in Canada, youth are often forced to choose between the pervasive notion of what constitutes a Canadian and the competing Latin American identity presented at home or within the family (Tairo, 2013). Participants indicated a sense of being positioned between the two, without being fully embraced by either, resulting in a sense of uncertainty in their Central American and Canadian identities. Some participants indicated an identity crisis as they tried to answer the question "Que soy yo?" (What am I?).

Conclusion

The interviews and photovoice projects revealed that first-and-a-half-generation and second-generation Central Americans struggle to develop a strong sense of belonging in Canada. Through ongoing discriminatory practices and micro-aggressions, Central American Canadians are constantly reminded that they are perceived as others in Canadian society. Pervasive narratives of multiculturalism veil ongoing experiences of racism, as Central American Canadians continuously encounter discourses rooted in Whiteness, rendering them hesitant to claim belonging in Canada. Their families' sudden displacement from Central America rendered it difficult to identify completely with the culture there. As a result, participants indicated feeling as if they belonged on the periphery of each culture.

Yet, as some of the photovoice projects indicate, newer generations of Central Americans in Canada are beginning to redefine their identities. We see from their projects how Central American youth have begun to reclaim the right to identify however they see fit. Some participants indicated that they went through a process of negotiation with themselves to accept a dual identity. Younger participants no longer felt as if they had to be either/or; instead, they understood their identities as fluid and rooted within themselves. These narratives were no longer rooted in acceptance by Canadian society; the participants alone defined where they belonged.

Acknowledgements

I want to acknowledge the work and support of my team, Morgan Poteet, Luis Carrillos, Giovanni Carranza, and Juan Carlos Jimenez. I am grateful to Marta Olivo, Henry Parada, Ana Leticia Ibarra Letona, and Marsha Rampersaud. I also wish to thank all the participants who shared their time and stories with us. This project was funded by the Social Sciences and Humanities Research Council of Canada (892-2018-0064 and 892-2019-1084), the Hispanic Development Council, and Mount Allison University.

References

Akuoko-Barfi, C., McDermott, T., Parada, H., & Edwards, T. (2021). "We were in white homes as black children": Caribbean youth's stories of out-of-home care in Ontario, Canada. *Journal of Progressive Human Services, 32*(3), 212–242. https://doi.org/10.1080/10428232.2021.1931649

Ali, M. A. (2008). Second-generation youth's belief in the myth of Canadian multiculturalism. *Canadian Ethnic Studies, 40*(2), 89–107. https://doi.org/10.1353/ces.2010.0017

Ansion, M., & Merali, N. (2018). Latino immigrant parents' experiences raising young children in the absence of extended family networks in Canada: Implications for counselling. *Counselling Psychology Quarterly, 31*(4), 408–427. https://doi.org/10.108 0/09515070.2017.1324760

Carranza, M. E. (2007). Building resilience and resistance against racism and discrimination among Salvadorian female youth in Canada. *Child and Family Social Work, 12*(4), 390–398. https://doi.org/10.1111/j.1365-2206.2007.00492.x

Carranza, M. E. (2012). Salvadorian ethnic pride: A bridge for reducing mother-daughter conflict due to acculturation into Canadian society. *Canadian Social Work Review, 29*(1), 61–85. http://www.jstor.org/stable/43486269

Carranza, M. E. (2015). Protesting against mothers' surveillance: Salvadorian mothers and their daughters negotiating adolescence in a foreign context. *Journal of Family Social Work, 18*(2), 106–122. https://doi.org/10.1080/10522158.2015.1005784

Castleden, H., Sloan Morgan, V., & Franks, A. (2016). Not another interview! Using photovoice and digital stories as props in participatory health geography research. In N. E. Fenton & J. Baxter (Eds.), *Practicing qualitative research in human geography* (pp. 167–189). Routledge.

Creese, G. (2019). "Where are you from?" Racialization, belonging, and identity among second-generation African-Canadians. *Ethnic and Racial Studies, 42*(9), 1476–1494. https://doi.org/10.1080/01419870.2018.1484503

Escobar Olivo, V., Parada, H., & Limón Bravo., F. (2022). Latin American youth and belonging at school in Ontario, Canada. In K. Tilleczek & D. MacDonald (Eds.), *Youth, education and wellbeing in the Americas. Youth, young adulthood and society series* (pp. 138–155). Routledge.

Escobar Olivo, V., Poteet, M., Carranza-Hernandez, G., & Jimenez, J. C. (2023). Our daughters: Central American women, intergenerational trauma, and the gender of caring. *Canadian Ethnic Studies, 55*(1), 25–45. https://doi.org/10.1353/ces.2023.0001

Galabuzi, G-E. (2011). Hegemonies, continuities, and discontinuities of multiculturalism and the Anglo-Franco conformity order. In M. Chazan, L. Helps, A. Stanley, & S. Thakkar (Eds.), *Home and native land: Unsettling multiculturalism in Canada* (pp. 58–82). Between the Lines.

García, M. C. (2006). *Seeking refuge: Central American migration to Mexico, the United States, and Canada.* University of California Press.

James, C. E. (2019). Adapting, disrupting, and resisting: How middle school Black males position themselves in response to racialization in school. *Canadian Journal of Sociology, 44*(4), 373–398. https://doi.org/10.29173/cjs29518

Kia-Keating, M., Santacrose, D., & Liu, S. (2017). Photography and social media use in community-based participatory research with youth: Ethical considerations. *American Journal of Community Psychology, 60* (3–4), 375–384. https://doi.org/10.1002/ ajcp.12189

Menard-Warwick, J. (2011). A methodological reflection on the process of narrative analysis: Alienation and identity in the life histories of English language teachers. *TESOL Quarterly, 45*(3), 564–574. https://doi.org/10.5054/tq.2010.256798

Méndez, M. J. (2019). The violence work of transnational gangs in Central America. *Third World Quarterly, 40*(2), 373–388. https://doi.org/10.1080/01436597.2018.1533786

Multiculturalism Act, RSC., 1985, c. 24 (4th Supp.).

Nichols, N. (2019). *Youth, school, and community: Participatory institutional ethnography.* University of Toronto Press.

Parada, H. (2012). The mestizo refuses to confess: Masculinity from the standpoint of a Latin American man in Toronto. In K. J. Moffatt (Ed.), *Troubled masculinities: Reimagining urban men* (pp. 21–41). University of Toronto Press.

Parada, H., Escobar Olivo, V., & Limón Bravo, F. (2021). "I just want to belong somewhere": Latinx youth's experiences in the education system in Ontario, Canada. *Journal of Latinos and Education, 22*(4), 1524–1537. https://doi.org/10.108 0/15348431.2021.1996366

Poteet, M., & Simmons, A. (2014). Schooling goals and social belonging among Central American–origin male youth in Toronto. *Canadian Ethnic Studies, 46*(3), 55–75. https://doi.org/10.1353/ces.2014.0047

Poteet, M., & Simmons, A. (2016). Not boxed in: Acculturation and ethno-social identities of Central American male youth in Toronto. *Journal of International Migration and Integration, 17*, 867–885. https://doi.org/10.1007/s12134-015-0442-0

Pottie, K., Brown, J. B., & Dunn, S. (2005). The resettlement of Central American men in Canada: From emotional distress to successful integration. *Refuge, 22*(2), 101–111.

Riaño-Alcalá, P. (2008). Journeys and landscapes of forced migration: Memorializing fear among refugees and internally displaced Colombians. *Social Anthropology, 16*(1), 1–18.

Simmons, A. B. (1993). Latin American migration to Canada: New linkages in the hemispheric migration and refugee flow system. *International Journal, 48*(2), 282–309. https://doi.org/10.2307/40202882

Simmons, A. B., & Plaza, D. E. (2006). The Caribbean community in Canada: Transnational connections and transformation. In V. Satzewich & L. Wong (Eds.), *Transnational identities and practices in Canada* (pp. 130–149). UBC Press.

Statistics Canada. (2022). *Data tables, 2021 census.* Government of Canada. https://www12.statcan.gc.ca/census-recensement/2021/dp-pd/dt-td/index-eng.cfm

Tairo, J. (2013). In-between cultures: Becoming Latin American Canadian [Unpublished MA thesis]. University of Toronto.

Veronis, L. (2007). Strategic spatial essentialism: Latin Americans' real and imagined geographies of belonging in Toronto. *Social and Cultural Geography, 8*(3), 455–473. https://doi.org/10.1080/14649360701488997

Veronis, L. (2010). Immigrant participation in the transnational era: Latin Americans' experiences with collective organizing in Toronto. *Journal of International Migration and Integration, 11*(2), 173–192. https://doi.org/10.1007/s12134-010-0133-9

Wilkinson, L. (2018). Second-generation immigrant youth and their sense of belonging in Canada. In S. Wilson-Forsberg & A. M. Robinson (Eds.), *Immigrant youth in Canada: Theoretical approaches, practical issues, and professional perspectives* (pp. 68–83). Oxford University Press.

Woodgate, R. L., & Busolo, D. S. (2021). African refugee youth's experiences of navigating different cultures in Canada: A "push and pull" experience. *International Journal of Environmental Research and Public Health, 18*, 2063–2076. https://doi.org/10.3390/ijerph18042063

Endnotes

1   The Mara Salvatrucha or MS-13 is one of the largest gang franchises in and from Central America, dealing largely in extortion and drug, human, and weapons trafficking (Méndez, 2019).

PART 5

BELONGING
in
FOREIGN SPACES

The chapters in this section consider the complex ways in which physical and socio-cultural spaces affect notions and feelings of "Canadian identity." The chapters examine the experiences of belonging of ethnically and linguistically minoritized groups within the following contexts: a neighbourhood in the east end of Toronto, a town in the Prairies, a church in Toronto, and Canada as a new home to Yiddish-speaking immigrants. Two points become evident: first, foreign space is a political place with the potential to exclude; second, individual agency can expand and redefine boundaries of belonging.

In Chapter 12, Anuppiriya Sriskandarajah argues that how belonging is studied, for the most part, is spatially decontextualized. Space is usually seen only as the backdrop for studies without looking at its analytical significance. Sriskandarajah aims instead to rescale belonging by examining the role of neighbourhoods, analyzing how individuals can simultaneously feel excluded at the national level and be attached to subnational spaces. Through a photovoice project, Sriskandarajah discusses how local neighbourhood space informs young Canadians' sense of belonging and citizenship, in which belonging is not just socially and culturally constituted but also produced through a sense of place.

In Chapter 13, Michelle Lam proposes a reconstruction of what it means to be Canadian by working toward a collaborative definition of belonging. The context of this chapter is rural communities, which often do not have the same access to settlement support services as cities and might not have populations for large ethnocultural community organizations. Rural communities are also largely under-represented in the literature on multiculturalism, identity, and belonging. Lam works with data from thirteen focus groups with immigrants in a rural Canadian city to discuss definitions of belonging, barriers, and pathways forward for new Canadians "in a place where size does matter."

In Chapter 14, Lisa Davidson engages with the question: what does a multicultural Canadian church mean to its ethno-racial congregants? Using two years of ethnographic fieldwork in multicultural and multiracial Presbyterian churches in Toronto, Davidson considers the narratives and experiences of racialized churchgoers from Guyana and the Philippines and their negotiation of recognition, assimilation, and integration into Canadian social life vis-à-vis a Christian worldview. Davidson argues that the uneven process of becoming Canadian and the ensuing experience of Canadian belonging are inseparable from identities both racialized and Christian. Davidson explores the challenge of "unifying diversity," endemic throughout multiple Canadian spaces and institutions, including churches.

In Chapter 15, Norman Ravvin demonstrates that, long before terms such as "multiculturalism" and "biculturalism" gained currency in Canada, Yiddish was a common third linguistic influence in urban and rural contexts across the country. By the late stages of Jewish immigration to Canada, the Yiddish cultural milieu had attained a global character. However, this narrative underwent a transformation following the Second World War. The key trends of the 1950s and later reflected an abandonment of the diverse and multinational Yiddish cultural context. In this way, assimilation of Canadian Jews into the mainstream ensured a shift away from uniquely Jewish forms of "cultural and linguistic diversity." Ravvin argues that, contrary to certain aspects of this volume's focus, the "Old World ideology" associated with Yiddish actually asserted a global multicultural worldview which, in the decades following the Second World War, was overwhelmed by Canadian assimilationist trends.

12

Reimagin(in)g Neighbourhood and Belonging:
Youth Citizenship in Practice

ANUPPIRIYA SRISKANDARAJAH

Most studies that examine belonging and citizenship focus on attachment to the nation (Yuval-Davis, 2006). This study diverges and aims to rescale belonging to examine the role of neighbourhoods in the experiences of belonging and citizenship for youth in marginalized neighbourhoods. Because youth for the most part have been viewed as "citizens in training they have not been included in discussions of citizenship and belonging" (Ríos-Rojas, 2011, p. 67). Through a photovoice project, this chapter examines how local neighbourhood spaces inform young people's sense of belonging and citizenship. I argue that citizenship and belonging for youth are not only socially and culturally constituted but also produced through a sense of place. There needs to be a reconceptualization of youth citizenship that centres spatial belonging.

This chapter lies at the intersection of Yuval-Davis's "politics of belonging" and Lefebvre's "right to the city." Yuval-Davis (2007, p. 561) argues that citizenship needs to be situated "in the wider context of contemporary politics of belonging which encompass citizenships, identities, and the emotions attached to them." A focus on status or rights and responsibilities does not consider how people are differently situated and how this engenders diverse forms of belonging. For Yuval-Davis, belonging is different from the politics of belonging; rather, "belonging is an emotional attachment" (2011, p. 4). However, it becomes "formally structured and politicized" when it is challenged: that is, the politics of belonging (2011, p. 4). Similarly, Lefebvre's concept shifts the focus of citizenship from legal ideals of rights to a more encompassing understanding of citizenship that not only views it as official status but also includes all those who live in the city. According to Lefebvre, urban residents have the "right to participation and the right to appropriation—to reconfigure the production of urban space and bring about a renewed transformation of urban life" (Lee, 2019, p. 79). I argue that the politics of belonging that underpin citizenship must incorporate the importance of spatial differences and the claim to public spaces.

Citizenship as Practice

To confine understandings of citizenship to the legal realm or rights does not capture the many ways in which citizens are differentiated even when they have official citizenship status. Thinking of citizenship as "relational" practice allows it to be understood as more than just official status, enables a focus on circumstances, and views it as an "active concept" that individuals can use to bring about change (Kurtz & Hankins, 2005, p. 3). "Active citizenship" centres agency and the ability to engage in projects that inform society (Johns et al., 2015, p. 173). This also allows the use of photovoice as a creative way to engage in practices of active citizenship.

Feminist researchers such as Ruth Lister (2003) argue that citizenship is a social process that regulates subjectivity and social relationships between individuals and states and between citizens. Viewing citizenship as a lived approach, as social relations, means recognizing that it is imbued with power relations that fragment and hierarchize its subjects along lines of difference. The liberal definition of citizenship looks at all citizens as the same without considering their differences (Yuval-Davis, 1997). A practice approach allows us to move past false ideas of universalism that underpin both categories of identity and ideas of citizenship. A practice approach, therefore, allows us to rethink this relationship between individuals and the state in terms of differentiated universalism; it allows us to link universalism (whereby everyone deserves the same rights bestowed by the concept of citizenship) while accounting for the particular lived experiences of individuals (Lister, 2003).

Space, Belonging, and Citizenship

Yuval-Davis (2011, p. 3) draws from Adrian Favel, who described the politics of belonging as "the dirty work of boundary maintenance." It is "dialogical" and includes negotiation of the practice aspect and the status aspect of citizenship (p. 3). According to Yuval-Davis, "social and political belonging" are composed of three key features: "social locations," "people's identifications and emotional attachments" to groups, and the "ethical and political value system with which people judge their own and others' belonging/s" (p. 5). These facets are interrelated. For Yuval-Davis, one of the major political projects of belonging is citizenship. Belonging is foundational; it is through belonging that all other aspects of citizenship—such as identity, political participation, status, and rights—are negotiated.

Lee (2019) argues that, to understand better those marginalized by dominant discourses on citizenship, it is best to examine how those on the margins make informal claims to the rights to the city. Lee refers to this as "corporeal citizenship," the "material, affective, and bodily dimensions of inclusion, belonging" (p. 80). For Erdal et al. (2018, p. 706), the "citizenship-belonging nexus" encapsulates the connection between "the institution of citizenship and individual and collective belonging."

For Hörschelmann and El Refaie (2014), if citizenship practices are reconceptualized through a relational understanding, then no one site of space would determine the formation of citizenship practices. Although their work focuses on transnational citizenship, I extend this argument for rescaling citizenship to focus also on the "microlocal," more specifically the neighbourhood level. Scholars have recognized the importance of space in studies of belonging (Youkhana, 2015). For Crath (2012, p. 46), belonging is "a spatialized layering of the discursive and materially manifested plays of power, the territorializing and deterritorializing practices that mobilise cultural and religious artefacts, values and sentiments, and the physical processes implicated in everyday practices of inter and intra-subjective formation."

Recently, there has been burgeoning academic interest in place and belonging, and this interest contests academic postulations that globalization would erase attachments to place (Cuervo & Wyn, 2014). Local communities continue to retain their own heterogeneous cultures, understandings, and identities despite homogenizing economic and cultural world processes (Harris, 2014; Leverentz, 2012). According to Benhabib (2007), processes of globalization have resulted in the decoupling of citizenship and national belonging and opened up space to explore citizenship at both global and local (neighbourhood) levels. A spatial focus allows an examination of how these multiple geographical scales of citizenship become linked.

Space is an important but often understudied aspect of citizenship (Yarwood, 2014). Barker (as cited in Yarwood, 2014) argues that citizenship is an unstable outcome of continuous struggle over how constructed categories of people come to be defined politically in space. Space is imbued with power relations that shape subjectivity, practice, and sense of belonging. It constructs certain forms of activities and sets of relations by configuring identities and understandings of people. Massey (2005) states that, since space is constructed through social relations, it is full of power and symbolism. Space and place are infused with socially constructed race, class, and gender meanings created both by people who live there through their spatial cultural practices and externally by the media and state. Space also has affective dimensions that shape feelings of security and belonging (Dillabough & Kennelly, 2010). Subjectivity and spatiality are dialogically constituted (Gulson, 2011).

Although my focus is on local spaces, the participants are by no means bounded. Neighbourhoods are sites where subjectivity connects to global spaces. Many of the young people in the study or their parents migrated from other places in the world. They continue to have transnational connections. They are also informed by a global youth culture, in particular American influences. Neighbourhoods are by no means insular. This mutual scalar exchange shapes how actors construct their identities and localities.

The study of space is not new in the field of youth studies (Ravn & Demant, 2017). However, space is usually seen as context, and Ravn and Demant (2017, p. 254) argue that space needs to be seen instead as "structuring" young people's subjectivities, and "performing subjectivities . . . in a social space is a way of producing that social space." Youth are particularly bounded by their local neighbourhoods because of restrictions on their movements and limited resources (Harris, 2009). Young people are more affected by their neighbourhoods than any other demographic group (Kintrea et al., 2010). Therefore, it is particularly important that we understand how youth subjectivity and sense of belonging are constituted through space.

The study of space and youth has an ambiguous history in youth studies. The moral panic that has accompanied the presence of youth in "deprived neighbourhoods" has been the focus of policy for more than two centuries (Browning & Soller, 2014, p. 166). "Collective fears" in city spaces have been centred on youth, particularly racialized young people (Boudreau et al., 2015, p. 335). In the contemporary context, Ugolotti and Moyer (2016) refer to this as "anxious politics," as demonstrated in their study of young people's use of public space in Turin, Italy. For Ugolotti and Moyer (2016, p. 203), "economic recession, crime, insecurity, undesirable difference, and terrorism ... [have] contributed to the justification and normalization" of othering certain groups of young people. Youth have been the focus of surveillance policies in the form of bylaws that discourage their use of public spaces or racial profiling that also deters them from accessing public spaces (Boudreau et al., 2015).

For young people, spaces become not only places for belonging but also "spaces of vulnerability," and this ambiguity is referred to as "social liminality" (Gonzales et al., 2020, p. 70). We see this in particular in the tensions that arise between adults and youth over the use of public spaces (Moris & Loopmans, 2019). Public spaces are "sites of cultural inclusion" and by extension exclusion (Ziemer, 2011, p. 233). Neighbourhoods' builds and social environments inform young people's sense of well-being (Teixeira & Zuberi, 2016).

Photovoice in Chester Le

This work is drawn from a larger, sixteen-month ethnographic study in two "priority neighbourhoods" (those identified by the City of Toronto as being underserviced with high rates of poverty and diversity). I focus on youth from one of the neighbourhoods, Chester Le, a small community in the east end of Toronto. It consists mostly of townhouses owned by the Toronto Community Housing Corporation (TCHC). The community was built in 1973 and mainly consists of 210 single-family townhouse units with a total of 968 residents (Qi, 2014). The townhouses are located in three places in the neighbourhood, all within walking distance from each other. There are also a few privately owned townhouses and detached homes and an apartment building. The majority of the neighbourhood is public housing. Most of the residents are racialized. The corporation revealed in its annual report that more than three-quarters of TCHC households earn less than $20,000 per year (Toronto Community Housing Corporation, 2014). Youth and children make up 67 percent of the tenants of the Chester Le TCHC housing (Qi, 2014), much higher than the city average of 26 percent (Hulchanski, 2010, p. 10).

I focus on a photovoice project conducted with eight youth in an after-school program in Chester Le. Photovoice is a participatory method that aims to rebalance the power relations between researchers and participants through a creative method. The youth in the study were in high school, with the exception of one participant who had recently graduated. There was also a youth who did not live in the neighbourhood but wanted to participate after hearing about the project. The youth were asked to take pictures of things that best represented their community with either their personal cameras or a disposable camera provided. Participants then discussed the images that they captured in a focus group and photo-elicitation interviews, which provided insights into how youth perceived, understood, interpreted, and engaged in their communities and how they imagined life in the city.

Shared Space and Un/Belonging

The photovoice project made it clear that shared neighbourhood spaces were a major source for the cultivation of belonging for the youth in the study. Through their photographs, the participants expressed the importance of communal spaces for their sense of belonging. The photographs were one way for them to lay claim to the city. They also discussed the need to cultivate actively a sense of community through shared public spaces such as community centres. For example, Faduma took a picture of an old community centre because for her it represented the importance of being involved in the civic life of her neighbourhood. The centre was her means of engaging in the neighbourhood.

> Anu: Why did you also take a picture of the [name of community centre] sign?
>
> Faduma: Because I think you should get involved in the community.

Figure 12.1. Faduma taking a picture of an old community centre. Courtesy of Photovoice study at University of Windsor.

The same public space had various meanings for different youth in the study. For example, Donte also took a picture of the old community centre, but he had a different opinion of the new centre compared with that of Faduma. For Donte, the old centre represented a more organic or grassroots sense of community. This was partially because it was situated in a house similar to where he lived. For the youth, the new larger centre represented a more bureaucratized space where those running the operations did not necessarily always connect with the young people in the neighbourhood. The participants expressed that their marginalization from the community centre became evident by rules that often limited youth access to the space if they were not registered in a program. As Donte said, "back when the old community centre was there or Community Corner was there it kind of brought us more together as a community than this space actually does." For him, the new centre highlighted wider issues faced by young people in the neighbourhood, for they were continuously marginalized from leadership roles. Donte wanted a more youth-oriented centre with more drop-in programs and genuine opportunities for young people's voices to be heard.

Donte: It is not youth friendly.

Anu: What would you do to make it more youth friendly?

Donte: Drop-in programs, get kids to try to run it, or make their voices heard.

Community centres as places of social interaction played an important role in the formation of spatially informed identity in the neighbourhood. Many of the youth in the study often felt that they belonged but simultaneously felt disconnected, as if they lived among strangers. Thomas's explanation of a photograph of a young man walking in his neighbourhood captured the ambiguity that accompanied life for youth in socio-economically marginalized communities. Thomas said that he took the picture because he was captivated by how deep in thought the subject of the picture was while walking in the neighbourhood. Although people lived close to each other, he thought that there was still the lack of a sense of community in his neighbourhood. There was a sense that people did not know their neighbours. But he quickly recognized that, because of social investments in public spaces in the neighbourhood, a sense of community was being revitalized. For Thomas, socio-economic disparities caused people to look inward. Through his photographs, he expressed how socio-economic inequalities affected how people related to others in these spaces.

Thomas: Like even though we live in the same community, we don't know what is going on with the guy living in the house next to you. . . . I think it is just like less than a sense of community than it was before. I feel like it is sort of coming back, like obviously it is, like spaces like [the name of the community centre] there is more investment in [the] community. . . . Because of the recession and all that stuff, a lot of people have been focused on keeping their own, holding their own, making sure they are well off, rather than worrying about the community. As long as they have a house to live [in], they have to worry about feeding themselves rather than are we taking care of the community gardens or how the youth are doing in the community. We need to engage them more.

Figure 12.2. A youth walking in the community. Courtesy of Photovoice study at University of Windsor.

Communities are sites of encounters (Stephens, 2010), and spaces have affective dimensions that inform belonging (Dillabough & Kennelly, 2010). The youth in the study highlighted the importance of shared public spaces such as community centres. However, they recognized that these encounters need to be genuine and that power needs to be redistributed in order for youth to feel a sense of leadership and ownership. They also recognized that these encounters are shaped by socio-economic marginalization, which informs how connected to each other they feel. Thomas indicated that positive place making must be cultivated and cannot be taken for granted.

Living in a shared space also had implications for a sense of relative disparity that often qualified their sense of belonging. The youth participants encountered spatial and social manifestations of disparity in mundane, taken-for-granted ways. For example, few of the participants took photographs of the "nicer" parts of their neighbourhood, the detached houses. Hakeem took pictures of the houses across the street from where he lived and referred to it as "the rich part." What

Figure 12.3. Privately owned detached homes in the neighbourhood. Courtesy of Photovoice study at University of Windsor.

he referred to as "rich" most Canadians in cities would consider typical middle-class homes. These were the everyday ways in which youth confronted their relative spatial disparity in their lives. For Hakeem, the rich houses motivated him to work hard so that he could buy his mother a similar house. For others, the relative disparity only heightened their sense of alienation.

> Hakeem: That is the rich part.
>
> Anu: That is a big house.
>
> Hakeem: That is the rich part of Chester Le. That is motivation.
>
> Anu: Motivation.
>
> Hakeem: One day.
>
> Anu: Two garages.
>
> Hakeem: So I can bring my mom to that house but in a different area.

The subjectivities of the young people in the study were constituted hierarchically in relation to how they were situated in their local space.

Figure 12.4. Canadian flag outside local public school. Courtesy of Photovoice study at University of Windsor.

Hakeem demonstrated how space structured young people's subjectivities. Space informed their sense of future possibilities. For Hakeem, for example, his neighbourhood experiences led to a yearning for upward mobility, as demonstrated by his desire to move his mother to a detached middle-class home in a different space.

Surveillance and Anxious Politics

For young people, their local neighbourhood spaces were also places of tension and feelings of alienation and unbelonging.

I asked Donte why he took a picture of a Canadian flag; he responded that "I am used to seeing it at school and because I am Canadian." In an earlier focus group, independent of the photovoice project, he had shared that he did not feel Canadian because of the everyday racism that he experienced, especially by the police. His seeming contradiction captured the ambiguous sense of Canadianness that many racialized youth experienced in Chester Le. They felt that they belonged while simultaneously feeling like outcasts. The youth were constantly reminded of their "otherness." One of the most common reminders, as highlighted by the photovoice project, was ongoing police harassment and state surveillance.

Figure 12.5. A police cruiser in the neighbourhood. Courtesy of Photovoice study at University of Windsor.

Almost every participant took a photograph of a police car in the neighbourhood, illustrating the constant police presence there. Most of the participants did not like the unwarranted presence and wanted to highlight their aversion to it.

> Hakeem: I don't like the police.
>
> Anu: How come?
>
> Hakeem: Because they are bad people, because they serve and protect themselves.

I asked Big why he took his photograph of the police.

> Big: Because cops around here always harass us.
>
> Anu: How come?
>
> Hakeem: Because they are jerks.

The constant police presence was not the only way that some participants felt over-surveilled in the neighbourhood. Donte discussed the constant surveillance and disciplining that young people in the

Figure 12.6. No loitering sign in the neighbourhood. Courtesy of Photovoice study at University of Windsor.

neighbourhood were subjected to as part of living in a public housing complex. He took a photograph of a sign found throughout the community that showcased some of the arbitrary rules imposed, which had racial implications. The subject of the photograph was a sign barring alcohol consumption and playing cards, dice, or dominoes in the common areas. Donte understood why smoking or drinking might be prohibited but did not understand the barring of dominoes. It is a popular pastime for those from the Caribbean, and this prohibition had racial and cultural implications for certain groups in the neighbourhood. The participants' interactions with state agents informed their sense of belonging. It is clear that young people in public spaces in Chester Le continue to cause concern, evidence of "anxious politics" (Ugolotti & Moyer, 2016).

Donte said that, "to be honest, I think it is a stupid rule about you can't play dominoes in the parking lot. I can understand no drinking, no smoking, no domino playing in the area is kind of stupid, and no trespassing."

Big also took a photograph of a sign notifying the neighbourhood of ongoing video surveillance.

Figure 12.7. Video surveillance sign in the neighbourhood. Photo courtesy of the student.

Youth have been the focus of surveillance policies that discourage the use of public spaces (Boudreau et al., 2015). As evident in this study, public spaces in neighbourhoods are "spaces of vulnerability" for young people (Gonzales et al., 2020, p. 70), where tensions arise when young people use public spaces. Photographs of the signs around Chester Le illustrate that the neighbourhood's physical and social environments inform young people's sense of well-being (Teixeira & Zuberi, 2016). Although young people in the study talked about the everyday tensions in their neighbourhood, it was also where they felt the most connected to others. Despite harassment, disciplining, and constant surveillance, the participants engaged in resistive practices, renegotiated dominant discourses that governed their existence, and laid claims to the city.

Rearticulation of Dominant Discourses: Rights to the City

Photovoice permitted participants to rearticulate dominant representations of their identities and their communities. Their photographs demonstrated both intentional and unintentional forms of resistance to dominant discourses.

For example, Yasmin took a picture of a father pushing his two children on the swings in the local park. The park signified different things for the participants, safety for some, a sense of home for others. When

Figure 12.8. A father with his children at the local park. Courtesy of Photovoice study at University of Windsor.

Yasmin was asked about the man in the photograph, she revealed that she did not know the father but nonetheless asked him if she could take the picture. She indicated that there was a sense of familiarity in their neighbourhood. Even though the father did not know her, she thought that he had probably seen her before in the neighbourhood and therefore agreed to be in the photo: "This is a park, they are with their dad, cause they are safe, ... [T]he playground is the most important thing in our community because every day, every single day, if it is raining, if it is snowing, you will see people there, you will see someone in the park. For example, me, I walk every day through the park to go to my school. So the park is the, when I look at the park, I am like finally I am home."

For many youth, as for Yasmin, Chester Le was a safe place to live, contrary to mainstream media representations. It was not a place of crime, absentee fathers, and moral decay, as often represented. The father in this picture captured this often unrecognized reality. In line with Lefebvre's (1996) right to the city, this is an example of how youth reconceptualize and assert what urban spaces mean to them. Donte took a similar photograph of the park, but he was explicit in his intention to dispel homogeneous representations of the neighbourhood. For him, the newness of the playground structure that replaced an old

Figure 12.9. Young people on a walk in the neighbourhood. Courtesy of Photovoice study at University of Windsor.

play structure signified the positive changes in the community that rarely got media attention. "I took a picture of the park because this neighbourhood is represented in a certain way. I took a picture of the playground because everyone views the neighbourhood the same way. It might not be the same way as a couple of years [ago]."

Resistance to and rearticulation of dominant discursive construc-tions were a constant theme within the photovoice project. None of the participants described the neighbourhood as unsafe or prone to crime. In fact, all said that it was safe. For example, when I asked Yasmin why she took a photograph of a group of youth walking in the community, she stated that she wanted to capture the positive aspects of everyday life in Chester Le: "Over here, friends chilling, walking by, they are safe, and it is good weather, there is nothing bad about it. Everyone is safe, you see cars over here, the houses."

These photographs illustrate how young people disrupt anxious politics by reframing what their spaces mean to them and disrupting how these spaces are typically portrayed. Here citizenship is not en-gagement in official acts but how youth negotiate their everyday realities and provide alternative narratives of their neighbourhood and in the process assert their right to space and mark their presence in the city.

Figure 12.10. An ill-maintained electricity meter box. Courtesy of Photovoice study at University of Windsor.

This is not to argue that participants had unadulterated utopian ideas of their neighbourhood. They did capture images of "rundown" or ill-maintained aspects of public spaces in it. By highlighting these elements, participants showcased what they wanted changed in their community.

Through their photographs, the participants asserted their desire to be seen and heard in their local spaces. For example, Thomas shared a photograph of his friend's graffiti work.

When asked why he captured that image, Thomas explained that it was because it highlighted the importance of art and the need to respect youth's voices. He stated that graffiti programs in the neighbourhood had declined. His friend got in trouble for tagging at school. But Thomas blamed this on the lack of places to practise graffiti. He argued that, instead of criminalizing graffiti, it should be seen as a legitimate art form that can beautify the city and allow youth to assert their legitimacy in public spaces. Thomas suggested creative ways to incorporate graffiti into the neighbourhood and make youth feel included. For example, he suggested that, instead of painting over electrical boxes that get tagged, graffiti could be used to decorate them. It was one example of the different ways that youth asserted their right to the city. The photo

Figure 12.11. Graffiti art on the side of a wall. Courtesy of Photovoice study at University of Windsor.

also illustrated how participants who recognized their marginality in the wider society found their own ways to lay claims to the city. The right to the city discourse conceptualizes citizenship to include those who live on the margins and take up spaces and engage in practices. For Lefebvre, the right to the city is "use value rather than exchange value" and "lies not in propagating ownership but *presence* in the city" (Bauder, 2016, p. 255). The examples above show how young people in these marginalized urban spaces appropriate and subvert dominant discourses about them and, as Lefebvre asserts, lay claim to them.

Conclusion

Lee (2019) argues that to see direct political actions only as resistance fails to capture the everyday work of those on the margins. Within a broader context marked by anxious politics, heightened globalization, greater diversity, intensified economic stratification, and increased surveillance of racialized young bodies in public spaces, I found in this study that neighbourhoods inform young people's sense of belonging and citizenship. I examined how racialized youth in a "priority neighbourhood" navigated belonging and citizenship within the wider discourses that circulate imaginings of their neighbourhood as dangerous, undesirable, and prone to crime. Through the use of photovoice, I found that shared public spaces were important in the constitution of belonging and citizenship for the participants. For example, the community centre was a key place through which the youth cultivated belonging and citizenship. Space informed their identities and their sense of futurity. Socio-economic marginalization informed how they connected with others. They recognized that the sense of positive place making needs to be cultivated. For the youth, their local neighbourhood spaces were also places of tension and unbelonging. They spoke about the overwhelming police presence in the neighbourhood that made them feel unwelcome in public spaces. The oversurveillance of youth was made evident by the photographs that showed the barring of playing cards, dice, and dominoes in public spaces, and constant reminders of the surveillance cameras around the housing complex qualified their sense of belonging. However, Boudreau et al. (2015) argue that "distancing" by youth from state figures such as the police is evidence not of disengagement but of a form of engagement. Such distancing allows them to cultivate their own alternative forms of engagement, for example graffiti art, as demonstrated by Thomas's picture.

The participants disrupted dominant representations that painted their neighbourhood as desolate, dangerous, and criminal. They presented framings missing from mainstream discourses that showed their community as safe, filled with love and spaces that cultivate a sense of belonging. I demonstrated in this chapter that confining understandings of citizenship to the legal realm or narrow conceptualizations of rights does not capture the many ways in which citizens are differentiated even when citizenship is granted. Citizenship thought of as universally inclusive in terms of national membership is unequal in its distribution of rights, most noticeable at the city level (Holston, 2008). I argued that a conceptualization of youth citizenship requires centring the importance of space in understandings of citizenship and belonging. The photographs revealed the centrality of the neighbourhood in the lives of these youth.

References

Bauder, H. (2016). Possibilities of urban belonging. *Antipode, 48*(2), 252–271.

Benhabib, S. (2007). Twilight of sovereignty or the emergence of cosmopolitan norms? *Citizenship Studies, 11*(1), 19–36.

Boudreau, J-A., Liguori, M., & Séguin-Manegre, M. (2015). Fear and youth citizenship practices: Insights from Montreal. *Citizenship Studies, 19*(3–4), 335–352.

Browning, C. R., & Soller, B. (2014). Moving beyond neighbourhood: Activity spaces and ecological networks as contexts for youth development. *Cityscape: A Journal of Policy Development and Research, 16*(1), 165–196.

Crath, R. (2012). Belonging as a mode of interpretive in-between: Image, place and space in the video works of racialised and homeless youth. *The British Journal of Social Work, 42*(1), 42–57.

Cuervo, H., & Wyn, J. (2014). Reflections on the use of spatial and relational metaphors in youth studies. *Journal of Youth Studies, 17*(7), 901–915.

Dillabough, J., & Kennelly, J. (2010). *Lost youth in the global city: Class, culture and the urban imaginary.* Routledge.

Erdal, M. B., Doeland, E. M., & Tellander, E. (2018). How citizenship matters (or not): The citizenship-belonging nexus explored among residents in Oslo, Norway. *Citizenship Studies, 22*(7), 705–724.

Gonzales, R., Brant, K., & Roth, B. (2020). DACAmented in the age of deportation: Navigating spaces of belonging and vulnerability in social and personal lives. *Ethnic and Racial Studies, 43*(1), 60–79.

Gulson, K. N. (2011). *Education policy, space and the city: Markets and the (in)visibility of race.* Routledge.

Harris, A. (2009). Shifting the boundaries of cultural spaces: Young people and everyday multiculturalism. *Social Identities, 15*(2), 187–205.

Harris, A. (2014). Conviviality, conflict and distanciation in young people's local multicultures. *Journal of Intercultural Studies, 35*(6), 571–587.

Holston, J. (2008). *Insurgent citizenship: Disjunctions of democracy and modernity in Brazil.* Princeton University Press.

Hörschelmann, K., & El Refaie, E. (2014). Transnational citizenship, dissent and the political geographies of youth. *Transactions of the Institute of British Geographers, 39* (3), 444–456.

Hulchanski, J. D. (2010). *The three cities within Toronto: Income polarization among Toronto's neighbourhoods, 1970–2005.* Cities Centre Press.

Johns, A., Mansouri, F., & Lobo, M. (2015). Religiosity, citizenship and belonging: The everyday experiences of young Australian Muslims. *Journal of Muslim Minority Affairs, 35*(2), 171–190.

Kintrea, K., Bannister, J., & Pickering, J. (2010). Territoriality and disadvantage among young people: An exploratory study of six British neighbourhoods. *Journal of Housing and the Built Environment, 25*(4), 447–465.

Kurtz, H., & Hankins, K. (2005). Guest editorial: Geographies of citizenship. *Space and Polity, 9*(1), 1–8.

Lee, C. T. (2019). Improvising "nonexistent rights": Immigrants, ethnic restaurants, and corporeal citizenship in suburban California. *Social Inclusion, 7*(4), 79–89.

Lefebvre, H. (1996). *Writings on cities* (E. Kofman & E. Lebas, Trans.). Blackwell.

Leverentz, A. (2012). Narratives of crime and criminals: How places socially construct the crime problem. *Sociological Forum, 27*(2): 348–371.

Lister, R. (2003). *Citizenship: Feminist perspectives* (2nd ed.). Palgrave Macmillan.

Massey, D. (2005). *For space.* SAGE.

Moris, M., & Loopmans, M. (2019). De-marginalizing youngsters in public space: Critical youth workers and local municipalities in the struggle over public space in Belgium. *Journal of Youth Studies, 22*(5), 694–710.

Qi, H. (2014). Designing for a safer public housing community: A case study of Chester Le, Toronto [Unpublished master's thesis]. Queen's University.

Ravn, S., & Demant, J. (2017). Figures in space, figuring space: Towards a spatial-symbolic framework for understanding of youth cultures and identities. *YOUNG, 25*(3), 252–267.

Ríos-Rojas, A. (2011). Beyond delinquent citizenships: Immigrant youth's (re)visions of citizenship and belonging in a globalized world. *Harvard Educational Review, 81*(1), 64–95.

Stephens, A. C. (2010). Citizenship without community: Time, design and the city. *Citizenship Studies, 14*(1), 31–46.

Teixeira, S., & Zuberi, A. (2016). Mapping the racial inequality in place: Using youth perceptions to identify unequal exposure to neighborhood environmental hazards. *International Journal of Environmental Research and Public Health, 13*(9), 844–858.

Toronto Community Housing Corporation. (2014). *Toronto Community Housing Corporation Annual Report.* https://torontohousing.ca/sites/default/files/2023-03/toronto_community_housing_annual_report_2014.pdf

Ugolotti, N. M., & Moyer, E. (2016). "If I climb a wall of ten meters": Capoeira, parkour and the politics of public space among (post)migrant youth in Turin, Italy. *Patterns of Prejudice, 50*(2), 188–206.

Yarwood, R. (2014). *Citizenship.* Routledge.

Youkhana, E. (2015). A conceptual shift in studies of belonging and the politics of belonging. *Social Inclusion, 3*(4), 10–24.

Yuval-Davis, N. (1997). Women, citizenship and difference. *Feminist Review, 57*, 4–27.

Yuval-Davis, N. (2006). Belonging and the politics of belonging. *Patterns of Prejudice, 40*(3), 197–214.

Yuval-Davis, N. (2007). Intersectionality, citizenship and contemporary politics of belonging. *Critical Review of Internal Social and Political Philosophy, 10*(4), 561–574.

Yuval-Davis, N. (2011). *Power, intersectionality and the politics of belonging.* FREIA Working Paper No. 75. Institut for Kultur og Globale Studier, Aalborg Universitet.

Ziemer, U. (2011). Minority youth, everyday racism and public spaces in contemporary Russia. *European Journal of Cultural Studies, 14*(2), 229–242.

13

Suppression for the Sake of Survival:
Multisectoral Rural Voices on Belonging and Anti-Racism

MICHELLE LAM

Despite equitable-sounding definitions of words such as *inclusion* and *integration*, for newcomers in a small prairie city, pathways to success are littered with a thousand hurtful "choices" that are not really choices at all: changing names to appear more anglicized on a résumé, adopting new regional accents, recertifying a certification already attained, changing styles of clothing, taking on new mannerisms, and making other decisions to "fit in" in a country that professes to adapt itself to a multicultural population. The realities for newcomers are "jettisoning" aspects of language, culture, and identity to find success in this new country or, as one participant described, "suppression for the sake of surviving."

Recognizing the disparity between the aims of a multicultural society and the realities on the ground, over the past year I co-led a community-based, collaborative research project that involved an interdisciplinary examination of what belonging and anti-racism might look like in a small city in rural Canada. Rural communities often do not have the same access as larger cities to settlement supports and services, and they might not have the populations for large ethnocultural community organizations. Rural communities are also largely under-represented in the literature on multiculturalism, identity, and belonging. Thus, a project that could shed light on the realities of belonging in a rural community, from a variety of perspectives, was necessary.

With data from thirteen focus groups discussing definitions of belonging, barriers and challenges, and pathways forward, in this chapter I lay out a path for similar community-based research initiatives as well as insights into how to create social change in a place where size does matter. I detail our community-based initiative and how we brought multiple voices to the table from broad sectors, such as health care, education, Indigenous communities, students, governments, and others. I describe the significant barriers and challenges identified and the opportunities for working together for a more equitable future.

This chapter contributes a reconstruction of what it means to be Canadian by working toward a collaborative definition of belonging. Although Canadian identity is often compared with a mosaic, in which every colour and shape has a place, voices on the ground indicate that "fitting in" requires jettisoning particular aspects of culture and adopting more dominant Anglo-Saxon norms. This chapter clearly defines the need to reconceptualize identity and belonging and calls readers to action within their own communities.

Words and Actions Misaligned (Or Why Equitable-Sounding Policies Do Not Result in Equity)

In 2007, Reitz and Banerjee measured levels of belonging, trust, Canadian identity, citizenship, life satisfaction, volunteering, and voting as ways to further understand the differences in how immigrants of various cohorts and generations experience social integration in Canada. They found a stark difference between White immigrants and racialized immigrants, which extends to the second generation, and that education and employment do not mitigate the discrimination and exclusion felt by the latter group. Reitz and Banerjee concluded with the striking comment that "policies have emphasized the laudable ideals of equal opportunity and opposition to racism, but they lack the features that would enable them to effectively bridge that racial divide" (p. 39). Simply put, equitable-sounding policies such as the Canadian government's definition of integration as a two-way process in which both the host society and the newcomer adapt to and benefit from one another are not realized on the ground.

To understand why policies that sound equitable do not result in equity, it is important to grasp the background of how they came to be. The "laudable ideals" mentioned by Reitz and Banerjee (2007, p. 39) are at the core of Canada's multiculturalism policy of 1971. Before 1961, 90 percent of all immigrants came from Europe (Kelley & Trebilcock, 2010). However, in the 1960s and 1970s, concepts such as equality and non-discrimination, combined with almost thirty years of a strong economy, led to high levels of immigration from increasingly diverse countries. The public sentiments of equality and anti-racism ultimately led to a points-based immigration system adopted in 1967, which selected immigrants based upon their human capital (Hiebert, 2006; Kelley & Trebilcock, 2010; Wong & Guo, 2018), including factors such as education, job skills, occupation, work experience, age, and knowledge of English or French (Wong & Guo, 2018).

In 1976, an Immigration Act was passed that marked a significant directional shift. For the first time, the goals of immigration were clearly laid out: reaching Canada's demographic aims, fostering a strong economy, facilitating family reunification, fulfilling international obligations to refugees, and upholding humanitarian traditions (Kelley & Trebilcock, 2010). The Act also required that provinces be included in consultations about annual admission numbers, and it detailed four classes of admission: family, assisted relatives, independent, and humanitarian. A business class was added two years later (Kelley & Trebilcock, 2010), designed to "secure off shore capital to support small- and medium-size businesses and commercial ventures that have difficulties in raising venture capital" (Li, 2002, p. 29). Although the points system might appear to be neutral, it has been criticized as still perpetuating racism by favouring some forms of human capital over others. For example, more heavily weighting points for language ability can be seen as "defining who potentially belongs or does not belong to Canada" (Wong & Guo, 2018, p. 3). Thus, even in attempts to create an equitable system that does not judge based upon ethnic origin, by weighting and allocating points for certain criteria the system decides who belongs and who does not.

Even after the arrival of immigrants, the settlement field is fraught with misalignment between aims and impacts. Again background is helpful. Before the Second World War, settlement services were viewed as the responsibility of newcomers themselves. After the war, those services were meant to help soldiers and war refugees adjust to Canadian life (Shan, 2015). In 1966, the services were discontinued since it was believed that newcomers would simply make use of existing services available to all Canadians. However, the changing demographics of newcomers arriving in the 1960s and 1970s because of the introduction of the points system described above (rather than the previous system, biased in favour of European countries) meant that the changing demographics were also raising questions about the identity of Canada as a nation (Shan, 2015). The policy of multiculturalism of 1971 was a response to these questions, and in 1974 government-funded immigrant settlement services were again established.

Although initially it was believed that "multiculturalism was most likely to succeed if newcomers could slide seamlessly into workplaces" (Robertson, 2005, p. 410), later research showed that "having more money does not necessarily bring a stronger sense of belonging" (Jedwab & Wilkinson, 2016, p. 26). Indeed, "work must be done to ensure the host society is ready and amenable to accepting the arrival of newcomers as integration takes place at the community level" (Wilkinson, 2013, p. 1). Access to settlement services is a significant step toward overcoming barriers in order to promote participation in all aspects of life in Canada (Ashton et al., 2016), but those services themselves can make distinctions that affect belonging. For example, within government-funded settlement programs, only particular groups of newcomers are eligible to receive services. Currently, international students, visitors, and those awaiting refugee decisions are all ineligible. The ideals of integration as a two-way process in which both host society and newcomers adapt to one another (Government of Canada, 2012; Wilkinson, 2013) are not always realized in practice (Shan, 2015). Needless to say, the concept of integration is more complex than the linear, measurable pathway envisioned (Guo, 2015; Li, 2003), and that pathway is less than smooth.

Public opinion also greatly affects belonging. As immigration numbers increase, infrastructure is challenged, and services are stressed by a sudden increase in numbers (Kandiah, 2018). Housing, health care, education, recreation, law enforcement, and local infrastructure are all affected (Burstein, 2010). Although seven of ten Canadians support current immigration numbers (Neuman, 2022), a significant proportion of the population still expresses concern about issues related to integration, viewing diversity as a threat to the prevailing culture and identity (Abu-Laban, 2015; Neuman, 2022).

Within rural communities, as locals leave in search of education or employment opportunities elsewhere, labour shortages are increasingly filled through the provincial nominee system. However, that can result in distrust and resentment among the local population, who believe that jobs have been "stolen" from long-time residents or their children. Thus, who belongs and who does not, who feels welcomed within a community, and who claims the role of "host" to recent newcomers are all dependent on a complex stew of factors, including public opinion, economic security, availability of resources, community connections, and whether the system was set up to favour particular people.

As a final point, it is necessary to point out, as do Sharples and Blair (2021), the problematic way in which Indigenous communities are lumped together under "multicultural" categories, ignoring how both White and racialized immigrants benefit from the ongoing dispossession of Indigenous peoples. Furthermore, by claiming the role of welcoming host, White Canadians continue to set the requirements for who is included. The Calls to Action from the Truth and Reconciliation Commission specifically address newcomers to Canada by requiring a more inclusive history and education and a reframing of the Oath of Citizenship to include treaty responsibilities (Calls 93 and 94). However, it is imperative to consider that the majority of settlement workers, language teachers, and educators continue to be non-Indigenous and that Indigenous voices are largely absent from welcoming ceremonies.

Changing Faces in Rural Places

Since most studies of immigrant integration and identity focus on large urban centres, rural areas have been largely left out of the conversation. But rural areas in Canada are becoming more culturally and linguistically diverse (Ashton, 2016; Carter et al., 2008; Hamm, 2015). This increasing diversity is happening for several reasons. First, "out-migration," or youth from small towns and smaller cities who depart in search of education and employment, can leave local communities with shrinking populations and the need for local labour. Responding to these needs, particularly in the prairie provinces, policy makers and local community leaders use immigration as a way to strengthen communities, fill shortages, rejuvenate local economies, and ease pressure on larger urban centres (Burstein, 2010; Krahn et al., 2005; Shields & Türegün, 2014), all of which result in increasing rural diversity. These workers are also from increasingly diverse source countries (Ashton et al., 2016), so in rural areas not only are newcomers increasing but also they are from increasingly diverse linguistic and cultural backgrounds. Second, communities outside major urban cities are attractive options for newcomers attracted by the lower cost of living, welcoming communities, and high quality of life (Hellstrom, 2018). Third, smaller communities play an important role in refugee resettlement, sponsoring refugees through the private sponsorship path (Hyndman et al., 2017). In addition, many smaller centres are destinations for government-sponsored refugees since the Canadian government is making efforts to disperse refugees outside Vancouver, Montreal, and Toronto. Yet, despite this increasing diversity, migration research remains concentrated in those three large cities.

Rural Canadians in areas that until recently have been largely homogeneous are "more apt to associate multiculturalism with part of a national, rather than local, identity" (Varma, 2003, p. 85). Long-term residents might view the success of immigrants in their communities with resentment, perceiving opportunities as "stolen from non-immigrants" (Varma, 2003, p. 94). This coincides with Clement et al.'s (2013) assessment of the realigned system of settlement services in Manitoba, which describes instances of racism and "negative backlash" (p. 53) that reduced retention rates in the initial years after arrival. Shields and Türegün (2014, p. 18) reiterate the need for community and social networks in integration, stating that "a welcoming environment is critical to their long-term integration and sense of belonging." Within education, responses to the arrival of newcomers are not always positive, and some people might view new students as a "threat to 'standards' and to the quality of education in schools" (Leung, 2016, p. 160). In a survey of Manitoba's Provincial Nominee Program participants, 19 percent said that their children have faced discrimination at school, and 33 percent said that they experienced racism or discrimination themselves (Carter, 2009).

Societies that focus on economic outcomes without a corresponding focus on other aspects of integration face problems that can extend beyond the first generation (Ali, 2008; Wilkinson, 2013). In addition, second-generation visible minority Canadians are less likely than both non-visible minorities and their parents to feel a sense of belonging in Canada (Ali, 2008; Bragg & Wong, 2016). In other words, "when immigrants are reduced to their labor-market contributions and ignored as people with families and plans and hopes for the future, it serves to alienate these immigrants from the nation in which they are settling and building their lives" (Bragg & Wong, 2016, p. 59). However, when host communities are supportive, newcomer language-learning outcomes improve, in turn promoting both economic and social integration (Derwing & Waugh, 2012).

For newcomers, concerns are not "just about surviving and thriving but also belonging," though considerations of belonging and identity need careful attention to "flexible identities" (Duff, 2015, p. 58, p. 71) or the recognition that identities shift and change. This process of creating a home is not linear or balanced (Wilkinson, 2013), for integration and newcomer trajectories are "multifaceted and complex" (Jedwab & Wilkinson, 2016). In other words, "home is not some end state, but rather a process" (Abu-Laban, 2015, p. 6). The importance of identity can be seen in a recent study showing that power dynamics in relationships between sponsored refugees and their sponsors can be alleviated by challenging victim and deficit stereotypes and recognizing refugees as people of agency and "self-rescue" (Kyriakides et al., 2018, p. 59).

Family reunification is tied to integration, identity, and belonging; however, with the government's emphasis on economic immigration, reunification with extended family becomes more difficult (Abu-Laban, 2015; Bragg & Wong, 2016). This has been evident recently since the program designed for immigrants to sponsor their parents and grandparents, a highly criticized lottery system, was changed to a first-come, first-served approach in 2018. In 2019, when the new system accepted expressions of interest, more than 100,000 people tried to access the form, and the program hit the limit of 27,000 application spots after only eleven minutes (CIC News, 2019; Harris, 2019).

What Rural People Think about Belonging and Anti-Racism

Recognizing this disparity between the aims of a multicultural society and the realities on the ground, and the need for a rural focus, I co-led a community-based, collaborative research project that involved an interdisciplinary examination of what belonging and anti-racism might look like in a small city in rural Canada. Our objective was to provide a space that could encourage dynamic, interdisciplinary, multidirectional perspectives on belonging and anti-racism that could be compiled and analyzed in order to provide constructive and meaningful feedback not only to participants as members of the community but also to organizations that attempt to create more equitable and welcoming spaces that can foster belonging.

The project was planned in collaboration with the Brandon Local Immigration Partnership and supported by the Brandon Friendship Centre and Westman Immigrant Services, an Indigenous friendship centre and a local settlement organization serving the city and surrounding areas in Manitoba. We began by inviting educators, practitioners, Indigenous leaders, government officials, newcomers, students, and community members at large to participate in an in-depth virtual discussion held via Zoom. We had more than 125 participants attend, and the event included a welcome and land acknowledgement from a local elder and spiritual leader, a welcome from the mayor, and some opening remarks from the Brandon Local Immigration Partnership and me. We then began two rounds of thirteen breakout room discussions, each one facilitated by an experienced researcher and research assistant. The event concluded with a wrap-up, the next steps, and an open Q&A discussion.

In particular, the event focused on questions that aimed to address belonging, identify barriers and challenges, and explore forward-looking developments and opportunities for the future. This local approach allowed for an exploration of many possible avenues for collaboration since it brought people together from varied backgrounds, organizations, and agencies. The discussion was a starting place from which further projects developed.

Defining Belonging

During the large group Zoom session, we asked participants to write one or two words in the chat to describe what belonging means to them. These words were then collected and compiled into a word frequency graphic in which larger words represent those used more frequently. The short phrases in the chat data were also elaborated within the focus group (breakout room) conversations. For example, one participant said that, "when I think about belonging, I think about those spaces where every person who enters that space truly feels that the collective can't get along without them, that their point of view, their voice, their experience is essential. Their happiness, their comfort, is essential to everyone in that collective." This sense of collectivity was reiterated by other participants (see Figure 13.1).

Figure 13.1. Word cloud of participant experiences. Created 26 March 2021. Powered by WordArt.com.

Belonging was also explored in relation to what it was not. Many participants discussed their feelings of a lack of belonging and used words such as *disconnected* and *on an island*. Taken together, these focus group conversations and chat words emphasized feelings of connection, freedom, safety, respect, and inclusion while emphasizing the need to combat isolation and disconnection. It is notable that this happened during the COVID-19 pandemic, which might have exacerbated feelings of loneliness because of the difficulties at that time.

Voices of Black, Indigenous, and People of Colour

Although we removed all identifying information from the transcripts, there were still many times when participants identified themselves as being Black, Indigenous, or People of Colour (BIPOC). By analyzing those comments separately, we found an additional focus on safety, risk, and exhaustion. Participants shared that spaces filled with well-meaning White people can feel exhausting, particularly if they have to spend time educating the people around them or address ongoing issues of discrimination. The risk of backlash had to be managed, and participants described feeling pressure to conform in order to feel safe. For example, one participant said that "we're scared every time we walk outside our doors." This admission is consistent with research on causes of activist burnout, which identified that one of the major stressors associated with activism for People of Colour is navigating the cumulative effects of racism in everyday life (Gorski, 2018). This racism is not only from people outside the activist movements but also, significantly, from those within the movements. As Gorski (2018, p. 672, citing Gorski & Chen, 2015) writes, "nearly every activist of colour they interviewed attributed their burnout in part to racism from white activists." Several participants suggested that having allies and advocates is important but desired "ethical spaces of engagement" (Ermine, 2007, p. 193) where they feel safe and believe that their voices and lived experiences are respected and valued. Power and emotional cost are significant barriers to belonging, as I will explore next.

Challenges and Barriers to Belonging

The current realities of racism, both personal acts of violence and systemic inequalities, were explored in detail within the focus groups as a significant barrier to belonging at the community level. Participants raised many examples, such as stereotyping, gaslighting, and making assumptions, misinterpretations, or demeaning comments. They thought that there was a general resistance to change, a lack of accountability, and ignorance that led to hurtful impacts. They also mentioned systemic barriers such as streamlining, zoning and demographic "bubbles," and credential recognition processes.

Although not a focus within the study questions themselves, when conducting the analysis we found many examples of words and phrases that further grouped people into those who belong and those who do not. We found examples of "us and them" language, which defines belonging and raises questions about issues of power. One participant noticed this within the group and called it out by saying that "I won't call it *our* community; it's *the* community." This is significant since it points to the demarcation between White Canadians and non-White Canadians that I described earlier, which persists despite Indigenous history and ongoing presence and despite multiple generations of non-White Canadians living in Canada.

The dynamic of in-group and out-group belonging can be understood additionally through a sociological examination. Anderson (2015) describes how many public spaces are still dominated by White individuals and termed "white spaces." When minorities enter these spaces, they must "do the dance" to demonstrate their trustworthiness and ability to belong. Their encounters in these spaces result in additional scrutiny and a feeling that they must be "on, performing before a highly judgmental but socially distant audience" (p. 14). They are viewed as the "perennial outsider[s]" (p. 18). Drawing from Dei (2001, p. 146), this exclusion persists because a dominant status makes it possible for the majority to view their own experiences, histories, knowledges, and backgrounds as "normal," thereby defining the criteria of inclusion and exclusion of who and what are accepted within that normal. For example, the dominant majority might determine that a certain level of English ability is required for acceptance into the system. Later, when newcomers adapt themselves to meet those requirements, the majority can change the criteria to include a more specific accent or demand it under the guise of "clear communication" (Lam, 2021a; Lam, 2021b). Using such nebulous phrases keeps the criteria vague, able to be redefined to include or exclude depending on the will of the majority. The same shifting criteria of inclusion/exclusion can be seen with the recent emphasis on "soft skills." If examining criteria for acceptance as set by the Canadian government through the Provincial Nominee Program and through the points allocations described earlier, then those targets are either met or not met by certain background certifications or qualifications. However, as newcomers from an increasingly diverse range of source countries began arriving, the "target" shifted, and suddenly they were excluded on the basis of a lack of soft skills or some other arbitrary measure as designed by the majority.

This shifting can be seen both through programmatic shifts at the settlement service level and through research using experiments to explore whether these shifts are racially motivated. In one famous example researchers sent out 5,000 résumés, some with White-sounding names and some with African American-sounding names, and found a 50 percent gap in which applicants received calls from potential employers (Bertrand & Mullainathan, 2004). This study looked only at callback rates, merely one step in the multistep process of getting a job. Thus, exclusion can be exacerbated with additional steps, such as an interview process that demands competency in White cultural norms or an employer who values only local experiences or requires local references. These aspects are also well documented in research. For example, Marom (2019) explored the concept of "professionalism" among job candidates.

She found that candidates were judged as more professional when they aligned with narrow stereotypes of what teachers looked like (dress code), spoke like (speech patterns), and taught like (knowledge, pedagogy, and assessment). In quoting a participant, she wrote that "those who are successful are usually a little more willing to assimilate" (p. 332).

Dei (2014, p. 246) reminds readers that they must "challenge the temptation to look to the dominant to seek validation, acceptance, and legitimacy in still-colonized spaces." This is important because it is difficult when the pathways to success demand "jettisoning aspects of language, identity and culture" (Lam, 2021b, p. 146). Newcomers must decide how to navigate this complexity given the need to find a job or put food on the table. Some choose to anglicize their names, others adopt different styles of dress, and some spend large sums of money on accent reduction coaching or other strategies for "fitting in" to the majority culture. This process was described by Hébert (2013, p. 5): "Today's citizen is yesterday's immigrant, the result of previous processes of adaptation contributing to a continuously evolving sense of Canadianness." However, we must examine whether this unidirectional process is in line with the promises of multiculturalism, which gives everyone a place to belong. If belonging is predicated on losing important aspects of who one is, then it is not true belonging. We teach this to our children when they begin to make friends: if their friends demand that our children act like them and talk like them and like the same things that they do, then they are not very good friends.

It is also important to point out that this gatekeeping, or as Dwayne Donald called it, this "pedagogy of the fort," in which certain people are included and others are excluded, is an ongoing erasure of Indigenous peoples. In relation to this chapter, then, we must question why, to borrow a term from Peter Li (2002), "old newcomers" have taken up the position of acting as hosts and welcomers of "new newcomers," which further marginalizes and erases the role of the original inhabitants of this land.

Opportunities for Ways Forward

As the conversation turned to descriptions of ways to move forward, participants mentioned the need for education, particularly in the areas of an all-encompassing anti-racism education, education that honours Indigenous and newcomer realities, and education that targets misinformation and stereotyping. Participants also desired both communication and action. There were many comments about the need to have more consultations like the one that they were currently involved in, but there was also some skepticism about whether these conversations alone would result in meaningful action. It is important to consider such conversations along with barriers to power and accountability when planning community-engaged research projects. Addressing issues of power, ownership, and control is important, for inviting diverse voices to the table is not enough, and there must be acknowledgement of the many intersecting barriers to full participation, such as the lack of safety described earlier as well as scheduling conflicts, costs, accessibility issues, and whether or not the purposes were collaboratively designed.

Additional ways forward identified by participants included further development in understanding who is responsible for accommodation, the need for pathways to address racism, and further support for newcomers, particularly in realizing equity in employment and recognizing professional certifications gained outside Canada.

Why This Matters

With data from thirteen focus groups discussing definitions of belonging, barriers and challenges, and pathways forward, this chapter laid out a path for similar community-based research initiatives as well as insights into what belonging means within a rural setting. I detailed one community-based initiative and how we brought multiple voices to the table from broad sectors, such as health care, education, Indigenous communities, students, governments, and many more. I described the significant barriers and challenges identified and the opportunities for working together for a more equitable future.

This chapter contributes a reconstruction of what it means to be Canadian by working toward a collaborative definition of belonging. Although Canadian identity is often compared with a mosaic in which every colour and shape has a place, voices on the ground indicate that "fitting in" requires jettisoning particular aspects of culture and adopting more dominant Anglo-Saxon norms. A lack of safety, racism, and systemic barriers create significant impacts on how people feel about belonging. This chapter clearly defines the need to reconceptualize identity and belonging and calls readers to action within their own communities.

References

Abu-Laban, Y. (2015). Transforming citizenship: Power, policy and identity. *Canadian Ethnic Studies, 47*(1), 1–10. https://doi.org/10.1353/ces.2015.0001

Ali, M. A. (2008). Second-generation youth's belief in the myth of Canadian multiculturalism. *Canadian Ethnic Studies, 40*(2), 89–107. https://doi.org/10.1353/ces.2010.0017

Anderson, E. (2015). The white space. *Sociology of Race and Ethnicity, 1*(1), 10–22. https://doi.org/10.1177/2332649214561306

Ashton, W. (2016). *Immigration in five rural Manitoba communities with a focus on refugees: Boissevain-Killarney case study*. Brandon University. https://www.brandonu.ca/rdi/files/2016/09/5MB-Boissevain-Killarney-Case-Study-2016.pdf

Ashton, W., Pettigrew, R. N., & Galatsanou, E. (2016). Assessment of settlement services systems in western and northern Canada: Perceptions of settlement provider organizations. *Canadian Ethnic Studies, 48*(3), 69–89. https://doi.org/10.1353/ces.2016.0026

Bertrand, M., & Mullainathan, S. (2004). Are Emily and Greg more employable than Lakisha and Jamal? A field experiment on labor market discrimination. *American Economic Review, 94*(4), 991–1013. https://doi.org/10.1257/0002828042002561

Bragg, B., & Wong, L. L. (2016). "Cancelled dreams": Family reunification and shifting Canadian immigration policy. *Journal of Immigrant and Refugee Studies, 14*(1), 46–65. https://doi.org/10.1080/15562948.2015.1011364

Burstein, M. (2010). *Reconfiguring settlement and integration: A service provider strategy for innovation and results*. Canadian Immigrant Settlement Sector Alliance. http://p2pcanada.ca/wp-content/uploads/2011/09/Reconfiguring-Settlement-and-Integration.pdf

Carter, T. (2009). *An evaluation of the Manitoba Provincial Nominee Program*. Manitoba Labour and Immigration Report. https://immigratemanitoba.com/wp-content/uploads/2017/11/pnp-manitoba-provincial-nominee-program-tom-carter-report-2009.pdf

Carter, T., Morrish, M., & Amoyaw, B. (2008). Attracting immigrants to smaller urban and rural communities: Lessons learned from the Manitoba Provincial Nominee Program. *Journal of International Migration and Integration, 9*(2), 161–183. https://doi.org/10.1007/s12134-008-0051-2

CIC News. (2019, 29 January). IRCC stands by parents and grandparents expression of interest process. *CIC News*. https://www.cicnews.com/2019/01/ircc-stands-by-parents-and-grandparents-expression-of-interest-process-0111802.html

Clement, G., Carter, T., & Vineberg, R. (2013). *Case study: The realigned system of settlement service delivery in MB 1999 to 2013*. Western Canadian Consortium on Integration, Citizenship, and Cohesion. https://umanitoba.ca/faculties/arts/media/CaseStudy_RealignedSystemMB2.pdf

Dei, G. J. S. (2001). Rescuing theory: Anti-racism and inclusive education. *Race, Gender and Class, 8*(1), 139–161.

Dei, G. J. S. (2014). Personal reflections on anti-racism education for a global context. *Encounters in Theory and History of Education, 15*, 239–249. https://doi.org/10.24908/eoe-ese-rse.v15i0.5153

Derwing, T. M., & Waugh, E. (2012). Language skills and the social integration of Canada's adult immigrants. *Institute for Research on Public Policy Study, 31*, 1–36.

Donald, D. T. (2009). *The pedagogy of the fort: Curriculum, Aboriginal-Canadian relations, and Indigenous Métissage* [Doctoral dissertation, University of Alberta (Canada)].

Duff, P. A. (2015). Transnationalism, multilingualism, and identity. *Annual Review of Applied Linguistics, 35*, 57–80. https://doi.org/10.1017/S026719051400018X

Ermine, W. (2007). The ethical space of engagement. *Indigenous Law Journal, 6*(1), Article 1. https://jps.library.utoronto.ca/index.php/ilj/article/view/27669

Gorski, P. C. (2018). Fighting racism, battling burnout: Causes of activist burnout in US racial justice activists. *Ethnic and Racial Studies, 42*(5), 667–687. https://doi.org/10.1080/01419870.2018.1439981

Gorski, P. C., & Chen, C. (2015). "Frayed all over": The causes and consequences of activist burnout among social justice education activists. *Educational Studies, 51*(5), 385–405. https://doi.org/10.1080/00131946.2015.1075989

Government of Canada. (2012, 31 October). *Annual report to Parliament on immigration, 2012—Section 4: Integration of newcomers and Canadian citizenship.* http://www.cic.gc.ca/english/resources/publications/annual-report-2012/section4.asp

Guo, Y. (2015). Language policies and programs for adult immigrants in Canada: Deconstructing discourses of integration. *New Directions for Adult and Continuing Education, 2015*(146), 41–51. https://doi.org/10.1002/ace.20130

Hamm, L. (2015). Hiring and retaining teachers in diverse schools and districts. In N. Maynes & B. Hatt (Eds.), *The complexity of hiring, supporting, and retaining new teachers across Canada* (pp. 40–61). Canadian Association for Teacher Education; Canadian Society for Studies in Education.

Harris, K. (2019, 28 January). Online applications to sponsor family immigrants hit limit in less than 11 minutes. *CBC News.* https://www.cbc.ca/news/politics/ircc-parent-grandparent-sponsorship-filled-2019-1.4995806

Hébert, Y. M. (2013). Cosmopolitanism and Canadian multicultural policy: Intersection, relevance and critique. *Encounters on Education, 14.* https://doi.org/10.24908/eoe-ese-rse.v14i0.4088

Hellstrom, M. (2018). Refugees discuss their settlement experience in New Brunswick [policy brief]. *Migration in Remote and Rural Areas,* 1–6. https://rplcarchive.ca/wp-content/uploads/2018/12/Hellstrom.-MIRRA-Research-Brief.pdf

Hiebert, D. (2006). Winning, losing, and still playing the game: The political economy of immigration in Canada. *Tijdschrift voor economische en sociale geografie, 97*(1), 38–48. https://doi.org/10.1111/j.1467-9663.2006.00494.x

Hyndman, J., Jimenez, S., & Payne, W. (2017). *The state of private refugee sponsorship in Canada: Trends, issues, and impacts.* Centre for Refugee Studies, York University. http://jhyndman.info.yorku.ca/files/2017/05/hyndman_et-al.-RRN-brief-Jan-2017-best.pdf

Jedwab, J., & Wilkinson, L. (2016). When it comes to migrant belonging and trust, it's not about the money, money . . . : A comparison of Canada's refugees and economic immigrants. *Canadian Diversity, 13*(2), 19–26.

Kandiah, L. (2018). Refugee mental health: A review of literature on treatment, practices and recommendations. *Journal of Ethics in Mental Health, 10*, 1–19.

Kelley, N., & Trebilcock, M. (2010). *Making of the mosaic: A history of Canadian immigration policy* (2nd ed.). University of Toronto Press.

Krahn, H., Derwing, T. M., & Abu-Laban, B. (2005). The retention of newcomers in second- and third-tier Canadian cities. *International Migration Review, 39*(4), 872–894. https://doi.org/10.1111/j.1747-7379.2005.tb00292.x

Kyriakides, C., Bajjali, L., McLuhan, A., & Anderson, K. (2018). Beyond refuge: Contested orientalism and persons of self-rescue. *Canadian Ethnic Studies, 50*(2), 59–78. https://doi.org/10.1353/ces.2018.0015

Lam, M. A. (2021a). "It's cold here": Lessons learned from the welcome perceived by newcomers to Brandon, Manitoba. *Diaspora, Indigenous, and Minority Education, 15*(4), 263–275. https://doi.org/10.1080/15595692.2021.1944086

Lam, M. A. (2021b). *Friendly Manitoba? A Brandon case study on welcoming newcomers outside the big city* [Doctoral dissertation, University of Manitoba]. https://mspace. lib.umanitoba.ca/xmlui/handle/1993/35327

Leung, C. (2016). English as an additional language: A genealogy of language-in-education policies and reflections on research trajectories. *Language and Education, 30*(2), 158–174. https://doi.org/10.1080/09500782.2015.1103260

Li, P. S. (2002). *Destination Canada: Immigration debates and issues.* Oxford University Press.

Li, P. S. (2003). Deconstructing Canada's discourse of immigrant integration. *Journal of International Migration and Integration, 4*(3), 315–333. https://doi.org/10.1007/s12134-003-1024-0

Marom, L. (2019). Under the cloak of professionalism: Covert racism in teacher education. *Race Ethnicity and Education, 22*(3), 319–337. https://doi.org/10.1080/13613324.2018.1468748

Neuman, K. (2022). *Canadian public opinion about immigration and refugees—Fall 2022.* Environics Institute. https://www.environicsinstitute.org/projects/project-details/canadian-public-opinion-about-immigration-and-refugees---fall-2022

Reitz, J. G., & Banerjee, R. (2007). Racial inequality, social cohesion and policy issues in Canada [policy brief]. *Institute for Research on Public Policy.* 1–57. https://irpp.org/research-studies/racial-inequality-social-cohesion-and-policy-issues-in-canada/

Robertson, H-J. (2005). Lost in translation. *Phi Delta Kappan, 86*(5), 410–411. https://doi.org/10.1177/003172170508600516

Shan, H. (2015). Settlement services in the training and education of immigrants: Toward a participatory mode of governance. *New Directions for Adult and Continuing Education, 2015*(146), 19–28. https://doi.org/10.1002/ace.20128

Sharples, R., & Blair, K. (2021). Claiming "anti-white racism" in Australia: Victimhood, identity, and privilege. *Journal of Sociology, 57*(3), 559–576. https://doi.org/10.1177/1440783320934184

Shields, J., & Türegün, A. (2014). *Settlement and integration research synthesis report.* CERIS. https://rshare.library.torontomu.ca/articles/report/Settlement_and_Integration_Research_Synthesis_2009-2013/23929164

Varma, M. (2003). Including immigration in the rural first aid kit. In R. Blake & A. Nurse (Eds.), *The trajectories of rural life: New perspectives on rural Canada* (pp. 85–100). Canadian Plains Research Centre.

Wilkinson, L. (2013). Introduction: Developing and testing a generalizable model of immigrant integration. *Canadian Ethnic Studies, 45*(3), 1–7. https://doi.org/10.1353/ces.2013.0038

Wong, L., & Guo, S. (2018). Canadian ethnic studies in the changing context of immigration: Looking back, looking forward. *Canadian Ethnic Studies Journal, 50*(1), 1–9.

14

Diversifying Unity and Unifying Diversity:
Christian Hospitality in Multicultural Presbyterian Churches in Toronto

LISA DAVIDSON

What makes for an inclusive church? In 2014, I met with Reverend Thomas,[1] a Scottish Canadian minister at an affluent Presbyterian church in downtown Toronto, who greeted me with a comment that he had just left a meeting with church elders over their growing concerns regarding the congregation's increasing ethnoracial population and the impact of diversity on denominational identity and congregational unity. Since the late 1960s, Canada's Protestant mainline denominations—national churches that travelled to Canada with European settlers in support of colonial efforts and consist of the United, Presbyterian, Anglican, and Lutheran churches—have been experiencing declining numbers and decreasing congregational participation by Anglo White Canadians (Clarke & Macdonald, 2017). With increasing participation of racialized Canadians and newly arrived immigrants from non-European countries, mainline denominations have been experiencing challenges to Eurocentric church culture as congregations are becoming less White and less European.

In 2010, World Vision, Canada's largest Christian development and advocacy agency, published a national study focusing on mainline Christian churches and their strategies to integrate the influx of immigrants into the churches. Canadian diversity, in terms of multiraciality and multi-ethnicity, is a major concern for mainline denominations, particularly those located in major Canadian cities. A common perception among personnel involved in church governance is that Canadian Christian churches, particularly those founded on Anglo-based traditions, are ill prepared to cope with the challenges and opportunities arising from the participation of a diversified population within urban denominations (World Vision, 2010, p. 13). These challenges are obliging many congregations to move away from their European roots and to identify as multicultural to make church life meaningful, relevant, welcoming, and inclusive for non-White migrants and racialized Canadians. Some of the strategies implemented by the Presbyterian Church are founded upon Christian understanding of hospitality, of making church space welcoming to outsiders.

Based upon two years of ethnographic fieldwork in multicultural and multiracial Presbyterian churches in Toronto, this chapter considers the narratives and experiences of racialized churchgoers and their negotiation of belonging, hospitality, and integration into Canadian social life vis-à-vis a Christian worldview. My argument is that the uneven process in becoming Canadian and the fraught experiences of Canadian belonging are inseparable from identities that are both racialized and Christian. Racialized Christians make sense of their transnational mobility, migration and labour experiences, and integration into Canada in terms of their relationship with God and what constitutes a good Christian life. Finally, and more broadly, my argument is an intervention into the celebratory framing of Canadian multiculturalism by demonstrating (1) how Protestant churches are engaging with Canadian multicultural socio-politics through a framework of Christian hospitality; (2) the challenge of "unifying diversity," endemic to multiple Canadian spaces and institutions; and (3) the tension among tolerance, compassion, and belonging experienced by racialized Christians.

Welcoming the Stranger: Hospitality and the Question of Dignity and Compassion

Christian hospitality is about ways of being together as diverse people united in a common faith. The ideas, key words, and actions that might appear to be emergent to multiculturalism, such as welcome and inclusion, are values associated with Christian hospitality. The ubiquitous phrase *welcoming the stranger* is an utterance widely used in churches to describe a statement of and process for transforming and stabilizing social relationships with those who are new to the church. What was emphasized to me that distinguishes Christian hospitality from state multiculturalism is the practice and intimacy of compassion and dignity within the church community and with strangers. However, what is at stake when engaging with a stranger? In biblical passages, the stranger is an ambiguous figure who has the potential and potency of the sacred since God is exemplified within the subjectivity of a stranger. Politically and socially, the stranger is fetishized as an outsider, an unknown person and a person without status and group membership. A stranger does not belong. As noted by Pitt-Rivers (1963), the status and identity of the stranger from their group of origin are not transferable to the new group, and the stranger is "othered." Because of their ambivalent status, strangers are looked at with suspicion and conceptualized as a category of hostility and violence by the new group (Ahmed, 2000; Derrida, 2000; Pitt-Rivers, 1992).

Sara Ahmed (2000) articulates that the crime prevention discourse of "stranger danger" defines what is safe and what is threatening. Strangers in this discursive domain are particular kinds of bodies marked in relation to a neighbour (who is safe), whereas a stranger is popularly imagined as an opaque figure lurking in the shadows awaiting nefarious opportunities. The stranger is thus perceived as dangerous because *"the outside is contained within a figure we imagine we have already faced"* (Ahmed, 2000, p. 2). In this formulation, a stranger is a predetermined body: it is already known, formed by what is already deemed unsafe, antagonistic, and inimical. Strangers are depersonified, and at times dehumanized, as they are detached from their own histories as a means of making them knowable to the host/receiving community. The act of welcoming produces the stranger because it already assumes that certain groups do not belong (Ahmed, 2000, p. 21).

Parallel to stranger danger is the alien stranger who is not only a relational encounter but also a spatial foreigner; the alien is the "outsider inside" (Ahmed, 2000, p. 3). The stranger is not only a relational quality but also a spatial attribute since there is an assumption that strangers desire to settle, thus bringing along with them their values, ideas, and beliefs to the receiving community (Simmel, 1950). Strangers stand out only if they stay; a stranger who remains mobile is more inclined to be welcomed by a community because acts of openness and hospitality do not necessarily entail expectations, permanence, or commitments of reciprocity (Simmel, 1950, p. 404). For host communities, the alien stranger strains the limits of hospitality since receiving such individuals cannot be thought of as a "welcome" given the potential for hostility and subsequent aggression, whether affective or physical, which thereby debases a person's dignity and sense of personhood, re-emphasizing that the person does not belong.

Derrida's writing on hospitality allows for a more nuanced understanding of the crux of hospitable relations, highlighting the tension of belonging and non-belonging. Although Derrida was inspired by Levinas's essays on the other, his thinking on hospitality was a response to Kant's work on the moral and legal cosmopolitan rights of people who cross the boundaries of their communities, specifically the moral and legal relationships between hosts and strangers (Derrida, 2000, p. 4). Hospitality for Derrida is a series of multiple double binds, rooted in the principle that universal hospitality cannot be conditional, and he focuses on distinguishing between "absolute hospitality" and "conditional hospitality" (Derrida, 2000; Still, 2010; Westmoreland, 2008).

Absolute hospitality, Derrida argues, is impossible because it is unconditional and immediate (Still, 2010, p. 8). By making the stranger (a foreigner) feel "at home," hosts (either citizens or states) must relinquish their sense of self and their sense of belonging and deprive themselves of their own identity. This, according to Derrida, is the crux and the double bind of hospitality. Ideologically, strangers are expected to make themselves at home; however, in actuality, this is a conditional form of welcome based upon the premise that the stranger will observe and obey the rules, conventions, and expectations of the host (Derrida, 2000, p. 12). A completely open welcome, at the core of absolute hospitality, is a welcome without limitation, invitation, or reciprocity (Derrida, 2000, p. 14; Still, 2010, p. 8; Westmoreland, 2008, p. 5). Ahn (2010, p. 250) thinks of this paradigm of hospitality as "a gift without gift" because it requires the surrender of "judgement and control over who will receive that hospitality." The act of inviting a stranger into one's domain (whether a church, a home, or even a country) is based upon conditional hospitality because an invitation presumes the presence of a door, a metaphorical or literal separation between strangers and hosts that must be crossed, and once crossed there is an expectation that outsiders will conduct themselves in a manner appropriate to hosts (Derrida, 2000, p. 2).

Although hospitality is generally recognized and experienced as a structure of reciprocity, whereby the host is recognized as a host through the guest's gratitude and perhaps eventual reciprocity, absolute hospitality entails no recognition, debt, or expectation of exchange since these are conditions of hospitality (Still, 2010, p. 15). This, for Derrida, is the crux of hospitality. In the act of depriving sovereignty to welcome and accommodate a guest, hospitality folds into the domain of hostility since hosts can no longer be true to themselves. The guest transforms into an enemy and is treated with hostility (Derrida, 2000, p. 4; Westmoreland, 2008). In other words, the host works to include the guest through practices that ensure the host's own exclusion. This is a unilineal flow of hospitality, a top-down model from host to guest.

The theoretical utility of Derridean hospitality is less as a resource to explain ethnographic data (Candea, 2012) than as a starting point to explain the fraught relationships arising from subjectivities that circulate among strangers, guests, and hosts. Indeed, people might find themselves situated within several categories of hospitality, moving from one subjectivity to another through the microprocesses of everyday acts of hospitality and more eventful moments of welcome. Strangers become less strange when they enter the domain of guests, guests might engage in host-like practices, strangers might interact with guests as if they were hosts, and hosts might become guests.

Toronto East Community Presbyterian Church: A Multicultural Congregation

Located in Don Valley Village, a gentrifying neighbourhood on the east side of Toronto, the Toronto East Community Presbyterian Church (TECPC) was established in the late 1870s in a working-class neighbourhood in East York, an area of Toronto east of the Don Valley. The simplicity of the 140-year-old brick church is a historical residual of the church's conservative and austere presence in a working-class past. Don Valley Village, where TECPC is located, was a low-income, working-class enclave, but today the neighbourhood is an eclectic mix of social housing, low-income Canadians and immigrants, young professionals, and affluent families. Older Anglo-Presbyterians expressed to me that hospitality is now hard work. Previously, the dominant perception was that all that had to be done was build a church and people would come together. Church members are now faced with the work of doing a plurality of hospitalities because of the ubiquity and salience of cultural, racial, and class differences, and this work is even more problematic both experientially and affectively because who is considered a stranger, guest, or host is not clear.

Within TECPC, racialized congregants outnumber White congregants, elderly members eclipse young members, and the number of underprivileged churchgoers exceeds economically well-off members. For church leaders, this kind of congregational diversity presents a set of challenges to a church experiencing declining membership and finances. A method for uniting a congregation that contains a plethora of differences, attitudes, experiences, hopes, and ambitions is what motivated the minister to label TECPC a multicultural church. "Multiculturalism" allows for an ideology of unity that forges common ground between White and racialized congregants and among congregants of various classes and generations. In practice, the term does not smooth over congregational differences, it does not ease uncomfortable interactions between long-term members and new members, and it does not address standards of church decorum that exclude certain groups from participating in the dominant White church culture: its governing structures and congregational activities. The hope is that the identifying marker of multiculturalism will relieve the initial anxieties of newcomers in order to join church activities in an era when many mainline congregations are experiencing spiritual, financial, and population decline. In Canada, multiculturalism is an ideology of benevolence, tolerance, and equality that advances celebrations to demonstrate recognition of cultures and cultural differences; however, it is also a state policy that effaces racial inequalities while perpetuating exclusions, occlusions, and displacements (Haque, 2012; McElhinny et al., 2012; Thobani, 2007).

Making Church Inclusive and Welcoming Difference: Racializing Ministry

Reverend Abraham Vellanueva, the teaching minister at TECPC, migrated from the Philippines to Canada in the 1980s to work as a chef in the Alberta tar sands. His calling to the Presbyterian Church and how he conducts his sermons and worship are grounded in theological social justice that grows out of his own experiences of labour migration, deskilling, and downward class mobility in Canada. Abraham did not migrate to Canada as a pastor; rather, it was his downward class mobility after he arrived and his precarious existence in Canada that allowed him to hear God's calling. Prior to his role as a preacher, he was the international director of operations for Kentucky Fried Chicken (a fast-food restaurant chain), travelling frequently between Atlanta, Vancouver, and Manila. When Abraham decided to relocate permanently to Vancouver, he found that his labour expertise and his educational credentials of an MBA and culinary chef offered no professional pathways. He worked in several low-wage jobs in the service sector before landing work in a kitchen for a mining company in Fort McMurray, a gateway town to the oil industry in northern Alberta.

Working in a remote area, separated from his family for extended periods of time, was a turning point for Abraham. His work required him to leave his family for twenty-four days a month, return to his family in Vancouver for thirteen days, and then return to the camp for another twenty-four-day cycle. He says that it was emotional and spiritual death for his well-being and sense of self: "Eventually, it killed me. It burnt me out. Shifts were 24/7, there was no Saturday or Sunday, we just kept cooking and cooking. . . . I just felt like I had a call to be somewhere else, and I started to look for seminaries on the internet." Returning to seminary was a spiritual and political choice and a pathway to reclaim his sense of humanity because he felt neither welcomed nor valued in Canada. Today Abraham sees himself as a "street preacher" because he refuses to separate his spiritual work as a minister from his political work with the homeless and migrant workers: "My entire reading of the biblical narrative is all political. It cannot be helped that, if I am telling a story from the Bible while here in the pulpit, I'm going to tell you that story using politics as the lens."

Abraham tries to bring to the church the synergy that he feels on the street, protesting in solidarity with other people and raising awareness of social justice and contemporary issues of inequality, which at the time of my fieldwork related to concerns about housing, migration, and the incarceration of transgendered men. He wants people to be "out there" rather than remaining confined to pews. For Abraham, the belief behind the saying "we are church" is that people, as the children of God, need to make change happen. In his emphatic words, "what does God want? God wants to change our world. He does not want suffering, starvation, and death. If we don't move, nothing is going to change." Welcoming others is thus not only about "guests" crossing the threshold of church doors but also involves the conduct of "hosts" in stepping outside God's domain to reach out to people categorized as strangers or outsiders because of their racialized and socio-economic differences. Radical hospitality is not a celebration of difference but an expression of compassion and love that takes on the question of being different and equal. However, not all congregants welcome his politics.

In one sermon, Abraham raised awareness of racialized immigrants in Canada. He purposefully refused White examples in his sermons to intervene in the normalcy and privilege of Presbyterian White experience. This tactic, however, was interpreted by more privileged congregants as an effective moment of White discrimination since it invalidated immigration and integration experienced through inclusionary tactics and the promise of upward class mobility. Joan, who migrated to Canada from Scotland, was irate with Abraham's refusal. Unable to identify with the experiences of racialized immigrants who entered Canada in the 1980s, she told me that

> what I find with Abraham is the emphasis on immigrants and the trouble they have in Canada. Abraham decided to do something of a talk to people, and he had a group of immigrants up in the front of the church. He passed the microphone [to them] and asked them what was it like coming to Canada and what kind of troubles did they have in settling in Canada etc. I kind of put myself in there because all of them are [a] different colour. And I felt they had to realize that immigrants are more than different colours, there is white too. So I snuck in there and sat down. When the microphone came to me and I said, "Well, I came to Canada as an immigrant, but I came as an educated person. I didn't have to worry about getting a job because I was a nurse. Everybody got a job in those days as a nurse. So we came here. We worked. We never took anything out of the system. We just worked! I couldn't even pay into unemployment insurance because nurses were never laid off."

What Joan found particularly problematic is the premise underlying the question of immigration as a homogeneously negative experience. She mentioned that "it is the premise that immigrants have to be in trouble that was irking me at the time. And it wasn't just me. When Abraham approached Enzi (a congregant who migrated from Swaziland), he said, 'I came here, and I have thoroughly enjoyed it ever since I got here, and I have never had any trouble.'" In making the church an explicit site of contestation for social equality and social change, Abraham experienced pushback from congregants who do not see themselves and their experiences within the same category of dehumanized migrant labour.

Another example of Abraham taking a non-traditional and more inclusive approach in Presbyterian ministering is how he changes his attire from week to week because the congregation is a socio-economic combination of professionals, working-class retirees, low-income people, and those without income who depend on government subsidies. One Sunday he would wear a Filipino *barong*, an embroidered, lightweight, long-sleeve shirt worn over a white undershirt; another Sunday he would wear a black-hooded sweatshirt and frayed jeans; other Sundays he would sport a Hawaiian-style T-shirt. Only on special occasions would Abraham wear his clerical robes, shirt, and tab collar insert, marking the importance of the sacrament of communion, Maundy Thursday (a Christian holy day commemorating the last supper of Jesus), Christmas Eve Mass, and Easter Sunday. When I questioned him about his attire, he laughed and asked me if I liked it. He followed up with a more serious tone, explaining to me that it was his attempt to intervene in overt class distinctions and racialized barriers within the church. By dressing in a variety of styles, the aim of his appearance was to make Sunday services and his sermons more accessible to all individuals, especially those who could not afford the formal wear of "Sunday best." By wearing a rumpled T-shirt and sweatpants, Abraham expressed that his own attire would diminish the stigmas and insensitivities associated with underprivileged and racialized disparities.

White Anglo church elders, who form a governing body within the church called the "session," are aware of the changes that Abraham is bringing to the church. They are uncertain, however, whether such changes will make the church "more ethnic" or whether they will do "something different, something new," to bring in new congregants. Such perceptions, however, convey that Abraham is moving church life away from normative Anglocentric practices. One elder, for example, remarked on the changes that Abraham made to holy communion. "The breaking of the bread is an old tradition in the church," she said. "Abraham breaks the bread from a solid lump of bread, and I was used to the little wafers." In a conservative church such as TECPC, elders experience his efforts to revitalize old traditions, such as making use of a new type of bread, as drastic changes. Unsure how to make sense of the modifications that Abraham is bringing to the church, the elders do not interpret these changes as cultural bridges, and they see these efforts not as cleavages with Canadian traditions but as personal nuances made by a minister. It is also arguable that his interventions were lost on many White members of the congregation. The point of his ministry is to guide the transformation of congregational relationships, within and outside church space, by presenting alternative ways of knowing and feeling church life and by making the unfamiliar less strange.

Making the Church Relevant: Belonging by Becoming

At a neighbouring, more affluent church, Queensview Presbyterian Church, the minister describes its organizational tradition as "very White, very male, and very professional." Diversifying the church from the perspective of its elders does not necessarily mean the inclusion of racialized congregants; rather, diversity and inclusion pertain to the activities that the church provides to racialized and underprivileged people within the surrounding community. White elders praised the humanitarian-based work of White Anglo congregants who developed English learning programs and services to members of the Chinese, Korean, and Vietnamese communities in neighbourhoods adjacent to the church. Racialized participants are mostly newly arrived international students from Korea and China and migrant labourers who have been in Canada for several decades yet have only basic-level English skills.

One strategy for community inclusion is through a church program called Monday Night in Canada, a play on words intended to be "fun and catchy," according to its organizers. When I spoke with racialized and immigrant guests who attended the dinners, it seemed that the humour of the name was lost on them. Most were unfamiliar with the TV program *Hockey Night in Canada* by the Canadian Broadcasting Corporation, its weekly broadcast of National Hockey League games on Saturday evenings.

The mission statement of this outreach program, according to the Monday Night in Canada pamphlet, is "to provide hospitality to new immigrants . . . [and] a chance for newcomers to experience common

Canadian cultural activities and to practice English while doing these activities." When I spoke with White volunteers, they noted that the program developed from requests by racialized churchgoers within the neighbourhood. They said that they wanted to improve their English so that they could better navigate Canadian society.

The goal of the program is an "intentional offer of hospitality" through social interaction. Organizers and volunteers distributed to each dinner guest conversation sheets listing various topics of discussion pertinent to Canadian food, holidays, habits, values, and beliefs. This was a way to help non-English speakers learn the language and a method for starting dialogue between immigrants and White Canadians. White volunteers demystified eastern Canadian colloquialisms such as "tube steak" and "2-4" and demonstrated the nuances of eating Canadian finger food, such as hamburgers and pizza. They also explained the symbols, customs, and values attached to national holidays such as Thanksgiving and Halloween. Guests at these dinners appeared to enjoy their time with church volunteers, smiling and nodding their heads, ostensibly indicating gratitude and appreciation. During these dinners, church space was a microcosm of White Canadian benevolence and hyper-nationalism.

Diversity and inclusion in these activities, however, are not about social justice or radical politics. Canadian multicultural hegemony underlies the affective and practical experience through recognition and tolerance. The exchange that transpired at Queensview Presbyterian between church hosts and community guests was normally unidirectional; White congregants dominated the floor, speaking to each other and trying to clarify each other's word definitions. At times, the interaction between the volunteers only added to the confusion of the participants. In one exchange between two White Canadian volunteers, Katherine and Louis, their turn-taking is best characterized as a ping-pong match. Katherine would cut off Louis from completing his definition of a word to reframe the definition. At other times, one would interrupt to complete the other's sentence. The turn-taking was very quick, and Chen, a student from China, had much difficulty gaining the floor to speak. He resolved the dilemma by pulling out his cell phone from his back pants pocket and using the Google translation app to help decipher the meaning of the word that Katherine and Louis were trying to interpret.

While White congregants tried to explain the nuances of Canadian food, idiomatic language, national holidays, and customs, there was little reciprocity in which newcomers were asked to share their own cultural values, languages, beliefs, and experiences. When Chen and his friend Ray, a fellow exchange student, revealed to Katherine that they were from China, she interjected during their turn to explain the history of Chinese migrants in Canada. She positioned herself as an expert who educated newcomers on the Canadian railway and the role of Chinese labourers in uniting Canada.

Welcome, in this instance, is to help support the integration and adaptation of non-Canadians into Canadian social life as opposed to listening to and learning from the experiences of newcomers. This is a multicultural rationale for belonging and inclusion as newcomers learn that an unaccented register of English might reduce discrimination against them and improve their participation in the Canadian labour force (Ameeriar, 2017). It is noteworthy that there was no Christian proselytizing during the community-based activities for racialized neighbours, and many of the guests told me that their only affiliation with Queensview Presbyterian was their participation in the Monday Night in Canada event. Church leaders pointed out that those who enter the church do so because they want to be involved with something that is culturally different, such as an Anglocentric and Canadian experience.

Unifying Diversity or Diversifying Unity?
Multicultural Belonging and Christian Hospitality

Among teaching elders, multiculturalism takes on divergent ideological strategies in pastoral care and ministry unity within congregations characterized by ethnoracial and class disparities. White church leaders are more inclined to reproduce neo-liberal multiculturalism, training racialized groups to become economic Christian citizens by inculcating an academic English-language register, denoting the possibility of prestige and privilege. Such strategies align with non-religious community programs that support language training, cross-cultural communication, and improvement of race relations (Allan, 2016; Das Gupta, 1999). For non-White church leaders such as Abraham, they are trying to challenge the Whiteness and uniformity of the church through innovative and overt tactics perceived to celebrate difference, such as narration of biblical passages and the singing of psalms in languages other than English, but are actually political and ethical practices that make the church hospitable and open to the histories of diverse racialized groups.

Each congregation has different practices of diversity and inclusion. More affluent congregations tend to deploy programs that emphasize state-centric multiculturalism by accentuating the assimilation and integration of racialized churchgoers into White Canadian culture: learning a professional register of written and spoken English and learning signs that index Canadian values, holidays, foods, and utterances. In such practices, multiculturalism is a unidirectional flow of learning and engagement. At TECPC, a less affluent congregation, multiculturalism is a tool for making the congregation open to differences based upon an ethic of justice and equality that grows out of the leadership of a racialized minister. This is an irregular endeavour, however, as congregants make sense of diversity, inclusion, and belonging through their experiences, hopes, and risks in migrating across borders and through their interactions with people who are racially, economically, spiritually, and culturally different.

Christian hospitality is about ways of being together as diverse people united in a common faith. Openness and welcome go hand-in-hand with faithfulness since they are ways for knowing God—a God for all people. Tom Selwyn (2000), a professor of anthropology at the University of London, details various scriptures throughout the Bible in which acts of hospitality are voluntary and altruistic, in which a relationship is not only established but also undergoes a process of transformation. Hospitality is a process of conversion in which strangers are made familiar, enemies become friends, and friends are turned into better friends (Selwyn, 2000, p. 35). Hospitality is a form of affective learning by engaging the heart and mind for mediating relationships. Affective learning is what some of my research participants called the "heart's mind," a way of knowing that collapses Cartesian mind-body dualism and the prioritization of knowing through the rational mind. Learning to attune oneself to feelings and senses allows for a deeper understanding of the Holy Spirit flowing through the body. For some congregants, affective moments crystallize the presence of God and the Holy Spirit to guide churchgoers to act with hospitality.

Ministers and congregants emphasized that mutuality is central to hospitality and foregrounds how Christians understand a Christian-infused sense of multiculturalism. Mutuality is about respecting differences by having conversations and relationships with others without assimilation. Assimilation, for some Presbyterians, is a transgression of God's love and gift of diversity. Letty Russell (2009, pp. 19–20), a feminist Presbyterian theologian, describes hospitality as a disposition that goes beyond the post-sermon offering of tea and cake: "Hospitality is the practice of God's welcome by reaching across difference to participate in God's actions bringing justice and healing to our world in crisis. . . . [H]ospitality can be understood as *solidarity with strangers*, a mutual relationship of care and trust in which we share in the struggle for empowerment, dignity and fullness of life."

Christian hospitality, accordingly, can be understood as inseparable from political action that requires individuals to reflect on whether they are "of" this world or "in" this world (Russell, 2009). Being of this world or community is required because it entails tactics of social and subjective reflection on injustices, yet self-reflection alone is inhospitable because it fails to include actions for just and peaceful relations. Hospitality, then, must be constantly cultivated and rethought to allow individuals and communities to shape how they flourish in extending the work of peace and justice, which characterizes being in the world (Russell, 2009, p. 15). This is a different framing of the prevalent Christian theme of being in but not of this world: Christians are of the Kingdom of God and are in the world to cultivate religious faithfulness (see Elisha, 2011, p. 193).

Being in this world is what makes hospitality a difficult ethical endeavour. Congregants understand the biblical rationale and ethics of Christian hospitality of being open and welcoming, but to put hospitality into practice in this worldly domain is to be influenced by everyday hostilities, arguments, restlessness, fears, and insecurities. Speaking to the tension and ambiguity of living in contemporary society while following the ways of Jesus, Abraham consistently reminded churchgoers that "God is calling us to be compassionate." He explains that to model oneself after the image of a compassionate God is to become a vessel of love and grace. For congregants, to be in this world is to follow Jesus in using the streets and valleys as spaces to show what compassion is in both word and action. The act of welcoming means that the host must venture beyond the security and comfort of church walls, must go out and interact with members of the community. Engaging in conversation transcends the visibility of difference, of otherness, and allows for rapport beyond the containment of church walls. Christian hospitality, then, is not confined to one momentous act or place; rather, it is a series of small, mundane acts that establishes and transforms social relations (Selwyn, 2000; Shryock, 2012).

It is arguable that state multiculturalism obstructs the church from becoming radically hospitable. Seeing difference alone does not inspire unity within diversity and ultimately ignores social justice issues (Russell, 2009). Russell emphasizes that an ethical Christian hospitality is not about saving, dominating, or controlling diversity, particularly strangers from colonized populations; rather, it is about loving differences. As Presbyterian congregants told me, God created diversity and difference throughout the natural world. Rather than meeting the strangeness of God's creations with ambivalence and fear, Christian virtue means meeting differences with love and openness. This is especially difficult in a multicultural city, such as Toronto, where people are situated in so many differences that the search for similarity and commonality appeals to those who feel isolated and who desire understanding and a sense of belonging.

References

Ahmed, S. (2000). *Strange encounters: Embodied others in post-coloniality*. Routledge.

Ahn, I. (2010). Economy of "invisible debt" and ethics of "radical hospitality": Towards a paradigm change of hospitality from "gift" to "forgiveness." *Journal of Religious Ethics, 38*(2), 243–267.

Allan, K. (2016). Self-appreciation and the value of employability: Integrating un(der) employed immigrants in post-Fordist Canada. In L. Adkhan & M. Dever (Eds.), *The post-Fordist sexual contract: Working and living in contingency* (pp. 49–70). Palgrave Macmillan.

Ameeriar, L. (2017). *Downwardly global: Women, work and citizenship in the Pakistani diaspora*. Duke University Press.

Candea, M. (2012). Derrida en Corse? Hospitality as scale-free abstraction. *Journal of the Royal Anthropological Institute, NS*, S34–S48.

Clarke, B., & Macdonald, S. (2017). *Leaving Christianity: Changing allegiances in Canada since 1945*. McGill-Queen's University Press.

Das Gupta, T. (1999). The politics of multiculturalism: "Immigrant women" and the Canadian state. In E. Dua & A. Robertson (Eds.), *Scratching the surface: Canadian, anti-racist, feminist thought* (pp. 187–206). Women's Press.

Derrida, J. (2000). *Of hospitality*. Stanford University Press.

Elisha, O. (2011). *Moral ambition: Mobilization and social outreach in evangelical megachurches*. University of California Press.

Haque, E. (2012). *Multiculturalism within a bilingual framework: Language, race, and belonging in Canada*. University of Toronto Press.

McElhinny, B., Davidson, L. M., Catungal, J. P., Tungohan, E., & Coloma, R. S. (2012). Spectres of (in)visibility: Filipina/o labor, culture and youth in Canada. In R. S. Coloma et al. (Eds.), *Filipinos in Canada: Disturbing invisibility* (pp. 5–45). University of Toronto Press.

Pitt-Rivers, J. (1963). The stranger, the guest and the hostile host: Introduction to the study of laws of hospitality. In J. G. Peristiany (Ed.), *Contributions to Mediterranean sociology: Mediterranean rural communities and social change* (pp. 13–30). Mouton & Company.

Pitt-Rivers, J. (1992). Postscript: The place of grace in anthropology. In J. G. Peristiany & J. Pitt-Rivers (Eds.), *Honor and grace in anthropology* (pp. 215–246). Cambridge University Press.

Russell, L. M. (2009). *Just hospitality: God's welcome in a world of difference* (J. S. Clarkson & K. M. Otts, Eds.). Westminster-John Knox.

Selwyn, T. (2000). An anthropology of hospitality. In C. Lashley & A. Morrison (Eds.), *In search of hospitality: Theoretical perspectives and debates* (pp. 18–37). Elsevier.

Shryock, A. (2012). Breaking hospitality apart: Bad hosts, bad guests, and the problem of sovereignty. *Journal of the Royal Anthropological Institute, NS*, S20–S33.

Simmel, G. (1950). *The sociology of Georg Simmel* (K. H. Wolff, Trans.). Free Press.

Still, J. (2010). *Derrida and hospitality: Theory and practice*. Edinburgh University Press.

Thobani, S. (2007). *Exalted subjects: Studies in the making of race and nation in Canada*. University of Toronto Press.

Westmoreland, M. W. (2008). Interruptions: Derrida and hospitality. *Kritike, 2*(1), 1–10.

World Vision. (2010). *Beyond the welcome: Churches responding to the immigrant reality in Canada: Final research report*. https://www.ureachcanada.ca/wp-content/uploads/2018/03/BTW_Report_Long.pdf

Endnotes

1   The names of the neighbourhood, church, research participants, and congregants are all pseudonyms.

15

Yiddish in Canada:
A Study of the Rise and Fall of a Unique Form of Cultural and Linguistic Diversity

NORMAN RAVVIN

In 1963, an order-in-council—an extra-parliamentary injunction by the prime minister's cabinet—empowered the Royal Commission on Bilingualism and Biculturalism to canvass the country about a new, more overt national program built upon bicultural and bilingual ideals. The Royal Commission that toured the country, tasked to prepare a report on these matters, was instructed to take account of the "contribution made by the other ethnic groups to the cultural enrichment of Canada" (Menkis, 2011, p. 285). This led a variety of ethnic communities to demand that they be acknowledged as equal to the commission's primary groups, the French- and English-language majorities. Yet the new federal catchwords and policies associated with bilingualism and biculturalism did not entice Jewish community leaders, represented most directly by the Canadian Jewish Congress.

These developments in what would lead to the federal policy known as multiculturalism took place at a time of successful assimilationist urges and accomplishments among Canadian Jews. They had found their way into social, economic, and educational roles that they had not previously held in meaningful numbers. At the same time, a major national cultural policy shift, which would define Jews as one among many other "ethnic" groups, was not viewed as a promising innovation for minority relations with the mainstream (Menkis, 2011, pp. 285–286).

Rebecca Margolis (2011–2012, p. 216) notes that, in the hearings on bilingualism and biculturalism, Jewish communal representation and requests for financial support were negligible. If language was to be among the deciding factors associated with a new federal policy on minority groups, then this development arrived as linguistic distinctiveness among Canadian Jews was on the wane. The 1961 census signalled a substantial drop in the number declaring Yiddish as their "mother tongue," the language used in their homes (Margolis, 2011–2012, p. 217). The Canadian reordering of national identity around issues of ethnicity, bound to language, took shape as Jews were reordering their own affiliations: home life in Yiddish was in eclipse; organizational and social life, undertaken in Yiddish in a variety of contexts since the early twentieth century, shifted to English; and Hebrew—the language of the State of Israel—replaced Yiddish among families who sent their children to Jewish day schools or part-time language programs at synagogues or community centres.

But Hebrew language would never parallel the centrality that Yiddish language had held in daily life. Communal leaders, most importantly those with the Montreal-based Canadian Jewish Congress, were most comfortable with Jewishness characterized in relation to religious identity. Jewish leftist organizations and language-focused Yiddishist groups continued to promote and insist on the centrality of "secular Yiddish culture" and "cultural pluralism" as the foundations upon which Canadian Jews should place themselves within the official framework of biculturalism (Margolis, 2011–2012, p. 217). Although the Yiddishist counterproposal was supported by a shrinking minority of Jews by the 1960s, it continued to play linguistic, social, educational, and political roles. It is this minority position—once among the most robust forms of identity among Canadian Jews—that I aim to address in this chapter in light of this volume's focus on diversity in recent constructions of Canadian identity.

My contribution to this discussion requires that I position myself within the historical and cultural shifts associated with Yiddish and the Canadian mainstream. I do this in part to highlight how a chapter about language and identity—though broad in scope—is refracted, from the outset, through the writer's personal and particular commitments and background. Born the year that the Royal Commission was struck, I am of the first Canadian-born generation in my immediate family. My parents, regardless of how fully Canadian they became, began as newcomers in Yiddish-speaking milieux: my father's family arrived in Calgary from Russia in 1922, and my mother's family alighted in Saskatchewan from central Poland in 1935. Both my parents were born into Yiddish-speaking families, though my mother's Vancouver home retained its Yiddish mother tongue, whereas my father's family abandoned it. Still, my father was sent in the late 1920s to the I. L. Peretz School, a secular, leftist-oriented, Yiddish-language day school in Calgary's downtown Jewish neighbourhood.

I have his Yiddish reader of that time, published on Grand Street in Manhattan, under the title *Unzer vort* (Our word). On the book's flyleaf, he double-inscribed himself. On the left, in Yiddish, he is Avraham Raveen (I transliterate to approximate the spoken Yiddish sound of his name). On the right, he is Albert Ravvin, signalling his youthful bilingualism. *Unzer vort* is a weighty tome for young readers—408 pages of literary and social-historical portraits with a distinctive leftist worker's slant and with youngster-oriented sections with titles such as "Worker-Children" and "The Jewish Child in the Old Country." The first poem on offer is "*Di noit*," by Mani Leib, a Russian-born, New York–based shoemaker who had been arrested by the czarist authorities for revolutionary activities ("*Di noit*" can be translated as "Hardship"). These details are evocative of what was on offer in Yiddish day schools across Canada in the interwar period—attentive study of a language and its literature brought from a variety of Eastern and Central European lands; an ongoing dedication to learning about and retaining a link with those past places; and a leftist ideology that had flourished among the large early-twentieth-century Jewish working class in the Russian Empire and post–First World War Poland. This picture of time and place, with its complex of cultural identification implied by the catchphrase "secular Yiddish culture," begins to define elements of a cultural milieu that no longer held sway among Canadian Jews as the 1963 Royal Commission on Bilingualism and Biculturalism entered mainstream discussions. Completed with the publication of its report in 1969, the commission ushered in the Canada that we live with today.[1]

Eastern European Global Networks

The foregoing polemical introduction allows me to introduce the main goal of this chapter: a recovery and reconsideration of Canadian secular Yiddish culture in the first half of the twentieth century as a unique case of cultural and linguistic diversity, which preceded the arrival of bicul-turalism, bilingualism, and multiculturalism while asserting a unique transnational set of networks and institutions Canadian in their focus, while remaining intimately linked with prior Eastern European mod-els. Since all of this developed (and then failed) in a pre-multicultural Canada, the fact and meaning of this countrywide phenomenon over a roughly six-decade period are not part of Canadian social history or self-identity.

The research that best illuminates the importance of Yiddish as the basis of a transnational Canadian Jewish culture is that of demogra-pher and community worker Louis Rosenberg. His oeuvre includes a compendium of his demographic studies, published in 1939 by the Canadian Jewish Congress, with the title *Canada's Jews: A Social and Economic Study of the Jews in Canada*. Using the ten-year-interval cen-suses of the early decades of the twentieth century, Rosenberg conveys the shifting social context of Canadian Jews, who numbered roughly 16,000 at the turn of the century but over 165,000 at the outbreak of the Second World War (Belkin, 1966, p. 211). The years of impressive population increase preceded the First World War, with a short period of recovery in the 1920s before the oncoming Depression and increas-ingly restrictive regulations put an end to this trend. Writing in 1939, the Polish-born American Yiddish writer Shmuel Niger further helps us to understand this historical period by highlighting a turning point in Jewish lives globally following the First World War.

Catastrophic events of that period, including the Russian Revolution and the Polish-Soviet War of the early 1920s, "changed the environ-ment which conditioned" Yiddish-language culture, presenting it with "new geographic boundaries" (Niger, 1939, p. 337). Niger's main interest is post–First World War Yiddish literature, but the trends that Niger highlights reflect "upheavals," as he puts it, in "the conditions of life, in the geographic, economic, political, and broadly cultural environment of world Jewry" (p. 337). His point is not to rehearse the well-known move-ment of great numbers to new geographic centres but to consider how the "changed" environment of Yiddish-inflected Jewish culture initi-ated and supported new forms of transnational Jewish communal and cultural experiences. The impact on Canada—with its small population and its founding settler context with a bicultural and bilingual charac-ter—of this "changed" Yiddish environment can be easily differentiated from that seen in the United States. This subject provides answers to the commonly asked but often unsuitably answered question regarding the differences between Canadian and American Jewish experiences.

The "changed" environment of Yiddish-speaking culture was not merely affected by geographical shifts. Ideological and political movements initiated in turn-of-the-century Russia and Polish lands motivated and underwrote the patterns that influenced transnational Yiddish institutions. The waves of emigration in the late nineteenth century and early twentieth century coincided with the rise of a secular Yiddishist ethos linked with the Jewish mass labour movement but represented as well by a deeper ideological shift in the direction of what was called diaspora nationalism. Its leading ideologue, Chaim Zhitlovsky, was influenced by the Russian revolutionary movement but dedicated his writing and organizing to the idea that a new secular Jewish identity should be founded upon a rebirth of Yiddish language and literature and on the belief that Eastern European Jews "constituted a distinct national group" (YIVO Institute for Jewish Research, n.d.). Zhitlovsky was central to the effort to declare Yiddish the national language of the Jewish people and to assert an essential non-religious Jewish identity, often referred to as *Yiddishkayt*.[2] Zhitlovsky moved to New York City in 1908 but continued to travel the world, offering lengthy stump speeches for projects such as secular Yiddish-language day schools.

The degree to which these Eastern European Yiddishist concerns influenced Canadian communities large and small is reflected by the remarkable number of visits that Zhitlovsky made to Canada. His first visit to Montreal, in 1910, to attend a labour Zionist conference resulted in a prophetic motion to found Yiddish secular day schools as well as to support the proto-multicultural ideal that "American democracy should not be a 'melting pot' (*shmeltstop*) but, instead, reflect the 'united peoples in the united states [*sic*]'" ("Chaim Zhitlovsky," 2016). Zhitlovsky spoke in Winnipeg in 1915, 1916, and 1917 and made semi-annual visits to Calgary in the 1930s. When he was not in Calgary, Yiddishists there organized fetes to honour his birthday, as they did for his seventieth birthday in 1935 (Switzer, 1999). His last visit to the city in 1943 had a planned length of two weeks to accommodate six public lectures; Zhitlovsky collapsed in the middle of one of these lectures at the Calgary Yiddish Peretz Shul and died at a local hospital. His body was transported to New York City by train under the watchful eye of his

Calgary host, Lou Pearlman, who sat on the memorial podium in New York next to the major Yiddish writer Sholem Asch (Switzer, 1999).

Zhitlovsky's efforts in the early decades of the twentieth century, in tandem with his contemporaries (writers, social activists, and educators), can be contrasted with the undertakings, in the early 1960s, that fostered the federal Royal Commission on Bilingualism and Biculturalism. Both efforts arose in a period of crisis: Zhitlovsky's Yiddish nationalism in response to czarist chaos and pogroms, the Royal Commission in response to the rise of intemperate Quebec cultural and political nationalism. In each case, too, language was the motivating factor for a much broader assertion of ideas about identity. The purpose of the commission, as the preamble to the act defined it, was "to inquire into and report on the existing state of bilingualism and biculturalism in Canada and to recommend what steps should be taken to develop the Canadian Confederation on the basis of an equal partnership between the two founding races, taking into account the contribution made by the other ethnic groups to the cultural enrichment of Canada and the measures that should be taken to safeguard that contribution" (Menkis, 2011, p. 285).

Similarly, Zhitlovsky and other key Yiddish cultural heroes, including the Warsaw-based writer I. L. Peretz, for whom the Calgary day school was named, were the leading voices at an epoch-making conference in Czernowitz, Bukovina, in 1908. There the attendees arrived at their guiding principle of making Yiddish the "national language of the Jewish people" (YIVO Institute for Jewish Research, n.d.). Two years later, in Montreal, it was this principle that motivated Zhitlovsky's call for a broad network of Yiddish day schools. One further crucial link and similarity can be noted in a consideration of his Yiddishism and the ethos that surrounded the Royal Commission on Bilingualism and Biculturalism. In both cases, language was the ground upon which a new kind of national identity came to the fore. Writing after the release of the report, John T. Saywell (1965, p. 379) acknowledged enthusiasm for a new Quebec, a "dynamic society fully formed if not fully clothed, a complete society and political reality determined to wrest from the twentieth century a place in the sun." As early as 1892, Zhitlovsky asserted the idea that "Jews constitute an independent people—'not 4% of one group to another, but 100% of themselves'" ("Chaim Zhitlovsky," 2016).

The ideological work of figures such as Zhitlovsky, supported by the steady years of immigration in the late nineteenth century and early twentieth century, contributed to the founding of what Rebecca Margolis (2009, p. 25) describes as an "international network of Yiddish cultural communities that peaked in the 1920s and 1930s." She adds that, by "the first decades of the twentieth century, Yiddish was a transnational cultural force with a consumer base of millions as well as writers, actors, singers, teachers, and activists spanning political, religious, and general ideological lines" (p. xvii).

The Yiddish centres, or capital cities, included Vilna, Warsaw, Lodz, Moscow, and New York. But the idea of a "cultural capital"—a *hoyptshtot*—was counteracted to a degree by the fact that the language and its attendant cultural creativity were viewed as a surrogate homeland writ large, following the idea that language defined Jews as a "national group," binding them together "across time and space" (Margolis, 2011, p. 11). One sees the lived outcome of this in Zhitlovsky's willingness to set out from his roost in the capital city of Yiddish life in America, New York City, to give repeated, sometimes marathon, talks in what would otherwise be considered far-flung places such as Calgary.

Canadian Yiddishism

An understudied aspect of this transnational network and its attendant ideologies is the place in them of bifurcated identity, not quite exile, and a sense of competing cultural homelands—not only a potentially creative but also a hazardous position from which to build a linguistic and cultural community. In the decades before the Holocaust, Eastern European–born Jews in Canada had a divided view of the world that they had left behind, with its intensely rich and long-established Jewish traditions experienced alongside a series of calamities. This divided view of the past is seen in the work of Montreal Yiddish writer and educator Yaacov Zipper. Like Zhitlovsky, Zipper was reared in a traditional religious Jewish context, which he abandoned in favour of leftist and Yiddishist idealism. His arrival in Montreal in 1925 gave him a kind of pioneer status as an early and influential teacher and principal devoted to the kind of Yiddish day school that Zhitlovsky promoted as part of the larger platform of *Yiddishkayt*.

Among this volume's concerns is the potential for Canadian educational contexts to address "plurilingual" speakers, "in alignment with

Canada's multilingual and multicultural society" (Tavares & Maciel Jorge, this volume). The Peretz School that Zipper oversaw confronted this challenge. As with similar schools in Toronto, Winnipeg, and Calgary, the Montreal Peretz School drew many of its pupils from immigrant families. In Montreal, the curriculum was "in keeping with the standards of the Protestant School Board" alongside a "full program of Jewish studies, which included classes in Jewish history and literature, Bible studies, and the Yiddish and Hebrew languages" (Zipper, 2004, p. xviii). The school offered a full-day stream as well as an afternoon program for students enrolled in Protestant public schools (Zipper, 2004, p. xviii). During Zipper's time as principal, there were no government subventions for a school like this, and its financial future was entirely in the hands of parents, many of whom could not pay for their children's tuition, and local community leaders. After the Second World War, when interest in Yiddish education and literacy was in decline, also in decline was the willingness by the community to view Yiddish schooling as a priority. As this shift took hold, Zipper's career as an educator and Yiddish idealist—a kind of arbiter of *Yiddishkayt*—was defined by shifting linguistic identification among Canadian Jews. As Hebrew and the State of Israel came to the fore in place of Yiddish ideologies and language, Zipper admitted in his diary a sense of personal failure, in line with his sense of being out of step with changes in the lives and cultural ideals of mainstream Canadian Jews. The goals and challenges associated with a "plurilingual education" remained central for him, yet key values associated with it had altered or evaporated. In the summer of 1960, Zipper (2004, p. 89) wrote in his diary that from "all sides there are cries: Yiddish education is bankrupt; Yiddish is doomed. Only Hebrew and a smattering of religion are significant. Here, a new generation struggles and asks, in English naturally: Can you furnish us with new supports and identifications without dogmatism or artificial orthodoxy[?]"

In effect, Zipper (2004, p. 89) and his colleagues were struggling to explain and promote an ideological and linguistic framework no longer widely supported: "I spend many hours with young fathers and mothers who want to understand our basic beliefs. . . . The supporters of Yiddish fight over a dictionary entry in a collapsing world."

The cultural divide encountered by Zipper in his workday life was further complicated by an enduring engagement with his Polish past—a set of divided loyalties that, in mid-century, did not lead to a return visit to Poland. Imaginary return was all that was available. In his diary, Zipper describes such a return in a dream:

> Couldn't fall asleep for a long time and tossed from side to side until I was striding up and down the hills of Tishevitz, down to the pasture-bridge, which lies partly collapsed a few feet from shore. I jump over the breech and a small, stony path appears between a stone fence and a blind wall that looks like a prison wall with small barred windows right at the top. It leads into a broad courtyard where [there is] a crowd of people, young and old, most of whom I know but cannot name. And it is clear to me that none of them is of this world. They surround me with magic that holds me in its spell because I can understand everything they say. . . . Opening my eyes in the darkness of the room, it seems to me that in my inner eye my memory is still unwinding the complete picture of that other world. (2004, pp. 257–258)

This is a post-Holocaust rumination, but its distinctive character is that of a prewar phantasm: the old home, its market crowds, "young and old, most of whom I know," beckon with a dark prophecy that "all will be revealed" (2004, pp. 257). We cannot appreciate what it could mean to dream over oceans of time to return, as Zipper did, to the place where he first encountered the enthusiasms that he would bring to his Canadian life and work. The Old World dream haunted the New World idealist and activist teacher. Faces of a catastrophically destroyed home reappeared as phantoms amid an effort to reassert language and values first encountered in the old home. These aspects of a bifurcated Canadian Jewish life, one might say, were debilitating, but they did not preclude putting one's shoulder to the wheel of *Yiddishkayt*.

My aim in this chapter is to convey how Yiddish ideologues, literary figures, and institutions asserted and sustained a transnational movement that developed its particular expression in Canada while remaining part of a global network, multilingual and multicultural in its resources and milieux. Among the key institutions whose raison d'être was to support this network was YIVO, whose acronym derives from its original Yiddish name and can be translated as Yiddish Scientific Institute. Founded in 1925 and based from 1927 to the Second World

War in Vilna in eastern Poland, it was the most important post–First World War response to what Niger (1939, p. 337) characterized as the "catastrophic events [that] changed the environment" and direction of Yiddish activities and daily life. Influenced by contemporary trends in the social sciences, linguistics, ethnography, and folklore studies, YIVO was a proactive cultural force as well as a promoter of salvage ethnography in its effort to collect written and published materials, recorded speech and song, folkways, and cultural artifacts—especially from small-town eastern Polish and Russian-Ukrainian communities—where collectors feared the disappearance of Jewish village and small-town life. Among its projects was a network of "amateur collectors"—*zammlers* in Yiddish—who gathered materials for YIVO's archives and library. Margolis (2011, p. 106) reflects on how these undertakings affected Canadian Jews: "The YIVO relied on both local and international correspondents to collect material, disseminate information about the organization and otherwise fulfill its mandate. In Montreal as well as in Toronto, Yiddish literati served as local correspondents for the YIVO throughout its American section." Zipper was among this group: he "submitted copies of rare journals, and established local contacts on behalf of YIVO" (Margolis, 2011, p. 106). On the latter front, he likely played a role in attracting Polish Yiddishists to give lectures in Montreal.

Calgary, at Once Faraway and Central

Having considered the early-twentieth-century Yiddishist ideal, alongside its particular Canadian developments, we now confront the turn, the retreat, the rejection of what Margolis (2011, p. 190) calls a "transnational modern Yiddish culture." In her book *Jewish Roots, Canadian Soil: Yiddish Culture in Montreal, 1905–1945*, she conveys this culture's status quo at its pinnacle of success, maintaining a focus on Montreal-based schools, newspapers, visiting writers, and many other Yiddishist pursuits whose outcome was a "well-developed and institutionally complete Yiddish cultural network," an "example of the cultural maintenance of a minority group on Canadian soil before the advent of Canada's official policy of multiculturalism in 1971" (p. 190). Similar patterns were established in other early-twentieth-century Canadian centres so that Yiddishism in Canada, at its height, foresaw key aspects of the national policy that came to be called multiculturalism. The countrywide influence of a formal Yiddishist network, with shared ideological and emotional enthusiasms, is conveyed by way of a portrait of a western Canadian alternative to Montreal.

In Calgary, proto-multicultural Yiddishist urges were nurtured by way of links to faraway Minsk, Vilna, and Warsaw and by the desire to remain fully engaged with a network of capital cities with Yiddish cultures. This is exemplified not only by the death of Zhitlovsky in Calgary in the midst of a strenuous speaking tour but also by a poet's romance. In 1918, the major Polish Yiddish playwright Peretz Hirschbein was in Calgary on his own lecture tour when he met the much younger, local, Byelorussian-born Esther Shumiatcher. A poet herself, she married Hirschbein in Calgary later that year, just as New York audiences and critics of the Yiddish press were toasting Hirschbein's play *A farvorfn vinkl* (A secluded corner).

His creative activities made Hirschbein a less direct ideological influence on global Yiddishism than Zhitlovsky, yet his presence in Calgary as a public speaker and his eventual bond with local Yiddishists by marriage allow us to see early-twentieth-century Calgary Yiddish idealists in the same light as Margolis viewed those in Montreal. Hirschbein's theatrical career began in Odessa, where a travelling troupe was founded with his name, which travelled through southern Russia, Belarus, and Lithuania in 1909. His own world travels took Hirschbein to Vienna, Paris, London, and New York, where he wrote for *Der tog*, one of the city's leading Yiddish newspapers. Lecture tours, as with Zhitlovsky, took him to far-flung centres such as Calgary (Hirschbein, n.d.). The writerly careers of Shumiatcher and Hirschbein were entwined by a set of remarkable world tours to the South Pacific, South America, and southern Africa, punctuated by regular return visits to Shumiatcher's Calgary home in the early Jewish downtown neighbourhood south of the Bow River.[3] In the spring of 1930, on one of these returns to Calgary, Hirschbein took part in an event memorializing Sholem Aleichem at the Calgary Peretz School. The *Calgary Daily Herald* noted that he had been "personally acquainted with the late author"—linking him with a kingpin of Yiddish literature—and described the event as follows: "The curtain rose on a bust of the late Scholom Aleichem with lighted tapers on each and a short silence in his memory was observed by the 400 people present. A concert programme was arranged by a committee. Gregori Garbovitsky's ladies' orchestra received a big ovation. Ester [*sic*] Schumiatcher, noted poetess, recited a number of her poems, entitled 'Jerusalem,' 'Grandmother' and many others, including a song"[4] (Jewish author, 1930, p. 20).

Shumiatcher took the stage on her own in 1945, once more at the I. L. Peretz School, speaking on the topic of "The Jewish Woman in Life and Literature." The poster for the event did not mention her roots in the city (no one in Calgary's Jewish community needed to be reminded of them). Instead, it touted her as "one of Jewry's leading daughters" (Alberta Jewish News, 2001).

One might say that after this date came the turn. In the spring of 1945, one knew fully the nature of the calamity that had largely obliterated Yiddish-speaking Europe. Survivors were making their way not home but to centres in the Americas and what would become the new State of Israel. The capital cities of Zhitlovsky's global *Yiddishkayt* were now German mass murder sites. After the war, official state Zionism would declare Hebrew the language of modern Israel. This shift in linguistic identity took root in Canada as it did in every other Jewish setting. Canada in the 1950s is well described by historian Frank Bialystok (2000, p. 69):

> The war was over, immigration barriers had been lifted, economic prosperity and the emerging welfare state had erased the vestiges of the Depression mentality, and Israel had been established as the national homeland for all Jews. These individuals were bent on advancing from the fringes of the Canadian mosaic into the mainstream of Canadian society. They were a community in transition, from the immigrant neighbourhoods to the suburbs, from the plethora of storefront synagogues, union halls, and ideological groups to large-scale congregations and service clubs. Yiddish culture, as presented in the ethnic press, the labour halls, the theatres, and most significantly, in street life, was vanishing in the 1950s.

Bialystok's portrait of the changes sought by Canadian Jews, and delivered by new social opportunities, shows Jews as part of the process that historian Harold Troper has called the "whitening of Euro-ethnics" (Bialystok, 2000, p. 69). These successes and the attendant "whitening" of Jews propelled them away from their own proto-multicultural undertakings. One might think of this period in terms of a film run backward (losing its pigment in favour of a black-and-white palette) as storefront Yiddish signs evaporated and the heady and hectic atmosphere of certain Jewish "cosmic spines," as novelist Matt Cohen dubbed Toronto's Spadina Avenue, were abandoned in favour of suburban anonymity and quiet. Cohen's (2000, pp. 42–43) sympathetic rendering of time and place—Toronto in the mid-1960s—carries with it an ironic undertone, based upon his own belated arrival at a late and faded stage of the Jewish main street: "On its southern stretch, you could have breakfast at the Crest Grill, lunch at Switzer's, dine, drink beer and listen to jazz at Grossman's Tavern. You could shoot pool on Spadina, walk with girlfriends on Spadina. . . . I myself had already lived at three Spadina addresses, eaten at a dozen Spadina restaurants, dressed in Spadina-bought clothes, even gone to my grandfather's funeral at a Spadina Avenue funeral chapel." Because his youthful years in Toronto are belated, Cohen does it all in the Canadian vernacular, not in Yiddish, though his tableau bears all the markings of the disappearing Yiddish-speaking past.

Yiddishism as Proto-Multiculturalism

Yiddish might be seen as the original disruption of Canada's dual linguistic mainstream. Yes, Nêhiyawêwin and Kanien'kéha (Plains Cree and Mohawk) and numerous other Indigenous languages long preceded it in the colonial dynamic, but these languages did not confront the urban mainstream as Yiddish did, on newsstands, in shop windows, in the cry of a shop boy selling to passersby, in community halls where hundreds honoured the Yiddish kingpins of Poland. Cohen's reverential account of Toronto's "cosmic spine" reminds us of the work that remains to be done—real archaeological digging and discovery—to recover a clear view of such spines as they existed in cities that have not received the attentive study applied by Cohen to Toronto and by Margolis to Montreal. On Calgary's multilingual streets—for Jews, the "spine" was Eighth Avenue at Centre Street—one might encounter community organizers and idealists such as Leo Paperny, who organized Peretz Hirschbein's celebratory talk on Sholem Aleichem in 1930s Calgary. In the early decades of the twentieth century, the marginality of Canadian Yiddish was central. What confirmed its marginality, whether in Jewish or in non-Jewish milieux, was its Old World linguistic and cultural connections, with its attendant ideologies—to the left and even all the way into anarchist territory—that were part of an inherited proto-multicultural, community-wide set of commitments.

The rejection of all this, beginning in the 1950s and in many ways complete in the 1960s, was guided by one crucial fact: in no way could this cultural tradition enter the Canadian mainstream. Evidence of this is found in a revealing document completed in 1965 by Canadian Jewish community leaders to be submitted to the Royal Commission on Bilingualism and Biculturalism under the title "Jewish Participation in Canadian Culture." Its author, Ruth Wisse, would go on to become both a Yiddishist and an American academic in the area of Jewish and Yiddish literature. But the Yiddishist status quo related to transnational motives is in no way the focus of Wisse's report. Rather, one of her chosen chapter titles, "Cultural Contribution: Into the Mainstream," reveals that the point of her document is not to highlight the Canadian contribution to a transnational, plurilingual, Yiddish culture. This theme was not timely, nor did it appeal to Jewish community leaders or Canadian biculturalists. Wisse's report is almost entirely weighted toward an account of the movement of Jewish writers, actors, scholars, and musicians into mainstream institutional roles across the country. It is a portrait of how successful the whitening of Euro-ethnics was circa 1965. Wisse highlights the English-language contributions of A. M. Klein, Mordecai Richler, and Leonard Cohen; the musical accomplishments of Harry Adaskin and the Hart House Quartet; and the presence of "approximately 175" Jewish professors and instructors in universities across the country (Wisse, 1965, p. 31, p. 34). Such a catalogue answers the Royal Commission's ideal—after its primary goal of addressing the French/English divide—of highlighting "the contribution by other ethnic groups to the cultural enrichment of Canada" (Temelini, 2003). In a late section titled "Jewish Culture: Within the Community," Wisse (1965, p. 51) takes account of the role of Yiddish as a "spoken language," as a basis for education, and sums up the value of "Yiddish Culture": "Given the relatively cohesive nature of Canadian Jewry, particularly in Montreal, Winnipeg and Toronto, it is not surprising that Yiddish cultural expression flourished for many decades, and though noticeably declining, still plays an important part in Jewish life." Following summaries of activity in literature, theatre, and the press, she cites telling statistics related to the "decline of Yiddish as a spoken language. The percentage of Jews giving Yiddish as their mother tongue dropped from 95.4 percent in 1931 to 76.2 per cent [*sic*] in 1941; from 50.6 percent in 1951 to 32.4 percent in 1961" (p. 57). The drop in the next decade, out of view of Wisse's report, would be that much more devastating. Her conclusion is that a study of culture within the Jewish community is a study of change: the language of expression was changing, the institutions were in a state of flux, and the modes of expression were being adapted to the requirements of a new, Canadian-born-and-bred population (p. 58).

What we find in "Jewish Participation in Canadian Culture" is its author's responsiveness to the goals of the Royal Commission, which Wisse (1965, p. 1) alludes to in a prefatory aside to her report: "Writing on the Jewish contribution to culture in Canada in these days of Bilingualism and Biculturalism is like coming as bridesmaid to the Wedding [*sic*]: your presence may be charming, but the marriage would go on without you." She echoes her community leaders' view that though the commission would define Jews "as an ethnic group ... they are also a religious group, or primarily a religious group," since "the religious basis of Judaism has remained the unbroken link between generations" (p. 59). Here the possibility that *Yiddishkayt* is a proto-multicultural model is jettisoned in favour of a newly asserted identity, better suited to what both Wisse and the leaders of her community imagined for their Canadian future.

References

Alberta Jewish News. (2021). From the archives of JHSSA: Esther and Peretz Hirshbein—Calgary's Yiddish celebrities. *Alberta Jewish News*. https://alberta-jewishnews.com/from-the-archives-of-jhssa-esther-and-peretz-hirshbein-cal-garys-yiddish-celebrities/

Belkin, S. (1966). *Through narrow gates: A review of Jewish immigration, colonization and immigrant aid work in Canada (1840–1940)*. Eagle Publishing.

Bialystok, F. (2000). *Delayed impact: The Holocaust and the Canadian Jewish community*. McGill-Queen's University Press.

"Chaim Zhitlovsky." (2016). *Yiddish leksikon*. http://yleksikon.blogspot.com/2016/09/chaim-zhitlovsky.html

Cohen, M. (2000). *Typing: A life in 26 keys*. Random House.

Hirschbein, P. (n.d.). Papers of Peretz Hirschbein. Center for Jewish History. https://archives.cjh.org/repositories/7/resources/3273

Jewish author is honored Wednesday (1930, 29 May). *Calgary Daily Herald*, p. 20.

Margolis, R. (2009). Negotiating Jewish Canadian identity: Montreal Yiddish literary journals in the interwar period. *Shofar: An Interdisciplinary Journal of Jewish Studies, 27*(4), 24–48.

Margolis, R. (2011). *Jewish roots, Canadian soil: Yiddish culture in Montreal, 1905–1945.* McGill-Queen's University Press.

Margolis, R. (2011–2012). Yiddish and multiculturalism: A marriage made in heaven? *Canadian Ethnic Studies, 43–44*(3–1), 213–225.

Menkis, R. (2011). Jewish communal identity at the crossroads: Early Jewish responses to Canadian multiculturalism, 1963–1965. *Studies in Religion, 40*(3), 283–292.

Niger, S. (1939). New trends in post-war Yiddish literature. *Jewish Social Studies, 1*(3), 337–358.

Rosenberg, L. (1939). *Canada's Jews: A social and economic study of the Jews in Canada.* Canadian Jewish Congress.

Saywell, J. T. (1965). Royal Commission on Bilingualism and Biculturalism. *International Journal, 20*(3), 378–382.

Switzer, J. (1999). Chaim Zhitlovsky dies in Calgary. *Discovery: The Journal of the Jewish Historical Society of Southern Alberta, 9*(1), 3–4.

Temelini, M. (2003). The first stage of the multiculturalism debate. *Canadian Issues.* https://www.proquest.com/central/docview/208699542/fulltext/FEA999D292AC4923PQ/2

Wisse, R. (1965). *Jewish participation in Canadian culture* [Essay commissioned by the Royal Commission on Bilingualism and Biculturalism].

YIVO Institute for Jewish Research. (n.d.). Czernowitz conference. In *YIVO encyclopedia of Jews in Eastern Europe.* https://yivoencyclopedia.org/article.aspx/czernowitz_conference

YIVO Institute for Jewish Research. (n.d.). Language: Yiddish. In *YIVO Encyclopedia of Jews in Eastern Europe.* https://yivoencyclopedia.org/article.aspx/Language/Yiddish

Zipper, Y. (2004). *The journals of Yaacov Zipper, 1950–1982* (M. Butovsky & O. Garfinkle, Eds.). McGill-Queen's University Press.

Endnotes

1   I was an unwitting witness of these shifts. In the early 1970s, I attended the Calgary I. L. Peretz School, half a century after my dad's tenure there (and at a different location; it had moved to the city's suburbs, far from its original downtown location). By the 1970s, the school had lost its leftist orientation but retained its attention to Yiddish language and literary culture and history associated with Eastern Europe. Our education represented a late-stage expression of key cultural, linguistic, and communal elements that the broader Jewish community was still in the process of jettisoning.

2   The dictionary meaning of *Yiddishkayt*—Jewishness, Judaism—conveys its all-encompassing potential.

3   Shaun Hunter's literary map of Calgary pinpoints the location of the family home at the following link: https://www.google.com/maps/d/viewer?mid=1KEMqq82O uqi0nvhKPrKtye-ON2EQX7eQ&ll=51.04838689999999%2C-114.0881243&z=18

4   Garbovitsky, a Russian-born Jew, directed the Calgary Symphony Orchestra and the Palace Theatre Orchestra.

PART 6

RETHINKING "CANADIAN IDENTITY",
FROM SOCIO-CULTURAL PERSPECTIVES
of
INCLUSION

The first two chapters in this section centre on race as a site of exclusion to "Canadian identity." Chapter 16 foregrounds research on the experiences of Black Canadians, and Chapter 17 focuses on Asian Canadians through an analysis of a journalistic article. The third and final chapter of this section considers race along with gender and nationality in the experiences of integration of immigrants to Quebec. These chapters not only demonstrate that discrimination is common among racialized groups but also contextualize these patterns of discrimination for different racialized groups. Together these chapters expand the discussion on "Canadian identity" by problematizing racial diversity in Canada.

In Chapter 16, with reference to George Orwell's *Animal Farm*, Joseph Mensah examines Black disillusionment regarding Canadian citizenship as evident from the experiences of racism in many spheres of Canadian life, notwithstanding the professed egalitarianism of Canadian citizenship. Black "Canadian identity" is set in a dialectical binary opposition to White "Canadian identity," thereby relegating Blacks to the periphery of what it is to be a *true* Canadian. To the extent that Black "Canadian identity" is often stereotyped as the dialectical opposite of "Canadian identity"—however nebulously both identities are conceptualized—it is unsurprising that Blacks bear much of the brunt of racism in Canada through discriminatory practices in several areas, such as the labour market, education, law enforcement, housing, and the COVID-19 pandemic. Within this context, Mensah makes the case that the Orwellian maxim—*all . . . are equal, but some are more equal than others*—is never too far from the minds of many Blacks in Canada.

In Chapter 17, Elena Chou unpacks *Maclean's* now infamous article originally entitled "Too Asian? Some Frosh Don't Want to Study at an Asian University." Chou explores the racial discourses in the article in order to investigate two related problems. First, how can the discourses and representations of Asians and Asian Canadians as abject and/or other in this article be used to explore assumptions underlying the logic of assimilation into Canadian multicultural society? Second, how has the increasing neo-liberalization of the Canadian social, political, and economic landscapes resulted in shifting perceptions and practices of Canadian multiculturalism? Furthermore, how do the discourses and representations of Asians and Asian Canadians in this article reflect this neo-liberal shift? Chou examines how race and practices of racialization continue to trouble commonly held ideas and national myths about inclusion/exclusion, assimilation, multiculturalism, and national identity in the Canadian context.

In Chapter 18, Marie-Laure Dioh and Julie Bérubé discuss the socio-professional integration of immigrants in Quebec with a focus on the obstacles to integration, including discrimination based upon national origin, gender, or skin colour. These barriers are exacerbated in regions with low immigrant density, where the local population is less prepared to receive newcomers. Moreover, the social debates currently under way in Quebec, related to Bill 21: An Act Respecting the Laicity of the State and, previously, to the bill on the Quebec Charter of Values, are rekindling conflicts and social fractures between the host society and immigrants. The cultural, religious, and linguistic identities of immigrants and the relationship to the other seem to be perceived as potential threats to "Quebec identity." Dioh and Bérubé offer a plea for intercultural mediation in order to reconcile the cultural identities and affiliations that make up today's Quebec, which entails immigrants and the host population working together toward a better experience for all.

"But Some Are More Equal than Others":
On Black Canadians' Sense of Belonging and Truncated Citizenship

JOSEPH MENSAH

In *Animal Farm* (originally published in 1945), George Orwell satirizes a communist revolution at a farm owned by one Mr. Jones, who, with his characteristic laziness and drunkenness, forgets to feed the animals, thereby provoking an uprising under the leadership of two pigs named Napoleon and Snowball. To help ossify the egalitarian ethos of the incipient revolution, the leaders change the name of the farm from Manor Farm to Animal Farm and promise to operate it in a way that benefits all animals on four legs equally. As a corollary, the leaders encapsulate the principles of their Animalist revolution, or Animalism, under seven commandments, which include the declaration that "all animals are equal." However, as the revolution becomes corrupted over time, the leaders reduce the seven commandments of Animalism to one: "All animals are equal, but some are more equal than others."

Analogized after *Animal Farm*, this chapter examines Blacks' disillusionment regarding Canadian citizenship as evident from their documented experiences of racism in many spheres of Canadian life—including education, law enforcement, employment, and housing (Abdi, 2005; Dei, 2005; Tanovich, 2006)—notwithstanding the professed egalitarianism of Canadian citizenship. Like most Western nations, Canadian citizenship is officially grounded in the ideals of liberal democracy, purportedly with no room for racial discrimination.

However, as this chapter demonstrates, the ideals of Canadian citizenship are not enjoyed equally, not even in the Canadian public sector (Nasser & Merali, 2021).

As the chapter shows, Black Canadian identity is set in a dialectical binary opposition to White Canadian identity, thereby relegating Blacks to the periphery of what it is to be a *true* Canadian. Unsurprisingly, Blacks bear much of the brunt of racism in Canada through a host of exclusionary and discriminatory practices. The level of discrimination faced by Blacks and other ethno-racial minorities in the Canadian labour market, in particular, has prompted one observer to insist, perhaps hyperbolically, that the country has a system of "economic apartheid" (Galabuzi, 2006). Racism remains a sore spot of and arguably an embarrassment to Canadian democratic citizenship. It points to the tensions between the professed universality of Canadian democracy and citizenship rights of freedom and equality and the evident inability of Blacks and other minorities to exercise such rights successfully.

The overarching argument of this chapter posits that, when it comes to citizenship, and its attendant sense of belonging, it is what obtains in the daily lived experiences of people that counts and not the grandiose words enshrined in any institutional document in Canada, be it the national Constitution, the Charter of Rights and Freedoms, or the Employment Equity Act. As a corollary, it is only in such practical terms that we can truly know whether or not we are all equal, as Canadians, or that some are more equal than others. As Zygmunt Bauman (2011, p. 14) aptly puts it, "if democratic rights, and the freedoms that accompany such rights, are granted in theory but unattainable in practice, the pain of hopelessness will surely be topped by the humiliation of haplessness; the ability to cope with life's challenges, tested daily, is after all the very workshop in which the self-confidence of individuals, and so also their self-esteem, is cast or is melted away." Indeed, Blacks are not the only racialized people who encounter racial abuse in Canada relative to their White counterparts; others, including Latinos, Asians, and First Nations people, face similar racial problems. At the same time, at the risk of indulging in an "Oppression Olympics," this chapter mounts a sustained, if not provocative, defence of a *uniqueness thesis*, of a sort, to show how anti-Black racism, arguably, is one of a kind in terms of its origins, ubiquity, prevalence, machinations, and cruelty.

Since citizenship and the sense of belonging that it engenders are often manifested in lived experiences, I use the philosophy of pragmatism to draw attention to the gaps between the expected and the observed realities of citizenship among Blacks in Canada. Additionally, I use the notions of *democratic racism* and *dialectics of enlightenment* to show how, regardless of the benevolent proclamations in liberal democracies such as Canada, it is not unusual to find the opposite manifestations in the lives of ethnoracial minorities in these societies. Also, I examine how Black Canadians and their identities undergird the formation of Canada's national identity. On the empirical front, I rely on previous studies to evince the extent of anti-Black racism in Canada, using it in three main spheres—employment, the criminal justice system, and the COVID-19 pandemic—as my working examples.

A Pragmatic Critique of Democratic Racism

Racism takes different forms. For instance, one can distinguish between individual racism, systemic (or structural or institutional) racism, and democratic racism. As the term suggests, "individual racism" is perpetrated by individuals; it can be overt or covert, but it is not embedded in institutional structures. "Systemic racism," conversely, is inherent in institutional structures and therefore hard to discern given its normalization and subtlety.

In the Canadian context, "democratic racism," the crux of my theorization here, is traced to the work of Henry et al. (1995) and Li (1998), who used it to describe the contradictory ways in which racist ideologies coexist with democratic principles in many social discourses. Democratic racism is often shrouded in liberal principles such as individualism, equal opportunity, and freedom of speech. An example here concerns the apparent contradictory situation in Canada in which the Charter of Rights and Freedoms—which seeks to protect minority rights—has ended up giving "legal ammunitions to extremists to advocate racial supremacism in the name of freedom of speech" (Li, 1998, p. 118). The issue here concerns the following vexing question. How can it be that in a liberal democracy such as Canada we still have racial oppression? An analogous concern is the focus of Theodor Adorno and Max Horkheimer's book *Dialectic of Enlightenment* (1944), in which they try to understand how, at the height of European civilization in the twentieth century, Europe could plunge, arguably, into the most regressive barbarism, culminating in two world wars and the Holocaust.

From the work of Adorno and Horkheimer, we know that the Enlightenment was not all positive: like democracy, it was somewhat self-undermining, self-destructive, and self-negating—hence their use of dialectics in examining it. In their view, the self-negation emanated mainly from the fact that the Enlightenment fostered differentiation, othering, domination, and moral apathy, notwithstanding its emphasis on scientific rationalism. As they observed, by shedding the trappings of superstition, tradition, and religion, the Enlightenment turned into fascism and promoted extreme forms of subjugation by separating people into those with power and those without it, or us versus them, and by seeing the latter as a mere instrument to be used in pursuit of the ends of the former. Accordingly, their "critique of enlightenment is intended to prepare the way for a positive notion of enlightenment which will release it from entanglement in blind domination" (p. xvi).

Relatedly, the coexistence of democratic principles and racism is nurtured by various systems of domination, not the least of which are forms of othering and dialectical negations as well as discursive practices entailing tactical denial, convenient forgetfulness, and the blaming of victims of racial oppression. We thus find some analysts of race relations in Canada (e.g., Tator & Henry 2006; Malhi & Boon, 2007) lamenting the fact that many among the majority seem to think that Canada is essentially a non-racist country and that instances of racism are isolated and perpetrated by a few bad apples. The conspicuous lack of any discussion of racism, Islamophobia, and issues regarding First Nations during the (latest) federal election of September 2021, in particular, is a telling example of the systemic and systematic neglect of racism by those who wield power in Canada.

As Sachedina and Taylor (2021, p. 5) put it, "at the English-language leaders' debate, where not a single Black person was invited to ask the Candidates a question, issues that impact Black Canadians were left unaddressed. The anti-Asian hate that has been on the rise since the COVID-19 pandemic began was also not a topic of discussion." It is only in the context of such strategic omissions that we can understand how and why we continue to have memorable moments of reckoning regarding issues of genocide, racism, and Islamophobia in Canada, yet nothing substantive changes. Our collective approach has been performative and symbolic, feeding into an orthodoxy that celebrates the problematic assumption that all Canadians, regardless of race, are equal in both theory and practice. Can we really say that the lived experiences of Blacks vis-à-vis Canadian citizenship are similar to those of Whites in pragmatic terms?

Traced genealogically to the works of Charles Sanders Peirce, William James, and John Dewey, in that order, pragmatism is the philosophical position that "truths are beliefs that are confirmed in the course of experience and are therefore fallible, subject to further revision" (Seigfried, 1995, p. 638). Simply put, "truth" is an idea that works in practice. In Peirce's view, we do not acquire truth simply by observing but by *doing* or putting an idea into practice—hence the name pragmatism. His pragmatic epistemology culminated in his *convergence theory* of truth, which posits that "a belief is true which the community of enquirers will converge upon over the long run" (Cahoone, 2010, p. 216).

Analogously, then, if we agree that democratic citizenship implies equal treatment under the law with no room for discrimination based upon race, how does this "truth" bear out in practice for Blacks in Canada? Would the community of enquirers affirm the fact that Blacks are treated as equally as Whites in Canada? And what does the prevalence of anti-Black racism say about democratic citizenship from the standpoint of convergence theory? As we will see in this chapter, racism persists in Canada under the cover of democracy, and it is only through an account of the lived experiences of Blacks and other racial minorities, by way of a tool such as pragmatism, that we can properly uncover it. Before I examine how racism plays out in the lives of Blacks in Canada, in the next section I discuss how the Black presence contributes to the formation of Canadian national identity.

Blacks in the Context of Canadian National Identity Formation

Even though the contributions of Blacks to Canada's socio-economic and -cultural development go back to the seventeenth century, many still see Black Canadians mainly in negative terms: as recent immigrants or refugees in need of humanitarian settlement, as immigrants coming from the long-embattled continent of Africa to take advantage of Canada's welfare system, or as people unable culturally to assimilate into mainstream Canada. Here I discuss how the prejudicial views of

Blacks feed into Canada's national identity formation and show the extent to which anti-Black racism undermines the citizenship and sense of belonging of Blacks in this country.

Although the term "nation" is hard to define precisely, Anderson's definition—that a nation is *"an imagined political community . . . inherently limited and sovereign"*—is more or less canonical in the literature (2006, p. 6; emphasis added). From this perspective, the nation is imagined in the sense that its members, regardless of how small the nation is, will never know most of its co-members. It is limited because it is always bounded geographically or made up of only a subset of the human population; it is sovereign because it seeks to be free, and the "gauge and emblem of this freedom is the sovereign state"; finally, it is a community, for regardless of the level of inequality in the nation it is characterized by the fraternity of its members (Anderson, 2006, p. 7).

Following Abdelal et al. (2009), I define the term "identity" here not as a stable entity but as a changeable phenomenon characterized by *content* and *contestation*: the former concerns what populates the self (or, in the present case, the imaginings of the nation), whereas the latter deals with the internal and external disagreements about the content of this national identity. In the context of modern nation-states, including Canada, one can hardly overlook the influence of immigration, race, ethnicity, religion, and so on, on both the content of and the contestations surrounding national identity formation. Although the content of Canada's national identity varies depending on the context and who is "populating" it, few analysts will dispute that Canada is fundamentally a northern country in both geographic and economic development terms, just as its history and present circumstances are couched in colonialism, Eurocentrism, multiculturalism, immigration, capitalism, and liberal democracy.

Given Canada's image as an essentially White, Eurocentric society, Blacks often serve as the putative polar opposite of the true Canadian in many popular and academic discourses with other ethnoracial groups sandwiched somewhere between these polarities. With this juxtaposition, Black Canadians often become the main symbolic and material reference point for Canada's national identity formation, especially per Hegelian negation: a dialectical move in which we grasp the meaning of a concept, say White or North, through what it is not, in this case Black or South, respectively. It is therefore unsurprising that there exists some rough correspondence among various cultural, socio-economic, political, and geographical identity markers of Blacks, on the one hand, and those of the Canadian nation-state, on the other (Mensah, 2015). Implicitly, then, Black identity is almost always drawn into the formation of Canadian national identity, at some level theoretical abstraction. For instance, feeding into the self-awareness of Canadian national identity as a White, Christian, Anglo-Franco, multicultural, settler nation are the attributes of the negated other as Black, Afro-Muslim or ethno-Christian, visible minority, refugee, immigrant, or foreigner. Similarly, shoring up Canada's international image as a rich, Western, developed country of the Global North is the identity of Blacks as poor, underdeveloped, working-class people from the Global South.

Adding to these identity markers are long-standing stereotypes of Blacks propagated through the discursive practices of intellectuals, the mass media, and kindred outlets of public opinion formation in the West (Nederveen, 1992). Within this schema, Blacks are seen as strangers, prone to criminality, lazy, and inferior from the standpoint of intellectualism but superior in sports and athletics (Fleras, 2011; Mensah, 2015), whereas the true Canadian is normalized as superior, White, immigrant host, law abiding, and hard working. These stereotypes are formed not through dialogue between Blacks and Whites but mostly through the domination of the former by the latter. More importantly, these unflattering stereotypes of Blacks serve to elevate the social status of Whites and thus accentuate the race-laced fissures between Blacks and Whites in Western societies such as Canada. Perhaps nothing sustains the efficacy of the stereotypes more than their inherent ability to operate in a self-fulfilling fashion: social representations echo social realities that in turn are modelled on social representations (Nederveen, 1992, p. 11). For reasons stemming from the preceding discussion, Blacks (and their identities) are intricately intertwined with the national identity formation of Canada, mostly because they serve as the polar opposites of Whites. Although some might have good reasons to dispute the argument that Blacks are the polar opposite of Whites in Canadian race relations—with the counterpoint that other minority groups face virtually the same racial discrimination as Blacks—there is at least an academic point to be made that the circumstances of Blacks are *unique*, not only because of their chromatic difference but also because of their legacy of slavery in North America and the attendant baggage of undesirable stereotypes.

At the same time, Frantz Fanon (1967, p. 86) had a point in observing that "it is utopian to try to ascertain in what ways one kind of inhuman behavior differs from another kind of inhuman behavior"; as he quipped, "is there in truth any difference between one racism and another?" Admittedly, any attempt to answer this arguably rhetorical question verges on "Oppression Olympics." Still, the prevalence, ubiquity, and cruelty associated with anti-Black racism around the world—the extreme form of which was epitomized by the murder of George Floyd in May 2020—can hardly escape the notice of even the most casual observer of global race relations. In fact, no less an authority than the United Nations Human Rights Council produced a report for the "promotion and protection of human rights and fundamental freedoms of Africans and people of African descent against excessive use of force and other human rights violations by law enforcement officers" following its forty-seventh session held from 21 June to 9 July 2021. Among other objectives, this report examined "the compounding inequalities that Africans and people of African descent face in all areas of life" (United Nations Human Rights Council, 2021, p. 1). In a candid admission, the UN commissioner for human rights acknowledged the "long-overdue need to confront the legacies of enslavement, the transatlantic trade in enslaved Africans and colonialism and to seek reparatory justice" (United Nations Human Rights Council, 2021, p. 1). Of course, one can still argue that anti-Black racism is different not in essence but in degree. Then again who would dispute that anti-Black racism is indeed unique, *just like any other form of racism*, and there lies the paradox implicated in any such thesis on uniqueness. In what follows, I examine how anti-Black racism is manifested in three specific spheres of Canadian life—employment, the criminal justice system, and the COVID-19 pandemic—to affirm my overarching argument that, when it comes to race relations in Canada, all are equal, but some are more equal than others.

Anti-Black Racism, Curtailed Citizenship, and Sense of Belonging

T. H. Marshall, to whom we can trace much of the contemporary theorization of citizenship, was rather too optimistic in his seminal work, *Citizenship and Social Class* (1950), when he predicted that the twentieth century would see the expansion of social rights (i.e., rights to basic

welfare and full participation in society) across Europe and by impli-
cation the Western world. As Reiter (2012) points out, Marshall did
not anticipate the globalization-induced mass migration of racialized
people from the Global South to the Global North and the resultant increase in xenophobia and racial discrimination in immigrant-receiving
countries such as Canada. There is evidence that non-White citizens in
many Western democracies find their civil and social rights truncated
by forces of racism to the point where analysts such as Balibar (2004),
Galabuzi (2006), and Massey and Denton (1993) can write justifiably
about an emergent apartheid system in Europe, Canada, and the United
States, respectively. In a similar vein decades ago, Brubaker (1992)
distinguished between *formal* and *substantive* citizenship. According
to him, the former connotes legal membership in a nation-state with
licit access to rights and duties of a citizen, whereas the latter points to
the extent to which those who have formal citizenship might or might
not enjoy the rights that ensure their full membership in a nation-state.

Thus, one can be a formal citizen but still struggle with substantive
citizenship, which speaks to how citizenship plays out, pragmatically,
in the lives of people. And if one accepts the pragmatist position that
concepts are meaningful based upon their practical utility (McDermott,
1977), then, as we shall soon see, for many Black Canadians citizenship
is nothing but an empty urn. Undoubtedly, Blacks are increasingly
tolerated in Canada, especially in symbolic cultural representations per
Canada's multiculturalism. Still, with insights from Žižek (2008, p. 660),
one can see tolerance as an ideology used to promote the "culturalization
of politics" in a bid to undermine genuine emancipatory political solu-
tions to many of the problems of today. As Brown (2006, p. 89) points
out, "the retreat from more substantive visions of justice heralded by
the promulgation of tolerance today is part of a more general depoliticization of citizenship and power and retreat from political life itself."

As far back as 1988, Peter Li found that Blacks suffered the most,
among all visible minority groups, regarding income inequality in the
Canadian job market after controlling for age, education, gender, nativ-
ity, social class, and so on. Almost two decades later Hum and Simpson
(2006) found that, for visible minority immigrant men, Blacks endure
the highest wage disadvantage of some 22.2 percent, relative to their
non-visible minority counterparts, after controlling for relevant con-
founding variables such as place of residence, age, education, et cetera.

Other visible minority immigrant men who experienced significant wage deficits include Indo-Pakistanis (13.1 percent), Arabs (13.7 percent), and Latin Americans (17.7 percent). Unfortunately, such racial inequalities in income are also found in Canadian universities (Henry & Tator, 2009; Li, 2012). In yet another study, Peter Li (2012) found that Black female professors in Canada suffer the most (among all visible minority female professors) when it comes to income inequality after controlling for relevant variables. The situation of Black male professors is not any better since they—together with Latin American and West Asian professors—were the most disadvantaged in this regard (Li, 2012).

Following the racial protests engendered by the murder of George Floyd, many Canadian universities have been caught flat-footed in their lack of Black faculty hires over the years. We now have leading Canadian universities—including York University, University of Toronto, McMaster University, and University of Waterloo—rushing shamelessly to embark on Black-only hires. The following excerpt from a recent University of Waterloo (2021, pp. 1–2) job advertisement is emblematic of the zeal with which these institutions are scrambling to hire Black scholars:

> The University of Waterloo is pleased to announce the cluster hiring of ten tenure-track/tenured academic appointments. ... All applicants to this cluster hiring opportunity must self-identify as Black in their cover letter. Because this is a special opportunity restricted to self-identified Black candidates, applicant self-identification information will be used for the purposes of screening and consideration.... The University regards equity and diversity as an integral part of academic excellence and is committed to accessibility for all employees. The University of Waterloo seeks applicants who embrace our values of equity, anti-racism and inclusion.

One wonders how the University of Waterloo (or, for that matter, any of the major Canadian universities) can justify the acute dearth of Black faculty members all these years. Why haven't Canadian universities been held accountable for their lack of Black faculty? Then, again, who would seek this accountability when the federal government itself is being sued for its own racial oppression of Black employees in the

Canadian civil service (Nasser & Merali, 2021)? At the time of writing this chapter, there was a report on a $2.5 billion class action lawsuit launched by Black federal workers against the federal government for alleged racial discrimination over the decades. This report contains allegations of senior civil servants praising the "good old days when we had slaves" (Nasser & Merali, 2021, p. 1). Perturbingly, the three Black women profiled in the report as plaintiffs—Carol Sip, Marcia Banfield Smith, and Michelle Herbert—worked as civil servants for twenty-six, nineteen, and seven years, respectively, and never received any promotion. Perhaps more worrisome is the fact that they endured repeated incidents of racial harassment and discrimination by supervisors and co-workers who maltreated them with impunity. Carol Sip, who worked at the Canada Revenue Agency (the former federal Customs Department) until her retirement, recalled, with considerable angst, how, whenever "they had a project with lifting boxes, only the Black ladies were chosen to lift the boxes" (Nasser & Merali, 2021, p. 3).

Similar to what obtains in the labour market, Canada's criminal justice system is wrought with systemic racism, notwithstanding its purported commitment to race-neutral operational standards. Studies (e.g., Sewell & Williams, 2021; Tanovich, 2006; Tator & Henry, 2006) suggest that Blacks and other visible minorities, as well as First Nations people, are treated worse than their similarly situated White counterparts at every stage of the Canadian criminal justice system—from points of surveillance through arrest to sentencing. In the case of Blacks, controversy has swirled in Toronto, in particular, around the police practice of contact carding, by which highly detailed personal information is extracted from civilians, most of whom are Blacks, in primarily non-criminal encounters. As Mensah and Williams (2017) note, Blacks, who comprise 8.1 percent of Toronto's population, account for 24 percent of those entered into the contact card database. The following quotation from the report by Justice Tulloch (2018, p. 42) shows how carding undermines the sense of belonging of some Black people in Canada: "During my consultations with members of the public and police, I heard of instances where groups of young Black men were asked for identifying information while playing basketball. Similarly, I heard from Black parents that when their children were hanging out with White friends, police would only ask their children for identifying information and not their White friends."

Additionally, available data show that Blacks, who formed only 2.5 percent of the total population of Canada by the 2006 census, constituted some 8.4 percent of the federal correctional population. This proportional share yields an odds ratio of 3.36, implying that Blacks were 3.36 times over-represented in the federal correctional population then relative to their share of the national population. The only group that had a higher over-representation than Blacks was Indigenous people. Even though correctional data at the provincial and territorial levels are scanty, estimates by Owusu-Bempah and Wortley (2014) show that in the four provinces for which data were available—Nova Scotia, New Brunswick, Ontario, and Alberta—Blacks were over-represented in the correctional populations with odds ratios of 6.6, 4.0, 4.5, and 3.6, respectively. Andrew Loku, Fran Anthony Berry, Michael Eligon, and Kwasi Skene-Peters were just some of the Black men whose deaths were caused by police shootings in Toronto since 2010. Undoubtedly, police killings of Black men are not as rampant in Canada as they are in the United States. Still, such killings occur every now and then, going as far back as the 1970s (Mensah & Williams, 2017).

With the ongoing COVID-19 pandemic, the ethnoracial fault line in Canada has been exposed as employment of Blacks and other racialized populations has become highly hazardous. Several studies have shown that Blacks and other visible minorities are over-represented in frontline occupations such as health care, education, sales, courier services, and farmwork, making them markedly vulnerable to the pandemic (Carman, 2020; George, 2020; Rocha et al., 2020). We also know from the work of Mensah and Williams (2017) that Black neighbourhoods in Toronto—including Jane-Finch, Black Creek, Mount Dennis, and Eglinton—have lower median incomes, higher unemployment rates, and higher proportions of households with unsuitable (or overcrowded) and inadequate (or "repair-needy") housing. These under-par conditions have created path dependencies by which Blacks (and other minorities) become more susceptible to COVID-19. For instance, data from the Mensah and Williams (2020, p. 132) indicate that, whereas Blacks comprised 9.28 percent of the population of Toronto by 30 September 2020, they accounted for almost a quarter (24 percent) of COVID-19 cases then. Contrast this with the case of Whites in Toronto, who comprised 49.64 percent of the population but only 21.66 percent of COVID-19 cases during the same period. Of course, as Butler (2020,

p. 5) notes, the virus itself does not discriminate, but "social and economic inequality will make sure that the virus discriminates [and
creates] a distinction between grievable and ungrievable lives, that is,
those who should be protected against death at all cost and those whose
lives are considered not worth safeguarding against illness and death."
Similarly, Foucault (2004), in his lectures on biopolitics, showed how
racism is used in the calculus of biopower to divide people into those
who must live and those who must die—this is yet another clear case
of some citizens being more equal than others.

Conclusion

With reference to Orwell's *Animal Farm*, in this chapter I have sought
to demonstrate that in Canada, as in the Animal Farm, some people
are indeed more equal than others, notwithstanding Canada's professed
liberal democratic ethos. As Orwell has it, the Animal Farm becomes
very prosperous and better organized at the end. However, the principles of Animalism, on which the revolution starts, change: not only
do some animals become more equal than others, but also they are led
to believe in the chorus "Four legs good, but two legs BETTER! Four
legs good, but two legs BETTER!" (Orwell, 2021, p. 95) after the pigs
learn to walk on two legs. Additionally, the egalitarianism on which the
farm operates changes seamlessly into a class system in which only the
pigs and their dogs enjoy life at the expense of the other animals, who
labour in the fields, often on empty stomachs, drink from the pool, and
are bothered by the cold in winter and the flies in summer. Worse still,
the title to the farm is owned only by the pigs, and even the practice of
calling each other Comrade is abolished at the end, just as the name
of the farm is switched from Animal Farm back to Manor Farm as the
pigs start to work on two legs like humans. Mr. Pilkington (the human
neighbour) and his friends confirm, after a visit to the farm, that "the
lower animals on Animal Farm did more work and received less food
than any animal in the county" (Orwell, 2021, p. 97). To the extent
that this fact is ascertained by a community of enquirers, its veracity
can be affirmed by the convergence theory of truth, as espoused by the
pragmatist.

A perfect analogy is almost utopian since every analogy breaks down
at one point or another. In this particular case, one cannot plausibly
argue that Canada has been under a communist revolution or that

Canadians have been expected to call each other Comrade. Still, the Animal Farm offers useful insights into why racism persists in Canada despite its democratic principles similar to those of Animalism. As we saw in the preceding discussion, democratic doctrines such as freedom of speech and equal rights have been upended to the disadvantage of racial minorities through convenient forgetfulness, tactical denials, and other underhanded discursive practices. Moreover, with a number of examples, I have shown how Black Canadians and their identities are drawn into the formation of Canadian national identity. For the most part, the negative stereotypes of Blacks are used to project the mainstream White population in a positive light through dialectical negation. Also, with the aid of pragmatism, I have demonstrated that what really matters are not magnanimous democratic proclamations but lived experiences of Black people. Indeed, I have shown that anti-Black racism is real in Canada, at least in the realms of employment, the criminal justice system, and the COVID-19 pandemic. Clearly, then, though Black Canadians might be formal citizens, their substantive citizenship—à la Brubaker (1992)—is found wanting, pragmatically speaking, and this corroborates the insistent premise of the chapter: *all are equal, but some are more equal than others.*

References

Abdelal, R., Herrera, Y. M., Johnston, A. I., & McDermott, R. (2009). Identity as a variable. In R. Abdelal, Y. M. Herrera, A. I. Johnston, & R. McDermott (Eds.), *Measuring identity: A guide for social scientists* (pp. 17–32). Cambridge University Press.

Abdi, A. A. (2005). Reflections on the long struggle for inclusion: The experiences of people of African origin. In W. J. Tettey & K. P. Puplampu (Eds.), *The African diaspora in Canada: Negotiating identity and belonging* (pp. 49–60). University of Calgary Press.

Adorno, T., & Horkheimer, M. (1944). *Dialectic of Enlightenment.* Social Studies Association.

Anderson, B. (2006). *Imagined communities: Reflections on the origin and spread of nationalism.* Verso.

Balibar, É. (2004). *We, the people of Europe? Reflections on transnational citizenship.* Princeton University Press.

Bauman, Z. (2011). *Collateral damage: Social inequalities in a global age.* Polity.

Brown, W. (2006). *Regulating aversion: Tolerance in the age of identity and empire.* Princeton University Press.

Brubaker, R. (1992). *Citizenship and nationhood in France and Germany*. Harvard University Press.

Butler, J. (2020). Capitalism has its limits. Verso. https://www.versobooks.com/blogs/4603-capitalism-has-its-limits

Cahoone, L. (2010). Rise of 20th century philosophy: Pragmatism [the Great Course, transcript]. In L. Cahoone (Ed.), *The modern intellectual tradition: From Descartes to Derrida* (pp. 210–219). The Teaching Company.

Carman, T. (2020). COVID-19 mortality rate higher in neighbourhoods with more visible minorities: StatsCan. *CBC News*. https://www.cbc.ca/news/canada/british-columbia/covid19-minorities-health-bc-canada-1.5801777

Dei, G. J. S. (2005). Racism in Canadian contexts: Exploring public and private issues in the educational system. In W. J. Tettey & K. P. Puplampu (Eds.), *The African diaspora in Canada: Negotiating identity and belonging* (pp. 93–110). University of Calgary Press.

Fanon, F. (1967). *Black skin, White masks*. Grove Press.

Fleras, A. (2011). *The media gaze: Representations of diversities in Canada*. UBC Press.

Foucault, M. (2004). *The birth of biopolitics: Lectures at the College de France, 1978–1979*. Picador.

Galabuzi, G. (2006). *Canada's economic apartheid: The social exclusion of racialized groups in the new century*. Canadian Scholars Press.

George, U. (2020, 27 October). Will Canada give its foreign essential workers their rights? *Open Democracy*. https://www.opendemocracy.net/en/pandemic-border/will-canada-give-its-foreign-essential-workers-their-rights/

Henry, F., & Tator, C. (Eds.). (2009). *Racism in the Canadian university: Demanding social justice, inclusion, and equity*. University of Toronto Press.

Henry, F., Tator, C., Mattis, W., & Rees, T. (1995). *The colour of democracy: Racism in Canadian society*. Harcourt.

Hum, D., & Simpson, W. (2006). Revisiting equity and labour: Immigration, gender, minority status and income differentials in Canada. In S. P. Hier & B. S. Bolaria (Eds.), *Race and racism in 21st century Canada: Continuity, complexity, and change*. (pp. 65–79). Broadview Press.

Li, P. (1988). *Ethnic inequality in a class society*. Thompson Educational.

Li, P. (1998). The market value and social value of race. In V. Satzewich (Ed.), *Racism and social inequality in Canada: Concepts, controversies and strategies of resistance* (pp. 115–130). Thompson Educational.

Li, P. (2012). Difference in employment income of university professors. *Canadian Ethnic Studies, 44*(2), 39–48.

Malhi, R. L., & Boon, S. D. (2007). Discourses of "democratic racism" in the talk of South Asian Canadian women. *Canadian Ethnic Studies, 39*(3), 125–151.

Marshall, T. H. (1950). *Citizenship and social class*. Doubleday.

Massey, D., & Denton, N. A. (1993). *American apartheid: Segregation and the making of the underclass*. Harvard University Press.

McDermott, J. J. (Ed.). (1977). *The writings of William James: A comprehensive edition*. University of Chicago Press.

Mensah, J. (2015). The Black, continental African presence and the nation-immigration dialectic in Canada. *Social Identities: Journal for the Study of Race, Nation and Culture, 20*(4–5), 279–298.

Mensah, J., & Williams, C. J. (2017). *Boomerang ethics: How racism hurts us all.* Fernwood.

Mensah, J., and Williams, C. J. (2022). Socio-structural injustice, racism, and the COVID-19 pandemic: A precarious entanglement among Black immigrants in Canada. *Studies in Social Justice, 16*(1), 123–142.

Nasser, S., & Merali, F. (2021, 16 September). "Enough is enough": Black civil servants vow to press on with discrimination suits as Liberals promise change. *CBC News.* https://www.cbc.ca/news/canada/toronto/black-federal-employees-canada-racism-1.6175910

Nederveen, P. J. (1992). *White on Black: Images of Africa and Blacks in Western popular culture.* Yale University Press.

Orwell, G. (2021). *Animal farm.* Mintz Classics. (Original work published 1945)

Owusu-Bempah, A., & Wortley, S. (2014). Race, crime, and criminal justice in Canada. In S. Bucerius & M. Tonry (Eds.), *The Oxford handbook on race, ethnicity, crime and immigration* (pp. 281–320). Oxford University Press.

Reiter, B. (2012). Framing non-Whites and producing second-class citizens in France and Portugal. *Journal of Ethnic and Migration Studies, 38*(7), 1067–1084.

Rocha, R., Shingler, B., & Montpetit, J. (2020, 11 June). Montreal's poorest and most racially diverse neighbourhoods hit hardest by COVID-19, data analysis shows. *CBC News.* https://www.cbc.ca/news/canada/montreal/race-covid-19-montreal-data-census-1.5607123

Sachedina, O., & Taylor, B. (2021, 18 September). "Really frustrating": Racialized people feel ignored in federal election campaign. *CTV News.* https://www.ctvnews.ca/politics/federal-election-2021/really-frustrating-racialized-people-feel-ignored-in-federal-election-campaign-1.5591309

Seigfried, C. H. (1995). Pragmatism. In *The Cambridge dictionary of philosophy.* Cambridge University Press.

Sewell, J., & Williams, C. J. (2021). *Crisis in Canada's policing: Why change is so hard, and how we can get real reform in our police forces.* James Lorimer & Company.

Tanovich, D. M. (2006). *The colour of justice: Policing race in Canada.* Irwin Law.

Tator, C., & Henry, F. (2006). *Racial profiling in Canada: Challenging the myth of "a few bad apples."* University of Toronto Press.

Tulloch, M. H. (2018). *Report of the independent street checks review.* Queen's Printer for Ontario. https://opcc.bc.ca/wp-content/uploads/2019/06/StreetChecks.pdf

United Nations Human Rights Council. (2021). *A report on the promotion and protection of the human rights and fundamental freedoms of Africans and people of African descent against excessive use of force and other human rights violations by law enforcement officers.* https://www.ohchr.org/Documents/Issues/Racism/A_HRC_47_CRP_1.pdf

University of Waterloo, Office of the Provost. (2021). Black excellence—Multiple faculty appointments open to all disciplines (tenure-track/tenured). https://uwaterloo.ca/provost/black-excellence-multiple-faculty-appointments-open-all

Žižek, S. (2008). Tolerance as an ideological category. *Critical Inquiry, 34*(4), 660–682.

17

Canadian Multiculturalism in the Neo-Liberal Era:
Discourses of Race, Asianness, and Assimilation in Maclean's *"Too Asian?"*

ELENA CHOU

In this chapter, I explore the racial discourses in *Maclean's* "Too Asian?" article (Finlay & Köhler, 2010) in order to investigate two related problems. First, I examine how the article's representations of Asians and Asian Canadians as abject (Kristeva, 1982) and/or "other" can be used to explore assumptions underlying the logic of assimilation into Canadian multicultural society in that the processes of assimilation work to reinforce the Whiteness of "core" Canadian culture (Bannerji, 2000) as hegemonic and normative, against which racialized bodies are continually contrasted and measured. Second, I argue that the increasing neo-liberalization of the Canadian social, political, and economic landscapes has resulted in shifting perceptions and practices of Canadian multiculturalism and that the representations of Asians and Asian Canadians in this article reflect this neo-liberal shift. Overall, the representation of Asians and Asian Canadians in the "Too Asian?" article highlights what Roland Sintos Coloma (2016, p. 363) argues is the "[paradoxical] position of Asian [Canadians] as a racialized minority: they are needed and rejected at the same time, desired and undesirable for inclusion and integration in educational and social institutions." This is emblematic of the effects of the neo-liberalization of both Canadian society and Canadian multiculturalism.

Representation of Asians/Asian Canadians in *Maclean's* "Too Asian?" Article

In November 2010, *Maclean's* magazine, in its Annual University Rankings issue, published an article entitled "Too Asian? Some Frosh Don't Want to Study at an Asian University" (Finlay & Köhler, 2010). The article claimed that a growing number of White Canadian students were consciously avoiding certain universities because of perceptions that they were "too Asian" and "so academically focused that some students feel they can no longer compete or have fun." As the authors noted, the phrase "too Asian" was "used in some U.S. academic circles to describe a phenomenon that's become such a cause for concern to university admissions officers and high school guidance counsellors that several elite universities in the U.S. have faced scandals in recent years over limiting Asian applicants and keeping the numbers of White students artificially high." Certain Canadian universities were identified by the White students at Havergal, the elite female private Toronto high school, who were interviewed for this article, as being "too Asian," including the University of Toronto and the University of British Columbia, often identified as among the most prestigious Canadian universities. The article also mentioned the University of California system as experiencing a similar problem with "too many" Asian American students among its ranks in proportion to the overall American population as well as the efforts, both implicit and explicit, to limit Asian and Asian American students in its system as well as in various Ivy League schools.

Organized primarily by the Chinese Canadian National Council and the Solidarity Committee against Anti-Asian Racism, the backlash to this article was swift, with immediate widespread condemnation of the article's racist representations of Asian and Asian Canadian students as "taking away" university spaces from White Canadian students. *Maclean's* and Rogers Communications (the parent company of *Maclean's*) were asked to apologize for the content of the article, and a boycott of both brands was attempted (Willetts, 2010). The *Maclean's* response was to quietly change the title of the article in its online edition of the magazine to "The Enrollment Controversy: Worries that Efforts in the U.S. to Limit Enrollment of Asian Students in Top Universities May Migrate to Canada" (though typing "*Maclean's*" and "Too Asian" in a Google search will still yield a link to the online version of this article with its new title) and did not recall any of the print versions of the issue. Numerous city councils across Canada—including Markham, Richmond Hill, Vancouver, and Victoria—voted in favour of motions to condemn the content of the article as racist and divisive (Heer, 2012, p. 5). In the end, both *Maclean's* and Rogers Communications refused to apologize or comment further on the matter.

The article has been the subject of numerous analyses over the years by Asian Canadian scholars. As they have noted, the framing of the issue or debate in the article set up a binary between Asian/ Asian Canadian and White students, with oppositional values and essentialized characteristics for both groups in which Asians/Asian Canadians were not depicted as "real" Canadians (Coloma, 2016; Cui & Kelly, 2013; Heer, 2012; Ho, 2014). The article represented Asian/ Asian Canadian students as overly studious and avoiding social and other non-academic activities in favour of academic work, in contrast to their White peers, represented as having more balanced lives and more fun (Finlay & Köhler, 2010; Ho, 2014). For example, the article included quotations from Diane Bondy, "a recently retired Ottawa-area guidance counsellor," who stated that "Asians get more support from their parents financially and academically" and added that "[the Asian/ Asian Canadian] kids were getting 98 per cent but they didn't have other skills" (Finlay & Köhler, 2010). As Coloma (2016, p. 367) notes, drawing from the arguments of Jeet Heer from an article published in *The Walrus* in 2010, the "Too Asian?" article homogenized all Asians as a monolithic group and Asian students as "socially dysfunctional nerds who lack any sense of fun, virtual robots who are programmed by their parents to study," so that the presence of Asian students is the "problem" rather than "social and cultural barriers that divide students."

Thus, Asian/Asian Canadian students were not depicted as exhibiting the traits of supposed "Canadian"—read White—students, represented as the cultural norm and standard against which Asian/ Asian Canadian as well as other racialized minority students were measured and defined. There was also the negative portrayal, perhaps unintended by Finlay and Köhler, of White students as interested more in partying than in studying. Furthermore, the article also represented Canadian universities as inundated or invaded by Asian students (Ho,

2014), drawing from older stereotypes of the late nineteenth and early twentieth centuries of Asians as the "yellow peril," in particular East Asians, who were viewed as a civilizational threat to the West because of their presence and perceived numbers in various countries.

In addition to promoting and entrenching these essentialized cultural stereotypes of Asians/Asian Canadians and their cultural values, the article discussed certain Asian ethnic groups but ignored others; students who appeared to have Chinese names or surnames were discussed or represented but not those from other Asian ethnicities: the article used "Chinese" as a synecdoche for all "Asians." In doing so, it ignored the intersectional power dynamics in which East Asian (Chinese, Korean, Japanese) and South Asian ethnic groups are often economically privileged compared with Southeast Asians (Filipinos, Laotians, Cambodians, Vietnamese) not only in Canada but also in other contexts, such as the United States (Budiman & Ruiz, 2021; Statistics Canada, 2019, 2020a).

Cui and Kelly (2013) add that the "Too Asian?" article, by essentializing supposed "Asian"—or Chinese—cultural values, uses cultural explanations rather than systemic or structural issues to explain individual behaviour such as hard work. Furthermore, Asian/Asian Canadian students are depicted as tending or even choosing to exclude themselves from mainstream (White) Canadian society without any analysis of why this might be happening, such as anti-Asian racism or the isolation of and/or lack of support for Asian international students as well as for international students from other ethnic or national backgrounds (Cui & Kelly, 2013). They also note that the article constructs and maintains White privilege in higher education by questioning merit and discounting the hard work of Asian/Asian Canadian students and thus maintains the existing privileged status of Whiteness and Eurocentric credentials by presenting Whites/White students as the victims.

Racialization of Asians/Asian Canadians in Canadian Multiculturalism

Asians occupy an ambiguous space in the racial hierarchy of White settler societies such as Canada. On the one hand, anti-Asian racism has a long and ongoing history in Canada, and Asians are still frequently the targets of racist violence, including during the recent COVID-19 pandemic. On the other hand, there is a common perception that

Whites, as well as other racialized minorities, view Asians as the model minority, as Asians are perceived as being able to achieve rapid upward social mobility in a relatively short period of time.

The term "model minority" was first used in 1966 by sociologist William Petersen in a *New York Times Magazine* story entitled "Success Story: Japanese American Style" as well as in an article for *U.S. News and World Report* in which he praised the success of Chinese Americans (Li & Wang, 2008, p. 3, p. 215). This is a stereotype in which a particular racial and/or ethnic group is seen as especially economically successful compared with other racial/ethnic groups. The premise of the model minority stereotype places a particular racialized group—in this case Asians—in a binary against other racialized or ethnic groups in which the former are depicted as hardworking, docile, family oriented, and law abiding in contrast to the "lazy" or "welfare dependent" families of other races, in particular African Americans (Li & Wang, 2008, p. 24). This term was used subsequently in the mainstream media to describe Asians as a super minority "outwhiting" Whites, in the words of *Newsweek* in 1971, replacing older media representations of Asians as the "yellow peril" (qtd. in Li & Wang, 2008, p. 3, p. 5).

Thus, as posed by Asian American scholars such as Mia Tuan (1998), are Asians then "honorary Whites"? This thesis is often backed by statistics showing that Asians on the whole in North America have higher rates of education (Abada et al., 2008; Budiman & Ruiz, 2021; Statistics Canada, 2021) and income (Budiman & Ruiz, 2021; Statistics Canada, 2019, 2020a, 2021), as well as increasing rates of intermarriage with Whites (Budiman & Ruiz, 2021; Milan & Chui, 2010) compared with other racial or ethnic groups, all of which are used to support the idea that Asians are becoming increasingly assimilated and therefore being closer to the dominant (Eurocentric) culture.

I argue that the discursive representation of Asian Canadians as the model minority necessitates a position of Asianness or an Asian racial identity defined and positioned in relation to Whiteness/White racial identity on the racial hierarchy in which Whites are at the top (Kim, 2007; Koshy, 2001; Li, 2004). This tension between assimilation and racialization highlights what Gayatri Chakravorty Spivak (1988) calls "recognition by assimilation," in which abject or "othered" bodies are recognized the closer they approximate the figure from the dominant or hegemonic culture.

Whiteness/Eurocentrism of Canadian Multiculturalism and Cultural Identity

Popular understandings and conceptualizations of Canadian multiculturalism function as commonsensical and naturalized myths (Barthes, 1972) that utilize and follow a circular logic: Canadians are tolerant and diverse because we are a multicultural society; Canada is multicultural because we are tolerant and diverse. However, racialized discourses are deeply embedded within Canadian culture despite proclamations of "diversity" and implied "racelessness" and "colour blindness." The discourse of multiculturalism in the Canadian context maintains a façade or impression of tolerance and diversity while masking racism and the institutions and structures that produce, maintain, and reproduce it, such as the media and the government (Bannerji, 2000; Henry & Tator, 2009; Mackey, 2002; Thobani, 2007).

In the late nineteenth century and into the twentieth century, Canadian immigration policy employed a "White Canada" approach, either overt or covert, until it ended in 1967 with the introduction of the "point system" of immigrant selection that rewarded applicants on the basis of education, skills, and other criteria rooted more in merit than in racial or ethnic origin (Jabukowski, 1999). Prior to the Second World War, Canadian officials promoted a strict hierarchy of races in which racial character and culture were seen as coterminous, with an emphasis on assimilation into the dominant culture (Mackey, 2002). After the war, though overt displays of antisemitism and racism became less socially acceptable, racial discourses, through coded language, were still propagated by Canadian public figures and government officials who focused on the "suitability" and "adaptability" of certain ethnic and racial groups to the Canadian climate (Jabukowski, 1999; Mackey, 2002).

Canadian multiculturalism policy originated in 1963 with the Royal Commission on Bilingualism and Biculturalism initiated by the Liberal government of Prime Minister Lester Pearson. The commission's work involved a series of consultations with various ethnocultural groups and organizations across Canada to discuss the viability of bilingualism and biculturalism in Canada. At the end, the commission recommended that Canada adopt an official policy of English and French bilingualism and biculturalism despite the wishes by the various ethnocultural groups and organizations for their cultural and linguistic contributions to be recognized and included in Canadian state policy, and it became official policy on 8 October 1971 through the Multiculturalism within a Bilingual Framework passed by the Liberal government now led by Prime Minister Pierre Trudeau. This framework asserted that, though Canada had two official languages, "there is no official culture, nor does any ethnic group take precedence over any other" (qtd. in Mackey, 2002, p. 64). However, the framework reinforced the Eurocentricity and Whiteness of Canada by erasing Indigenous peoples as founding peoples in Canada in favour of only the English and French (Abu-Laban & Gabriel, 2002; Haque, 2012; Thobani, 2007). As Eve Haque (2012) argues, this emphasis on the English and French as the foundational cultures in Canada was used by the Canadian government to argue that English and French were the language groups that could help to assimilate other ethnic groups even as doing so relegated these groups to the margins; language therefore functioned as the modality through which a racial hierarchy based upon differential inclusion could be maintained. Haque adds that the commission's goal was to create a model for nation building that could preserve the existing White settler hegemony while it disavowed racialized minority populations, in which racial differences are elided at the same time that language is used as a universal form of community building.

Scholars of Canadian multiculturalism have also argued that the introduction of multiculturalism as official Canadian policy and discourse was a response by the political and economic elite in Canada to the changing demographics in post–Second World War Canada, in which, rather than "trying to erase difference and construct an imaginary community based on the assimilation to a singular notion of culture, the Canadian state attempted to institutionalize various forms of difference, thereby controlling access to power and simultaneously legitimating the power of the state" (Mackey, 2002, p. 50), while also presenting a version of Canada on the international stage as "urbane, cosmopolitan, and at the cutting edge of promoting racial and ethnic tolerance among western nations" in light of its foreign policy goals to present itself as an emerging leader on the global geopolitical stage (Thobani, 2007, p. 144). Multiculturalism, these scholars argue, was used as a device to manage differences within the nation rather than any form of public policy that emerged from the benevolence or progressiveness of the Canadian state (Bannerji, 2000; Mackey, 2002; Thobani, 2007). Furthermore, the initiation by Pearson of the Royal Commission on Bilingualism and Biculturalism was intended to deal more with quelling the emerging nationalist movement in Quebec than with offering any state benevolence (Haque, 2012; Winter, 2011).

Much of the criticism of or backlash to Canadian multicultural discourse and policy is often the result of the perception that multiculturalism is a zero-sum game among different groups of people in competition for a finite amount of resources, whether real (e.g., representation) or symbolic (e.g., recognition). Embedded in this backlash has been White anxiety about the loss of power and resources, whether real or symbolic, to non-Whites.

However, the terms "multiculturalism" and "diversity" are empty signifiers (Bhabha, 1994). As Gunew (2004, p. 19) argues, multiculturalism is a concept onto which various groups project their desires and fears. For example, among the right wing in Canada, the term "multiculturalism" is used as a signifier for "racialized" or "non-White" people, particularly those from non-European cultures seen as "foreign" to or "incompatible" with "Canadian" culture (Bannerji, 2000; Ryan, 2010). Bannerji (2000) adds that the term "diversity" appears to be neutral and even positive but is a covert way of "managing difference" without examining the real horizontal power relations in Canadian society that marginalize non-White others seen as threats to hegemonic Eurocentric Canadian cultural identity.

Indeed, some critics of multiculturalism argue that, though racial, ethnic, and cultural diversity in demographic terms is promoted and celebrated through Canadian multicultural policy, multicultural ideology and policy itself does not support anti-racist or equity measures, such that diversity exists only on a banal or visual level rather than on the level of equitable social and power relations (Bannerji, 2000; Dhamoon, 2009; Mahtani, 2002; Thobani, 2007). Therefore, it could be argued that Canadian multicultural policy from the beginning has been a colonial project focused on the assimilation of racialized ethnocultural minority groups rather than on any meaningful recognition of or attempt to introduce genuine diversity, inclusion, or equity measures that would materially affect the lives of ethnocultural groups in terms of challenging racism, socio-economic inequality, sexism/patriarchy, and so forth (Bannerji, 2000; Dhamoon, 2009; Thobani, 2007).

Race, Racialization, and Asians/Asian Canadians under Neo-Liberal Multiculturalism

In terms of the broader social, economic, and political factors that have contextualized the racialized discourses in the "Too Asian?" article, the increasing neo-liberalization of the Canadian social, political, and economic landscapes over the past thirty years has resulted in shifting perceptions and practices of Canadian multiculturalism, which in turn have affected conceptualizations and discourses of race, ethnicity, and practices of racialization in Canada. I argue that this neo-liberal turn in Canadian society has resulted in an increasingly neo-liberal multiculturalism that has implications for popular and commonsensical ideas about "race" in Canada. Liberal multiculturalism was exemplified in the era roughly between 1971 and 1993 and emphasized how ethnocultural groups in Canada could maintain their cultural traditions, often with the discursive and economic support of the Canadian state (Abu-Laban & Gabriel, 2002; Mackey, 2002). With liberal multiculturalism, the focus of discourse and policy was placed on the representation as well as the visibility of racial, ethnic, and cultural differences, vis-à-vis racial, ethnic, and cultural pluralism, within the Canadian collective. Yet, under neo-liberal multiculturalism, though the visibility of racial, ethnic, and cultural pluralism was still emphasized, there was a discursive and policy shift to highlight cultural difference, instead of race and ethnicity, as markers of difference and cultural difference to determine and assess notions of "civilization" and the degree of appropriate assimilation into Canadian culture and its attendant values.

In an increasingly neo-liberal climate in Canada, this has meant de-emphasizing issues related to race, ethnicity, and equity in favour of "colour-blind" approaches to individual merit and social mobility. I further argue that there is a tension between the logic of neo-liberal multiculturalism and the continued importance placed on diversity as a key part of our Canadian cultural identity, for there is the simultaneous racialization and deracialization of bodies in which race is made visible yet at the same time erased symbolically and epistemically.

There are many ways in which neo-liberalism as policy and discourse has affected various aspects of Canadian public policy in regard to race and ethnicity. In terms of multicultural discourse and policy, beginning in the late 1980s, there was already a shift to promote multiculturalism as a "selling point" for Canada, to use ethnic and cultural diversity as a means to increase international trade, which we continue to see today. Starting in the 1980s, the neo-liberalization of the Canadian economy began in earnest when the Canadian government aggressively pursued foreign capital and investment, particularly from Asia and specifically from Hong Kong (Abu-Laban & Gabriel, 2002; Mitchell, 2009). For example, the "business immigrant" category was created in 1984 to target Hong Kong capital, prior to the handover back to China in 1997, in which investors were required to invest a certain amount of money in Canada, and in turn their applications for residency were given priority and expedited (Mitchell, 2009).

In 1986, the Brian Mulroney–led Conservative government held the Multiculturalism Means Business conference, which explored how Canadian multiculturalism could be utilized to serve Canadian business and economic interests (Abu-Laban & Gabriel, 2002). We still see how narratives of Canada as one of the most diverse countries in the world, and how Canada consistently ranks as one of the best places in the world to live in part because of its ethnic and cultural diversity, are used to market the country to promote foreign trade and investment or to increase the number of international students rather than to foster meaningful cultural exchange or celebration (see Remitly, 2020; U.S. News and World Report, 2021).

The neo-liberalization of multiculturalism in Canada involves changes in several areas in relation to race, ethnicity, and racial and ethnic relations, including immigration policy, and was precipitated by the neo-liberalization of Canadian society as well as the effects of economic globalization and shifting global geopolitics. Abu-Laban and Gabriel (2002, p. 106) note that policy shifts between 1993 and 2001 emphasized the economic value of multiculturalism along with loyalty and "attachment to Canada." During this period, multicultural policy was also heavily criticized by those opposed to multiculturalism, including how it is divisive by encouraging and emphasizing differences rather than commonalities, and how the expression of ethnic minority cultures and languages should be relegated to the private sphere, where the Canadian state should not provide public funding to support the private matter of culture (Abu-Laban & Gabriel, 2002; Kwak, 2019; Ryan, 2010; Winter, 2011; Wong & Guo, 2015).

In terms of specific immigration policy and discourse, there has been a shift toward an increasingly market-oriented immigration policy to increase the numbers of highly skilled, highly educated, and economically self-reliant immigrants not deemed to be a financial burden or drain on the state. Although Canada eliminated its explicitly racist immigration selection criteria in 1967 in favour of the point system, it has been argued that this system was neo-liberal from the beginning since it predetermines and assumes a particular class of immigrants who can contribute economically to Canada (Bauder, 2003; Root et al., 2014). In the past twenty years, investor immigrants as well as wealthier immigrants have been favoured over immigrants in the family reunification and refugee streams, and newer policies such as the Canadian Experience Class and increasing use of the Temporary Foreign Worker Program are examples that highlight the economic focus of Canadian immigration policy as developed with the goal of meeting Canadian economic or labour needs rather than developing potential Canadian citizens from permanent residents or citizens (Bauder, 2003; Root et al., 2014).

The deracializing and individualizing mechanisms in neo-liberal multiculturalism are what allowed the Conservative government led by Stephen Harper to rhetorically support multiculturalism as a way to mobilize political support for the party among socially conservative immigrants (Kwak, 2019; Ryan, 2010). When Jason Kenney became the federal minister of Citizenship, Immigration, and Multiculturalism in 2009, he actively courted social conservative racialized immigrants (particularly Asian and South Asian religious and social conservatives) (Kwak, 2019; Ryan, 2010). One of Kenney's first acts was to change citizenship rules in light of the 2006 evacuation of Lebanese Canadians residing in Lebanon during a conflict between Israel and Hezbollah to avoid "Canadians of convenience" (Ryan, 2010), perceived under neo-liberal multiculturalism as a financial burden on the state. This emphasizes what Laura Kwak (2019, p. 15) observes under neo-liberal multiculturalism: "Racelessness ultimately offers a reordering of racial rule wherein racial populations are either folded into state representation or pathologized as [a] threat to the state." Hence, even though neo-liberalism emphasizes racelessness and colour blindness, if a racialized minority group is perceived in any way to be a threat to the dominant and hegemonic Eurocentric status quo whether economically, socially, politically, or some combination, then its difference is highlighted, and the entire group is pathologized.

Theorizing Race and Analyzing Anti-Asian Racism under Neo-Liberalism

Some scholars of race and racialization have argued that, rather than attempting to understand how processes of neo-liberalism produce specific instances of racism, neo-liberalism itself is fundamentally racist, working to normalize racism by enforcing, reproducing, and modifying existing forms of racism (Davis, 2007; Giroux, 2005, 2008; Goldberg, 1993, 2009; Roberts & Mahtani, 2010). In other words, race and neo-liberalism are co-constitutive and work in tandem (Roberts & Mahtani, 2010). Under the individualizing and privatizing logic of neo-liberalism, race is no longer presented as an important factor in or determinant of an individual's success; however, as these scholars argue, racism and processes of racialization are effaced under neo-liberal regimes so that racism is normalized while making it appear that race is no longer important.

David Goldberg (2009, pp. 334–335) argues that the more neo-liberal the state, the "more likely race would be rendered largely immune from state intervention so long as having no government force behind it," since neo-liberalism recreates social relations but with increased forms of control. He claims that neo-liberalism can be read as "a response to the concerns about the declining power of Whiteness, in that it was a short step from privatizing property to privatizing race through the removal of racial categories and conceptions from the public to private realm" (p. 335). Goldberg also suggests that neo-liberalism "works to produce an increasing 'racial secularization' by ensuring that race and race discourse [are] ... purged from public administration while remaining alive and unaddressed in the private realm" (p. 341).

If neo-liberalism, as Goldberg claims, is a "response to the concerns about the declining power of Whiteness," then we can read how the anti-Asian comments expressed in the "Too Asian?" article are a deep psychic expression by Whites about the failure of neo-liberalism to manage and control the racial other. In other words, if the neo-liberalization of multiculturalism has meant, or resulted in, a deracialization of multicultural policy and discourse in favour of individual enterprise and credentialism devoid of race/racial politics and discourse, then the academic success of Asians as the model minority works simultaneously to support the notion of meritocracy championed by neo-liberal discourse and to disrupt the subordinate position of Asians in the racial hierarchy.

The anti-Asian sentiments expressed in the "Too Asian?" article exhibit White resentment toward or anxiety about Asians that has not been resolved by the project of multiculturalism, whose goal was to manage and control the other, as well as the failure of neo-liberalism to secure, or to resecure, White power. Thus, neo-liberalism, with its emphasis on individual enterprise and meritocracy, has failed to eradicate the problem of race and thus failed to maintain White hegemony.

David Eng and Shinhee Han (2010, p. 61) discuss how Homi Bhabha's (1994) concept of mimicry refers to the "social imperative to assimilate" resulting from colonialism. They argue that the model minority stereotype is one that Asian Americans/Canadians are forced to embody in order to gain recognition by Whites in the racial hierarchy. However, as Bhabha (1994) suggests, mimicry is simultaneously a partial success and a partial failure since it is both resemblance and threat, a poor imitation of Whiteness. In the "Too Asian?" article, we can see how the figure of the model minority Asian/Asian Canadian student is represented by Whites as a mimicry of Whiteness, almost the same but not White, which serves to highlight the ambiguous position of Asians in the settler colonial racial hierarchy. Whereas Asians/Asian Canadians excel academically to the point where they are "taking away" spots from White Canadians, Asians/Asian Canadians are still rendered as abject or other since they are unable to replicate all aspects of Whiteness in that they are unable to do anything other than study, and thus unable to "have fun," as Finlay and Köhler (2010) describe. However, despite the consternation and racial anxiety expressed by White Canadians about the presence of Asian students in Canadian universities, whether they are domestic or international students, Asian international students are heavily recruited by Canadian postsecondary institutions. They (along with other international students) are perceived and treated as "cash cows" by postsecondary administrators since their higher tuition fees compared with those of domestic Canadian students make up the funding shortfalls and decreasing financial investments from federal and provincial governments because of the neo-liberalization of public education (CBC Radio, 2016; Crawley, 2017; Kim & Kwak, 2019; Statistics Canada, 2020b). Asians/Asian Canadians are thus both desired and undesired as students in Canadian educational institutions, yet the People's Republic of China has been the top source country for international students in terms of numbers in the past decade, and only recently has it been supplanted by students from India (Kim & Kwak, 2019; Statistics Canada, 2020b).

Conclusion

The logic and processes of assimilation fit well with the logic of neo-liberalism since both demand similar processes of deracialization. Thus, Canadian multiculturalism in the neo-liberal era continues the project of racial management in which race is erased from public discourse yet left simmering under the surface, as the anti-Asian comments in the *Maclean's* article demonstrate. This deracialization as the result of neo-liberalism also effaces the existing asymmetrical power relations in Canada as well as its White settler colonial roots in order to maintain White settler colonial hegemony.

References

Abada, T., Hou, F., & Ram, B. (2008). *Group differences in educational attainment among the children of immigrants*. Business and Labour Market Analysis Division.

Abu-Laban, Y., & Gabriel, C. (2002). *Selling diversity: Immigration, multiculturalism, employment equity, and globalization*. University of Toronto Press.

Bannerji, H. (2000). *The dark side of nation: Essays on multiculturalism and gender*. Canadian Scholars Press.

Barthes, R. (1972). *Mythologies*. Hill & Wang.

Bauder, H. (2003). "Brain abuse," or the devaluation of immigrant labour in Canada. *Antipode, 35*(4), 699–717. https://doi.org/10.1046/j.1467-8330.2003.00346.x

Bhabha, H. (1994). *The location of culture*. Routledge.

Budiman, A., & Ruiz, N. G. (2021, 29 April). Key facts about Asian Americans, a diverse and growing population. Pew Research Group. https://www.pewresearch.org/fact-tank/2021/04/29/key-facts-about-asian-americans/

CBC Radio. (2016, 18 November). Hefty fees from foreign students are bailing out Canadian universities—and that's not good. https://www.cbc.ca/radio/sunday/hefty-fees-from-foreign-students-are-bailing-out-canadian-universities-and-that-s-not-good-1.3854036

Coloma, R. S. (2016). Too Asian? On racism, paradox and ethno-nationalism. In R. S. Coloma & G. Pon (Eds.), *Asian Canadian studies reader* (pp. 363–382). University of Toronto Press.

Crawley, M. (2017, 12 July). Universities growing more reliant on foreign student fees. *CBC News*. https://www.cbc.ca/news/canada/toronto/international-students-universities-ontario-tuition-1.4199489

Cui, D., & Kelly, J. (2013). "Too Asian?" Or the invisible citizen on the other side of the nation? *Journal of International Migration and Integration, 14*(1), 157–174. https://doi.org/10.1007/s12134-012-0235-7

Davis, D-A. (2007). Narrating the mute: Racializing and racism in a neoliberal moment. *Souls, 9*(4), 346–360. https://doi.org/10.1080/10999940701703810

Dhamoon, R. (2009). *Identity/difference politics: How difference is produced and why it matters.* UBC Press.

Eng, D. L., & Han, S. (2010). A dialogue on racial melancholia. In J. Y. W. S. Wu & T. Chen (Eds.), *Asian American studies now: A critical reader* (pp. 55–79). Rutgers University Press.

Finlay, S., & Köhler, N. (2010, 10 November). Too Asian? Some frosh don't want to study at an Asian university. *Maclean's.* https://macleans.ca/news/canada/too-asian/

Giroux, H. (2005). The terror of neoliberalism: Rethinking the significance of cultural politics. *College Literature, 32*(1), 1–19. https://doi.org/10.1353/lit.2005.0006

Giroux, H. (2008). *Against the terror of neoliberalism: Politics beyond the age of greed.* Paradigm Publishers.

Goldberg, D. T. (1993). *Racist culture: Philosophy and the politics of meaning.* Blackwell.

Goldberg, D. T. (2009). *The threat of race: Reflections on racial neoliberalism.* Blackwell.

Gunew, S. (2004). *Haunted nations: The colonial dimensions of multiculturalism.* Routledge.

Haque, E. (2012). *Multiculturalism within a bilingual framework: Language, race, and belonging in Canada.* University of Toronto Press.

Heer, J. (2012). Introduction. In R. J. Gilmour, D. Bhandar, J. Heer, & M. C. K. Ma (Eds.), *"Too Asian?" Racism, privilege, and post-secondary education* (pp. 1–13). Between the Lines.

Henry, F., & Tator, C. (2009). *The colour of democracy: Racism in Canadian society* (4th ed.). Nelson Education.

Ho, R. (2014). Do all Asians look alike? Asian Canadians as model minorities. *Studies on Asia, 4*(2), 78–107.

Jabukowski, L. M. (1999). "Managing" Canadian immigration: Racism, ethnic selectivity, and the law. In E. Comack (Ed.), *Locating law: Race/class/gender connections* (pp. 98–124). Fernwood Publishing.

Kim, N. Y. (2007). Critical thoughts on Asian American assimilation in the whitening literature. *Social Forces, 86*(2), 561–574.

Kim, A. H., & Kwak, M-J. (2019). Introduction. In A. H. Kim & M. J. Kwak (Eds.), *Outward and upward mobilities: International students in Canada, their families, and structuring institutions* (pp. 3–22). University of Toronto Press.

Koshy, S. (2001). Morphing race into ethnicity: Asian Americans and critical transformations of whiteness. *Boundary 2, 28*(1), 153–194. https://doi.org/10.1215/01903659-28-1-153

Kristeva, J. (1982). *The powers of horror: An essay on abjection.* Columbia University Press.

Kwak, L. J. (2019). "New Canadians are new Conservatives": Race, incorporation and achieving electoral success in multicultural Canada. *Ethnic and Racial Studies, 42*(10), 1708–1726. https://doi.org/10.1080/01419870.2018.1508734

Li, D. L. (2004). On ascriptive and acquisitional Americanness: *The Accidental Asian* and the illogic of assimilation. *Contemporary Literature, 45*(1), 106–134. https://doi.org/10.2307/3593557

Li, G., & Wang, L. (2008). *Model Minority myth revisited: An interdisciplinary approach to demystifying Asian American educational experiences.* Information Age Publishing.

Mackey, E. (2002). *The house of difference: Cultural politics and national identity in Canada.* University of Toronto Press.

Mahtani, M. (2002). Interrogating the hyphen-nation: Canadian multicultural policy and "mixed race" identities. *Social Identities, 8*(1), 67–90. https://doi.org/10.1080/13504630220132026

Milan, A., Maheux, H., & Chui, T. (2010). *A portrait of couples in mixed unions.* Statistics Canada. http://www.statcan.gc.ca/pub/11-008-x/2010001/article/11143-eng.htm

Mitchell, K. (2009). In whose interest? Transnational capital and the production of multiculturalism in Canada. In S. Mookerjea, I. Szeman, & G. Faurschou (Eds.), *Canadian cultural studies: A reader* (pp. 344–365). Duke University Press.

Remitly. (2020). Where the world wants to work: The most popular countries for moving abroad. https://www.remitly.com/gb/en/landing/where-the-world-wants-to-live

Roberts, D. J., & Mahtani, M. (2010). Neoliberalizing race, racing neoliberalism: Placing "race" in neoliberal discourses. *Antipode, 42*(2), 248–257. https://doi.org/10.1111/j.1467-8330.2009.00747.x

Root, J., Gates-Gasse, E., Shields, J., & Bauder, H. (2014). *Discounting immigrant families: Neoliberalism and the framing of Canadian immigration policy change: A literature review.* RCIS Working Paper No. 2014/7. https://rshare.library.torontomu.ca/articles/journal_contribution/Discounting_Immigrant_Families_Neoliberalism_and_the_Framing_of_Canadian_Immigration_Policy_Change_A_Literature_Review/14636169

Ryan, P. (2010). *Multicultiphobia.* University of Toronto Press.

Spivak, G. C. (1988). Can the subaltern speak? In C. Nelson & L. Grossberg (Eds.), *Marxism and the interpretation of culture* (pp. 271–313). University of Illinois Press.

Statistics Canada. (2019). *Data tables, 2016 census.* https://www12.statcan.gc.ca/census-recensement/2016/dp-pd/dt-td/Index-eng.cfm

Statistics Canada. (2020a). *2011 National Household Survey: Data tables.* https://www12.statcan.gc.ca/nhs-enm/2011/dp-pd/dt-td/Index-eng.cfm

Statistics Canada. (2020b, 25 November). *International students accounted for all of the growth in postsecondary enrolments in 2018/2019.* https://www150.statcan.gc.ca/n1/daily-quotidien/201125/dq201125e-eng.htm

Statistics Canada. (2021). *Asian Heritage Month . . . by the numbers.* https://www.statcan.gc.ca/en/dai/smr08/2021/smr08_250

Thobani, S. (2007). *Exalted subjects: Studies in the making of race and nation in Canada.* University of Toronto Press.

Tuan, M. (1998). *Forever foreigners or honorary whites? The Asian ethnic experience today.* Rutgers University Press.

U.S. News and World Report. (2021). 2021 best countries ranking. https://www.usnews.com/news/best-countries

Willetts, K. (2010, 2 December). UVSS plans consumer boycott of *Maclean's. The Martlet.* https://issuu.com/martlet/docs/issue_16_volume_63

Winter, E. (2011). *Us, them, and others: Pluralism and national identity in diverse societies.* University of Toronto Press.

Wong, L., & Guo, S. (2015). Revisiting multiculturalism in Canada: An introduction. In S. Guo & L. Wong (Eds.), *Revisiting multiculturalism in Canada: Theories, policies and debates* (pp. 1–14). Sense Publishers.

18

Intercultural Mediation:

A Necessity for Identity Reconstruction Observed in Contemporary Quebec

MARIE-LAURE DIOH AND JULIE BÉRUBÉ

Canada prides itself on being an international exemplar when it comes to welcoming landed immigrants. There is no doubt that the country is a pioneer in its immigration and integration policies and practices. However, particular attention should be paid to the discrimination, systemic racism, and exclusion that often have been described in several provinces, including Quebec, with respect to immigrants. Moreover, the social conflicts observed in Quebec society lead us to question certain ideological postulates and to discuss practices to ensure better social acceptance of cultural diversity and the creation of a common culture.

This is the societal background for the reflections set out in this chapter, divided into four parts. The first part presents literature highlighting the barriers to social and professional integration experienced by immigrants to Quebec. The second part examines the social debates currently under way in the province, which crystallize the conflicts and social fractures that divide the host society and immigrants. In the third part, we examine interculturalism, the model for immigration and integration applied in Quebec, and its potential role in the social problems observed. The argument is that it is not in tune with the diverse cultural composition of Quebec's population today. At the same time, it does not express concrete practices by which newcomers can adhere to the dominant culture. In the fourth part, we offer an optimistic vision for the future with a plea for urgent intercultural mediation to reconcile Quebec's culturally diverse society.

Barriers to Immigrants' Social and Professional Integration in Quebec

Migration flows to Canada have been steadily increasing ever since the country proclaimed itself a land of immigration. The Canadian government's three-year plan reiterates its willingness to welcome more than one million people between 2021 and 2023 (Statistics Canada, 2021). On this basis, Canada is often cited as an international exemplar for its policy on welcoming and integrating immigrants (OECD, 2021). However, at the national level, their integration has been the subject of several studies by the academic community and has given rise to debate within Canadian society and specifically in Quebec. As several studies have shown, immigrants have always encountered difficulties that affect their integration in Quebec (Chicha, 2009; Lenoir-Achdjian et al., 2009), and this is still the case. Immigrants, especially racialized people, often experience discrimination (Namululi et al., 2018; Otmani, 2020; Piché & Renaud, 2018). For example, the study by Namululi and colleagues (2018), which examined the intersectionality of gender and race to explain the unequal situation of Congolese women in the job market, particularly in Quebec, highlighted the exclusion and discrimination that they experience because of their skin colour, ethnic origin, and gender.

Other authors, such as Otmani (2020), even use the term "systemic discrimination" to describe this inequality in the labour market. According to Otmani, the confusion surrounding the hiring process highlights the institutional barriers faced by physicians of Algerian origin, which lead to their marginalization in accessing their profession. They are accused of not having the knowledge and skills that Quebec standards demand. In other cases, it is a matter of structural problems within organizations, linked, for example, to a lack of knowledge of professional nomenclatures in the candidates' countries of origin. This creates barriers to finding jobs that match their qualifications and skills, even in sectors with labour shortages (Dioh 2020; Dioh & Racine, 2017). Triki-Yamani (2020) highlighted the fact that immigrants face several challenges in advancing in professional careers in Quebec. Recruitment and selection practices, implicit rules and norms related to promotion, and the attitudes of human resource managers and union representatives result in unequal treatment.

Immigrants also experience systemic racism in their social integration in Quebec. Racial profiling is observed in institutions such as the police and cities such as Montreal (Drudi, 2020). With this in mind, the Conseil interculturel de Montréal is working on a report on the conditions for a successful policy to make Montreal an intercultural city. Other authors (Hamisultane, 2020) have also highlighted the micro-aggressions that immigrants experience in social interactions, which they tend to keep quiet to avoid exclusion. These problems of discrimination and exclusion have been criticized for several years and lead us to question seriously the welcome that immigrants receive once they have settled in Quebec. Barriers to integration are exacerbated in areas with low immigrant densities, where local populations are less prepared to receive them (Guilbert et al., 2013). In fact, since the 1990s, a policy of regionalization of immigration applied by the Quebec government has sought to attract immigrants to these regions and to retain them there to revive economic and social life. But here again difficulties affecting socio-economic integration are observed, and immigrants must implement bypass strategies to make progress in their projects, such as deskilling or returning to school (Albert & Lazzari Dodeler, 2020; Dioh et al., 2020; Dioh & Racine, 2017).

Immigrants also experience discrimination in their social relations (Dioh et al., 2021), and the role of local communities in being open and welcoming them is often mentioned, especially since newcomers find themselves without social and ethnic networks in their new environments. This situation has an impact on their sense of belonging and their desire to settle in the region permanently. Consequently, though difficulties related to integration are similar in all regions of Quebec, they are more likely to be observed in localities where immigrants are a minority and where such characteristics affect ethnocultural relations (Dioh et al., 2021; Guilbert et al., 2013).

Social Debates in Quebec on Immigrants' Cultural Membership

In addition to these academic studies critiquing the social and professional difficulties affecting the integration of immigrants in Quebec, many debates have taken place in the province in recent years regarding their integration into the host society, rekindling conflicts and social fractures within the population. Bill 60: Charter Affirming the Values of State Secularism and Religious Neutrality and of Equality between Women and Men, and Providing a Framework for Accommodation Requests was already the subject of heated social debates. The bill aimed to define the values considered to be Quebec values: the equality of all in the eyes of the state, the equality of women and men, the religious neutrality of the state, and respect for Quebec's cultural and historical heritage (Gouvernement du Québec, 2013). But the bill also had effects on the perception and representation of certain categories of the population, including those whose cultural differences were visible (Le Gallo, 2018). According to Potvin (2017), the debate on the Charter of Quebec Values in 2013–2014 triggered a process of radicalization of public opinion, which became visible in polls and in an increase in hate crimes.

Other authors (Beaman & Smith, 2016; Romdhane, 2013), who have focused on the societal issues that arose in the wake of the charter project, have shown that the statements made in the National Assembly and the discussions that followed contributed to stigmatizing segments of the population, such as Muslim women, presented as in need of protection and as people who do not integrate into Quebec's free and democratic society and threaten its identity (Romdhane, 2013). The wounds created by these debates (Beaman & Smith, 2016) were undoubtedly reopened by the current debate on Bill 21: An Act Respecting the Laicity of the State (Pineda, 2019).

Bill 21 creates doubt in people's minds about whether Quebec society is willing to allow space for identity and religious affiliations and claims. On the one hand, immigrants denounce policies that seem to impose ethnocentric beliefs, values, and ways of doing things to which they must adhere and conform. On the other hand, a segment of the host population maintains that immigrants must integrate into Quebec culture and embrace all its customs. Moreover, events such as the mosque shooting in Quebec City in 2017, which caused the deaths of six people and several casualties, and the media treatment that followed, have turned social media into instruments of propaganda. This allows populist groups in Quebec to propagate hate speech on the grounds of race, ethnicity, and religion (Potvin, 2017), putting a strain on the social climate and creating a feeling of rejection and fear of immigrants. Their cultural, religious, and linguistic identities and general otherness appear to be perceived as potential threats to Quebec identity (Meintel, 2018). In other words, these social fractures reinforce perceptions of and anxieties about identity loss and lead to cultural misunderstandings between the host society and immigrants. Indeed, the differences highlighted in this kind of discourse are not only related to ethnicity; the host society has also been complaining about a divergence in the two groups' universes of meaning, giving the impression that their respective cultural referents are irreconcilable.

Is Quebec's Model of Interculturalism at the Root of These Societal Issues?

Quebec interculturalism is an ideology distinct from Canadian multiculturalism. From the point of view of the leaders who instituted it, multiculturalism relegates the people of Quebec to the standing of a mere "cultural community" on the same level as other communities, without recognizing their status as one of the founding peoples of Canada (Le Gallo, 2018). Interculturalism therefore proposes an attitude toward cultural diversity and inclusion that would recognize the achievements of Quebec society while promoting the inclusion of cultural communities and immigrants to form a united society (Bouchard, 2012; Le Gallo, 2018). To this end, it advocates for interaction among different cultures and integration into a dominant majority as well as respect for fundamental Quebec values. According to Bouchard (2012, p. 6; our translation), "interculturalism should encourage interactions, reconciliation, discussions, [and] initiatives . . . and ensure that these discussions contribute to bringing together not only minorities, but also members of the majority with minorities. . . . [T]hese interactions have a general objective of integration. They tend to bring together or reconcile different or even divergent values and norms; they contribute to reducing stereotypes and false categorizations that feed into discrimination and exclusion; they are a prerequisite for participation in public debates; and they create a favourable ground for negotiating conflicts."

This ideology is well received by many Quebecers because it seems to promote openness to cultural pluralism, but some authors (Mc Andrew, 2006) have questioned the series of controversies that it has stirred up, which call into question its tolerance and acceptance of difference. From our perspective, there is no doubt that its macro-social conception in terms of orientations is laudable, but by the founding author's own admission this model never reached the micro-social level and specified how to implement ways of living with ethnocultural diversity in the daily life of public and private institutions (Bouchard, 2012). Interculturalism has never been the subject of a government policy statement that would define its philosophy and determine its practice. It also seems to create inconsistencies by advocating openness to cultural communities while requiring them to conform to the values and customs of the majority culture. This contradiction probably explains why immigrants do not recognize themselves in this model, which they criticize for homogenizing values by emphasizing those of the dominant culture, based upon Western civilization. Similarly, the host society does not appear to be able to figure out how to assert a majority culture without falling into assimilationism. This situation leads us to believe that, in Quebec today, the interculturalist ideology creates divisions because immigrants believe that their backgrounds and identities are under attack.

In a survey conducted by Bouchard and Roy (2007, p. 69), 63.8 percent of 141 Quebec respondents stated that Quebec culture was in crisis, as reflected in a loss of reference points, blurring perceptions of self and other, the definitions of individual and collective aims, memory, and vision of the future. From this point of view, the authors agreed that the young Quebec nation, unlike old Western nations, was still in search of its identity. In our view, it might be appropriate to consider the current identity transformation taking place in the province. We must accept that the face of Quebec is changing and that its population no longer shares a homogeneous culture. Also, since so many complex questions arise from the coexistence of groups with diverse cultural backgrounds on the same soil, it is perhaps time to look at today's Quebec and to build tomorrow's Quebec by better recognizing this pluralist culture and the richness of each component. It is time to embrace these social and cultural changes and to work toward a common vision born from a journey toward and renewal of an inclusive Quebec identity.

Intercultural Mediation as an Avenue for Better Community Life

Based upon research and the social realities presented earlier in this chapter, we therefore enter a plea for intercultural mediation (Dioh et al., 2020; Drudi, 2020). This would help to reconcile the different identities and cultural affiliations; sensitize Quebec's host population to other ways of being, doing, and thinking; and guide immigrants in acquiring the rules and values of the host culture. In fact, both immigrants and the host population must work toward a better way of living together through a dynamic of conversation, coexistence, and discussion (Appiah, 2005, 2006), which would lead to the creation of a collective identity (Raney, 2009): namely, shared values, ideals, and cultural references. Basically, we can assume that the values defended in Quebec can also be found in other cultures. It is therefore necessary to move beyond this era of divisive debates, crises, and discrimination to focus on a process that will unite the entire Quebec nation. In the conception of interculturalism, a common culture would serve several functions according to Bouchard (2012, p. 72; our translation): "(1) to serve integration, guarantee minorities and newcomers the assurance of full citizenship, and protect them from exclusion; (2) to reduce the We-They dichotomy; (3) to allow members of the majority and ethnic minorities who fear being confined to an ethnic 'ghetto' to renegotiate their original belonging; (4) to allow for a meeting place, where diversity can be expressed and valued; (5) to create a sense of belonging in order to support social ties."

This rapprochement and creation of a common vision is possible thanks to intercultural mediation practices (Gagnon et al., 2020; Guilbert, 2004). Intercultural mediation can be defined as the set of psychological, relational, collective, and institutional processes generated by the interactions of cultures, in a relationship of reciprocal exchange, and with a view to safeguarding the relative cultural identities of the partners in the relationship (Leanza, 2012). It helps to establish or re-establish social links among people from different cultures. It allows them to modify their representations of each other, to build a space for dialogue, and to move toward a common, welcoming, inclusive culture. According to Beauregard and Borri-Anadon (2019), the first step in intercultural mediation is decentring. It requires those in the relationship to become aware of the frame of reference with which they perceive the other and then to decentre it. In other words, they must examine their own cultural referents (beliefs and values) upon which they base their perceptions. Then they can identify "hot spots" that highlight what they take for granted. This kind of detachment leads to the second step: the discovery of the other's frame of reference, the point at which each person seeks to understand how other people's perceptions of the world influence their practices. The third step is the meeting with the other, involving a negotiation so that neither party imposes its perspective. Intercultural mediation would therefore promote better inclusion of immigrants in the Quebec population while creating a process of reflecting on their plural citizenship. It would also be a question of mutual recognition (Ricoeur, 2004) in an intercultural approach.

This process of reconciliation is possible when we take for granted that migration inevitably leads to a reconstruction of identity for immigrants. This process is accentuated when children are born in the host country (Plivard, 2010). Moreover, direct, continuous contact between cultures necessarily creates changes (Camilleri, 1989) in both immigrants and members of the host society, though both groups need to refer to fundamental values and representations. In this process of cohabitation, we therefore learn what constitutes ontological maintenance and what comprises pragmatic adaptation (Plivard, 2010). In this logic, there is room for coalescing around common values: accepting changes in certain values but keeping a solid base of other values essential to the construction of an inclusive identity.

Conclusion

We have pointed out that the difficulties that immigrants face in integrating into Quebec society, socially and professionally, have been decried by a number of studies in recent years, thus raising questions about the Quebec population's policies, practices, and attitudes with respect to the people the province receives. The social debates that have been raging since the introduction of the Charter of Quebec Values, which intensified after the mosque shooting in Quebec City, and which currently focus on Bill 21: An Act Respecting the Laicity of the State, have only accentuated the social divide between these two groups of the population, thus calling into question the social appropriation of the interculturalist ideology specific to Quebec society. It is imperative to consider a solution to reconcile the various members of that society. In other words, the dominant identity must be combined with other identities to reflect the cultural composition of contemporary society. For this reason, an intercultural process of mediation is envisaged to help the different groups change their representations of each other and to build a space for dialogue that should lead to a common culture.

This chapter is not intended as a harsh criticism of Quebec's immigration policy, its interculturalist model, its identity, or its openness to immigration. The chapter calls for awareness of and reflection on current societal issues that are detrimental to social cohesion and a sense of belonging among Quebecers who have been in the province for different lengths of time and that are leading to unfortunate outcomes. Continued government action against social and employment discrimination, systemic racism, and hate speech is crucial. Furthermore, intercultural mediation practices between host society populations and immigrants need to be supported and deployed throughout Quebec, not only in the major centres where most initiatives originate. These intercultural mediation practices are means of preventing and intervening in cultural disputes. They will promote more harmonious community life by encouraging unity but not imposing uniformity and by respecting personal identity while also leading to collective identity. The dynamics observed within the youngest generations of Quebecers composed of native born and second generation lead us to believe that this mediation and this collective culture will become self-evident in building the future of Quebec, where the inclusion of all will be an essential value.

References

Albert, M-N., & Lazzari Dodeler, N. (2020). L'entrepreneuriat immigrant de nécessité au sein d'une région où il n'existe pas d'enclaves ethniques. *Projectics/proyéctica/projectique, 25*(1), 107–130. https://doi.org/10.3917/proj.025.0107

Appiah, K. A. (2005). *The ethics of identity.* Princeton University Press.

Appiah, K. A. (2006). *Cosmopolitanism: Ethics in a world of strangers.* W.W. Norton & Company.

Beaman, L., & Smith, L. (2016). "Dans leur propre intérêt": La *Charte des valeurs québécoises*, ou du danger de la religion pour les femmes. *Recherches sociographiques, 57*(2–3), 475–504. https://doi.org/https://doi.org/10.7202/1038436ar

Beauregard, F., & Borri-Anadon, C. (2019). La médiation interculturelle: Une approche pour soutenir la relation parents immigrants-orthophonistes au niveau primaire. *La revue internationale de l'*éducation familiale, *45*(1), 47–67. https://doi.org/10.3917/rief.045.0047

Bouchard, G. (2012). *L'interculturalisme: Un point de vue québécois.* Boréal.

Bouchard, G., & Roy, A. (2007). *La culture québécoise est-elle en crise?* Boréal.

Camilleri, C. (1989). La culture et l'identité culturelle: Champ notionnel et devenir. In C. Camilleri & M. Cohen-Emerique (Eds.), *Chocs de cultures: Concepts et enjeux pratiques de l'interculturel* (pp. 21–73). L'Harmattan.

Chicha, M-T. (2009). *Le mirage de l'*égalité: Les immigrées hautement qualifiées à Montréal. http://www.metropolis.inrs.ca/le-mirage-de-legalite-les-immigrees-hautement-qualifiees-a-montreal/

Dioh, M-L. (2020). L'agentivité des immigrants comme vecteur d'intégration socioprofessionnelle au Québec. *Canadian Ethnic Studies, 52*(2), 99–114. https://doi.org/10.1353/ces.2020.0007

Dioh, M-L., Gagnon, R., & Racine, M. (2021). Le récit de vie comme voie d'accès à l'expérience vécue par des personnes immigrantes en processus d'intégration dans la région des Laurentides. *Recherches qualitatives, 40*(2), 81–100. https://doi.org/10.7202/1084068ar

Dioh, M-L., Guilbert, L., & Racine, M. (2020). L'immigrant actif: Étude du parcours de vie comme cadre d'analyse pour une compréhension globale du projet migratoire. *Alterstice, 9*(1), 39–50. https://doi.org/10.7202/1075249ar

Dioh, M-L., & Racine, M. (2017). Insertion professionnelle des immigrants qualifiés en technologies de l'information à Québec: À l'encontre des mythes, témoignages d'immigrants. *Relations industrielles, 72*(4), 763–784. https://doi.org/10.7202/1043175ar

Drudi, G. (2020). L'avis du Conseil interculturel de Montréal (CIM) sur la problématique du profilage racial à Montréal: Un appel à la rencontre interculturelle. *Nouvelles pratiques sociales, 31*(2), 241–250. https://doi.org/10.7202/1076654ar

Gagnon, R., Thiaw, M-L., & Fernandes, F. (2020). Le travail de réflexivité de femmes immigrantes au service de la formation de futures sages-femmes … et de leur propre intégration. *Alterstice, 9*(1), 69–81.

Gouvernement du Québec. (2013). *Parce que nos valeurs, on y croit. Document d'orientation: Orientations gouvernementales en matière d'encadrement des demandes d'accommodement religieux, d'affirmation des valeurs de la société québécoise ainsi que du caractère laïque des institutions de l'état.* https://sisyphe.org/IMG/pdf/Document_d_orientation.pdf

Guilbert, L. (2004). Médiation citoyenne interculturelle: L'accueil des réfugiés dans la région de Québec. In L. Guilbert (Ed.), *Médiations et francophonie interculturelle* (pp. 199–222). Presses de l'Université Laval.

Guilbert, L., Vatz-Laaroussi, M. L., Bernier, E., & Ansòn, L. (2013). *Les collectivités locales au coeur de l'intégration des immigrants: Questions identitaires et stratégies régionales.* Presses de l'Université Laval.

Hamisultane, S. (2020). Personnes descendantes de migrants racisées face aux micro-agressions: Silence, résistance et communauté imaginaire d'appartenance. *Nouvelles pratiques sociales, 31*(2), 163–181. https://doi.org/10.7202/1076650ar

Le Gallo, S. (2018). Imaginaire national et laïcité: Penser l'identité avec le projet de *Charte des valeurs. Communiquer, 24*, 17–35.

Leanza, Y. R. (2012). *Exercer la pédiatrie en contexte multiculturel: Une approche complémentariste du rapport institutionnalisé à l'autre.* Georg.

Lenoir-Achdjian, A., Arcand, S., Helly, D., Drainville, I., & Vatz Laaroussi, M. (2009). Les difficultés d'insertion en emploi des immigrants du Maghreb au Québec. *Choix IRPP, 15*(3), 1–42.

Mc Andrew, M. (2006). Projet national, immigration et intégration dans un Québec souverain: Dix ans plus tard, l'analyse proposée tient-elle toujours la route? *Sociologie et sociétés, 38*(1), 213–233. https://doi.org/10.7202/013715ar

Meintel, D. (2018). La religion en question. In D. Meintel, A. Germain, D. Juteau, V. Piché, & J. Renaud (Eds.), *L'immigration et l'ethnicité dans le Québec contemporain* (pp. 104–123). Presses de l'Université de Montréal.

Namululi, N., Bagaoui, R., & Hemedzo, K. (2018). Analyse intersectionnelle des défis et enjeux des inégalités sociales sur le marché du travail: L'expérience de vingt femmes congolaises résidant au Québec et en Ontario. *Reflets, 24*(1), 98–126.

OECD. (2021). *International migration outlook 2021*. https://doi.org/10.1787/29f23e9d-en

Otmani, R. (2020). Discrimination à l'embauche et sentiment de racisme: Le cas des médecins algériens à Montréal. *Nouvelles pratiques sociales, 31*(2), 82–100.

Piché, V., & Renaud, J. (2018). Un nouveau regard sur la discrimination. In D. Meintel, A. Germain, D. Juteau, V. Piché, & J. Renaud (Eds.), *L'immigration et l'ethnicité dans le Québec contemporain* (pp. 60–87). Presses de l'Université de Montréal.

Pineda, A. (2019, novembre 27). Décision attendue de la cour d'appel du Québec sur la *Loi sur la laïcité de l'état*. *Le Devoir*. https://www.ledevoir.com/politique/quebec/567842/laicite-la-cour-d-appel-entend-la-demande-d-injonction-contre-la-loi-21

Plivard, I. (2010). La pratique de la médiation interculturelle au regard des populations migrantes . . . et issues de l'immigration. *Connexions, 93*(1), 23–38. https://doi.org/10.3917/cnx.093.0023

Potvin, M. (2017). Discours racistes et propagande haineuse: Trois groupes populistes identitaires au Québec. *Diversité urbaine, 17*, 49–72.

Raney, T. (2009). As Canadian as possible . . . under what circumstances? Public opinion on national identity in Canada outside Quebec. *Journal of Canadian Studies, 43*(3), 5–29.

Ricoeur, P. (2004). *Parcours de la reconnaissance*. Gallimard.

Romdhane, S. B. (2013). *Charte des valeurs québécoises*: Un mariage forcé entre laïcité et invisibilité des différences? *Éthique publique, 15*(2). https://doi.org/10.4000/ethiquepublique.1269

Statistics Canada. (2021). *Notice—Supplementary information for the 2021–2023 immigration levels plan*. https://www.canada.ca/en/immigration-refugees-citizenship/news/notices/supplementary-immigration-levels-2021-2023.html

Triki-Yamani, A. (2020). La progression en emploi dans le secteur privé du Grand Montréal: Les minorités visibles face à des inégalités de traitement. *Nouvelles pratiques sociales, 31*(2), 38–65.

PART 7

GENDERED, RACIALIZED,
and
TRANSNATIONAL IDENTITIES
RECONSTRUCTING "CANADIAN IDENTITY"

Intersectional scholars of immigration have stressed the importance of considering gender, race, ethnicity, class, and immigration status in combination when it comes to understanding trajectories of identity (re)construction among immigrants to Canada. The two chapters in this section are bound together by their intersectional approach to the analysis of experiences of immigrants of a minoritized background in Canada when the cultural and linguistic knowledge that they possess is delegitimized by monocultural ethics in an (officially) bilingual and multicultural country.

In Chapter 19, Sepideh Borzoo and Pallavi Banerjee illustrate how occupation and migration trajectories intersect with race, class, and gender in the formation of Canadian identities among immigrant women. Their case involves immigrant women employed in beauty work selling cosmetics and is based upon qualitative interviews with fifteen immigrant women of colour. Borzoo and Banerjee demonstrate that, despite the devalued, low-wage, and feminized job of selling cosmetics, the immigrant women of colour find it agentic. By centring the stories of their marginalization in Canada and their challenges at work, the authors discuss how the immigrant women converted their otherwise undervalued jobs into social currency and attempted to reconstruct their identities at the margin of a dominant "Canadian identity."

In Chapter 20, Gertrude Mianda explores the experiences of immigrant francophone Canadians from Sub-Saharan Africa in that they rarely benefit from the symbolic capital of speaking French even though it is one of Canada's two official languages. Mianda demonstrates that the discrimination that these immigrant Canadians face in the labour market in the Greater Toronto Area brings to light the intersection of race, language, gender, and class as they relate to the devaluation of their colonized status. Mianda therefore questions the essence of multiculturalism that promotes (an exclusionary) bilingualism since the employment experiences of these immigrants in the francophone health-care and education systems show the triple marginalization of francophone African Canadian immigrants.

19

Self-Employment among Immigrant and Migrant Women and Reconstruction of Canadian Identity from Intersecting Marginal Positions

SEPIDEH BORZOO AND PALLAVI BANERJEE

Intersectional scholars of immigration have posited the importance of gender, race, religion, ethnicity, class, and immigration status for identity formation among immigrants and migrants in North America (Banerjee, 2019; Banerjee et al., 2020; Shams, 2020; Valdez, 2011). These intersectional identities are crucial to the lives and interactions that marginalized immigrants have in the host society, but they take on different meanings in the context of self-employment and entrepreneurship, especially among immigrant women of colour. Previous research has shown that self-employment and entrepreneurship can be empowering for such women, and they often deploy resources that their intersectional identities extend to them to access and claim agency (Banerjee, 2013, 2019; Valdez, 2011). Although there is research that explores the intersectional experiences of immigrant women who work in beauty businesses (Kang, 2010; Otis, 2016), little research has studied beauty businesses owned by immigrant women of colour and how these businesses fit into the larger landscape of the beauty industry, which has been dominated by White middle-class women employers and clients and owned by White men (Peiss, 2011; Walker, 2007).

For this chapter, we studied local, smaller beauty businesses owned by women of colour. We conducted fifteen interviews with immigrant women of colour self-employed selling cosmetics in Canada. Our goal was to explore how these businesses differed from big-box stores and what purposes these businesses serve for women of colour within the beauty industry. We found that, despite the devalued and feminized job of selling cosmetics, immigrant women of colour find the work agentic. We thus argue that the same oppressive labour of selling cosmetics and beauty products simultaneously gives the women owners a form of capital within the social arena of their diasporic community. By centring stories of marginalization experienced by these business owners and the challenges that they face in the beauty industry, we show how they converted their otherwise undervalued work into a matter of pride and community uplift.

Literature Review

Immigration and Identity Negotiation

Immigration as a process necessitates transformation of the self and the social status of the migrant (La Barbera, 2015; Madsen & Naerssen, 2003; Rabiau, 2019). In the Canadian context, the literature has shown that such transformations happen in the immigrant subject's sense of belonging, sense of self, gendered and racialized identity, and transnational interactions and identities (Byers & Tastsoglou, 2008; Goitom, 2017; Rashid et al., 2013; Somerville, 2019; Tastsoglou & Petrinioti, 2011; Tastsoglou, 2019). The fluidity of identities is visible in Tastsoglou and Petrinioti's (2011) study on identity formation among second-generation Lebanese youth in Halifax. Their article unravels the conflicting feelings of immigrant Canadian-born youth who feel trapped between their families who insist on Lebanese culture and values and the mainstream Canadian culture that others them. According to the authors, the youth learn to develop hybrid identities by accepting certain values from both mainstream culture and ethnic culture. However, their article does not explore in depth the depletion of selfhood that often occurs in the process of hybridity as expounded by scholar of postcolonialism Homi Bhabha (2015).

In a different study, Goitom (2017) examined identity formation among second-generation Ethiopian and Eritrean youth in Toronto. The author showed how the formation of identity among young people is informed by family, community, school, policy, and so forth. As these immigrant Black youth were othered and excluded by mainstream Canadian culture, they developed a strong sense of ethnic belonging as their main identities. Goitom emphasized racial exclusion as the most important reason for adopting a collective identity among Ethiopian and Eritrean youth. The study moved away from hybridity to show how the East African youth were able to develop ethnic identities separate from Canadian identities, perhaps possible only in a multicultural context such as Canada.

Along the same line, a study of African immigrants in Alberta shows how, in the case of francophone immigrants, they are pushed to negotiate multiple identities because of their racial and cultural locations and to reinterpret their identities to counter racism (Madibbo, 2016). Another study of Sudanese and Ghanaian youth in Calgary shows how they experienced discrimination in the labour market because of racial and ethnic identity markers such as their names and how Canada's policy of multiculturalism did not protect them from exclusion (Zaami & Madibbo, 2021).

The intersectional analysis centres the multiplicative ramifications of identities on experiences of marginalization and privilege (Crenshaw, 1991). Intersectional feminist scholars in the past two decades have included immigrant identity in the matrix of analytics (Banerjee, 2022; Bannerji, 2000; Compton-Lilly et al., 2017; Ku, 2019; La Barbera, 2015; Purkayastha, 2005; Somerville, 2019; Sundar, 2008; Tastsoglou, 2019). Sundar (2008) explores the use of ethnic identities among immigrant South Asian young people in the Canadian context as a tool of empowerment. The author explains how the class, gender, and religious status of South Asian Canadians can affect their racial exclusion and identity formation. To subvert the relations of power, the participants in this study built upon their multiple identities—such as class status (middle class), gender (for men), and/or religion (for Christians)—to mitigate racial disadvantages. The fluidity of identity along with its deployment as a tool of empowerment as a theoretical construct is prominent in papers about the identities of immigrants in North America. One of the pioneering renditions of this theory is in Purkayastha's (2005) book on second-generation South Asian Americans. Purkayastha shows how these young people of Indian, Pakistani, Bangladeshi, and Nepalese origin develop a pan–South Asian ethnic identity through the adoption of ethnic labels, reinventing pan–South Asian traditions and consumption of ethnic products. Similar trends have been found among Canadian immigrants, especially youth in several of the studies alluded to here.

Building upon intersectional scholars of immigration, this research attempts to show how the act of self-employment of immigrant women intersects with the different layers of their identities (race, ethnicity, and gender) toward the reconstruction of their identities.

Self-Employment, Identity Negotiation, and Immigrant Women

The intersectional literature on migrant entrepreneurs suggests that self-employed women and men form their identities in relation to their gendered, racialized status, nationality, and class (Akbar & Preston, 2021; Banerjee, 2019; De Clercq & Honig, 2011; Johnson, 2000; Maitra, 2013; Rehn et al., 2013; Teixeira, 2001; Valdez, 2016; Zhang & Chun, 2018). For instance, Zhang and Chun (2018), in their study of identity construction among Chinese immigrant entrepreneurs in Canada, show that Chinese immigrants used entrepreneurship to resolve identity-based conflicts that they experienced after migration and to search for new selves. The authors argue that migration led to immigrants' disconnections from their pasts, resulting in deep dissatisfaction and uncertainty about the future. Such experiences led immigrants to look for new and possible selves by exposing themselves to new networks, practices, and skills. The research shows that entrepreneurship emerged along with construction of new selves and identities among these immigrants. In a foundational study that centred ethnic identities within the intersectional frame, Valdez (2016) examined how class, family ideology/structure, access to entrepreneurial capital, and family labour facilitate entrepreneurial activities of family members in the United States. The research shows that men benefited from family ideology and traditional gender norms in working-class families that expected daughters to drop out of college but gave sons greater access to education. Whereas working-class women were expected to drop out of school, children in middle-class households were encouraged to get a college degree regardless of their gender. In the Canadian context, ethnicity has been the key axis of identity formation among self-employed immigrant entrepreneurs.

Some scholars have explained self-employment among immigrant people of colour as a result of experiencing exclusion from the Canadian labour market (Johnson, 2000; Maitra, 2013). Maitra's (2013) study of South Asian self-employed women shows how gender and racial discrimination in the Canadian labour market forced these women to start ethnic businesses using their cultural resources. However, self-employment has provided these women with opportunities to develop networks within the community and to contribute to community empowerment and development. Johnson's (2000) study of Southeast Asian refugees in Canada shows that a lack of English fluency and a lack of transferable skills are some of the important reasons for refugees to start ethnic businesses. The author shows that refugee entrepreneurs depend highly on family cultural and social capital. Having access to family labour is an important factor in minimizing labour costs. The research shows that family members who exchange social capital in the form of networks and common languages can compensate for the lack of education or cultural capital such as English-language skills. In a study of the spouses of highly skilled Bangladeshi men in Toronto, Akbar and Preston (2021) illustrated how these immigrants adopted diverse pathways to entrepreneurship to overcome marginalization experienced in the Canadian labour market. The authors argue that women in these families were key to their economic survival. Although these women experienced the same economic barrier, the diversity in class status and gender norms within Bangladeshi families channelled these women to different pathways, home-based businesses or businesses outside the home.

The common theme in this body of literature is an exploration of self-employment through the lens of intersectionality. Intersecting axes of inequality (gender, race, class, immigration status) can limit immigrants' access to resources. However, the deployment of aspects of immigrant identities combined with self-employment creates opportunities for immigrants to use their ethnic/racial status to foster social and economic mobility. Building upon the two bodies of literature, we ask whether and how self-employment among immigrant women of colour intersects with their other identities to construct new identities among them. We also explore the process of this identity formation.

Methodology

We draw from in-depth qualitative interviews based upon snowball sampling conducted with fifteen women entrepreneurs in the beauty industry in Canada. These interviews are part of Borzoo's larger study of the work experiences of mostly immigrant women of colour in the retail sector of the cosmetic industry. Borzoo conducted interviews with women to explore their experiences in the beauty companies in which they were working, performances of gender and race in the workplace as the women interacted with co-workers and customers, and whether the structure of the business affected their gender and racialized performance. This chapter is based upon fifteen interviews with women who owned and worked in the local beauty boutiques, given that the entrepreneurial aspect of their identities was most noticeable in these interviews.

The women in this sample had at least a college degree, and most of them self-identified as middle class in Canada. They identified as belonging to different nationalities, including Indian, Nigerian, Ghanaian, Filipino, and El Salvadoran. They were first-, second-, or third-generation immigrants. These women were self-employed or worked for the companies at the time of the interviews and planned to remain in the businesses in the future. Of the fifteen participants, only one had a part-time job besides her business. On average, the women had been in business for five years. Of the fifteen participants, six were married and had children, five were married without children, and four were single. The average age was thirty-five. Participants were recruited from Calgary, Edmonton, Toronto, Vancouver, and Winnipeg.

The interviews ranged in length from approximately forty minutes to ninety minutes. They were conducted via Zoom or WhatsApp during the first phase of the COVID-19 pandemic. The participants were asked about their backgrounds and education, how they entered the beauty industry, their experiences interacting with clients, the impacts of their gender and race on the business, the challenges of working in the industry, and so forth. In responding, the women talked at length about the process of setting up their businesses, working in them, and how doing so shaped their identities. The data were thematically coded and analyzed to understand how self-employment affected their lives, especially their core identities. We used constant comparative methods as our analytical approach, which oriented us to make connections between the literature and the interview transcripts. Reading through the interview transcripts multiple times, writing analytical notes, and comparing data with the literature helped us to analyze the transcripts. Initially, open coding (Williams & Moser, 2019) was used to identify the main themes and concepts. The second phase of coding involved the identification of themes that merged with each other, which we categorized as core themes. Finally, the core themes were analyzed using the theoretical lens of intersectionality.

Findings

Self-Employment as a Marker of Intersectional Empowerment

Much like previous studies, our analysis revealed that self-employment was transformative for the women engaged in the business. Most of the women in the study considered their businesses as a way to change their lives and have a positive impact on other people's lives. Gabriel's story explicates these emotions in nuanced ways. Gabriel is a first-generation immigrant from El Salvador who came to Canada with her parents when she was young. She graduated from broadcasting and communication studies and used her expertise to train beauty and cosmetic brands consultants to increase their sales through communication and marketing. In the meantime, she was able to build a strong network with people working in the field of beauty and with customers. As she consulted with more people, Gabriel found an opportunity to become a business owner herself. In one such interaction, she met another immigrant entrepreneur who produced green skincare products. Gabriel consulted with her to promote her products among clients in Vancouver and eventually entered a business partnership with her former client. She continued collaborating with her partner as a certified cosmetologist and dermo-cosmetic educator. Gabriel was not motivated merely by financial needs. She was proud of building a business from scratch and dispelling the controlling image of immigrant women engaged only in "low-skilled or unskilled work." Her pride flowed through in this self- and community-affirming statement: "An Indian woman, a Latino woman, a Filipina woman, a Black woman in a luxury store? Because we always got used to seeing people like that being a nurse or cleaning. . . . We want to do what we can to leave a mark. . . . And if we are a drop in the bucket to make a change in the beauty industry, to change the narrative in the beauty industry, that's something that I'd be super proud of."

Like many of the women in the sample, Gabriel was proud of what she was able to build. This was particularly relevant in the context of her class and racial status in Canada that minoritized her like many immigrant women of colour. Growing up in a working-class family, Gabriel saw her self-employment status in a predominantly White, middle-class industry as a way to subvert her class and racial marginalities: "I grew up in a single-mother family. I grew up in a very poor neighbourhood, and I saw the outcome of many families, you know, people my age who grew up in that and continued that cycle of poverty and addiction. I didn't want that for myself. I feel so proud working in this company and being able to break that cycle."

Being in the business of producing ethical skincare products on a larger scale gave Gabriel a sense of moral purpose both in terms of her business and in terms of empowering other immigrant women of colour by creating access for them to luxury, ethically produced, and high-quality skincare products that had been available primarily to White middle-class women. Self-employment thus became a conduit for immigrant women like her to pronounce their agency in affirming ways. Her use of the phrase "we leave a mark" is profound in this regard. Gabriel uses the royal "we" specifically to create agentic solidarity with other women of colour in the industry. To her, her presence in the industry is not only about her own mobility, journey, and growth but also about changing the racialized landscape of the industry as predominantly White. It is also about changing the dominant perception of immigrant women workers as low-wage care workers. It is noteworthy that Gabriel alludes to two feminized low-wage jobs (cleaning and nursing) as attached to immigrant women. Both occupations are feminized and associated with care work. In many ways, it can be argued that the beauty industry and her own work in it also fall into the category of feminized labour (consulting and producing beauty products). Gabriel, however, distinguishes her work not only because she owns the business but also because she creates products for other women of colour and pushes the boundaries of an industry corporatized globally and dominated by White men. She is a change maker in her own way and evokes pride in her positionalities (Borzoo, 2023).

Along similar lines, Isabella, a Filipina woman and part of Gabriel's company, was concerned about changing how people view immigrant women of colour as suitable only for low-status, dirty jobs. To her, though growing the business and increasing profit were important parts of the job, it was less about her own ambition to become rich and more about the survival of a business that could alter how people view immigrant women of colour. She asserts that, "yes, of course we have to make money, we always want to increase our sales. But we also want to make an impact. We want to tell the world that we are not only good for doing the grunt work of running a company. We can lead these companies. We can build these companies."

Isabella's assertion that a business run by an immigrant woman of colour is about much more than making money—it is centrally about changing the makeup of the industry itself while also shifting perceptions of immigrant women—projects the sense of empowerment that Isabella and other women workers of colour can experience. Although this rhetoric of empowerment is present in previous research, the confidence in these narratives is certainly absent in previous research. Williams (2005) used the term "glass ceiling" to discuss the barriers that prevent women from achieving elevated positions in their workplaces. The narratives of the women in this study project a future for immigrant women of colour in which they can confront that ceiling. Entrepreneurship provides the women in our study with resources to change their socio-economic status while also making larger societal changes, at least in their own view.

Most of the women in this research considered themselves as inspirational to women in their communities and other immigrant women of colour. These immigrant entrepreneurs believed that they set examples for other women in their communities to push the boundaries associated with their gender and racial status. Self-employment thus became the women's way of resisting the intersectional oppressive identities that relegated them to the realm of low-wage, occupationally immobile work while creating the new identity of the inspirational immigrant women of colour Canadian entrepreneurs.

Contribution to Community Development

Entrepreneurship went beyond individual ambition for the women in this study. It expanded intrinsically to contribute to their own communities and the larger collective of women of colour in the public sphere in Canada and to change the landscape of the beauty industry. The most common contributions cited by participants were providing jobs for other immigrant women, advertising for other women-owned immigrant businesses, and creating awareness of colonial beauty standards.

Such standards reflect Eurocentric paradigms of beauty for cis women that eulogize lighter skin colour, blue eyes, straight blonde hair, and a certain body type, whereas all other paradigms of beauty are pitched as undesirable or exotic compared with the colonial paradigm (Murray, 2015; Robinson-Moore, 2008).

Nadina, a first-generation Nigerian immigrant, launched her beauty brand in 2014. A few years later she opened a beauty salon in partnership with three other entrepreneurs. She intentionally hired immigrant Black women. Nadina admitted that providing jobs for new immigrants and advertising for other Black-owned local businesses comprised a big part of her agenda. According to Amal, her employee, Nadina never advertised her own beauty products to customers. She always asked makeup artists to use other Black-owned beauty products on customers despite the high quality of her own products.

This account of Nadina's business practices is not merely a reflection of an entrepreneur whose livelihood comes from running the business. Her business is intended to uplift other immigrant women and their businesses. Her business ethics are entrenched in her consciousness of gender and racial justice, a mark of intersectional awareness of injustice. Although Nadina mostly employed other women of colour, her non-Black immigrant women employees of colour also saw how her business was transforming their lives and identities.

Amal is a Syrian refugee woman who recently came to Canada with her husband and her son and works for Nadina. She shared that "I was new in Canada and needed a job very badly. One day I was walking in the street and saw an ad for this beauty company. I went there, and I had to go to a couple of workshops. Because I was very interested in doing makeup and learning new things, she decided to hire me. She helped me because I was really struggling. She supported me on my path of grief after leaving my country." This explanation that Nadina hired Amal because she was struggling as a new immigrant and that the job allowed her to work through the trauma of her past is at the core of forging a new identity. But this was possible only because Nadina set up a business with an explicit goal of uplifting other women of colour.

Beyond the project of equalizing race and gender, women of colour entrepreneurs engaged in the beauty business strove to create awareness of colonial beauty standards. Lily, a third-generation Black immigrant who runs a small beauty company along with her mother and her older sister, discussed feeling responsible for educating clients about the beauty industry. According to her, because of being exposed to the Eurocentric ideal of beauty, many women of colour customers perceive that they are not beautiful. As she shared, "I think for us . . . what we've been taught about beauty doesn't represent us. . . . A lot of people would come in and would be like, even something as simple as red lipstick, 'Oh, with my skin tone, I can't really wear red lipstick.' . . . So it was very important for us to educate people."

Thus, educating customers about the idea of beauty was part of an empowerment project that these businesses adopted. Trying to fill the gap in the cosmetics industry by producing products for different skin tones, these women have been able to change the hegemonic beauty standards by giving Black women the confidence to try different colours and "step out of their comfort zones." Lily added that "people are being told 'Oh, it's gonna be very hard for you to find what works for you.' We've worked with people who, when they came into the store, they . . . [didn't] wear makeup at all. And right now, if you see them, they're trying new colours. They're like 'You guys have really given me the confidence to wear makeup. I'm gonna step out of my comfort zone.'"

Empowering Black women to try new makeup reveals how these women indirectly decolonize customers' grooming decisions and practices. For immigrant women of colour, self-employment became the tool to disrupt the racial exclusivity in the cosmetic industry that can directly or indirectly affect community members by "helping them [to feel] . . . confident with who they are and being comfortable in their own skin," as Lily put it.

Self-Employment and Integration of Multiple Identities

Self-employment is a practice through which immigrant women often reconcile and integrate multiple identities. The women entrepreneurs in this study believed that they were expected to negotiate their multiple identities (women, racialized women, community members and contributors, mothers, successful businesspersons, and so forth) seen as distinct from and often in conflict with one another. For instance, as racialized women, their familial and caregiving responsibilities were seen as distinct from their identities as business owners. However, we found that the women resisted this distinction since their entrepreneurial journeys allowed them to make sense of all their identities as co-constituted. According to Courtney, a mother of three children and an entrepreneur, "it was through the hard process of becoming a mother that I learned if I wanted to create something I could do that." Courtney blurred the line between motherhood and work commonly seen as oppositional spheres. She also fused her two identities by equating reproductive labour with productive labour, much like the women who worked in ethnic businesses in Banerjee's (2013) study.

Many of the immigrant women in the study showed awareness of systemic racism and built their businesses based upon countering racial inequality. For instance, Lily's mother, a Black woman, launched a beauty brand because she and her sister were unable to find the right products that matched their skin tone. Later they opened a store and created an online platform to network with Black-owned entrepreneurs. As Lily indicated, speaking about the experiences of Black entrepreneurs and sharing their struggles as Black women are big parts of the discussions on their Instagram platform. According to her, their products tell a story that resonates with other Black women's struggles. The business meant not only creating a brand that caters to Black women but also building a space to counter the racial exclusion that they experienced both as customers and business owners in the beauty industry. For immigrant women of colour, self-employment therefore turns into a tool that fosters racially diverse beauty standards in the Canadian context. As Lily stated, "We help people feel confident in being who they are, being comfortable in their own skin. We've had people who were crying when they found their foundation. They're literally in tears. Like, 'Oh, my gosh, I can't look like this.' We've had brides who afterwards cry. A lot of people would give up and say 'I'm not wearing makeup. They're not bringing shades for me, so let's just forget about it.' We had to come in and grab people who weren't wearing makeup."

Thus, encouraging Black women to wear makeup fosters a more diverse image of beauty within and outside ethnic communities. Self-employment has created the opportunity for these women not only to integrate their multiple identities but also to contribute to the construction of a more racially diverse landscape of the industry in the Canadian context (Borzoo, 2023). Isabella stated that

> a few years ago I was approached by [the name of the company] to be a model for their Self-Care Campaign. I was

flabbergasted—I was the one who helped to get women ready behind the camera, not the woman in front of the camera. That photoshoot helped me to see myself differently, and now that I work for [the name of the company] I continually am able to fully see who I am as a woman of colour. I am valued, I am seen, I am beautiful. . . . And as a Filipina, I can be the face of a campaign for a luxury, green, skincare brand.

Isabella's statement illustrates how immigrant women of colour entrepreneurs in this study are creating spaces where racially diverse beauty standards are possible and even welcomed. Her statement that, "as a Filipina, I can be the face of a campaign for a luxury, green, skincare brand" reveals the racial exclusivity of the upscale ethical section of the beauty industry and how being the face of the company as an immigrant woman of colour can contribute to the decolonization of Eurocentric standards of beauty. Given that the women in the study are from different cultural backgrounds, they have access to various ethnic and cultural resources that can make their businesses distinctive.

Linda, a second-generation Indian immigrant, self-identified as middle class and shared that, having been born and raised in Canada, "I always see myself as a Canadian, but in my life having parents from India was such a part of who I was and how I was raised—what we ate and what we did and how we managed everything." According to Linda, spirituality has always been part of having Indian parents. Growing up, she would see her dad practising yoga and doing meditation. Although she did not have any background in the beauty industry, she decided to build a business based upon Indian Ayurvedic science. She started producing skincare products that had been around for generations and that her parents used. The beauty brand was built upon her ethnic capital, which made her products interesting and sophisticated for clients outside her community. According to her, "I have a range of clients. I didn't design it for South Asian people, and I never wanted that. I want everybody to buy it. Everybody loves learning about Ayurveda, but I feel non-Indian clients really appreciate it."

Linda is proud that her clientele extends beyond her co-ethnics for a product that is decidedly Indian. Although she had no training in this field, she used her biography and her derived expertise in Ayurveda based upon her ethnic background to claim legitimacy in her chosen business track. Much like the women in Banerjee's (2019) study, Linda marshalled her capital associated with her ethnic identity not only to start her business but also to establish authority in the field. By sharing her ethnic capital with customers beyond her co-ethnics and introducing beauty products based upon Indian tradition, she is contributing to changing the racial context of the beauty industry.

Self-employment for these women has become an identity integrated with their other identities—gender, ethnicity, race, and class—and often become a resource that the women have deployed to sustain their businesses. More importantly, they have produced skincare and cosmetic products to counter the oppressions that they and other women of colour have experienced at the intersections of gender, race, and class in Canada. Self-employment has turned into a tool for these women not only to voice their experiences as immigrant women of colour but also to enhance racially and ethnically diverse beauty practices and ideals. They have done so by actively resisting hegemonic beauty ideals while constructing their own identities as successful immigrant women entrepreneurs in a heavily gendered and racialized industry.

Conclusion

Our analysis of entrepreneurship among immigrant women of colour associated with the beauty industry reveals two points of convergence with the previous literature and some important points of departure. As far as convergences are concerned, we find that self-employment is a tool of empowerment for immigrant women of colour in line with the body of literature on this topic (Banerjee, 2019; Johnson, 2000; Maitra, 2013; Teixeira, 2001; Zhang & Chun, 2018). We also find, as indicated in the literature (Akbar & Preston, 2021), that intersectional identities and experiences of race, ethnicity, and gender became agentic for the women entrepreneurs in their work.

The points of departure in our analysis, however, are far more important and have critical theoretical and empirical implications. Unlike previous work on immigrant women entrepreneurs, who often used self-employment primarily to support their families and social and economic mobility for themselves, we found that the women of colour entrepreneurs in the beauty industry in Canada were acutely aware of the racial and gender inequities in the industry and larger Canadian society. They used this awareness to construct Canadian identities for themselves that went beyond, and even confronted, the dominant, multi-culturally defined identities of immigrants and immigrant workers based upon ethnicity. Both immigrant women entrepreneurs and beauty workers in this study intentionally placed their Canadian identities in an intersectional frame in which race, gender, and class were as important to their self-employed status as their ethnic identities.

This intentionality meant that their businesses became conduits of social change in an industry that remains oppressive to women and excludes people of colour. In centring their own identities in their businesses, the women made their businesses intersectional projects at the local level along the lines of racial projects (Omi & Winant, 2015) to push against the systemic barriers faced by women of colour in the industry by hiring other women of colour and promoting the products and businesses of women of colour who, in a strictly business sense, were their competitors. This is important theoretically because it highlights an identity construction that goes beyond emplacing the immigrant in the host country, in this context Canada. The identity construction is rather a deep commitment to social justice that is not exhibitionist and beyond the usual profit orientation of businesses. Another departure that we observed was in the merging of social and entrepreneurial identities in creating more diverse and inclusive beauty practices. The fused identities reconstructed the entrepreneurs as individuals who oriented their businesses to social justice issues and demonstrated deep business acumen through the strategy of pitching their businesses as having identity-based niches in the industry. This resulted in an identity formation ensconced in pride and purpose and geared to transformation of the self, Canadian society, and the industry.

References

Akbar, M., & Preston, V. (2021). Entrepreneurial activities of Canadian Bangladeshi women in Toronto: A family perspective. *Journal of Ethnic and Migration Studies, 49*(4), 1–20.

Banerjee, P. (2013). Paradoxes of patriarchy: South Asian women in ethnic labor markets. In N. F. Gonzales, A. R. Guevarra, G. Chang, & M. T. Morn (Eds.), *Immigrant women workers in the neoliberal age* (pp. 96–116). University of Illinois Press.

Banerjee, P. (2019). Subversive self-employment: Intersectionality and self-employment among dependent visas holders in the United States. *American Behavioral Scientist, 63*(2), 186–207.

Banerjee, P. (2022). *The opportunity trap: High-skilled workers, Indian families, and the failures of the dependent visa program.* New York University Press.

Banerjee, P., Chacko, S., & Piya, B. (2020). Paradoxes of being and becoming South Asian single mothers: The enclave economy, patriarchy, and migration. *Women, Gender, and Families of Color, 8*(1), 5–39.

Bannerji, H. (2000). The paradox of diversity: The construction of a multicultural Canada and women of color. *Women's Studies International Forum, 23*(5), 537–560.

Bhabha, H. (2015). *Debating cultural hybridity: Multicultural identities and the politics of anti-racism.* Zed Books.

Borzoo, S. (2023). *FOR ALL THE BEAUTIFUL SHADES OF YOU: How race, gender, and embodiment shape the retail beauty work* [Doctoral dissertation, University of Calgary].

Byers, M., & Tastsoglou, E. (2008). Negotiating ethno-cultural identity: The experience of Greek and Jewish youth in Halifax. *Canadian Ethnic Studies, 40*(2), 5–33.

Compton-Lilly, C., Papoi, K., Venegas, P., Hamman, L., & Schwabenbauer, B. (2017). Intersectional identity negotiation. *Journal of Literacy Research, 49*(1), 115–140.

Crenshaw, K. (1991). Mapping the margins: Intersectionality, identity politics, and violence against women of color. *Stanford Law Review, 43*(6), 1241–1299.

De Clercq, D., & Honig, B. (2011). Entrepreneurship as an integrating mechanism for disadvantaged persons. *Entrepreneurship and Regional Development, 23*(5–6), 353–372.

Goitom, M. (2017). "Unconventional Canadians": Second-generation "Habesha" youth and belonging in Toronto, Canada. *Global Social Welfare, 4*(4), 179–190.

Johnson, P. J. (2000). Ethnic differences in self-employment among Southeast Asian refugees in Canada. *Journal of Small Business Management, 38*(4), 78–86.

Kang, M. (2010). *The managed hand: Race, gender, and the body in beauty service work.* University of California Press.

Ku, J. (2019). Journeys to a diasporic self. *Canadian Ethnic Studies, 51*(3), 137–154.

La Barbera, M. C. (2015). *Identity and migration in Europe: Multidisciplinary perspectives.* Springer.

Madibbo, A. (2016). The way forward: African francophone immigrants negotiate their multiple minority identities. *Journal of International Migration and Integration, 17*(3), 853–866.

Madsen, K. D., & Naerssen, T. V. (2003). Migration, identity, and belonging. *Journal of Borderlands Studies, 18*(1), 61–75.

Maitra, S. (2013). Points of entry: South Asian immigrant women's entry into enclave entrepreneurship in Toronto. *South Asian Diaspora, 5*(1), 123–137.

Murray, C. (2015). Altered beauty: African-Caribbean women decolonizing racialized aesthetics in Toronto, Canada. *Revue YOUR Review* (York Online Undergraduate Research), *2*, 57–67.

Omi, M., & Winant, H. (2015). *Racial formation in the United States.* Routledge.

Otis, E. (2016). China's beauty proletariat: The body politics of hegemony in a Walmart cosmetics department. *Positions, 24*(1), 155–177.

Peiss, K. L. (2011). *Hope in a jar: The making of America's beauty culture.* University of Pennsylvania Press.

Purkayastha, B. (2005). *Negotiating ethnicity.* Rutgers University Press.

Rabiau, M. A. (2019). Culture, migration, and identity formation in adolescent refugees: A family perspective. *Journal of Family Social Work, 22*(1), 83–100.

Rashid, R., Gregory, D., Kazemipur, A., & Scruby, L. (2013). Immigration journey: A holistic exploration of pre- and post-migration life stories in a sample of Canadian immigrant women. *International Journal of Migration, Health and Social Care, 9*(4), 189–202.

Rehn, A., Brännback, M., Carsrud, A., & Lindahl, M. (2013). Challenging the myths of entrepreneurship? *Entrepreneurship and Regional Development, 25*(7–8), 543–551.

Robinson-Moore, C. L. (2008). Beauty standards reflect Eurocentric paradigms—So what? Skin color, identity, and Black female beauty. *Journal of Race and Policy, 4*(1), 66–85.

Shams, T. (2020). Successful yet precarious: South Asian Muslim Americans, Islamophobia, and the model minority myth. *Sociological Perspectives, 63*(4), 653–669.

Somerville, K. (2019). Intergenerational relations and gendered social surveillance of second-generation South Asians. *Canadian Ethnic Studies, 51*(3), 95–115.

Sundar, P. (2008). To "brown it up" or to "bring down the brown": Identity and strategy in second-generation, South Asian–Canadian youth. *Journal of Ethnic and Cultural Diversity in Social Work, 17*(3), 251–278.

Tastsoglou, E. (2019). Transnational, feminist and intersectional perspectives on immigrants and refugees in Canada: An introduction. *Canadian Ethnic Studies, 51*(3), 1–16.

Tastsoglou, E., & Petrinioti, S. (2011). Multiculturalism as part of the lived experience of the "second generation"? Forging identities by Lebanese-origin youth in Halifax. *Canadian Ethnic Studies, 43*(1), 175–196.

Teixeira, C. (2001). Community resources and opportunities in ethnic economies: A case study of Portuguese and Black entrepreneurs in Toronto. *Urban Studies, 38*(11), 2055–2078.

Valdez, Z. (2011). *The new entrepreneurs*. Stanford University Press.

Valdez, Z. (2016). Intersectionality, the household economy, and ethnic entrepreneurship. *Ethnic and Racial Studies, 39*(9), 1618–1636.

Walker, S. (2007). *Style and status: Selling beauty to African American women, 1920–1975*. University Press of Kentucky.

Williams, J. C. (2005). The glass ceiling and the maternal wall in academia. *New Directions for Higher Education, 2005*(130), 91–105.

Williams, M., & Moser, T. (2019). The art of coding and thematic exploration in qualitative research. *International Management Review, 15*(1), 45–55.

Zaami, M., & Madibbo, A. (2021). "You don't sound Black": African immigrant youth experiences of discrimination in the labor market in Calgary. *International Journal of Intercultural Relations, 83*, 128–138.

Zhang, Z., & Chun, D. (2018). Becoming entrepreneurs: How immigrants developed entrepreneurial identities. *International Journal of Entrepreneurial Behaviour and Research, 24*(5), 947–970.

20

Migration and the Paradox of Canadian Bilingualism:
The Experience of Sub-Saharan African Francophone Immigrants in the Minoritized Francophone Community of the GTA

GERTRUDE MIANDA

Bilingualism serves alongside multiculturalism as a shared, distinctive characteristic of Canadian identity and citizenship (Shapiro, 2010). Scholars nevertheless argue that, regardless of multiculturalism, bilingualism in Canada embodies a project that promulgates the hegemony of the two founding settler groups (Haque, 2012; Shapiro, 2010). Bilingualism in Canada, however problematic, has never been reflected in the equal use of English and French. Instead, outside Quebec, English has always occupied a dominant position, seeming to swallow up the French language. Cooper (2000) pointed out that, though women of African descent came to Canada speaking various European languages other than English, it was assumed that they were anglophone. Compared with English, French has been disadvantaged because the francophone population has been marginalized economically, even within Quebec, where, until the 1960s and 1970s, wealthy, powerful elites were principally drawn from the anglophone population (Charbonneau, 2012). The Official Languages Act adopted in 1969 was intended to counter the historical marginalization of francophones by granting equal status to both French and English (Charbonneau, 2012; Ricento, 2013). Whatever the intention, Fleming (2016) observes that

Canadian immigration and language policies are well articulated to absorb other languages and cultural diversity.

Like Fleming (2016), I contend that Canadian immigration and language policies contribute to maintaining the dominant position of English-language speakers despite efforts to increase the use of French. Immigration policies designed to increase the number of francophones in Canada, rather than improving linguistic and cultural diversity, reproduce neo-colonial and racialized patterns of contemporary international migration. In particular, the immigration of skilled francophone women from the Global South is accompanied by their downward mobility upon arriving in Canada. A great number of francophone women from Africa who migrate to Canada end up concentrated in care services, working in health care, education, and social work. In this chapter, I use the lived experiences of francophone immigrants of Sub-Saharan African origin in the francophone minoritized community of the Greater Toronto Area (GTA) to shed light on how immigration and language policies perpetuate discrimination, inviting highly skilled women who then carry out low-wage social reproductive labour.

My analysis relies on critical anti-Black racism (Crenshaw, 1991, 2005; James, 1999; James et al., 2010; Mensah, 2002), decolonial theorizing (Dei, 2017; Lugones, 2010; Tamale, 2020), and feminist approaches to social reproduction (Bhattacharya, 2017; Ferguson, 2008, 2016; Hirtz, 2019; Verschuur, 2013). Each perspective speaks to different aspects of systemic discrimination against Black people, particularly women, at the intersection of race, gender, and class, as embodied in the structural fabric of Canadian society and in pro-francophone immigration policies. Taken together, these approaches make visible neo-imperialistic, patriarchal dynamics that facilitate the exploitation of women from the Global South through migration processes intended to support official bilingualism.

I begin the chapter with a discussion of bilingualism and francophone African immigrants in Canada, specifically in Ontario, focusing on the importance of francophone immigration to the maintenance of French. In the second section, I expose the workplace experiences of francophone immigrant women of Sub-Saharan African origin by examining how they become positioned in the niches of health care and education in the labour market of the GTA. Overall, I problematize official immigration policies in support of the French language, laying bare the intersecting ways that francophone African women are encouraged to migrate to Canada only to face quadruple discrimination on the grounds of their race, gender, class, and francophone language once here.

Bilingualism, Migration, and Francophone African Immigrants in the Minoritized Francophone Community in Canada

As noted, Canada adopted English and French as its two official languages with the Official Languages Act in 1969 with the aim of increasing the number of French speakers and challenging the marginalized position of the francophone minority in the country. Major modifications to the Act concerning minority language groups, particularly anglophones living in Quebec and francophones living outside Quebec, were introduced in 1988. Article 4 of Part 7 of the Act, in particular, instructs the Canadian government "to adopt positive measures to support the development and vitality of official languages in the minority communities and to promote both official languages in Canada" (Fraser & Boileau, 2014, p. 8). In a similar spirit, beginning in 2003, the federal government established a target to ensure that 4 percent of francophone immigrants entering Canada would settle outside Quebec (Fraser, 2015). Since that time, other measures have been introduced, such as Express Entry in January 2015 and the Mobilité francophone stream in June 2016, to support the immigration of skilled workers and to continue boosting francophone immigration in majority anglophone contexts (Immigration, Refugees and Citizenship Canada, 2019). Canada was projected to reach a target of 4.4 percent by 2023 for new francophone immigrants outside Quebec (Immigration, Refugees and Citizenship Canada, 2019, p. 2).

The demographic growth of the francophone population outside Quebec is essential not only to the cultural, social, and economic vitality of these communities but also to the future of French as one of the two official languages. Immigration therefore becomes a fundamental channel for making Canadian claims to French-English bilingualism a meaningful reality, especially in majority anglophone contexts. For francophone immigrants, Canada is an attractive destination given its French-English bilingual identity; the fact that Canada is among the few Western countries with a large francophone population; and since—following Morocco, Algeria, the Democratic Republic of Congo, and France—it is inhabited by the fifth largest francophone population in the world (Barber, 2014, p. 3, p. 11). Yet trends indicate a steady decline in the demographic weight of francophones as a percentage of the total population, from 27.5 percent in 1971 to 22.8 percent in 2016 (Patrimoine canadien, 2019). This means that immigration plays a critical role in maintaining and revitalizing a French-language population in Canada.

Outside Quebec, the need to stabilize and increase the number of francophones is even greater if French-English bilingualism is to be maintained, since francophone communities in the rest of Canada decreased from 6.1 percent of the population in 1971 to 3.8 percent in 2016 (Patrimoine canadien, 2019). By 2019, the francophone population outside Quebec made up just 2.8 percent of the country's total population. The same pattern prevails in Ontario, which now receives the largest share of francophone immigrants outside Quebec and where the demographic weight of francophone speakers decreased from 6.2 percent in 1986 to just 4.7 percent in 2016 (Ontario, Ministère des affaires francophones, 2016). Hence, francophone migration outside Quebec is crucial to reversing the shrinking French-speaking population of Canada.

If immigration matters to the Canadian francophonie, then this is not only a matter of numbers but also a matter of who is coming to Canada and from where. Historically, Europe was the continent that provided the largest number of francophone immigrants to Canada. However, in the two decades since the 1990s, the number of francophone immigrants coming to Canada from non-European regions has grown. The proportion of immigrants of European origin decreased from 37 percent in 2011 to 28 percent in 2016, when the proportion of francophone immigrants from Africa represented 35 percent of the total (Ontario, Ministère des affaires francophones, 2016). Among the 4,400 francophone immigrants who settled outside Quebec in 2016, nearly 2,400 chose to live in Ontario, accounting for 2.2 percent of the total 110,019 newcomers in the province in 2016 (Keung, 2017). Taking other source countries for francophone immigrants into account, such as those in South Asia, the Middle East, and the Caribbean, the faces of francophone immigrants to Canada are changing; most are now visible minorities.

The increasing number of immigrants from Sub-Saharan Africa is a result of changes in Canadian immigration policy introduced in 1967 with the creation of the points system to recruit immigrants based upon professional qualifications, age, education, and potential contribution to Canada. Skilled Black individuals were able to enter Canada based upon their own merits for the first time in the history of Canadian immigration policy because skilled applicants from all countries were assessed equally (Mensah, 2002, p. 71). This change in immigration policy did not totally eradicate racial discrimination, which can occur through mechanisms such as recognition of foreign credentials. The refusal to consider immigrants' foreign credentials and experience is a major factor impeding immigrants' successful labour market integration in Canada (Lochhead & Mackenzie, 2005, p. 104). Nonetheless, if Black persons are downwardly mobile given racism in Canada, they are now entering Canada as part of the immigrant francophonie in greater numbers than ever before.

Like other highly skilled immigrants, African francophones are invited to Canada to take up certain professions that fill the country's labour market needs (Lochhead & Mackenzie, 2005; Schellenberg & Hou, 2005). This means that, if there is a linguistic motivation behind encouraging francophones to immigrate to Canada, there are economic motives as well: priority is given to those who can fill shortages in specific occupations (Kustec, 2012, p. 10). Interestingly, this labour market emphasis has meant that the goal of increasing the number of francophones in Canada outside Quebec is less robust than it might seem. In the case of Express Entry, for example, additional points are given to francophone individuals who demonstrate good English skills (Immigration, Refugees and Citizenship Canada, 2019, p. 3). This is presumably meant to encourage broader labour market opportunities in an anglophone environment. As for the Mobilité francophone stream, a French-speaking worker does not need to work in a francophone job. Francophone immigrants who settle outside Quebec and need employment in a mainly English-speaking environment might adopt English over time (Corbeil & Lafrenière, 2010, p. 8; Fraser & Boileau, 2014, p. 8; Morency et al., 2017, p. 40), especially if they face difficulties entering the resident Canadian francophone communities' labour markets (Mianda, 2018–2019).

Overall, the policy of official bilingualism and associated efforts to encourage highly skilled francophones to immigrate to Canada have had ambiguous effects with respect to francophone African migrants. They are supposed to contribute to strengthening the francophonie in Canada, especially outside Quebec. Yet in practice the immigration measures that bring French-speaking workers to English-speaking communities and labour markets encourage francophone migrants to switch to English to find employment. Moreover, as we will see below, francophone Africans, especially women, tend to end up in low-paid social reproductive labour, so their ability to speak French, usually understood as desirable cultural capital, and their educational credentials and professional skills do not spare them from the intersectional inequities of race, class, gender, and language once in Canada.

Race, Language, and the Experiences of Black Francophone Immigrants of Sub-Saharan African Origin in the Canadian Labour Market

If African francophone migrants are encouraged to come to Canada to buttress official French-English bilingualism, once here they face anti-Black racism, not least in the labour market. Numerous scholars have documented the segmentation based upon race, gender, and class characteristics of the Canadian labour market. They have indicated that Blacks experience greater discrimination than other groups in that market (Javdani et al., 2012, pp. 9–10; Mensah, 2002; Musisi & Turrittin, 1995, 2006). Black immigrants are mostly concentrated in jobs defined, during the COVID-19 pandemic, as "essential services," including clerical work, janitorial work, supply chains, and orderlies and nursing assistants (McKenzie et al., 2020). If the COVID-19 pandemic has brought to the surface the extent to which those socio-economically marginalized in Canadian society are affected (Bowden, 2020), the marginalization of Blacks is long-standing, occurring well before the pandemic.

An examination of Blacks' socio-economic situation between 2001 and 2016 reveals their labour market marginalization (Houle, 2020). An overview of Black workers aged twenty-nine to fifty-nine in 2016 indicated an unemployment rate of 10 percent for men as well as women, higher than that of 7 percent for men and 6 percent for women in the same age range in the rest of Canada's population. Moreover, the employment rate of 78 percent for Black men and 71 percent for Black women was lower compared with that of the rest of the Canadian population, in which 83 percent of men and 76 percent of women were employed (Houle, 2020). Notably, among Black immigrants, the situation of those from Africa is worse than that of any other Black group (Houle, 2020). Data on the situation of Black immigrants aged twenty-five to fifty-nine collected from 2001 to 2015 reveal that unemployment among immigrants from Africa is higher than that of immigrants from the Caribbean, Latin America, and other regions (Houle, 2020, p. 19).

For francophone African immigrants, there are additional challenges. Notably, in majority anglophone contexts outside Quebec, a lack of proficiency in English is a major obstacle preventing immigrants from accessing good jobs (Lochhead & Mackenzie, 2005; Sadiq, 2005). However, because of the decline in the relative size of the francophone population, combined with the federal government's effort to boost francophone immigration, one would expect that speaking French would be an asset. Moreover, the ability to speak French is often understood as a form of desirable cultural capital (Bourdieu, 1979) because it can facilitate one's labour market integration, especially in the minoritized francophone community. Curiously and paradox-ically—as noted earlier—even Express Entry, meant to boost franco-phone immigration, requires newcomers to demonstrate sufficient fluency in English. Is this kind of contradiction not at the heart of the measures that contribute to reinforcing English-language hegemony? Language is not only a medium of communication. It carries power relations too.

Here we might usefully draw from Bourdieu to understand the complex social position of African francophone migrants, especially how they are unable to capitalize on their sought-after ability to speak French. According to Bourdieu (1977, p. 23), a language is worth what those who speak it are worth. There is a relationship between a language and who speaks it (Chudzinski, 1983). Whether popular or standard speech, there is a hierarchy in how people speak that is socially legit-imated. Furthermore, each way of speaking is associated with a value linked to the speaker's gender, so that women's language practices tend to be devalued compared with men's. A speaker's accent is also a locator of that speaker's social class (Bourdieu, 1977), and higher-class accents are typically valued over lower-class ones. In addition, as Armand and Dagenais (2005, p. 99) point out, "language proficiency and the presence of accent, like other visible markers of difference," can be used to discriminate "based on the negative representations of the languages and the speakers of those languages." All of this has consequences for African francophone migrants once they arrive in Canada.

As is well known, Africa has a negative image across the world because it has been represented as "located at the bottom of (the) racialized social hierarchy" (Dei, 2018, p. 123). Moreover, francophone as well as anglophone Africans acquired French and English through the colonial education system with its mission to "civilize" them. Although historically Africans acquired cultural capital by speaking French or English in school, they were educated in the languages of the colonizers for the purpose of being subaltern to Whites (Mudimbe, 1994a; wa Thiong'o, 1987, pp. 16–17). As cultural capital, their mastery of French or English is not considered to have the same weight as it does for White colonizers, to whom French and English are seen to belong. Instead, French and English are associated with White colonizers and their higher position in colonial space. Mudimbe (1994a) underlined the fact that the introduction of French established a new criterion of stratification; it divided "civilized" Whites from "non-civilized" Africans. Languages, he noted, became arranged hierarchically, with French, the language of the "master," at the top of the pyramid. French was the "property" of the elite, and knowledge of it was meted out with great cautiousness (Mudimbe, 1994b, pp. 130–131).

Today Africans speak French with accents coloured by their local African languages, a process that has given rise to a diversity of French languages (Baghana et al., 2020). Rather than being understood as an enrichment of French, this multiplicity of French coloured by local African languages was excluded from and did not influence the education curriculum. Instead, "standard French," meaning that spoken by the colonizers, was the language of education, unsurprisingly, since the curriculum was most often designed and implemented by the colonial order (Baghana et al., 2020) and saturated with ideas of the African other as ontologically and thus culturally inferior. Even today more highly educated Africans speak standard French or standard English.

There are continuities with the contemporary context of the reception of francophone Africans in Canada. Too often they are associated with the enduring and negative colonial or neo-colonial image of Africa. Because they are Black, the French that they speak is perceived as not belonging to them, and they are accepted not as culturally competent French speakers but as imitators of "real" (White) francophone migrants from European nations. This compounds the labour market discrimination that they already experience based upon race, gender, and class. Hence, both in daily life and in the workplace, French within Canadian bilingualism has its own hierarchy based not only upon race but also upon African origin, which contradicts the official support for French across Canada and especially in majority English contexts.

This social context means that mastering the French language is not sufficient for acceptance, much less social mobility, of francophone African immigrants in the minoritized francophone community in Canada. Indeed, for those who do not speak English, they also need to master it and therefore be (at least) bilingual to increase their opportunities to access employment (Mianda, 2018–2019). Put differently, to be a francophone immigrant from Sub-Saharan Africa is to be confronted with discrimination based upon race, gender, and language since one's accent adds to one's minoritized situation (Mianda, 2018–2019). A racialized francophone immigrant expressed this clearly and eloquently by saying that "francophone immigrants are an invisible minority within a visible minority. Our needs are overlooked" (Keung, 2017).

In sum, encouraged to come to Canada as francophones, African migrants are the locus of multiple inequities, and too often their specific needs remain unmet in the context of gendered, anti-Black, and anti-African racisms that exacerbate failures to recognize their francophone abilities as critical cultural capital in the labour market and in broader communities.

In the next section, I illustrate the experiences of Sub-Saharan African francophone immigrant women who work in early childhood francophone education or as personal support workers in the francophone care system in the GTA. These women encounter gendered racism and discover the paradox of bilingualism that in fact privileges speakers of English.

The Experiences of Francophone Sub-Saharan African Immigrant Women Working in the GTA

So far, I have discussed how race, national origin, and language play into the inequities experienced by francophone African migrants, and I have mentioned but not systematically explored gender. Putting gender at the centre of an intersectional lens helps us to focus on the experiences of women in particular. According to the 2006 census, immigrant women in Canada comprised 20.3 percent of the female population (Chui, 2011, p. 5). About 55 percent of these women belonged to racialized or visible minority groups, the largest being South Asian (28 percent) followed by Chinese (23 percent) and then Black (11 percent) (Chui, 2011, p. 10). Immigrant women from Africa comprised 10 percent in 2006, up from 8.5 percent in 2001 (Chui, 2011, p. 10). The significant presence of immigrant women in Canada corresponds to the phenomenon of the feminization of international migration, notably including an increase in the number of women who migrate as skilled labourers (Kofman, 2004; Sassen, 2010).

Examining the situation of immigrant women, including visible minority women in Canada, reveals that they are highly represented in precarious and low-paid employment (Block & Galabuzi, 2011; Chui, 2011), confirming the gendered dimension of labour market segmentation that persists along racial lines. Of particular relevance to francophone African immigrants, recent data show that Black women aged twenty-five to fifty-nine are concentrated in the health-care and social assistance sector. In 2016, 33 percent of these women were working in this sector compared with 21 percent for the rest of the female population (Houle, 2020, p. 21). No other sector employed as many Black women. Immigrant women from Sub-Saharan Africa specifically were widely represented in this sector, with 12 percent from West Africa, 12 percent from Central Africa, and 8 percent from East Africa (Cornelissen, 2021, p. 3). Many of these women work in this sector because they had difficulty entering other sectors of the labour market, and many entered it by deskilling their credentials (Cornelissen, 2021, p. 2).

Among these women, francophone immigrant women from Rwanda and the Democratic Republic of Congo made up the third and fourth largest percentages of workers in the health-care and social assistance sector, behind immigrant women from Haiti, who contributed the largest percentage, and from Jamaica, the second largest percentage (Houle, 2020, p. 34). This reflects the situation of immigrant women from the Global South in the contemporary system of international migration in which they are confined to care services in the Global North, ensuring the work of social reproduction (Beneria, 2010; Bhattacharya, 2017; Hirtz, 2019; Kofman, 2004, 2012; Sassen, 2010; Teeple Hopkins, 2017; Verschuur, 2013). The situation in Canada illustrates the contemporary face of the global economy, which exploits racialized women from the Global South to such a degree that it appears to reproduce a kind of colonial power (Quijino, 2007) and gender (Lugones, 2010). If the colonial era is formally over in Africa and the Caribbean, its hierarchies based upon race, gender, and class endure, and it can be said that there is a coloniality or neo-coloniality marking contemporary migration.

Illustrative of the ways that francophone Sub-Saharan African women are incorporated into the labour market in Canada is the shortage of educators that occurred in early childhood education in 2010, following the introduction of the Programme d'apprentissage à temps plein de la maternelle et du jardin d'enfant (see PAJE: The Full-Time Kindergarten Program, 2016) for children aged four and five.[1] Becoming aware of the need for French-speaking early childhood educators, many francophone African immigrants struggling to find a job—given the intersecting racisms explored earlier—seized the opportunity to enrol in Boreal College, which offers a two-year program to train such educators. In this way, francophone African immigrant women hoped to earn credentials in a relatively short period of time that would allow them to get jobs in the francophone milieu. Most of them did so by deskilling their credentials. This is characteristic of how francophone Sub-Saharan African women become downwardly mobile within the Canadian context.

Another example of how such women are channelled into a few sectors is their uptake of work as personal support workers (PSWs). Across Canada, there is a constant shortage of workers in the health-care sector in francophone communities because of the continuous need to deliver health care to elders and the existence of an important francophone population among older Canadians. Although some work as nurses, many francophone Sub-Saharan African immigrant women find themselves working as PSWs, deskilling their credentials as a way to secure work (Mianda, 2018–2019). Indeed, becoming a PSW was not most of these women's choice but a decision that they were constrained to make to survive because of the lack of openness to Black immigrant women in other job market sectors (Cornelissen, 2021, p. 2). The option of getting additional training through Boreal College was a shortcut to access work as a PSW because such training took only six months in the early 2000s. From that perspective, it can be argued that in some ways these educational institutions function within unequal global and national contexts to facilitate the reproduction of economic precariousness for numerous francophone immigrant women of Sub-Saharan African origin.

Conclusion

Francophone Sub-Saharan African immigrants come to Canada as part of the government's efforts to maintain French-English bilingualism in the context of declining resident French speakers. Yet experience in Canada indicates that they receive a rude awakening once here since they must navigate anti-African and anti-Black racisms and deskilling of their educational and professional qualifications while enduring neo-colonial prejudice because of their accents. Indeed, if speaking French is usually associated with high cultural capital, francophone African minorities rarely benefit from that capital. Instead, they encounter marginalization at the intersection of race, gender, class, and French accent, for Sub-Saharan African French is viewed as deviating from White and European accents considered the desirable "standard." Moreover, the kind of bilingualism articulated in some of Canada's immigration measures tends to support English-language hegemony, and to dilute efforts to ensure that francophone immigrants continue to speak French, since immigration measures are diminished by maintaining a strong requirement for fluency in English.

There is, in short, a paradox at the heart of Canada's official bilingualism and associated immigration policies. Rather than strengthening a rich, diverse francophonie in Canada, immigration policies and persistent inequities tell a story of enduring racisms, prejudice against Africans and their accents, and discriminatory failures to recognize African educational credentials and professional skills. Whether francophone or anglophone, immigrants of Sub-Saharan African origin experience discrimination based upon race, gender, class, and the accents with which they speak either of Canada's two official languages. Discrimination against them based upon race and accent tends to indicate that Canada's two dominant and legitimate languages are associated not with racialized people but with Canada's original (White) settlers. Canada's language and immigration policies reproduce and reinforce socio-economic and -cultural inequities. They send a message of exclusion that contrasts with the demographic and linguistic diversity that characterizes Canada and thus exposes the paradox of Canadian bilingualism and multiculturalism.

References

Armand, F., & Dagenais, D. (2005). Languages and immigration: Raising awareness of language and linguistic diversity in schools. *Canadian Issues, Spring,* 99–102.

Baghana, J., Slobodova, N. K., & Birova, J. (2020). The French language in Sub-Saharan Africa: Revisited. Research result. *Theoretical Applied Linguistics, 6*(1), 54–64.

Barber, K. (2014). *Ontario francophone immigrant profile: Immigration trends and labour outcomes.* RCIS Report, Ryerson Centre for Immigration and Settlement.

Beneria, L. (2010). Travail rémunéré, non rémunéré et mondialisation de la reproduction. In J. Falquet, H. Hirata, D. Kargoat, B. Labari, F. Sow, & N. Le Feuvre, (Eds.), *Le sexe de la mondialisation: Genre, classe, race et nouvelle division du travail* (pp. 71–84). Presses de la Fondation nationale des sciences politique.

Bhattacharya, T. (Ed). (2017). *Social reproduction theory: Remapping class, recentering oppression.* Pluto Press.

Block, S., & Galabuzi, G. E. (2011). *Canada's colour-coded labour market: The gap for racialized workers.* Canadian Centre for Policy Alternatives.

Bourdieu, P. (1977). L'économie des échanges linguistiques. *Langue française, 34,* 17–34.

Bourdieu, P. (1979). Les trois états du capital culturel. *Actes de la recherche en sciences sociales, 30*(1), 3–6. https://doi.org/10.3406/arss.1979.2654

Bowden, O. (2020, 2 May). Canada's lack of race-based COVID-19 data hurting Black Canadians: Experts. *Global News.* https://globalnews.ca/news/6892178/black-canadians-coronavirus-risk/

Charbonneau, F. (2012). L'avenir des minorités francophones du Canada après la reconnaissance. *Revue internationale d'études canadiennes, 45–46,* 163–186.

Chudzinski, Y. (1983). À propos de ce que parler veut dire. *Bulletin du CERTE, 2,* A30–A37. https://doi.org/10.4000/edc.3326

Chui, T. (2011). *Immigrant women, Women in Canada: A gender-based statistical report.* Statistics Canada. Catalogue No. 89-503-X.

Cooper, A. (2000). Constructing Black women's historical knowledge. *Atlantis, 25*(1). https://journals.msvu.ca/index.php/atlantis/article/view/1544

Corbeil, J. P., & Lafrenière, S. (2010). *Portrait des minorités de langue officielle au Canada: Les francophones de l'Ontario.* Statistiques Canada. No. 89-642-X au catalogue—no. 001.

Cornelissen, L. (2021). *Profile of immigrants in nursing and health care support occupations.* Statistics Canada. Catalogue No. 75-006-X.

Crenshaw, K. W. (1991). Mapping the margins: Intersectionality, identity politics and violence against women. *Stanford Law Review, 43*, 1241–1298.

Crenshaw, K. W. (2005). Carthographies des marges: Intersectionnalité politique de l'identité et violence contre les femmes de couleur. *Cahiers du genre, 39*, 51–82.

Dei, G. J. S. (2017). *Reframing Blackness and Black solidarities through anti-colonial and decolonial prisms.* Springer.

Dei, G. J. S. (2018). "Black like me": Reframing Blackness for decolonial politics. *Educational Studies, 54*(2), 117–142.

Ferguson, S. (2008). Canadian contributions to social reproduction feminism, race and embodied labor. *Race, Gender and Class, 15*(1–2), 42–57.

Ferguson, S. (2016). Intersectionality and social-reproduction feminisms toward an integrative ontology. *Historical Materialism, 24*, 38–60.

Fleming, D. (2016, December). Canadian bilingualism, multiculturalism and neo-liberal imperatives. Scholars Speak Out. *Journal of Language and Literacy Education, 12.* http://jolle.coe.uga.edu/wp-content/uploads/2014/01/SSO-December_Fleming.pdf

Fraser, G. (2015). *Rapport annuel 14/15.* Commissariat aux langues officielles, no. De cat., SF 1F-PDF.

Fraser, G., & Boileau, F. (2014). *Agir maintenant pour l'avenir des communautés francophones: Pallier le déséquilibre.* Rapport conjoint. Commissaire aux services en Français de l'Ontario (CSFOntario).

Haque, E. (2012). *Multiculturalism within a bilingual framework: Language, race, and belonging in Canada.* University of Toronto Press.

Hirtz, N. (2019). Travailleuses migrantes et transformations du marché de l'emploi. *Gresea échos, 100.* https://gresea.be/Travailleuses-migrantes-et-transformations-du-marche-de-l-emploi

Houle, R. (2020). *Changes in the socioeconomic situation of Canada's Black population, 2001 to 2016.* Ethnicity, Language, and Immigration Thematic Series. Statistics Canada. Catalogue No. 89-657-X2020001.

Immigration, Refugees and Citizenship Canada. (2019). *Faits et chiffres 2015. Profils des immigrants de langues officielles: Résidents permanents d'expression française.* Recherche et évaluation.

James, C. (1999). *Seeing ourselves: Exploring ethnicity, race and culture* (2nd ed.). Thompson Educational Publishing.

James, C., Este, D., Bernard, W. T., Benjamin, A., Lloyd, B., & Turner, T. (2010). *Race and well-being: The lives, hopes, and activism of African Canadians.* Fernwood Publishing.

Javdani, M., Jacks, D., & Pendakur, K. (2012). *Immigrants and the Canadian economy.* Metropolis British Columbia. Centre of Excellence for Research on Immigration and Diversity, Working Paper Series.

Keung, N. (2017, 31 May). A cold bienvenue for francophones. *Toronto Star.*

Kofman, E. (2004). Genre et migration internationale: Critique du réductionnisme théorique. *Les cahiers du CEDREF, 12.* http://cedref.revues.org/543

Kofman, E. (2012). Le care au cœur des migrations genrées à l'ère de la mondialisation. In C. Cossée, A. Miranda, N. Ouali, & D. Séhili (Eds.), *Le genre au cœur des migrations* (pp. 59–88). Éditions Petra.

Kustec, S. (2012). *Migrant and labour market in Canada*. CIC, Research and Evaluation. Ref. No. RR 201 20705.

Lochhead, C., & Mackenzie, P. (2005). Integrating newcomers into the Canadian labour market. *Canadian Issues, Spring*, 103–106.

Lugones, M. (2010). Toward a decolonial feminism. *Hypatia, 24*(4), 742–759. https://doi. org/10.1111/j.1527-2001.2010.01137.x

McKenzie, K., Boozary, A., & Roberston, A. (2020, 14 April). We need data to protect those most vulnerable to the coronavirus. *Toronto Star*, A14. https://www.thestar. com/opinion/contributors/we-need-data-to-protect-those-most-vulnerable-to-the-coronavirus/article_5c2635db-bd6e-5860-a3d1-9555e483bc07.html

Mensah, J. (2002). *Black Canadians: History, experience, social conditions*. Fernwood Publishing.

Mianda, G. (2018–2019). Genre, langue et race: L'expérience d'une triple marginalité dans l'intégration des immigrants francophones originaires de l'Afrique subsaharienne à Toronto. *Francophonies d'Amérique, 46–47*, 27–49. https://www.erudit.org/en/ journals/fa/2018-n46-47-fa04895/1064886ar/

Morency, J. D., Malenfant, E. C., & MacIsaac, S. (2017). *Immigration et diversité: Projections de la population du Canada et de ses régions, 2011 à 2036*. Statistiques Canada. Catalogue No. 1-551-X.

Mudimbe, V. Y. (1994a). *Les corps glorieux des mots et des êtres: Esquisse d'un jardin africain à la bénédictine*. Présence africaine.

Mudimbe, V. Y. (1994b). *The idea of Africa*. Indiana University Press.

Musisi, N., & Turrittin, J. (1995). African women and the metropolitan Toronto labour market in the 1990s: Migrating to a multicultural society in a recession. https://web. archive.org/web/20090507150619/http://ceris.metropolis.net/Virtual%20Library/ community/Musisi/Musisi1.html

Musisi, N., & Turrittin, J. (2006). Knocking at the door: Professional African immigrant and refugee women's experiences in the Canadian labour market. In K. Konadu-Agyemang, B. Takyi, & J. Arthur (Eds.), *The new African diaspora in North America: Trends, community building and adaptation* (pp. 209–233). Lexington Books.

Ontario, Ministère des affaires francophones. (2016). *Profil de la population francophone de l'Ontario—2016*. https://www.ontario.ca/fr/page/profil-de-la-population-francophone-de-lontario-2016

Patrimoine canadien. (2019). *Statistiques sur les langues officielles au Canada*. Numéro de catalogue CH14-42/2019F-PDF. https://www.canada.ca/fr/patrimoine-canadien/ services/langues-officielles-bilinguisme/publications/statistique.html

Programme d'apprentissage à temps plein de la maternelle et du jardin d'enfant. (2016). https://d2khazk8e83rdv.cloudfront.net/books/edu_the_kindergarten_program_ french_aoda_web_july28.pdf

Quijino, A. (2007). Coloniality and modernity/rationality. *Cultural Studies, 21*(2), 168–178.

Ricento, T. (2013). The consequences of official bilingualism on the status and perception of non-official languages in Canada. *Journal of Multilingual and Multicultural Development, 34*(5), 475–489.

Sadiq, K. D. (2005). Race, ethnicity, and immigration in the workplace: Visible minority experiences and workplace diversity initiatives. *Canadian Issues, Spring*, 61–66.

Sassen, S. (2010). Mondialisation et géographie globale du travail. In J. Falquet (Ed.), *Le sexe de la mondialisation: Genre, classe, race et nouvelle division du travail* (pp. 27–42). Presses de la Fondation nationale des sciences politiques.

Schellenberg, G., & Hou, F. (2005). The economic well-being of recent immigrants to Canada. *Canadian Issues, Spring*, 49–52.

Shapiro, B. J. (2010). Bilingualism: A Canadian challenge. *Learning Landscapes, 3*(2), 137–140. https://doi.org/10.36510/learnland.v3i2.349.

Tamale, S. (2020). *Decolonization and Afro-feminism*. Daraja Press.

Teeple Hopkins, C. (2017). Mostly work, little play: Social reproduction, migration, and paid domestic work in Montreal. In T. Bhattacharya (Ed.), *Social reproduction theory: Remapping class, recentering oppression* (pp. 131–147). Pluto Press.

Verschuur, C. (2013). Reproduction sociale et *care* comme échange économico-affectif: L'articulation des rapports sociaux dans l'économie domestique et globalisée. https://books.openedition.org/iheid/5944?lang=en

wa Thiong'o, N. (1987). *Decolonizing the mind: The politics of language in African literature*. Zimbabwe Publishing House.

Endnotes

1   The program was implemented in September 2010. It started with 35,000 children in a certain number of schools; in 2013, 184,000 children attended the program. The Programme d'apprentissage à temps plein de la maternelle et du jardin d'enfant (PAJE) created a need for additional classroom educators to work alongside teachers. Boreal College offers a two-year program to train such educators.

CONTRIBUTORS

Jennifer Adese is Otipemisiwak/Métis and the Canada Research Chair in Métis Women, Politics, and Community and an associate professor in the Department of Sociology at the University of Toronto–Mississauga. She is the co-editor, with Robert Alexander Innes, of *Indigenous Celebrity: Entanglements with Fame* (2021), and her book *Aboriginal*™ was published in 2022.

Anwar Ahmed is an assistant professor in the Department of Language and Literacy Education at the University of British Columbia in Vancouver. His recent book is *Exploring Silences in the Field of Computer Assisted Language Learning* (Palgrave, 2022). Anwar's current research focuses on affect/emotion in second-language teaching and teacher education.

Pallavi Banerjee is an associate professor in the Department of Sociology and a University Research Excellence Chair at the University of Calgary. Her research is situated at the intersection of immigration, gender, family, unpaid and paid labour, intersectionality, and transnationalism. Her recent book *The Opportunity Trap: High-Skilled Workers, Indian Families and the Failures of Dependent-Visa Policy* was published by NYU Press in 2022.

Julie Bérubé is an associate professor at the Université du Québec en Outaouais. Her research interests include issues of equity, diversity, and inclusion in cultural industries and the role of cultural organizations in addressing these issues.

Sepideh Borzoo is a postdoctoral fellow with the YARI-Collective in the Department of Sociology at the University of Calgary. She received a bachelor's degree in French literature from Isfahan University and a master's degree in sociology from Tehran University. Her research interests are gender and feminist studies, immigration, critical race theory, work and organization, and qualitative methods.

Elena Chou is a PhD candidate in the Department of Sociology at York University. Her research focuses on the intersections between race and racialization, identity and representation, cultural studies, and media and popular culture, particularly as they pertain to Asian diasporas in Canada.

Lisa Davidson is an assistant professor, Teaching Stream, in the Department of Anthropology at York University. Her teaching and research focuses on multiculturalism, racialization, and migration. Currently, her research involves Filipinos and other racialized church-goers and their work to create and sustain a sense of place, community, and belonging among and between newly arrived immigrants, second- and third-generation racialized Canadians, and multiracial congregants in Canadian Protestant congregations. She is a co-editor and contributing author of *Filipinos in Canada: Disturbing Invisibility* (University of Toronto Press, 2012).

Marie-Laure Dioh, a work and organizational psychologist, is an associate professor at the Université du Québec en Outaouais. Her research focuses on the socio-professional integration of immigrants, skilled workers, and refugees in Quebec using a qualitative approach.

Augie Fleras received a PhD in Maori studies and social anthropology from Victoria University in Wellington, New Zealand. He taught at the University of Waterloo for nearly forty years. His major focus remains on social inequality, immigration and multiculturalism, and the politics of race, ethnic, and Indigenous peoples' relations in Canada. He received a lifetime achievement award from the Canadian Ethnic Studies Association and has authored or co-authored thirty books.

Shamette Hepburn is an associate professor in the School of Social Work, York University, Toronto. Her current research explores geographies of aging, critical analyses of the migratory life course as a visual and cultural artifact, community education, intervention research, and an array of settlement processes and experiences at the distal end of the migratory life course. Her theoretical, methodological, and practice approaches are grounded in critical transnationalism, postcolonialism, interpretive gerontology, and participatory methods.

Michelle Lam lives in Brandon, Manitoba, located on the traditional homelands of the Dakota, Anishinaabe, Cree, Oji-Cree, Dene, and Métis peoples. She is the director of BU CARES Research Centre, an applied research institute in the Faculty of Education at Brandon University. She is interested in newcomer settlement and integration, education for anti-racism, and rural equity.

Catherine Longboat, PhD, is First Nation born in Canada and an assistant professor in the inaugural Department of Indigenous Educational Studies, Faculty of Education, Brock University, St. Catharines, Ontario.

Maria João Maciel Jorge is an associate professor in York University's Department of Languages, Literatures and Linguistics. She holds a PhD from the University of Toronto. Her research interests and publication record in English, Spanish, and Portuguese include early modern Iberian literature, colonial encounters, and contemporary island culture.

Irene Marques holds a PhD in Comparative Literature, a master's in French Literature, a master's in Comparative Literature, and a Bachelor of Social Work. She is a bilingual writer (English and Portuguese) and lecturer at Toronto Metropolitan University where she teaches literature, literary theory, and creative writing in the Department of English. She is the author of several works of fiction. Her most recent publications include *Daria* (novel, 2021), and *Uma Casa no Mundo* (novel, 2021), which won Prémio Imprensa Nacional/Ferreira de Castro in Portugal. She is also the author of numerous academic publications including the book *Transnational Discourses on Class, Gender and Cultural Identity* (Purdue University Press, 2011). Her fourth collection of poetry, *The Bare Bones of Our Alphabet*, will be published in 2024 (Mawenzi House).

Joseph Mensah is a professor and the former chair of the Department of Geography at York University. His research focuses on globalization and culture, dialectics, race and employment, and African development. Best known among his publications is *Black Canadians: History,*

Experience, and Social Conditions (Fernwood, 2002 and 2010). His latest book (co-authored with Christopher Williams) is *Boomerang Ethics: How Racism Affects Us All* (Fernwood, 2017).

Gertrude Mianda is a sociologist and professor in the Gender and Women's Studies Program at Glendon Campus and in the School of Gender, Sexuality and Women's Studies at York University. Formerly she served as director of the Tubman Institute for Research on Africa and its Diasporas, and chair of the School of Gender, Sexuality and Women's Studies at York University. Her research interests focus on gender and development, globalization, postcolonialism, de-colonialism, and women's rights including SGBV in the DRC, and the migration of francophone Africans to Canada living in the minoritized francophone community in Canada (Ontario). She is the author of *V. Y. Mudimbe, les Africaines, le genre et l'ordre social* (Paris: Editions du Cygne, 2021) as well as several articles that examine francophone African immigrants' experiences in the minoritized francophone community in the GTA and Ottawa.

Jacqueline Ng is an associate professor in the Department of Languages, Literatures and Linguistics (DLLL), York University, Canada. In the context of EAP teaching, she is particularly interested in researching multiliteracies pedagogy, technology-enhanced teaching and learning, translanguaging, and culture and identity. Her recent research explores how ELL learners may enhance their academic literacy skills and reaffirm their identity construction by integrating their linguistic and cultural knowledge with multimodal practices and experiential education.

Snežana Obradović-Ratković, PhD, is originally from Serbia and a research officer and instructor in the Faculty of Education, Brock University, St. Catharines, Ontario.

Veronica Escobar Olivo is a research associate with the Rights for Children and Youth Partnership based at Toronto Metropolitan University's School of Social Work. She has previously worked as a research member for the Toronto Metropolitan University Centre of Immigration and Settlement and the research project Picturing Our Realities. Her experience includes working with Latinx diaspora youth in Canada on issues of immigration, belonging, and settlement. Her research interests include immigration, youth rights and well-being, coloniality, identity and belonging, dynamics of power, and violence against women and children. She is the co-author (with Henry Parada and Kevin Cruz) of *Central American Young People Migration: Coloniality and Epistemologies of the South* (Routledge).

Judith Patouma is a socio-linguist and didactician of languages. An associate professor in the Faculty of Education Sciences at Université Sainte-Anne, Pointe-de-l'Église, Nova Scotia, she ensures the professional training of student teachers in language didactics. Her research interests include language and cultural mediation, multilingualism, pluriculturalism, identity construction, and language teaching in diverse contexts.

Norman Ravvin is a writer, critic, and professor based in Montreal at Concordia University's Department of Religions and Cultures. His recent novel of Poland and Vancouver is *The Girl Who Stole Everything* (Linda Leith), and his most recent academic volume is the co-edited and bilingual collection *Kanade, di goldene medine? Perspectives on Canadian-Jewish Literature and Culture/Perspectives sur la littérature et la culture juives Canadiennes* (Brill). This volume was the outcome of an international conference that took place in Łódź, Poland, that reflected his ongoing collaboration with Canadianists and literary scholars in that country. Ravvin's essays on North American and European Jewish writers examine the works of Philip Roth, Bruno Schulz, Saul Bellow, Leonard Cohen, and Mordecai Richler. Some of these essays were collected in *A House of Words: Jewish Writing, Identity, and Memory* (McGill-Queen's University Press, 1997). His recent research is on immigration to Canada in the early 1930s and forms of integration and new identities in Jewish lives on the Prairies at that time.

Anuppiriya Sriskandarajah is an assistant professor in the Children, Childhood and Youth program at York University. Her research interests include transnationalism, gender, difference, youth belonging, and racialization. Recently, she published the edited book *Rethinking Young People's Lives through Space and Place*.

Vander Tavares holds a PhD in linguistics and applied linguistics from York University. He is currently a postdoctoral research fellow in the Faculty of Education at Høgskolen i Innlandet (Inland Norway

University of Applied Sciences). His more recent work focuses on the internationalization of higher education, the international student experience, second language education, and identity in multicultural contexts. He is the author of *International Students in Higher Education: Language, Identity and Experience from a Holistic Perspective* (Lexington Books) and the editor (with Inês Cardoso) of *Teaching and Learning Portuguese in Canada* (Boa Vista Press).

Reshma Rose Tom is originally from India and a graduate of the MEd program, Faculty of Education, Brock University, St. Catharines, Ontario.

Esther Wainaina is originally from Kenya and a graduate student and teaching assistant in the Faculty of Education, Brock University, St. Catharines, Ontario.